W9-BLL-619

CONTENTS

★ ★

© Filippo Bacci / Getty Images

FOREWORD

★ ★ ★ ★ ★ ★ ★ ★

ANDREW ZIMMERN

Lonely Planet has once again created a must-have guide for any serious road trip junkie, any family looking for cool itineraries to put in play at the next family gathering, or a road warrior with time on their hands at the next sales conference. *The Unique States of America* delivers on its promise. Here are the experiences, well catalogued, that make our 50 states so wonderful to visit and spend real time in. Far from a listicle in a magazine, these entries have heft. Even a cursory glance is bound to intrigue, inspire and encourage any curious traveler. What I feel duty bound to offer up is why I think you all should have this volume on your shelf.

I've visited all 50 states, and I have to tell you that my domestic travel experiences are beyond compare to any other I have ever undertaken. The most enduring, exciting, memorable and impactful travels of my life have all been 'right around the corner', in my own back yard, in my country, the place I have lived my life and raised my family. Here's why.

I believe that travel is transformative. We become the best versions of ourselves on the road. We step out of our comfort zone, that's how we grow. Travel forces us in the best way possible to try new things. That's a vital piece of what makes us human. Through it, we experience real humility, empathy and happiness. Travel puts life in perspective and gives us all a greater appreciation for our blessings and a better understanding of how to help our fellows. Travel exposes us to different ideas about life, and increases the diversity of our friendships. If I never left home the only people I would know are the ones in my neighborhood, the people most inclined to think and act like I do. That would be a life of such massive limitations with no learning of any kind that I couldn't bear it. Travel allows us to experience the unimaginable. From the natural beauty of Yellowstone to a sunrise over

New York City, from Big Sur to Okefenokee... seeing the incomparable beauty of our natural world, and the manmade (I see you Mr Museum!) is a spiritual experience. The development of attachment of that type yields immeasurable benefits. Travel allows us to learn new languages, and in this day and age any way we can find to connect with others, to understand each other better is a good thing.

So, given all that, the most rewarding experiences and benefits of travel are the ones found by journeying into and throughout our own country. Your carbon footprint is smaller, you can learn more about your own heritage, you can save money and plan more trips. All true. Most urgently, at this point in time, in our own country if we want a better future for all, we must seek to understand, rather than be understood. The benefits of travel are more important now than ever before. Seeing our own nation, up close and personal, is an adventure learning experience that has never been more vitally urgent. We have become increasingly a country defining ourselves by our differences rather than our commonalities. This alone is reason enough to change our collective future by actually getting out and seeing for ourselves the truth, that we have way more in common with each other than at any time in our history. We all have the same hopes and dreams, we all want to be happy and of service, we all want to celebrate our communities and find connection with each other.

You don't have to journey abroad to learn new lessons: they are all available to us here at home. And I would insist its more important to know those closest to us. The adventure learning experience of a lifetime is in your hands, in the pages of this book. EMPHASIS ON ADVENTURE. Life is supposed to be fun, and these 50 United States have all the fun you can handle.

And it goes without saying that the true Biggest Ball of String is in Minnesota.

©Matt Munro / Lonely Planet

INTRODUCTION

★ ★ ★ ★ ★

From one coast to another, the country stretches out in infinite variety. Covering it all is a daunting, herculean task. A single city like Los Angeles or Houston, Seattle or Chicago could easily fill a whole book themselves, but we've restricted our selections and will leave it to readers to disagree with them (half the fun of any list). Rather than provide an exhaustive survey of every place you might visit, we've carefully chosen a range of highlights from each corner of every state, spanning roadside attractions to world-class museums and everything in between. You'll discover surprising pockets of nature on the crowded Northeast corridor, mural installations in Fort Smith Arkansas, beckoning waters in Voyageurs National Park near the Canada border, and tucked-away tribal communities in the Navajo Nation. There's an incredible bounty of character within every state, and surprises even in your own backyard.

Follow the Blue Ridge Parkway and explore bluegrass as you pass from Shenandoah National Park to the Great Smoky Mountains; chase Ernest Hemingway's ghost through Key West; witness the picturesque charms of New Hampshire's seemingly endless covered bridges. Architecture buffs may want to make a pilgrimage to Frank Lloyd Wright's creations, while art lovers may make the trek to Marfa, Texas or Tippet Rise Art Center, Montana. The scenic byways, musical traditions, memorials to a troubled, unresolved past, immigrant communities, and ever-varying landscapes come together to create a richly varied tapestry. Historical sites and museums honor the struggles along the way, from the Civil War to integration battles. Whether you track the course of the Lewis and Clark Expedition or go back to the days of the Thirteen Colonies, relish the Americana-overdose of Gatlinburg and Dollywood, pick up a wave in Hawaii, don a hat for the Kentucky Derby or hit the slopes of the Rockies, there's no end of options. Upscale or down-home, adrenaline-pumping or relaxing: whatever you're looking for, it's out there.

You'll find choices for each state's iconic eats at the start of each entry, from Kansas City barbecue to Maryland blue crab, Maine blueberries to some good old ears of Iowa corn. Even in today's chain restaurant times, regional food thrives across the country. We've called out everything from Cincinnati chili to the North Dakota kuchen passed down by German immigrants, Somali food brought by the growing diaspora in Minneapolis, Delta hot tamales, and New Mexican sopapillas and green chiles. As a whole, vegans and vegetarians, or those with gluten and dairy sensitivities, may find that these traditional menu items run on a rather carnivorous line, but rest assured that college towns and cities across the country have richer options on offer than ever before. Not to mention a new outgrowth of vineyards, distilleries, breweries, and coffee roasters, no longer restricted just to California's Napa Valley or Portland's buzzing cafes. Even places like Salt Lake City have their own Beer Bar, with 140 beers on the menu. For the under-21 crowd, child-friendly attractions round out the picture.

While *E Pluribus Unum* is an ideal that's never perfectly met, each state's unique flavor adds to the diversity of the many, and traveling across them is the perfect way to celebrate the country's differences and explore it commonalities. We hope you'll take it as a challenge not just to visit every state, but to see them with fresh eyes.

© canadastock / Shutterstock

ALABAMA

★ ★ ★ ★ ★ ★ ★ ★ ★ ★ ★ ★ ★ ★ ★ ★ ★ ★ ★ ★

POPULATION: 4.8 million | **SIZE**: 52,419 sq miles | **STATE CAPITAL**: Montgomery
LARGEST CITY: Birmingham | **WEBSITE**: https://alabama.travel

FROM THE SMALLEST HUNTING CAMPS TO CITIES BUILT ON THE STEEL INDUSTRY, AND FROM the forested hills of the upland north to the long, low sweep of flooded forest and white sand beaches of the Gulf Coast, Alabama is fiercely unique. Everywhere you can feel a regional passion that constantly animates Alabama's arts, food, culture and, of course, sports, an institution that informs all levels of society in this state. History runs deep in the Yellowhammer State. The Mississippian Native American culture built great mound cities, the remains of which still dot the landscape. Mobile, home of the USA's oldest Mardi Gras celebrations, is dotted with Franco-Caribbean architecture. Finally, for many people, Alabama is synonymous with the American civil rights movement, which is interpreted via a slew of excellent museums and monuments.

© W. Drew Senter / Getty Images

FOOD & DRINK

ALABAMA BBQ Whether you go with Dreamland BBQ in Tuscaloosa, Saw's Juke Joint in Birmingham or any other of the endless barbecue options in the state, you'll find some of the most mouthwatering smoked meat in the country. Try smoked chicken with a tangy local white sauce, but you can't go wrong whatever you pick. Plates usually come with the traditional slices of white bread, and don't forget sweet iced tea to round out the meal.

BANANA PUDDING Other states in the South might plausibly lay claim to having America's best banana pudding – Georgia and North Carolina are both devotees. Nonetheless, while you're frequenting Alabama barbecue spots and down-home buffets, you'll find an excellent banana pudding is almost always the star of the dessert menu, whether at Miss Myra's Pit Bar-B-Q in Birmingham or Sisters' Restaurant in Troy.

BOILED PEANUTS Freshly harvested 'green peanuts' that have been boiled in salty water until they soften are a beloved roadside snack across the Deep South. To try these salty, addictive indulgences, head to Luverne in September for the World's Largest Peanut Boil, where some 60,000 pounds of peanuts go into the drink. www.crenshawcochamber.com/peanutboil

FRIED GREEN TOMATOES Made famous by Fannie Flagg's novel *Fried Green Tomatoes at the Whistle Stop Cafe* and the subsequent 1991 film adaptation, fried green tomatoes still rule the roost in Alabama. Made from unripe green tomatoes prepared in a crispy cornmeal jacket, this treat turns summer bounty into decadence. You can even pretend it's healthy.

GULF SHRIMP & GRITS A visit to Gulf Shores or nearby Orange Beach wouldn't be complete without an order of gulf shrimp and grits. Alabama gristmill McEwen & Sons and access to the Gulf of Mexico's fisheries put this classic southern dish a head above other fare, though seafood gumbo, oysters and fried seafood po'boys all compete with gulf shrimp for attention at mealtimes along the Alabama Gulf Coast.

SPORTS BARS College football is close to a religion here. If you can't get one of the 70,000 seats at the University of Alabama's Bryant-Denny Stadium or you want to watch the Iron Bowl among rabid fans of the Alabama Crimson Tide or Auburn Tigers, you'll have options. Stop into Houndstooth Sports Bar in Tuscaloosa, where they bleed crimson, or check out one of the sports bars along Auburn's College Street.

YELLOWHAMMER TURKEY Turkey is Alabama's official state game bird: there are more wild turkeys per acre here than anywhere else in the US. Hunters might request a license for the spring season, but casual visitors can stop in at the restaurant attached to Bates Turkey Farm. Set off I-65 between Mobile and Montgomery, Bates House of Turkey in Greenville serves a full Thanksgiving meal year-round.

★ ★ ★

MUSCLE SHOALS

The South has many ties to music history, but not everyone knows about northern Alabama's biggest claim to fame. The towns known as greater Muscle Shoals, including Muscle Shoals itself, Sheffield, Florence and Tuscumbia, were home to recording studios that created records for the world's most iconic musicians. Local FAME Studios and Muscle Shoals Sound Studio worked with artists of all races in the segregated 1960s, backing their vocals with distinctive rhythm sections that developed the legendary 'Muscle Shoals Sound.' Artists like the Rolling Stones, Cher, Etta James, Paul Simon and Aretha Franklin recorded hits here. There has been renewed interest in these studios thanks to the documentary *Muscle Shoals*, and both offer tours. The beat goes on with modern artists, including Alicia Keys and the Black Keys, who continue to record here.

© Kevin C. Cox / Getty Images; Left: © Leona Jims / Alamy Stock Photo

★ ★ ★

THE IRON BOWL

Football is breakfast, lunch, dinner, water, air and the very essence of existence in Alabama. All right, we're exaggerating, but only just. There are plenty of football traditions that define this state, but the Iron Bowl – the annual game between Auburn University and the University of Alabama – is the bone-crunching culmination of one of the most fiercely contested rivalries in American college sports. The game is traditionally played on Thanksgiving weekend; if you're visiting around then, the entire state will briefly seem to vanish for a few hours as folks head inside to watch the game.

NATURAL ESCAPES

DISMALS CANYON This sandstone gorge, tucked away in the deep woods of northern Alabama near Phil Campbell, has been thoughtfully developed into a tourism destination that focuses on the quiet appreciation of a beautiful wilderness space. At night local 'Dismalites' (glowworms – the larval stage of a local fly) pepper the sides of the canyon with blue-green constellations of bioluminescence. *901 County Rd 8*

SPLINTER HILL BOG Blankets of white-topped pitcher plants can be found in Bay Minette on a 2100-acre plot of land owned and protected by the nonprofit Nature Conservancy. Walk into the pitcher-plant bogs and you may notice that the midges, mosquitoes and flies so common in southern woodlands are busily being digested by a graceful field of wildflowers. *Co Rd 47*

ARTS, HISTORY & CULTURE

BIRMINGHAM CIVIL RIGHTS INSTITUTE Powerful audio, video and photography exhibits tell the story of racial segregation in America and the civil rights movement at this institute, part of the city's Civil Rights District. There's an extensive exhibit on the 16th Street Baptist Church (located across the street), which was tragically bombed in 1963. *www.bcri.org, 520 16th St N*

CIVIL RIGHTS MEMORIAL CENTER With a circular design crafted by Maya Lin, this haunting memorial in Montgomery focuses on 40 martyrs of the civil rights movement. From Dr Martin Luther King Jr to many 'faceless' deaths along the way, both white and African American, their lives and deaths are honored here. An on-site museum expands on the memorial's mission. *www.splcenter.org/civil-rights-memorial, 400 Washington Ave*

From left: The Alabama Crimson Tide line up against the Auburn Tigers at the Iron Bowl; a fishing pier on the Gulf of Mexico; Vulcan Park in Birmingham. Previous page: Gulf Shores.

© dbimages / Alamy Stock Photo

DEXTER AVENUE PARSONAGE The Montgomery home of Dr Martin Luther King Jr and Coretta Scott King has been frozen in time, a snapshot of a mid-20th-century home. The most fascinating part of the tour is King's old office, which still contains some of the books that influenced his theology, philosophy and activism. *www.dexterkingmemorial.org/tours, 309 S Jackson St*

EDMUND PETTUS BRIDGE Few sites are as iconic to the American civil rights movement as the Pettus Bridge in Selma, where Alabama state troopers and their dogs charged into nonviolent marchers in 1965 as news cameras captured the state-sponsored violence. Nearby museums flesh out the history of the Jim Crow South and the struggle against legalized segregation. *Broad St and Walter Ave*

THE NATIONAL MEMORIAL FOR PEACE AND JUSTICE/LEGACY MUSEUM This 6-acre memorial in Montgomery stands in honor of the 4400 African American victims of lynching in the US. Nearby, an 11,000-sq-ft museum examines how this violence, far from being a relic of the past, informs racial segregation into the 21st century. *https://museumandmemorial.eji. org, 115 Coosa St (museum), 417 Caroline St (memorial)*

SLOSS FURNACES From 1882 to 1971, this was a pig iron–producing blast furnace and a cornerstone of Birmingham's economy. Today it's a National Historic Landmark, a red mass of steel and girders rusted into a Gothic-looking monument to American industry. Quiet pathways pass cobwebbed workshops and former production lines. A small museum on-site explores the furnaces' history. *www.slossfurnaces.com, 20 32nd St N*

US SPACE & ROCKET CENTER If you ever entertained dreams of playing Major

FUN FACT

While Mardi Gras is most associated with New Orleans, the Alabama city of Mobile is where the tradition originated in the US.

© Mike Skowronski / 500px; Right: ©Bob Pool / Shutterstock

While there are midsize domestic airports in Mobile and Montgomery, the most common air entry to Alabama is via Birmingham-Shuttlesworth International Airport. If you're driving, Birmingham is about 150 miles from Atlanta and 200 miles from Nashville. Alabama's beautiful Gulf Coast is barely an hour from some of the most popular beaches of the Florida Panhandle.

Tom to someone's ground control, head to Huntsville, birthplace of America's space program. The Smithsonian-affiliated museum here boasts one of the world's largest collections of space artifacts, from rockets to shuttle components. There are simulator rides for kids and adults (try the G Force simulator!). *www.rocketcenter.com, 1 Tranquility Base*

FAMILY OUTINGS

FLORENCE INDIAN MOUND AND MUSEUM

This attractive museum in Florence takes a deep look at the culture and history of the indigenous peoples of the Tennessee River valley. Arrowheads, soapstone carvings and old pipes constitute part of the massive artifact and archaeology collection. The experience aims to make visitors feel as if they have entered the underground chambers of a ceremonial space. The museum is set by a 43ft-high earthen mound dating to 500 BCE. *www.facebook.com/FlorenceIndianMoundMuseum, 1028 S Court St*

GULF SHORES

With its warm, light-blue waters, white sand beaches and endless horizons stretching over the Gulf of Mexico, the town of Gulf Shores represents a particular kind of oceanside fantasy. But there is more to this area than the comfortable amenities and high-rise condos of the waterfront. Visit nearby Bon Secour National Wildlife Refuge to find the oak woodlands, coastal prairie, wetlands and scrub forest that once covered the entire coast. *www.gulfshores.com*

ITINERARY

Days 1 & 2
Start in Birmingham, where you can begin with a visit the Civil Rights Institute before walking the Civil Rights Memorial Trail. That evening, make sure to indulge in the city's excellent dining and nightlife scene, but try not to go too wild. The next day you'll want your energy up for exploring the monumental grandeur of the Sloss Furnaces and hiking around Vulcan Park.

Day 3
Drive down to Montgomery, another seminal location for the civil rights struggle; don't miss the National Memorial for Peace and Justice, and take a tour of the Dexter Avenue Parsonage.

Day 4
Drive to Selma along the same route used by civil rights activists in the 1960s.

Day 5
Swing north through western Alabama, making sure to stop by Tuscaloosa on your way to Muscle Shoals. As you round out your trip, pop into Dismals Canyon and say hello to all of the glowworms.

RAILROAD PARK Birmingham's Railroad Park, which occupies some 19 acres of downtown real estate, is a stroke of planning brilliance that celebrates the industrial and artistic heritage of the city. As urban green lungs go, this park with its miles of pathways, public art and pretty lighting is fantastic, and a central gathering place. *www.railroadpark.org*

VULCAN PARK Imagine Christ the Redeemer in Rio de Janeiro but made of iron and depicting a beefcake Roman god of metalworking. Vulcan is visible from all over Birmingham – it is actually the world's largest cast-iron statue – and the park he resides in offers fantastic views, along with an observation tower. A small on-site museum explores the city's history. *www.visitvulcan.com, 1701 Valley View Dr*

From left: Tuscaloosa's Dreamland BBQ; Sloss Furnaces in Birmingham.

ALASKA

★ ★

POPULATION: 738,000 | **SIZE:** 663,268 sq mi | **STATE CAPITAL:** Juneau
LARGEST CITY: Anchorage | **WEBSITE:** www.travelalaska.com

ALASKA IS THE US SUPERSIZED. EVERYTHING IS UNUSUALLY LARGE HERE, FROM THE GLACIERS to the bears to the ice-crusted mountains, many of which tower over anything in the Lower 48. In a nation obsessed with the 'Wild West,' this is the last true frontier, a place where big fauna outnumbers people, locals still hunt for subsistence and the capital city remains refreshingly disconnected from the main road network. While the state doesn't lack historical sites or endearing fishing villages, most people venture here for big, bold wilderness. Only in Alaska can you see giant bears without the aid of binoculars, test your navigation skills in national parks without trails or dip an oar into steep-sided inlets with names like Fords Terror or Misty Fjords. Luxury cruise ships have opened the state, once the domain of gutsy gold rush prospectors, to all comers, yet it remains intriguingly remote and wild.

© Piriya Photography / Getty Images

FOOD & DRINK

ALASKAN BREWS Alaska has a vibrant, thriving brewery scene. Harboring what is possibly the best small-town drinking scene in the US, Haines (population 1700) has a microdistillery, an annual beer festival, several old-school Alaskan dive bars and a shiny new microbrewery with an attached tasting room. In Anchorage, dip into Humpy's Great Alaskan Alehouse to try its wide range of Alaskan beers on tap.

KING CRAB Any viewer of *Deadliest Catch* is familiar with the allure of Alaskan king crab, but to really understand the appeal, you need to try some fresh. Tracy's King Crab Shack in Juneau is one of the most popular spots to chow down on the delicacy, but it's available just about everywhere, including Ray's Waterfront in Seward and Bridge Seafood in Anchorage.

RUDOLPH FOR DINNER Bid adieu to gourmet food and say hello to reindeer sausage. Imported from Siberia in the late 1800s, reindeer became a hearty Alaskan staple, and you can try out reindeer sausage at Tiki Pete's Alaskan Dogs food cart in Anchorage. Be on the lookout for caribou steak as well, though this native species isn't farmed and can only be found as game meat.

SALMON Alaska's five salmon species are so key to the state's identity that sustainable fisheries are mandated by the state's constitution. From the prized Chinook, or king, salmon to red sockeye and silver coho, the salmon here is a point of pride and a way of life. Alaska Fish House in Ketchikan always has fresh-caught fish, or try Alaska Salmon Bake in Fairbanks for a traditional Alaskan dinner in Pioneer Park, open seasonally from May to September.

NATURAL ESCAPES

ANIAKCHAK NATIONAL MONUMENT & PRESERVE A mysterious collapsed volcano in the Aleutian Range regularly hooded in mist and patrolled by the planet's largest bears, Aniakchak is little known, even among Alaskans. Those with the wherewithal (and bravery) to hike in will encounter wilderness of the highest order along with a unique, if spine-chilling, opportunity to raft the fast-moving Aniakchak River to the sea. *www.nps.gov/ania*

CHICKEN A study in remoteness and eccentricity, the 'town' of Chicken (population 7-ish) is a throwback to the days of gold rushes and gritty Jack London tales. True to its history as a mining town, there aren't many home comforts in this rough but delightfully authentic collection of gold dredges and clapboard saloons, unless you count the enormous cinnamon buns served at the local cafe. Visit in summer; come winter, the highway closes. *www.chickenalaska.com*

CHILKOOT TRAIL Way more than just an adventurous hike, the 33-mile Chilkoot Trail is a walk through the annals of history. Following the route of the 1897 Klondike Gold Rush stampeders, the steep but spectacular trail from Dyea, Alaska to Lake Bennett, Canada is littered with the

★ ★ ★

NORTHERN LIGHTS

Given Fairbanks' clear skies and extreme northern latitude, there are few better places in the US to see the ghostly colors of the aurora borealis (northern lights) than this Alaskan city, where the phenomenon is on show for around 240 nights of the year. The trade-off: you may have to brave the winter cold because the lights aren't viewable on ultra-long summer nights when it never gets properly dark. Fortunately several travel companies can minimize the chill, organizing tours to heated yurts and cabins or incorporating dogsledding adventures into the mix. Early fall to April is the best time to visit to view the aurora.

© Dustin Montgomery / Shutterstock; Left: © Benny Marty / Shutterstock

★ ★ ★

MT MARATHON RACE

There are longer races held in more remote places, but few running events match the brutal intensity of this short blitz up and down Alaska's Mt Marathon near Seward, held every year on July 4. A lethal mix of punishing climbs and knee-bashing descents up and down the 3022ft peak, ever since 1915 this 5k mountain race has been known to sorely test even the strongest of contenders.

memories of the 19th century's 'last great adventure' and framed by magnificent lakes, mountains and alpine beauty. *www.nps.gov/klgo*

COLUMBIA GLACIER Prince William Sound is famous for the tidewater glaciers that empty their rivers of ice directly into the sea. The big daddy of them all is the Columbia, easily visited on a day trip out of Valdez. Daredevils organize kayaking trips around the bergs of Columbia Bay; the less athletically inclined sightsee by boat. *www.anchorage.net/discover/glaciers/ prince-william-sound*

DENALI The aptly named 'Great One' doesn't just stand tall over the bushy taiga of Alaska – it towers over all other peaks in North America. Climbing the mountain is a significant feat of endurance. Consequently most visitors settle for admiring it from the comfort of an Alaska Railroad train or one of the numerous buses that ply the surrounding Denali National Park. *www.nps.gov/dena*

FERRY TO THE ALEUTIANS In a state renowned for deluxe cruise liners, the 'Trusty Tusty' is a cheaper, more authentic alternative, a utilitarian state-run ferry where the thrills are less in the onboard entertainment and more in the ethereal coastal landscapes. The Tustumena sails seasonally from Homer through the necklace of islands between the Alaska Peninsula and Russia, amid smoldering volcanoes and choppy seas. *www.dot.state.ak.us/amhs*

KATMAI NATIONAL PARK In the Lower 48 you need binoculars to catch a safe glimpse of a bear. In Katmai National Park & Preserve you'll see dozens of them up close, plucking fat salmon out of fast-moving Brooks Falls. Although its remote wilderness is expensive to reach, Katmai is considered a trip of a lifetime for aspiring bear watchers. Most visitors admit that it's money well spent. *www.nps.gov/katm*

MCCARTHY The Wild West spirit lives on in the pinprick, one-horse town of McCarthy,

From left: Historic store in Wrangell–St Elias National Park; Denali National Park; a grizzly sow in Denali. Previous page: Aurora borealis near Fairbanks.

©Jacob W. Frank/Getty Images

encased within Wrangell–St Elias National Park & Preserve. Stay in the clapboard Ma Johnson's Hotel or compare beard growth (and beers) at the Golden Saloon before venturing off on a no-holds-barred wilderness adventure. *www.mccarthylodge.com*

PARK ROAD The sole road in Denali National Park winds for 92 unrelentingly gorgeous miles through scrubby tundra flanked by some of the continent's highest mountains. With private cars banned, visitors must transfer onto special park buses to view one of the greatest wildlife spectacles on earth, dominated by bears, moose, caribou, Dall's sheep and, if you're lucky enough to see them, wolves. *www.nps.gov/dena*

ARTS, HISTORY & CULTURE

ANCHORAGE MUSEUM When the elements have worn you out, take a day off from outdoor adventure at the state's largest museum. Recently upgraded, this super-modern facility in Anchorage offers a perfect précis of Native Alaskan art and culture backed with 10,000 years of human history. There's also a kid-friendly Discovery Center and planetarium. *www.anchoragemuseum.org, 625 C St*

KLONDIKE GOLD RUSH NATIONAL HISTORICAL PARK Part of a three-pronged park with additional branches in Seattle and Dawson City, this Skagway outpost captures the gold rush at its most feverish and volatile. Incorporating numerous downtown buildings with the nearby 'ruins' of Dyea and the cross-border Chilkoot Trail, it has been wonderfully preserved by the National Park Service, which brings it to life with free historical walks. *www.nps.gov/klgo*

SITKA NATIONAL HISTORICAL PARK Alaska's 125-year union with Imperial Russia seems all but forgotten until you dock in Sitka on Baranof Island. Here, in a forested park, the site of a critical 1804 battle between Russian fur traders

FUN FACT

Not only is Alaska the largest state in the country (more than twice as large as Texas), Wrangell–St Elias National Park & Preserve covers a larger area than nine US states.

© James + Courtney Forte / Getty Images; Right: © Justin Foulkes / Lonely Planet

and native Tlingit has been preserved along with slender totem poles, a visitors center and one of the oldest ecclesiastical buildings in the state. *www.nps.gov/sitk*

FAMILY OUTINGS

ALPENGLOW Glamping might seem a bit posh for rough-and-ready Alaska, but this small collection of canvas tents on mile 102.5 of the Glenn Highway doesn't appear too over the top with its hotel-quality beds, cedarwood hot tub and spirit-reviving views of the Matanuska Glacier. Communal breakfasts and coffee on tap ease the urban-to-wilderness transition. *www.alpenglowluxurycamping.com, 31090 W Glenn Hwy*

DALTON HIGHWAY EXPRESS The only bus route to the Arctic Ocean in North America is a rutted, 450-mile lifeline linking the city of Fairbanks with the frigid outpost of Deadhorse. Watch out for herds of musk oxen, sporadic truckers and the odd brave cyclist during your 16-hour, summer-only bus journey north to the top of the world. *www.daltonhighwayexpress.com*

HURRICANE TURN One of the world's most distinctive railroad rides, the Hurricane Turn is a rare flagstop train: passengers can get on or off anywhere along the 57-mile route between Talkeetna and Hurricane Gulch. You can disembark for a short hike in the Alaskan wilderness and flag the train down on its return journey. *www.alaskarailroad.com*

MT ROBERTS TRAMWAY There aren't many mechanical aids in the Alaskan wilderness apart from this gravity-defying cable car in Juneau that takes you from the cruise dock to the tree line in a mere six minutes. The top station has a restaurant, raptor center and trails flanked by alpine flowers. *www.mountrobertstramway.com, 490 S Franklin St*

★ ★ ★

GETTING THERE & AROUND

A lack of roads makes ferries and airplanes the best way to explore Alaska. The Alaska Marine Highway acts as the primary transport artery in the southeast; the main airport is in Anchorage. Trains run between Seward, Anchorage and Fairbanks. Small minibuses ply the interior. Alternatively, rent a 4WD car.

ITINERARY

Days 1 & 2
Start in the small
port of Seward, a fine
embarkation point for
sea-kayaking excursions
in Resurrection Bay
that look out for marine
life and eagles as well as
glaciers toppling off the
Harding Icefield.

Day 3
Take the train north to
Anchorage where time
can be spent visiting
the Anchorage Museum
(the state's best) and
enjoying a surprisingly
perky coffee and micro-
brewing scene.

Days 4 & 5
Continue on the train
to Denali National Park
while being treated to
unparalleled views of
North America's tallest
mountain on the way
(weather permitting).
Stay over in the small
service center of Canyon
and spend a day travel-
ing by bus along the 90-
mile Park Road as you
witness Alaska's finest
wildlife extravaganza.

Day 6
Head by train to cusp-
of-the-wilderness Fair-
banks for sunny nights,
relaxing river floats
and the comprehensive
Museum of the North.

**From left: Exploring
Kenai Fjords National
Park; Chicken, Alaska.**

ARIZONA

★ ★

POPULATION: 6.9 million | **SIZE:** 113,998 sq miles | **STATE CAPITAL:** Phoenix
WEBSITE: www.visitarizona.com

AMERICA MAY BE A YOUNG COUNTRY, BUT ARIZONA'S LAND IS ANCIENT. EACH TWIST IN THE ROAD leads further back in time, past vintage Route 66 motels, Wild West ghost towns, clifftop Hopi pueblos built last millennium, and the deeps of the Grand Canyon. Zoom around a 50,000-year-old crater, where a meteor crashed and blew back the hair of the giant sloths living here at the time. Or picnic in the Petrified Forest like dinosaurs did when these trees were alive, 25 million years ago. And let's talk about that road – the lonesome one cowboys always sing about, the one lined with wind-sculpted red rocks shown in car commercials. It's the highway that haunts your wildest American dreams, that turns truckers into philosophers and neon-lit diners into the promised land, and inevitably ends in the Grand Canyon. That road is all Arizona, and it's wide open.

© Alexey Suloev / Shutterstock

FOOD & DRINK

CHIMICHANGAS AND NUEVO MEXICAN
From the invention of the chimichanga (or fried burrito) in Tucson through today, Mexican classics are constantly reinvented by Arizona's ubiquitous taquerias and its best bistros. Tucson's top chef Suzana Davila invents Nuevo Mexican dishes daily as fresh ingredients and inspiration arrive at her Cafe Poca Cosa. All over Arizona you can pair tacos with cactus margaritas, while the annual Desert Botanical Garden's Chiles and Chocolate Festival in Phoenix celebrates cross-border flavors.

CROSSROADS CUISINE
Where Route 66, the Santa Fe Railway and Native pathways converge, Arizona's crossroads cuisine thrives. Brake for roadside diners selling crossover taste sensations like fry bread tacos and bison burgers, and detour to Winslow and La Posada Hotel's legendary Turquoise Room for crossroads favorites: Hopi piki bread with bad-dap-suki (tepary bean hummus), blackberry barbecue ribs with Native corn polenta, and caramelized prickly pear cactus bread pudding.

GHOST-TOWN DINING
You won't strike it rich in Arizona's 200 mining ghost towns, but you'll find killer happy hours in Prescott and Tombstone, and decadent dinners in Bisbee and Jerome. 'No straitjacket required' deadpans the menu at Asylum Restaurant in Jerome's notoriously haunted Jerome Grand Hotel. Still, Asylum's Wine Spectator award-winning wine list is no joke, and that Big Bad Chocolate Cake for Two is to die for, twice.

NATIVE AMERICAN EATS
Native Americans have cultivated heirloom crops in Arizona for a millennium. Traditional crops are making a comeback on Native Seeds/SEARCH Foundation's Conservation Farm, and many Native ingredients grace menus in the state – look for saguaro-blossom honey, cholla buds, scarlet runner beans and violet-grain mustard. Trailblazing Native restaurant Kai ('seed') in Phoenix even uses Gila River Reservation–grown heirloom ingredients.

RANGE TO TABLE
Farm to table comes with a cowboy kick in Arizona; the barbecue is free-range, beans are campfire-cooked, and flavors are wild. At Arizona range-to-table outposts like Flagstaff's Brix Restaurant, you'll find racks of roast elk and coffee-rubbed duck breast with craft cocktails.

SONORAN DOG
The beloved Sonoran dog, a kind of Tex-Mex chili dog, is wrapped in bacon and grilled before being topped by pinto beans, onions, tomatoes, mayo and more. You can get this authentically delicious treat from vendors around Tucson, or try stopping in at one of the El Güero Canelo locations in Tucson.

NATURAL ESCAPES

CANYON DE CHELLY NATIONAL MONUMENT
Wind and water sculpted this spectacular canyon from a stone plateau, but it took human ingenuity to establish ancient civilizations among 1000ft-high cliffs. Prehistoric petroglyphs show that this remote Navajo Reservation valley has been inhabited for 5000 years. Take in the

★ ★ ★

VOLUNTEERING AT THE GRAND CANYON

Ready for a challenge? Help preserve archaeological sites on five-day service trips with the Grand Canyon Field Institute. *www.grandcanyon.org/classes-tours*

Not much time? Take educational hikes, share your photographs, sign petitions to stop uranium mining, or replant eroded slopes with the Grand Canyon Trust. *www.grandcanyontrust.org*

Still in school? Volunteers aged 15+ conserve natural wonders through the Student Conservation Association. *www.thesca.org*

Just a kid? In one activity-packed afternoon, kids aged 4–14 become park advocates and earn the esteemed title of Junior Ranger. *www.nps.gov/grca/learn/kidsyouth*

Want to make it a career? Become an official volunteer or park ranger with the National Park Service. *www.volunteer.gov*

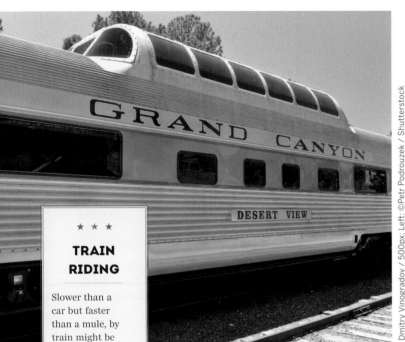

© Dmitry Vinogradov / 500px; Left: ©Petr Podrouzek / Shutterstock

★ ★ ★

TRAIN RIDING

Slower than a car but faster than a mule, by train might be the best way to cover Arizona's scenic routes. On the vintage Grand Canyon Railway, chug from the Williams depot to the Grand Canyon's South Rim while a costumed sheriff chases outlaws through the train and banjo players lead sing-a-longs in the parlor car. Get your kicks on Route 66 aboard Amtrak's South-west Chief, which covers the distance from Kingman to Winslow in time for dinner at the legendary Turquoise Room. For more adventures, Amtrak's Sunset Limited stops at Yuma, Arizona en route to LA (5¾ hrs) and New Orleans (41 hrs).

six viewpoints along 16-mile South Rim Drive before towering Spider Rock, where you can stay overnight in a traditional hogan. For horseback trips or cave hikes, hire authorized Navajo guides. *www.nps.gov/cach, Chinle*

COLORADO RIVER The Colorado is the thrill of a lifetime for outdoor adventurers, covering the Grand Canyon through rolling rapids and hushed side canyons. White-water rafting trips on the river run mid-April to November, and recommended trips include conservation-minded journeys with Colorado River & Trail Expeditions, photography trips with Arizona Raft Adventures, family-friendly float-paddle tours with OARS, history and ecology-focused options with Grand Canyon Expeditions, and quick trips with gourmet food from Hatch River Expeditions.

GRAND CANYON NATIONAL PARK The Grand Canyon in northwestern Arizona opens 18 miles wide and dares you to look a mile straight down, past two billion

years of striped rock formations to the dazzling Colorado River. Drive-up selfies can't capture such monumental grandeur: 360-degree vistas reward short hikes to Ooh Aah Point and Hermit's Rest. The North Rim is closed in winter, and visitors should take care in the off-season. *www.nps.gov/grca*

MONUMENT VALLEY NAVAJO TRIBAL PARK You'll recognize this scene-stealing scenery from movies, cartoons and car commercials, but you still won't believe your eyes. Just below the Utah border, red sandstone monoliths rise 1200ft from the desert floor in strangely familiar shapes: look for the Mittens, Eagle, Elephant, Owl, Bear and Rabbit. Allow 1½ hours for the drive off Highway 163, or take a Navajo-led guided tour on foot or horseback. *www.navajonationparks.org, Indian Rte 42*

MT LEMMON Arizona's craggy skyline is a standing invitation to rock climbers, with special marks to the Wilderness of Rock where Mt Lemmon awaits. More

From left: The Grand Canyon train; Saguaro National Park; the stunning interior of Taliesin West.
Previous page: The Milky Way over the Grand Canyon.

© Matt Munro / Lonely Planet

than 9000ft above sea level in the Santa Catalina Mountains, this is part of the unique 'sky island' ecosystem in southern Arizona, remnants of what was once a volcano; it's now part of the Coronado National Forest. Climbers may also be tempted to try their grip in Flagstaff to the north. www.fs.usda.gov/coronado

PATAGONIA PRESERVE Birders swap stories of rare migratory bird sightings in southern Arizona, especially at the Nature Conservancy–run Patagonia Preserve. This scenic canyon 4.2 miles southwest of Patagonia is the most famous birding spot in the state, where you may spy canyon wrens and the rare rose-throated becard. www.nature.org

SAGUARO NATIONAL PARK Waving a shy hello to all who pass through Arizona, the prickly saguaro cactus is the Southwest's most lovable curmudgeon. Saguaro take 50–80 years to grow 10ft, but this park 15 miles from downtown Tucson is full of stately elders. Lucky April–June visitors might spot the elusive white saguaro flower, which blooms for only 24 hours. www.nps.gov/sagu

SEDONA Mystical red rocks form a ring around Sedona and its resident free spirits and their sundry previous incarnations. Many believe mysterious vortices radiate the earth's power around Sedona at Bell Rock, Cathedral Rock, Airport Mesa and Boynton Canyon, but even skeptics feel the pull of this magnetic landscape. Scenic spas, New Age centers and sublime restaurants soothe body and soul here. https://visitsedona.com

ARTS, HISTORY & CULTURE

BIOSPHERE 2 Like an alien greenhouse has touched down in Tucson's Sonoran Desert, Biosphere 2's surreal complex of glass bubbles and ziggurats contains everything needed to sustain human life in outer space. Eight volunteers lived inside Biosphere 2 for two years, and you can see how they survived the experiment on a tour

FUN FACT

Don't get too close (ouch!) or scratch initials in saguaro cactus; fines for cactus graffiti run up to $5000.

© aaronj9/Shutterstock; Left: ©ronnybas/Shutterstock

© aaronj9/Shutterstock; Left: ©ronnybas/Shutterstock

★ ★ ★

VISITING NATIVE AMERICAN NATIONS

Many of Arizona's iconic attractions are on Native American land, including the Grand Canyon and the some of the state's most scenic campgrounds. While in the area, why not try Native foods, hire Native guides and visit Native trading posts? Even if you're just passing through a reservation, the money spent locally on art, souvenirs, food or accommodations directly supports the Native people who sustain this ancient land. Most reservations ban alcohol, and many prohibit videos, photography, drawing and other recordings. Always ask first and expect to pay a fee or tip. At a powwow or ceremonial dance, modest dress is customary, and elders should be shown deference.

of the sci-fi-esque facilities, now a research facility for the University of Arizona. *http://biosphere2.org, 32540 S Biosphere Rd, Oracle*

COSANTI How do you live sustainably in a desert? To radical Frank Lloyd Wright protégé Paolo Soleri, the obvious answer was underground, in cavernous open-air rooms sculpted with earth-cast concrete. You're free to walk around this Scottsdale site on weekdays, but guided morning tours let you ask questions and glimpse bells being hand-poured in the on-site foundry. *https://arcosanti.org/visit/cosanti, 6433 E Doubletree Ranch Rd*

HEARD MUSEUM Artistic masterpieces and immersive exhibits offer deep insights into Native American life, history and culture at this Phoenix highlight. Prepare to be wowed by the unparalleled collections of Hopi kachina dolls, Navajo carpets and inlaid Zuni jewelry, but nothing can prepare you for the harrowing stories of government-run boarding schools for

Native children in the powerful Away from Home exhibit. *www.heard.org, 2301 N Central Ave*

HOPI RESERVATION Three vast, windswept mesas are home to the Hopi people, and their thousand-year-old stone pueblo at Walpi is still used for ceremonial dances. Find master Hopi silversmiths, kachina (spirit) doll carvers and basket weavers on the Hopi Arts Trail, and get first-person introductions with Experience Hopi guides. To join Hopi-led tours of mesa villages, stop by First Mesa Consolidated Visitor Center in Polacca. *www.hopi-nsn.gov, off AZ State Rte 264*

NAVAJO NATIONAL MONUMENT The rose-gold walls of Tsegi Canyon are hiding a secret: deep inside sandstone alcoves are the Ancestral Puebloan cliff dwellings of Betatakin and Keet Seel, built around AD 1250–1300. Take the easy half-mile Sandal Trail to a sweeping vista point or join a rigorous ranger-led hike for a closer

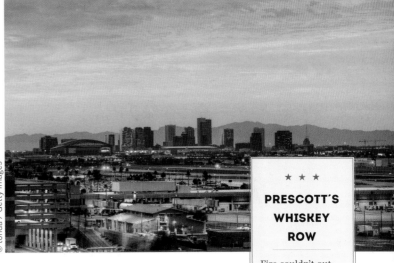

From left: Monument Valley at dusk; looking out on the rocks of Sedona; the skyline of downtown Phoenix.

© tonda / Getty Images

peek at these stunning ancient villages in the northwest portion of the Navajo Nation. *www.nps.gov/nava, Shonto*

TALIESIN WEST World-famous architecture keeps a low profile at Taliesin West in Scottsdale, the winter retreat of modernist pioneer Frank Lloyd Wright. His boulder walls and angled wood frames are widely imitated today, but this harmonious desert hideaway remains breathtakingly original: it's hard to believe it dates from 1938 to 1940. The 90-minute Insights Tours explain building techniques and let you sit in Wright's favorite chair. *www.franklloydwright.org, 12621 N Frank Lloyd Wright Blvd*

FAMILY OUTINGS

ARIZONA DUDE RANCHES Not long ago, the only way to reach Arizona's remote corners was by horse, and it's still the best way to appreciate the unbroken silences and immense skies of this majestic landscape. The small town of Wickenburg,

outside Phoenix, features a number of dude ranches to get you out on horseback, including Rancho de los Caballeros and others. For cookouts, trail rides and lodge stays at a working cattle ranch, head to the Sonoran Desert's Flying E Ranch or Sedona's M Diamond Ranch. If you'd rather sit back and relax, take horse-drawn wagons and sleigh rides through Coconino National Forest's fragrant Ponderosa pines with Hitchin' Post Stables. To get the full movie-star treatment, follow your sunset ride with spa massages at Hacienda del Sol, the 1930s ranch hideaway of Clark Gable, Katharine Hepburn and other Hollywood greats.

ARIZONA-SONORA DESERT MUSEUM
Cartoons can't compare to this museum in Tucson, where you can see a real Wile E Coyote, Roadrunner and friends in their natural habitat. Home to cacti, coyotes and palm-sized hummingbirds, this 98-acre ode to the Sonoran Desert is one part zoo, one part botanical garden and one part museum – a trifecta that will entertain

★ ★ ★

PRESCOTT'S WHISKEY ROW

Fire couldn't out-run the drinkers of Prescott's Whiskey Row: when flames hit the boomtown in 1900, regulars rescued the Palace Saloon's 24ft-long Brunswick Bar. Today the doors still swing at Prescott's infamous Victorian Palace, where Doc Holliday and Wyatt Earp once held court at the indestructible Brunswick Bar, and occasional historical plays and honky-tonk bands supply amusement. Whiskey Row pub crawls are daunting, with 40 saloons to quench local thirsts. The nearby Arts Prescott Gallery overflows with local artwork.

© Daniel ViÒE Garcia / Getty Images; Right: © Carol Polich / Lonely Planet

Phoenix's Sky Harbor International Airport handles most air traffic, but Tucson International Airport services 22 destinations. Amtrak trains link Tucson, Winslow and Flagstaff with destinations near (Albuquerque and El Paso) and far (Los Angeles and New Orleans). Greyhound's interstate bus route options cover Phoenix, Flagstaff and Tucson, but nostalgic drivers have the chance to visit Arizona's Route 66 roadside attractions.

young and old for easily half a day. Follow trails into caves, through aviaries and around ponds to meet sociable prairie dogs, curious coatis, goofy otters and other Arizona critters among the cacti. *www.desertmuseum.org, 2021 N Kinney Rd, Tucson*

KARTCHNER CAVERNS STATE PARK

This drippy subterranean castle was 330 million years in the making, yet it remained Arizona's best-kept secret until it opened as a park in 1999. On 90-minute educational tours through this underground Gothic fantasyland, you might hear the squeak of migrating bats in the Big Room cave (October–April) or feel like a royal troll in the column-lined Throne Room. Reservations are recommended. It's also a designated International Dark Sky Park. *https://azstateparks.com/kartchner, 2980 AZ-90, Benson*

LOWELL OBSERVATORY Arizona's desert skies are so clear that you'll swear you can pluck the stars right out of the Milky Way. With an arid environment, the state is a hotbed for professional telescopes like the ones at Kitt Peak near Tucson. You can see all the way to Pluto at Flagstaff's Lowell Observatory; in fact the first sighting of Pluto was here in 1930. There is regular programming for visitors. *https://lowell.edu, 1400 W Mars Hill Rd*

PETRIFIED FOREST NATIONAL PARK

Back when dinosaurs stomped through what is now eastern Arizona, it was lush green forest. Fast-forward 225 million years, and the once lush trees have turned into massive fossils glittering like gemstones with hints of pink, blue and yellow. Giant Logs is an easy walk from the Rainbow Forest Museum, and Blue Mesa Scenic Drive loops past towering logs and Painted Desert

badlands – ideal backdrops for family holiday photos. *www.nps.gov/pefo*

OLD TUCSON 'Hollywood in the Desert' set the stage for hundreds of classic Western movies since 1939, featuring stars from Clint Eastwood to Leonardo DiCaprio. Now it's your turn for adventure in this movie studio and theme park, with costumed stunt shows, high-kicking saloon dances, stagecoach rides, and after-dark ghost tours for Halloween. *http://oldtucson.com, 201 Kinney Rd, Tucson*

From left: On horseback through the desert landscape; Antelope Canyon.

ITINERARY

Day 1
At the Heard Museum in Phoenix, get to know your hosts: the Native American tribes who shaped the Southwest. Hit the highway to Tucson; once you see giant cacti wave hello at Saguaro National Park, you've officially arrived. Act like a movie star in a Western at Old Tucson theme park and studio, and head to your Hacienda del Sol hideaway for sunset horse rides and spa massages.

Day 2
Enter the future at Tucson's Biosphere 2, the sci-fi lab where volunteers inhabited a self-contained biodome. Take the scenic route through Tonto National Forest outside Phoenix, or head directly to Holbrook to get your kitsch on Route 66. Vintage neon marks classic roadside diners and the Wigwam Motel's cheerfully inauthentic concrete tepees.

Day 3
Ascend Hopi First Mesa to tour millennium-old Walpi pueblo, or traverse the Navajo Nation from historic Hubbell Trading Post to secluded Canyon de Chelly. Pause at Spider Rock to pay respects to the mighty Navajo Spider Woman, weaver of the universe.

Enter Monument Valley Navajo Tribal Park to see towering sandstone buttes glow like campfire embers.

Day 4
Brake for beauty at Navajo National Monument on your way west from Monument Valley and spot Ancestral Puebloan villages tucked into canyon walls. Then brace for the monumental impact of the Grand Canyon, which can't be captured in selfies: you just have to be here. Hike to South Rim viewpoints or venture into the canyon.

Day 5
Return to Flagstaff and follow the Red Rock Scenic Byway to mystical, appealing Sedona, where good vibes abound and stars shine bright.

Day 6
Detour to Jerome on your way back to Phoenix, the copper-mining ghost town turned hippie art colony. Check out Jerome Artists Cooperative Gallery or check into Asylum Restaurant for chilling ghost stories. Just don't be late for a dinner reservation in Phoenix at Kai, where sensational Native American flavors leave you craving more.

ARKANSAS

★ ★

POPULATION: 3 million | **SIZE:** 53,179 sq miles | **STATE CAPITAL:** Little Rock
WEBSITE: www.arkansas.com

FROM THE ROLLING MOUNTAINS OF THE OZARKS AND THE OUACHITAS TO THE LOWLAND FORESTS and prairies that give way to the Mississippi River Delta, Arkansas fully embraces its nickname as the Natural State. Hundreds of miles of hiking and mountain-biking trails and seemingly endless lakes, rivers and streams make for an outdoor adventurer's paradise. Arkansas history is part western frontier forts, part enterprising Ozark pioneers and part Old South heritage, creating a complex regional identity (and that's before accounting for Native American tribes). Visitors can stand at the foundations of the original Fort Smith and retrace the steps of civil rights pioneers at Little Rock Central High School. The state is also home to industry giants like Walmart and Tyson Foods, and educational institutions which are creating hubs of innovation, art and culture that hark back to Arkansas' wild and independent roots.

© Sean Pavone / Alamy Stock Photo

FOOD & DRINK

CATFISH FRY Visitors can't go too far in Arkansas without spotting a restaurant dedicated to the state's favorite meal, fried catfish. Whether you're at a friendly fish fry in a park or in the beloved booths of Little Rock's Flying Fish, this is a classic way to celebrate the most iconic sport fish in the Natural State. The first state to develop a commercial catfish industry has lakes and waterways that abound with 'river kitties.'

NATURAL ESCAPES

BLANCHARD SPRINGS CAVERNS This 'living' cave system of stalactites and stalagmites has three levels, two of which are open for guided tours. The half-mile Dripstone Trail travels through two huge rooms, while the 1.2-mile Discovery Trail's 700 stair steps explores the cave's middle level. A Wild Cave Tour is available too. *www.blanchardsprings.org, 704 Blanchard Springs Rd, Ozark-St Francis National Forests*

CRATER OF DIAMONDS STATE PARK An average of 600 diamonds are found each year at one of the only places in the world where visitors can search for real diamonds and keep what they find. This park in Murfreesboro boasts several notable finds including the over 40-carat Uncle Sam, the largest diamond ever uncovered in the US. *www.arkansasstateparks.com, 209 State Park Rd*

MT MAGAZINE STATE PARK At 2753ft, Mt Magazine is the highest point in Arkansas. Besides taking in sweeping vistas, nature lovers can hike, ride a horse or hop in an ATV, bike and rock climb. The park also offers hang-gliding launch areas. While there's plenty of space for camping, visitors can stay at the Lodge at Mt Magazine and dine at Skycrest Restaurant. *www.arkansasstateparks.com, Paris*

WHITE RIVER REFUGE One of the largest remaining bottomland hardwood forests in the lower Mississippi River valley boasts 300 lakes connected by streams, swamps and bayous that are home to a myriad of wildlife. Visitors to this site near St Charles can hike hundreds of miles of trails or paddle a canoe trail. *www.fws.gov/refuge/white_river, 57 S CC Camp Rd*

ARTS, HISTORY & CULTURE

CHAFFEE BARBERSHOP MUSEUM It was the haircut heard around the world as Elvis Presley got his first GI cut at Fort Chaffee after enlisting in the army in 1958. This museum in Fort Smith steps back in time to the day Elvis lost his locks, and documents the military base's history. *www.fortsmith.org/elvis-barbershop-museum*

CRYSTAL BRIDGES MUSEUM OF AMERICAN ART Founded by Walmart heiress Alice Walton and nestled between trees and spring-fed ponds, this ambitious museum in Bentonville has a permanent collection spanning five centuries of American masterworks from the Colonial era to contemporary art. Iconic images by Norman Rockwell, Andy Warhol, Georgia O'Keeffe and others reveal the evolution of the American aesthetic. Who says the

★ ★ ★

America's first
NATIONAL RIVER

At 153 free-flowing miles, the Buffalo National River is one of the few remaining undammed rivers in the contiguous United States. Its national river status was established by Congress in 1972 thanks to the efforts of Arkansas conservationists determined to protect the river from a US Army Corps of Engineers plan to dam it.

The Buffalo is popular with hikers, kayakers and canoers due to its dramatic topography of caves, springs, massive exposed bluffs and other rock formations. The 209ft-tall Hemmed-In-Hollow Falls, Hawksbill Crag, Granny Henderson's Cabin, the abandoned town of Rush and the Big Bluff Goat Trail can all be found in the surrounding wilderness. The river is also home to Arkansas' only elk herd, which can be seen roaming Boxley Valley at dawn and dusk.

© Zack Frank / Shutterstock; Left: © Erik Pendzich / Alamy Stock Photo

Little Rock, Hot Springs, Fort Smith and northwest Arkansas all have city and regional bus systems, but most destinations in cities and throughout the state are best reached by car. Bill and Hillary Clinton National Airport in Little Rock, Northwest Arkansas Regional Airport in Bentonville and Fort Smith Regional Airport are the state's main airports, apart from dozens of smaller regional and municipal airstrips.

coasts have all the best culture? *https://crystalbridges.org, 600 Museum Way*

JOHNNY CASH'S BOYHOOD HOME
Before he was the Man in Black, Johnny Cash grew up in the Dyess Colony, a federally funded town created by the WPA to give hundreds of impoverished families a fresh start. Arkansas State University has been restoring significant buildings in Dyess, starting with the Cash family home. *http://dyesscash.astate.edu, 110 Center Dr*

LITTLE ROCK CENTRAL HIGH SCHOOL
In 1957 nine black students stepped up to the front lines in the battle for civil rights when they desegregated Little Rock Central High School. Today the school is a National Historic Site that still educates students; it offers guided tours, but book in advance. *www.nps.gov/chsc, 2120 W Daisy L Gatson Bates Dr*

OZARK FOLK CENTER STATE PARK
This state park in Mountain View is dedicated to preserving the music, crafts and culture of Ozark pioneers. The Craft Village is home to more than 20 working artisans, and southern mountain music fills the air during live concerts. *www.arkansasstateparks.com, 1032 Park Ave*

SPA CITY
Set in the rolling hills of the Ouachitas, Hot Springs has been everything from a Major League Baseball training ground that saw the likes of Babe Ruth to a gambling mecca that was a favorite of Al Capone during Prohibition. It's nicknamed Spa City because of its thermal springs, many of them in Hot Springs National Park to the north, that led to the construction of the bathhouses on Bathhouse Row. *www.hotsprings.org*

THE UNEXPECTED PROJECT
Since 2015, The Unexpected Project has brought internationally renowned street artists here to create a walkable outdoor gallery, breathing new life into downtown Fort Smith. There are dozens of murals on view, as well as nearby cafes, restaurants and boutiques. *www.unexpectedfs.com*

FAMILY OUTINGS

EUREKA SPRINGS Tucked into the Ozark Mountains, sitting just below the outstretched arms of the Christ of the Ozarks statue, Eureka Springs is a maze of steep, winding streets lined with colorful Victorian homes. Packed into this tiny town are the architecturally marvelous Thorncrown Chapel, the haunted Crescent Hotel, Lake Leatherwood City Park and a bustling community of artists. *www.eurekasprings.org*

RIVER MARKET DISTRICT Little Rock's downtown is anchored by the natural beauty of the Arkansas River. History buffs can visit the Clinton Presidential Library and Museum as well as the Old State House Museum. For foodies there's Ottenheimer Market Hall, with an array of international cuisines under one roof. Meanwhile, art lovers can enjoy a walking tour of more than 100 sculptures in the area. The Metro Streetcar provides local transport. *www.rivermarket.info*

From left: Historic Little Rock High; waterfall at Hot Springs National Park. Previous page: The Little Rock skyline at sunset.

ITINERARY

Day 1
Start your two-day visit to Little Rock by venturing to the Clinton Presidential Library and Museum and the Heifer International headquarters' village and urban farm before taking a stroll through the William E 'Bill' Clark Presidential Park Wetlands. To get around the River Market District, the convenient Metro Streetcar has a 3.4 mile network that operates between Little Rock and North Little Rock.

Day 2
Spend day 2 going back in time at the Historic Arkansas Museum and Old State House Museum before jumping back to the present with a visit to the Arkansas State Capitol.

Day 3
Trek an hour west to historic downtown Hot Springs and take in the fascinating past of the city with a walk along Bathhouse Row and the Hot Springs Baseball Trail. Then take a peek inside the Arlington Hotel and visit the Gangster Museum of America for a look at the city's mobster era. Grab food at the Ohio Club, which in the 1920s was a speakeasy that attracted patrons like Al Capone.

Day 4
Drive north to visit the Chaffee Barbershop Museum at Fort Chaffee before heading to downtown Fort Smith for a walking tour of The Unexpected Project. Enjoy taking in the nearby cafes and boutiques and break up your mural sightseeing with a stop at the Fort Smith National Historic Site and Fort Smith Museum of History.

Day 5
In northwest Arkansas, start in Fayetteville with a visit to the Clinton House Museum and a stroll around the downtown square and the University of Arkansas campus before heading to Bentonville for a visit to the Crystal Bridges Museum of American Art, the best museum in the entire region.

Day 6
Drive east into the Ozark Mountains for a jaunt through Eureka Springs. Start at the Christ of the Ozarks for a panoramic view of the town, then drive down the winding roads to take in the Victorian homes of this arty small town escape. Take a walk downtown before wrapping up the day with a ghost tour at the famously spooky Crescent Hotel.

CALIFORNIA

★ ★ ★ ★ ★ ★ ★ ★ ★ ★ ★ ★ ★ ★ ★ ★ ★ ★

POPULATION: 39.8 million | **SIZE:** 163,696 sq miles | **STATE CAPITAL:** Sacramento
LARGEST CITY: Los Angeles | **WEBSITE:** www.visitcalifornia.com

RIDE INTO THE SUNSET AND EVENTUALLY YOU'LL ARRIVE IN CALIFORNIA, AMERICA'S DREAM state. Follow Pacific Coast Highway 1 past movie-star mansions and hippie homesteads, and you can mark the exact spots where California dreams became real. Here are the sunny suburbs where Black Power and Facebook were founded; there are the misty vineyards where prized wines are made by Cesar Chavez–unionized farmworkers. Above are lofty mountaintops proclaimed as national parks; below are freeway underpasses reclaimed by renegade skateboarders. California drives the nation's food trends as well as its entertainment; without California, America's menu would be drab and predictable. You'll recognize California from the movies, but just when the California scenery looks familiar, new horizons appear. Here at the outer edge of the continent, every sunset is an open invitation to keep dreaming.

© Corey Jenkins / Getty Images

FOOD & DRINK

CALIFORNIA CUISINE NorCal (Northern California) hippies started a 'back to the land' organic farming revolution in the 1960s, and chef Alice Waters has served that revolution on a platter since 1971 at her landmark local, seasonal, sustainable restaurant Chez Panisse. The secret to California's creative, ultra-fresh food is dirt. This mineral-rich coastal terrain yields almost all of America's specialty produce, from artichokes to zebra tomatoes. Look for ingredient-forward menus proudly crediting local farmers, with sustainable sourcing footnotes. Get extra avocado with your meal to give it that extra local flavor.

FISH TACOS Originally from Mexico's Baja peninsula, this simple dish crossed the border to become a SoCal (Southern California) speciality. Fried white fish and shredded cabbage are wrapped in a corn tortilla, drizzled with crema (a thin sour cream sauce), and squirted with lime for a handy beach bite. Californian Ralph Rubio gets credit for opening San Diego's first fish taco stand in 1983; Rubio's is now a multi-outlet chain. Every San Diegan has a beloved fish taco, whether from a taco truck, beach vendor or sit-down restaurant. To find your own favorite, sample your way from Salud or El Paisa in Barrio Logan to Pacific Beach Fish Shop, then north to Las Olas up in Cardiff-by-the-Sea.

IN-N-OUT BURGER While San Francisco may have the most Michelin stars and restaurants per capita of any US city, Californians still swear by fast-food mainstay In-N-Out Burger even as the number of top-notch chefs in the state explodes. Gourmet and farm-fresh may be California bywords, but In-N-Out has had a good thing going since 1948: prime chuck beef processed on-site, plus fries and shakes made with ingredients you can pronounce, all served by employees paid a living wage. Consider ordering yours off the menu 'Animal style,' cooked in mustard with grilled onions.

LA FOOD TRUCKS Movie stars bow before the altar of SoCal cuisine: the food-truck order window. East LA loyalties are divided between shrimp tacos and ceviche tostadas at Mariscos Jalisco and Mariscos 4 Vientos, but Korean short rib burritos unite LA at chef Roy Choi's Kogi Korean BBQ trucks. Food trucks cover SoCal beachfronts, nightclub parking lots and movie back lots; track nearby trucks on the website Roaming Hunger.

MISSION BURRITO Oversized and stuffed with flavor, these massive burritos are synonymous with California's Cal-Mex food. This isn't a fad – Cal-Mex has been California's most popular food since before statehood, when California still belonged to Mexico. Debates rage over the definitive NorCal burrito in San Francisco's Mission District and beyond – taste-test them yourself (keeping them intact is a notorious challenge) and pick a favorite.

PACIFIC RIM SOUL FOOD From Chinese noodles to Peruvian cocktails, Californian cooks have catered to cosmopolitan cravings since the gold rush. Californian chefs continue to invent Pacific Rim trade-route dishes: recent standouts include Ravi

★ ★ ★

California's
5
WILDEST
BEACHES

La Jolla Dive into marine biology studies at San Diego-La Jolla Underwater Park Ecological Reserve, a 6000-acre wonderland of sea caves and tide pools.

Venice Unicyclers, bodybuilders and tattoo artists are glimpsed in their natural habitat at this alterna-beach scene.

Año Nuevo Little compares to this elephant seal hot spot north of Santa Cruz, where you'll witness alpha-male brawls and scrawny adolescents loudly barking.

Point Reyes National Seashore North of San Francisco, a lonesome lighthouse sits in 100 sq miles of coastal wilderness.

Lost Coast Pacific sunsets over black sand beaches reward hikers traversing California's most rugged, remote stretch of northern coastline, protected by the Bureau of Land Management.

California's
BEST LIVE MUSIC

Mega Music Festivals CA's marquee music event is Coachella in Indio, drawing 250,000 attendees over three April weekends to see major headliners. SF's Golden Gate Park hosts Outside Lands, NorCal's biggest festival, with chart-topping acts in August, and Hardly Strictly Bluegrass, October's free (yes, free) roots music jamboree.

West Coast Jazz LA's Central Avenue was the stomping ground of Charlie Parker and Charles Mingus, while San Francisco's North Beach clubs swung with the Beat poets and Dave Brubeck. Monterey Jazz has showcased international talent since 1958, and SFJAZZ Center is America's biggest dedicated jazz venue.

World-Class Classical Frank Gehry's design for Walt Disney Concert Hall echoes the thundering LA Philharmonic inside, while San Francisco Symphony holds more Grammys than Adele, and San Francisco Opera premieres original works.

© Mark Read / Lonely Planet

© Mark Read / Lonely Planet

Kapur's Hawaiian tuna poke with Peruvian quinoa at SF's Liholiho Yacht Club, Bryant Ng's Vietnamese 'sunbathing' prawns with Fresno chilies at Cassia in Santa Monica, and Charles Phan's Japanese Wagyu beef atop Vietnamese cellophane noodles at Slanted Door in SF.

SAN DIEGO BREWPUBS Drink like a picky sailor on shore leave in San Diego, home to 100-plus craft brewers. Begin with brewpubs in the San Diego Brewers Guild, host of November's Beer Week, which actually lasts 10 days (and no one's complaining). Standouts include Ballast Point Tasting Room and Kitchen for tastings with beer-steamed mussels, and beer-battered fish taco pairings at Stone Brewing World Bistro, aptly located in Liberty Station's former Navy mess hall.

WINE COUNTRY FEASTS Cheese pairings and wine tastings are warm-ups to Wine Country's main event: a sit-down gourmet extravaganza. Napa Valley is just 30 miles long, but it's lined with bistros – especially

in Yountville, the most Michelin-starred village on the planet and home of Thomas Keller's landmark French Laundry. Save room for Sonoma County, where culinary stars are converging around pioneering sustainable farmstead restaurants Farmhouse Inn, Single Thread and Backyard.

NATURAL ESCAPES

BIG SUR On California's most poetic stretch of coastline, from Carmel to San Simeon, rainbows rise from cliffside waterfalls at Julia Pfeiffer Burns State Beach, whales glide past the lighthouse at Point Sur State Historic Park, wild ideas swirl around Henry Miller Memorial Library, and nude stargazers contemplate mysteries of the universe in cliffside hot tubs at Esalen Institute. *www.parks.ca.gov*

DEATH VALLEY NATIONAL PARK Tumble down Mesquite Flat Dunes at dawn, walk on water at salt-encrusted Badwater Basin, find inspiration in the semiprecious-

© Denise Taylor / Getty Images

From left: Selection of seasonal food in Sonoma; driving in Death Valley; lifeguard tower at Malibu Beach. Previous page: La Jolla Cove in San Diego.

stone scenery of Artist's Drive and sleep under starry skies amid singing sands and whispering palms. Just over the Nevada border, Death Valley is America's hottest place – but when valleys erupt with wildflowers in spring, no place feels more alive. www.nps.gov/deva

JOSHUA TREE NATIONAL PARK Green pom-poms wave from desert trees at this park where the Mojave Desert and Colorado Desert face off. Beyond the eponymous trees, which can live up to a thousand years, you might spot jackrabbits, desert turtles, bighorn sheep, night lizards, and even a howling coyote. Test your bouldering skills at Skull Rock and brave spiky Cholla Cactus Nature Trail to see the desert bloom; it's an easy road trip from LA and a good add-on to Palm Springs. www.nps.gov/jotr

LAKE TAHOE The topaz-blue crown of the High Sierra never fails to dazzle, year-round. Glide down epic snowy slopes in winter, paddle pristine mountain waters in summer or hike and mountain-bike to historic cabins anytime. Tahoe is a standing invitation to explore and toast nature's wonders over hot chocolate or manzanita-berry cocktails. https://visitinglaketahoe.com

LASSEN VOLCANIC NATIONAL PARK Ominous signs for Bumpass Hell lead to Lassen's totally twisted natural wonders. Mud pots burp, fumaroles hiss steam, and turquoise springs boil in sulfur-yellow riverbeds. Gold rush pioneer Bumpass didn't strike it rich in northern California's remote volcanic landscape, but he did find the ideal spot for gazing at summer meteor showers and winter cross-country snowshoeing. www.nps.gov/lavo

MALIBU Even without celebrity beach houses, sunset cocktail patios or iconic surfers, Malibu, west of LA, would be a sight to see. Seaside bluffs hug sandy coves along 23 miles of protected coastline, with million-dollar views accessible to all at public beaches,

FUN FACT

California is the world's fifth-largest economy, ahead of the UK and France and behind Germany, Japan, China and the US overall.

© Trinette Reed / Getty Images; Left: © Christopher Kimmel / Getty Images

★ ★ ★

CALIFORNIA
Pride

Come out wherever you are for LGBTQ Pride parades, events and parties from San Diego to Eureka. No place in this solar system shows Pride quite like San Francisco, where monthlong June celebrations include the binge-worthy LGBTQ Frameline Film Festival and the joyous parade, 1.2 million strong. Why stop there, though? Celebrate from April to October with these classic California Pride events:

➤ Play gay beach volleyball at **Laguna Beach**.

➤ Score Disneyland discounts for LGBTQ families in **Anaheim**.

➤ Take selfies with megastars in **West Hollywood**.

➤ Toast LGBT solidarity at **Santa Barbara** beach picnics.

➤ Hug trees and fellow LGBTQ hippies at **Humboldt County**'s Redwood Pride.

park canyon trails and surfer-paradise campgrounds. For surf reports, wildfire advisories and coastal road conditions, check the visitors bureau. *www.visitcalifornia.com*

REDWOOD COAST California redwood trees can reach 22 stories high and 1500 years old, but their endurance isn't only a natural wonder: it's a tribute to Californians who have protected these giants for a century. The Redwood Coast begins north of San Francisco at Muir Woods National Monument, stretches through Sonoma and Mendocino to Humboldt County's Avenue of the Giants, and sprawls across vast Redwood National and State Parks to reach ancient Jedediah Smith Redwoods State Park. *www.visitredwoods.com*

YOSEMITE NATIONAL PARK The living glaciers of Yosemite have exposed the Sierra Nevada mountains' soft spot, splitting granite cliffs to reveal an enchanted valley. Here waterfalls glow fiery red at sunset, and giant sequoia groves

make humans shrink in comparison. Book ahead to camp under crystalline stars in this Unesco World Heritage Site, and emerge with a renewed sense of wonder before returning back to San Francisco three hours west. *www.nps.gov/yose*

ARTS, HISTORY & CULTURE

CALIFORNIA'S MISSION TRAIL Take Highway 101 from San Diego to Sonoma and you'll pass California's 21 Spanish missions. Franciscan founder Junípero Serra imagined local converts would run the missions, but European-introduced diseases decimated Native American populations, and California's missions closed by 1834. Mission San Juan Capistrano is the best restored, and San Juan Bautista is recognizable as the church from Alfred Hitchcock's *Vertigo*. *www.parks.ca.gov/?page_id=22722*

GETTY CENTER Money can't buy taste, people say – until they visit this minimalist

From left: A hiker looks up through the sunlight at a giant redwood tree in Stout Grove, Jedediah Smith Redwoods State Park; Palm Springs bliss; a barista pours a nitro coffee at Lo/Cal Coffee in Santa Monica.

© Bob Berg / Getty Images

white marble temple in LA, lined with Rembrandts, Van Goghs and modern photography masterworks. Some might find the French furniture collection glitzy or the reflecting pools over the top. But you can't argue with these panoramic views of LA, or the price: the Getty is open to the public free of charge.
www.getty.edu, 1200 Getty Center Dr

HISTORIC CHINATOWNS Fleeing China's Opium Wars, Chinese immigrants were early arrivals in California's 1848 gold rush. Despite anti-Chinese laws restricting them to ethnic enclaves, Chinese Californians pioneered transcontinental railroads, international telephone service and national civil rights movements. San Francisco's Chinatown has historic alleys and LA's Chinatown has galleries galore, but the wildest Chinatown in the West is Locke, the Prohibition-speakeasy boomtown outside Sacramento.

LANDMARK MURALS Colorful murals have covered California since the 1930s, when Diego Rivera's murals at San Francisco Art Institute and City College inspired Coit Tower's Social Realism Public Works murals, now a national landmark. David Alfaro Siqueiros' 1932 anti-colonial *América Tropical* mural on LA's Olvera Street was whitewashed within a decade of its unveiling, but it's been painstakingly restored by the Getty Center. Today mural walking tours cover neighborhoods including San Francisco's Mission District, Downtown LA and Venice Beach.

LOS ANGELES COUNTY MUSEUM OF ART In Los Angeles, duck under the 340-ton boulder also known as Michael Heizer's Levitated Mass and enter the biggest art museum in the West. Sprawling LA-style from the east-end Japanese Pavilion to LACMA West's converted department store, this complex covers art history from ancient southwestern Mimbres ceramics to contemporary Islamic art, plus selfie-worthy surprises à la Chris Burden's Urban Light installation of vintage LA streetlamps.
www.lacma.org, 5905 Wilshire Blvd

★ ★ ★

COFFEE CULTURE

Coffee is no simple brew here: it sets global trends. CA pioneered 'third wave coffee,' or specialty coffee sourced direct from small-scale growers, roasted on-site at cafes. Today the CA-based Coffee Review website covers cult roasters ranging from Santa Cruz' venerable Verve to scrappy 'micro-roasters' like Oakland's pedal-powered Bicycle Coffee. Fourth wave coffee bars raise coffee craft to the next level with siphoning, pour-overs, cold brewing and microfoaming. Visit fourth wave SF icons Blue Bottle and Ritual, and you'll agree: when the coffee's this good, sleep is overrated.

© Chris Rogers / Getty Images ; Left: © Kurt Preissler / Getty Images

★ ★ ★

California's OTHER WINE COUNTRIES

Napa and Sonoma are California's marquee wine destinations, but California has been graced with vineyards statewide since the 1800s. Santa Barbara's coastal mists lead to its signature pinots, and Mendocino County is now as famous for its sparkling pinot noir as for its other feel-good cash crop: pot. Paso Robles is cowboy country, and there's no finer rib-eye pairing than its down-to-earth local syrahs and barnstorming Rhône red blends. Head to the Sierra Foothills to uncover a wealth of old-vine zinfandels and robust cabs.

PALM SPRINGS The desert oasis that put mid-century modern architecture on the map remains Hollywood's favorite hideaway, from Elvis' honeymoon to Beyoncé's Coachella after-parties. But the permanent scene-stealers here in the Coachella Valley are Palm Springs Art Museum and Modernism Week, when modernist dream homes open to visitors. Tiki bars are ubiquitous and the LGBTQ scene is legendary, from poolside drag brunches to The Dinah, America's biggest women's party. *www.visitpalmsprings.com*

SAN FRANCISCO MUSEUM OF MODERN ART Get lost in Richard Serra's rusted-metal lobby maze and discover new favorite artists at SFMOMA's recent $500 million extension. The now triple-sized SFMOMA hosts sprawling new-media installations by hometown favorite Matthew Barney, a corner sanctuary for Agnes Martin's minimalist masterpieces, and a center dedicated to America's finest photography collection, from gold rush daguerreotypes to Dorothea Lange's government-censored WWII photos, as well as rotating special exhibitions. *www.sfmoma.org, 151 3rd St*

FAMILY OUTINGS

ALCATRAZ In SF, on the ferry ride across San Francisco Bay to this former island jail, visitors plot their escapes. If you were a convict sent to Alcatraz, would you dig a tunnel or hide in the laundry? Hear the stories of real-life escape attempts on a riveting cellblock audio tour featuring former prisoners and guards – or if you have kids up for a dare, book ahead for a twilight tour. *www.nps.gov/Alcatraz, Alcatraz Landing at Pier 33*

DISNEYLAND Generations bond in Anaheim over the Magic Kingdom's storybook characters and spellbinding charms. Main Street, USA is a promenade/gauntlet of musical numbers, mascot hugs and ice cream leading to classic 1950s attractions: Cinderella's Castle, Mickey's Toontown and Tomorrowland. Here,

From left: Vineyard in Santa Barbara County; Exploratorium in San Francisco; Comic-Con in San Diego.

© Justin Baker / Getty Images

Star Wars shuttles zoom over Tatooine deserts, and visitors can embrace gleeful inauthenticity and enjoy Big Thunder Mountain Railroad's mining-themed roller coaster, Indiana Jones Adventure's geographically challenged safari, and Pirates of the Caribbean hijacking high jinks. *https://disneyland.disney.go.com, 1313 Disneyland Dr*

EXPLORATORIUM Step off a San Francisco pier into a world of wild possibilities, where you can stop time, interrupt a tornado, and find your way through total darkness using only your sense of touch. Push the boundaries of science and art at this experimental museum, where resident MacArthur fellows (individuals selected for the foundation's 'genius grants') invite you to bend rules and make discoveries with hands-on, eye-popping, mind-boggling exhibits. *www.exploratorium.edu, Pier 15*

GOLD COUNTRY'S HIGHWAY 49 Time travel along Highway 49 starting in Sonora,

established by gold miners from Mexico's Sonora region. When Sonoran miners struck it rich, California imposed taxes on immigrants – but the tax backfired when they returned to Mexico, and California's economy collapsed. Costumed actors reenact gold panning at Columbia State Historic Park, and Marshall Gold Discovery State Historic Park shows where the gold rush started. Historic Nevada City is booming with California's newfound natural resources: wine and marijuana. *www.visitcalifornia.com/attraction/highway-49*

HEARST CASTLE Be the VIP guest of eccentric millionaire and media mogul William Randolph Hearst, who spent a fortune on this 165-room mansion in San Simeon to impress his girlfriend and entertain movie stars. California's first licensed woman architect, Julia Morgan, took on the monumental task of making Hearst happy with Spanish banquet halls, Roman pools and a private zoo at Hearst Castle. Look for zebras at neighboring

★ ★ ★

Comic-Con
& ON

Fans of comics, fantasy, and sci-fi series need no introduction to Comic-Con, the mega pop culture convention held each summer in San Diego. Costumes are highly encouraged and make it easy to spot fellow travelers among the 130,000 attendees gathered to meet comics legends, anime giants, and superhero movie stars. Since this summer blockbuster is so popular, there's a sequel: Wonder-Con in Anaheim is timed for spring break, with epic autograph sessions and game tournaments. Silicon Valley's Comic Con is an unabashedly nerdy celebration, costumes required.

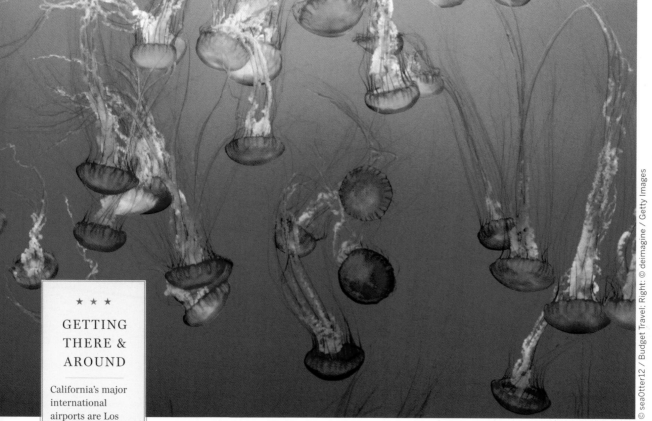

© seaOtter12 / Budget Travel; Right: © deimagine / Getty Images

★ ★ ★

GETTING THERE & AROUND

California's major international airports are Los Angeles International in Southern California and San Francisco International in Northern California; domestic airlines serve California's smaller regional airports. City traffic is notorious: take public transit in and around SF and LA whenever it's possile. Amtrak takes the scenic route up and down the state (and runs legendary transcontinental routes ending in the state), but to taste that iconic California flavor, some driving up the Pacific Coast Highway is a must.

Hearst Ranch, and sea life at William Randolph Hearst State Beach. *http://hearstcastle.org, 750 Hearst Castle Rd*

MONTEREY BAY AQUARIUM Walk underwater in this aquarium built right into Monterey Bay, with domed sardine ceilings and walls of glowing jellyfish. Learn about the role people play in Pacific sea life as you make friends with a shy pink octopus, clap along with a band of rescued sea otters and pick up ballet moves from fluttering golden sea dragons. *www.montereybayaquarium.org, 886 Cannery Row*

SANTA CRUZ Surf's up on Main Beach, where kooks (newbies) learn from pros and catch waves at Beginners' Lane. Families flock to Santa Cruz Beach Boardwalk for old-timey rides perfect for holiday photos

– and rickety enough to make hearts race, especially the 1924 Giant Dipper coaster. Hit Municipal Pier for lunch with sea lions or visit the Sant Cruz Surfing Museum at Lighthouse Point to salute Gidget, TV's teen surfer girl, who popularized the sport in the 1960s. *http://www.santacruz.com*

UNIVERSAL STUDIOS Hollywood Summer blockbusters can't match action-packed tram tours through Universal Studios' backlot theme park in Universal City. Dart through sets from jungly Jurassic Park to spooky Bates Motel, narrowly dodge flash floods, earthquakes and alien attacks, and miraculously survive close encounters with Jaws and King Kong. For your grand finale, ride coasters through the Wizarding World of Harry Potter. *www.universalstudioshollywood.com, 100 Universal City Plaza*

VENICE SKATEPARK When neighborhood tweens were edged out of prime surf spots by older kids in the 1970s, they put wheels on wood and invented California's original extreme sport: skateboarding. Today's LA skaters don't have to sneak into empty pools to practice ollies and grabs: this park in Venice features 17,000 sq ft of challenges, including an old-school skate run and pool. *www.veniceskatepark.com, 1500 Oceanfront Walk*

From left: Monterey Bay Aquarium; Venice Skatepark.

ITINERARY

Day 1
An ambitious trek hugging California's coast from bottom to top starts with a beach-crawl from La Jolla's tide pools near San Diego to Venice's Muscle Beach in LA, stopping for surf breaks, fish tacos and sandy yoga poses along the way: dude, you're a Californian already. In LA, get high culture at the Getty or keep a low profile with star chefs at Santa Monica Farmers Market, and then hit Sunset Strip hot spots.

Day 2
Driving north from Los Angeles, hug the coastline on the Pacific Coast Highway, passing Malibu beach houses and Santa Barbara villas. Go further north to Pismo Beach Monarch Butterfly Grove, and explore Hearst's Castle in San Simeon before stopping in Big Sur.

Day 3
In Big Sur, discover poetic views at Julia Pfeiffer Burns State Park and Beat poetry at Henry Miller Memorial Library along Highway 1, which meanders past woodsy Carmel. Visit the wondrous Monterey Bay Aquarium and bond with sea otters over sustainable seafood lunches along Cannery Row; then

head to Santa Cruz for surf lessons and vintage coaster rides at Beach Boardwalk. Follow Highway 1 north to San Francisco.

Day 4
In SF, start at SFMOMA or the Exploratorium before you drive north and drift past Sonoma's Russian River, two hours north. Stop for wine tasting along Sonoma's Dry Creek Valley and in the booming vineyard scene of Mendocino's Anderson Valley on your way to the Mendocino Coast.

Day 5
Brunch and bookshops await in Mendocino village, and botanical gardens and local crafts just north in Fort Bragg. But the star attraction is the Redwood Coast, from staggering 'sea stack' rocks to Humboldt's redwood-lined Avenue of the Giants. Escape modern life along Lost Coast hiking trails, then retreat to the hippie haven of Arcata overnight.

Day 6
Continuing north from Arcata, stop in Trinidad for waterfront whale-watching and picnic supplies, then lose track of time in the ancient groves at lovely Jedediah Smith Redwoods State Park.

COLORADO

★ ★ ★ ★ ★ ★ ★ ★ ★ ★ ★ ★ ★ ★ ★ ★ ★ ★ ★ ★

POPULATION: 5.6 million | **SIZE:** 104,094 sq miles
STATE CAPITAL: Denver | **WEBSITE:** www.colorado.com

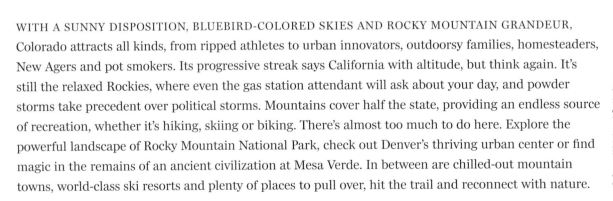

WITH A SUNNY DISPOSITION, BLUEBIRD-COLORED SKIES AND ROCKY MOUNTAIN GRANDEUR, Colorado attracts all kinds, from ripped athletes to urban innovators, outdoorsy families, homesteaders, New Agers and pot smokers. Its progressive streak says California with altitude, but think again. It's still the relaxed Rockies, where even the gas station attendant will ask about your day, and powder storms take precedent over political storms. Mountains cover half the state, providing an endless source of recreation, whether it's hiking, skiing or biking. There's almost too much to do here. Explore the powerful landscape of Rocky Mountain National Park, check out Denver's thriving urban center or find magic in the remains of an ancient civilization at Mesa Verde. In between are chilled-out mountain towns, world-class ski resorts and plenty of places to pull over, hit the trail and reconnect with nature.

© Steve Whiston / Getty Images

FOOD & DRINK

CANNABIS With the legalization of retail marijuana, weed tourism is a booming business in Colorado. Denver and Boulder have the highest concentration of dispensaries in the state; there are more dispensaries in Denver than there are Starbucks or McDonald's locations. Dispensaries of all kinds require a valid ID to enter; once you make it past the waiting room, offerings from lollipops to gummies and extracts tempt visitors with their formerly off-limits bounty. Dosage isn't federally regulated, so use caution!

CHILE VERDE With one of the largest Hispanic populations in the country, Colorado has a Mexican food scene that is understandably thriving. Its influence stands out in Colorado's signature chile verde (green chili), a state favorite that's packed with flavor from plenty of green chilies and tomatillos, usually simmered with a slow-cooked pork shoulder.

COLORADO-RAISED LAMB The state is one of the country's top lamb producers, and its lamb is known around the world. Whether you sample it as a lamb chop or in a lamb stew, it's a range-raised delicacy every spring. Flagstaff House in Boulder serves lamb in particularly notable fashion as a rack, shank or jus, with the meal heightened by the views of the Denver metro area.

DENVER CENTRAL MARKET Set in a repurposed warehouse, this gourmet marketplace wows with its style and breadth of options that represent the diversity and bounty of Colorado. Eat a bowl of handmade pasta or an artisanal sandwich; consider a wood-fired pizza or street tacos. Or just grab a cocktail at the bar and wander between the fruit stand and chocolatier. There are communal tables and a street-side patio. *https:// denvercentralmarket.com, 2669 Larimer St*

MICROBREWS Colorado's prolific crop of breweries is the exact opposite of juggernaut Coors Brewing Company, so long associated with the Rocky Mountains. Times have changed, and the state's endless IPAs and rich stouts richly reward visitors who explore the thriving and innovative beer culture. Try New Belgium brewery, which brings you face-to-face with the freewheeling essence of Fort Collins: a hoppy passion for beer, bicycles and sustainability. The tour guides are knowledgeable, smart and playful, and the special selection of beers is among the nation's best.

MOUNTAIN TROUT The wild waters of the Rocky Mountains teem with silvery trout, their flesh tender and succulent and sweet. The best way to try some? Catch it yourself. Learn fly-fishing, a state obsession, by hiring a guiding company like Duranglers (*https://duranglers.com*). It's an indelible local experience that takes full advantage of the state's mountain streams and lakes.

NATURAL ESCAPES

ARKANSAS RIVER RAFTING Brace yourself for the icy splash as you plunge into a roaring set of big waves. Running

---

★ ★ ★

A LEAN AND GREEN STATE

Flying the green sustainability flag is a point of fervent Colorado pride. Cue the local, grass-fed, fair-trade and organic options on any brunch menu. The EPA recognizes Colorado as having some of the cleanest air and water in the country. It's also a leader in renewable energy, with more LEED-certified buildings than any other state. Travelers can whiz from Denver's airport to downtown via light rail. And there's more to come. A revamp of Highway 36 between Denver and Boulder rewards alternative transportation, with tolls on single-occupant cars, an express shared-vehicle lane and dedicated bus and bike lanes (the first phase of the revamp cost a cool $312 million). New bike-share programs in Front Range cities will help maintain the state's status as the nation's slimmest, all while saving on fuel use.

© Dan Ballard / Getty Image ; Left: © Chip Kalback / Lonely Planet

★ ★ ★

FROZEN DEAD GUY DAYS

Macabre, bizarre and wonderful, this festival brings 15,000 souls to Nederland in early March. A three-day blowout event first begun in 2002, Frozen Dead Guy Days celebrates Norwegian Grandpa Bredo Morstoel, who was cryogenically frozen and transported to a local shed to await reanimation (lots of dry ice helps). Live bands, coffin races, salmon tossing and polar plunges make this a local curiosity.

from Buena Vista through Browns Canyon National Monument to rocket through the spectacular Royal Gorge, the Arkansas River is the longest, most diverse river in the state. American Adventure Expeditions, based in Buena Vista, has trips to suit both families and thrill seekers. *www.americanadventure.com, 12844 Hwy 24*

COLORADO NATIONAL MONUMENT

Witness the sinking sun set fire to otherworldly red-rock formations, hike stark and beautiful high-desert trails and watch lightning storms roll across the distant plains. These canyon walls rise 2000ft above the Colorado River to reveal the twinkling lights of Grand Junction. It's a startling juxtaposition, even before you remember that this landscape was once patrolled by dinosaurs. *www.nps.gov/colm*

DUDE RANCHES With its wide-open ranges, wildflower meadows and snow-kissed peaks, Colorado as seen from the saddle is a whole other world. Visitors will find ample opportunity to do so. You can try your hand at herding cattle, venture out to a sustainable bison ranch or ride horses in the luxuriant Rocky Mountain retreat of Devil's Thumb Ranch in Tabernash. *https://duderanch.org/listings/states/colorado*

GREAT SAND DUNES NATIONAL PARK

Sculpted by wind and seemingly straight out of Arabia, these 55 sq miles of sand dunes in southern Colorado appear out of nowhere. Ringed by mountain peaks and glassy wetlands, the tallest dunes in America (up to 750ft) are both eerie and amazing. Hike in to camp under the Milky Way or just have fun careening down these pillowy hills on your own two feet. *www.nps.gov/grsa*

MESA VERDE NATIONAL PARK You don't just walk into the past at Mesa Verde, the site of 600 ancient cliff dwellings. You scramble up 10ft ladders, scale rock faces and crawl through tunnels on one exhilarating adventure. All the while you

From left: Mesa Verde; Great Sand Dunes National Park; the Denver Art Museum. Previous page: Maroon Bells, Aspen.

© Will Dozier / Getty Images

will be puzzling out the archaeological and cultural clues left by the Ancestral Puebloans who vacated the site in AD 1300. The towns of Cortez and Mancos have amenities for your visit. www.nps/gov/meve

ROCKY MOUNTAIN NATIONAL PARK
With elk grazing under granite walls, alpine meadows rife with wildflowers, and a winding road inching over the Continental Divide, the natural splendor of 415-sq-mile Rocky Mountain National Park packs a wallop. Don't get stuck behind a row of RVs on Trail Ridge Road – lace up your hiking boots instead. Trails range from epic outings up Longs Peak to elk-spotting ambles. Estes Park and Grand Lake make good bases. www.nps.gov/romo

STEAMBOAT MOUNTAIN RESORT Also
known as Ski Town, USA, this sprawling resort in Steamboat Springs has excellent powder and trails for all levels, including gentle open glades, that make for some of the best skiing in the US. In summer check out the Steamboat Bike Park. The town is also a western-style village with plenty of activities to entertain families. www.steamboat.com

ARTS, HISTORY & CULTURE

BRECKENRIDGE ARTS DISTRICT
Breckenridge doesn't just offer world-class skiing. Explore this block-long stretch of historic Breckenridge enlivened by a burgeoning arts scene with events, exhibits and workshops. There's a live-work art space for visiting artists and a ceramics studio (Quandary Antiques Cabin), as well as exhibition space in buildings like the Breckenridge Theater. Some permanent sculptures are on display outside the buildings. www.breckcreate.org/explore/arts-district, S. Ridge St & E. Washington Ave

CENTRAL CITY OPERA Head to
Central City in the hills west of Denver for a summer opera performance at this gorgeous, ornate 19th-century opera house built by miners. The ceiling fresco alone is

FUN FACT

The 13th step leading to the entrance of the Colorado State Capitol in Denver is exactly 1 mile above sea level.

★

© Deb Snelson / Getty Images

remarkable. Founded in 1932, Central City Opera is one of the oldest opera companies in the country. *www.centralcityopera.org, 124 Eureka St*

DENVER ART MUSEUM This isn't some stodgy old art museum, though its holdings can compete with the best. With one of the largest Native American art collections in the US, a fabulous western American art section, and multimedia exhibits on everything from British art to Star Wars costumes, DAM is amazing. The best part is diving into the interactive exhibits. *www.denverartmuseum.org, 100 W 14th Ave*

DENVER PERFORMING ARTS COMPLEX Not sure what you want to do in Denver on a given night? Come here and something may spark your interest. This massive complex has 10 venues in the space of four city blocks, including the historic Ellie Caulkins Opera House and the Boettcher Concert Hall. It's also home to the Colorado Ballet, Denver Center for the Performing Arts, Opera Colorado and the Colorado

Symphony. *www.artscomplex.com, 14th St and Champa St*

RED ROCKS AMPHITHEATER Once a Ute camping spot, this natural open-air amphitheater in Morrison produces pristine acoustics for your favorite band. Just ask U2, who filmed *Under a Blood Red Sky* here. No wonder it's seen as America's best small outdoor venue. With the setting sun aflame on the rock formations and music thrumming, it's one captivating experience. *www.redrocksonline.com, 183000 W Alameda Pkwy*

FAMILY OUTINGS

ASHCROFT GHOST TOWN Visiting a ghost town provides a window onto Colorado's stark and hardscrabble pioneer past. It's a trip to wander through this 1880s silver-mining town, with its miners' cabins, broken-down wagons, abandoned post office and saloon. Just outside sleek Aspen, it's a stark contrast to that high-end resort town, and the access point to the

★ ★ ★

Ask a Local

'The best way to make the most of summer in the mountains is with a trip to Telluride. Festivals like Telluride Bluegrass or Blues & Brews bring together an awesome community, and they're so much fun. When you need a break from the crowds, walk a few blocks off Main Street and the San Juan mountains are right there to explore.' – *Annie Ramirez, teacher*

From left: Telluride; inside the Denver Museum of Nature and Science; taps at the Great American Beer Festival.

© Xinhua / Alamy Stock Photo; Left: © Sharon Wildie / Shutterstock

breathtaking Castle Creek Valley; in winter you can access it on cross-country skis. *www.aspenhistory.org, Castle Creek Rd*

CHAUTAUQUA PARK This historic park is the gateway to Boulder's Flatirons, the rock formations that are the signature icon of Boulder. This magnificent slab of open space has oodles of hiking trails. There are also on-site cabins, a concert venue and a lush lawn for picnics. Stop in the Ranger's Cottage for free nature discovery packs with binoculars, field guides and activities. *www.chautauqua.com, 900 Baseline Rd*

CHILDREN'S MUSEUM OF DENVER This is the hottest ticket in Denver for kids, and is one of the best children's museums in the country. After a recent expansion, highlights include an enclosed three-story climbing structure (helmets provided), a kids' kitchen with hands-on cooking classes, a 2300-sq-ft art studio, a maker space, and a huge outdoor playground to romp in. *www.mychildsmuseum.org, 2121 Children's Museum Dr*

COORS FIELD On a summer night in Denver, there's no better place to be than the ballpark. With an on-site brewery and cheap tickets for same-day seats in the Rockpile section, Coors Field in the revamped LoDo (Lower Downtown) neighborhood is the signature stadium of the West. The Colorado Rockies play from April to September. Stadium tours, available year-round, include access to the field and Press Club. *www.mlb.com/col/ballpark, 2001 Blake St*

DENVER MUSEUM OF NATURE & SCIENCE Located on the edge of Denver's City Park (also home to the Denver Zoo), this classic natural-science museum has excellent temporary exhibits that bring to life topics like the biomechanics of bugs, Pompeii and mythical creatures. Permanent exhibits are equally engaging and include an exceptional array of those cool dioramas we all loved as kids. The IMAX Theater and Gates Planetarium are especially fun for visitors. *www.dmns.org, 2001 Colorado Blvd*

★ ★ ★

GREAT *American* **BEER FESTIVAL**

Colorado has more microbreweries per capita than any other US state, and Denver's hugely popular fall Great American Beer Festival at the Colorado Convention Center sells out in advance. More than 500 breweries are represented, from the big players to the home-brew enthusiasts.

© Image Source / Alamy Stock Photo

★ ★ ★

GETTING THERE & AROUND

Almost all visitors to Colorado by air come through Denver International Airport, with its light rail link to downtown. There's decent bus service on the Front Range, but to explore further, it's best to rent a car, which is cheaper away from the airport. When driving in the mountains, proceed with caution and be aware of the weather.

DINOSAUR NATIONAL MONUMENT

There are few places on earth where you can literally get your hands on a dinosaur skeleton. Dinosaur National Monument has one of largest dinosaur fossil beds in North America. Explore its desert trails, examine ancient rock art or raft the Yampa River through the serene landscape of its twisting red-rock canyons. The site, an International Dark Sky Park, extends into Utah. *www.nps.gov/dino*

PEARL STREET MALL
The highlight of downtown Boulder is this vibrant pedestrian zone filled with kids' climbing boulders and splash fountains, bars, galleries and restaurants. You'll find soaked children cavorting in the pop-jet fountains when the temperatures rise. Street performers, out in force on weekends, captivate crowds; the people-watching is extraordinary. *www.boulderdowntown.com, Pearl St between 9th and 15th Sts*

ROYAL GORGE DINOSAUR EXPERIENCE
This museum, which debuted in 2016, is highly recommended for fans of the Jurassic period and anyone interested in the evolution of life on the planet. In Cañon City, it features interactive science-focused displays where visitors get hands-on with genuine dinosaur fossils, life-size fossil casts and convincing animatronic beasties. A multistory ropes course completes the fun. *www.dinoxp.com, 44895 W. Hwy 50*

Above: Chautauqua Park's distinctive Flatirons from the trailhead.

ITINERARY

Day 1
Start in Denver with an outing to Coors Field ballpark. While away the evening knocking around downtown and strolling River North Art District (RiNo), with an exquisite dinner at one of the neighborhood's landmark restaurants and nightcaps at a craft brewery.

Day 2
Immerse yourself in culture with a trip to the Denver Art Museum and its landmark Frederic C Hamilton Wing, an angular modern masterpiece. In the evening, take in a concert at Red Rocks Amphitheater.

Day 3
Careful city planning in Boulder means the foothills are your playground. Hike to the Royal Arch in Chautauqua Park or rent a cruiser to explore the Boulder Creek Path. Spend your evening browsing the Pearl Street Mall, visiting the Dushanbe Teahouse or sipping creative cocktails at happy hour. And if urban adventures aren't your thing? On landing in Denver, rent a car and head west, away from the densest part of the state and towards Mesa Verde, where you can spend the first three days of your trip exploring Colorado's wild side.

Day 4
Drive the Peak to Peak Highway to Rocky Mountain National Park. Leave your car in a lot and take a shuttle to the Bear Lake trailhead for a hassle-free start. There's a range of trails for all abilities here; make for the namesake pine-rimmed lake for your first taste of alpine wonder.

Day 5
Dress warm to drive Trail Ridge Road over the Continental Divide, but leave the car to explore the open views and meadows exploding with wildflowers in spring where Estes leads to the Rockies. In wintertime, head up into the ski slopes of Steamboat Springs or Breckenridge for the night to get a taste of Colorado's amazing powder on any number of ski runs.

Day 6
Winding your way back to Denver, either detour to Fort Collins for a tour of the excellent New Belgium Brewery or head back via Lyons, a scenic foothills village that comes alive each August when it hosts the down-home Rocky Mountain Folks Festival.

C O N N E C T I C U T

★ ★

POPULATION: 3.6 million | **SIZE:** 5543 sq miles | **STATE CAPITAL:** Hartford
LARGEST CITY: Bridgeport | **WEBSITE:** www.ctvisit.com

CONNECTICUT STRADDLES TWO REGIONS OF THE COUNTRY. ITS WESTERN CORNER IS ORIENTED toward the Mid-Atlantic and especially New York City, with Bridgeport, New Haven and affluent suburbs like Greenwich sitting on the Metro-North commuter line. Head further east and inland, and you'll realize you are in New England – it's the region's southernmost state – with village greens and historic sites that date back to the Colonial era. For a small state (only Rhode Island and Delaware are smaller in size), Connecticut has a surprising diversity of landscapes and experiences, from seaside towns along Long Island Sound to rolling hills along the Massachusetts border. Its cities – especially New Haven and Hartford – were early centers of industrialization, while it's easy to imagine yourself back in the 19th century in some of its New England villages.

© Allard One / Shutterstock

FOOD & DRINK

CLAMBAKE Connecticut is not alone in claiming the clambake as a local specialty. The meal of clams, lobsters and mussels, along with corn and potatoes, all traditionally steamed in layers of seaweed, is popular throughout New England. Clambakes are popular summer parties but if you don't get invited to one, the Place in Guilford, open from May to October, offers a casual clambake experience.

CLAM CHOWDER Connecticut straddles an important culinary divide between New England (cream-based) and Manhattan (tomato-based) chowders. Dunville's in Westport, along I-95, serves up excellent versions of both. A casual clam shack, the Clam Castle in Madison, is known for its Rhode Island-style chowder made with a clear broth.

HAMBURGERS Connecticut is home to some must-dine destinations for those who love burgers. Louis' Lunch in New Haven, open since 1895, boasts that it is where the hamburger was invented. Its version is served on white bread with only cheese, onion and tomato, allowing the flavor of the meat to stand out. Steamed hamburgers, drenched in steamed cheese, are a central Connecticut specialty. Ted's Restaurant in Meriden is a good place to try one.

LOBSTER ROLLS You may think first of Maine when you think of the lobster roll, though many believe it was invented in Connecticut. At New London's take-out-only Captain Scott's Lobster Dock, open seasonally from April to October, you can try two variations: warm with melted butter or cold with mayonnaise. Knapp's Landing in Stratford serves its rolls along with Housatonic River views.

NEW HAVEN PIZZA The rivalry between two New Haven pizza restaurants on Wooster Street stretches back decades: Pepe's opened in 1925, and Sally's Apizza followed in 1938, both fueled by coal-fired ovens. Don't be discouraged by the lines; it's worth the wait for some of the best thin-crust pizza anywhere. Order a clam pizza, or 'pie,' a Connecticut specialty.

PORTUGUESE CUISINE In the late 19th and early 20th centuries, thousands of Portuguese immigrants settled in New England's fishing ports, and over time many made their way to Hartford. Primavera and O Camelo are two popular choices in this city with a surprisingly thriving Portuguese culinary scene. Danbury, Stonington and Waterbury all have their own annual Portuguese festivals where you can try a variety of dishes.

NATURAL ESCAPES

HAMMONASSET BEACH STATE PARK Set on two miles of beachfront in the charming small seaside town of Madison, this shoreline park on Long Island Sound is one of the biggest draws in the state. Set on land once used by Native American tribes for farming, the park opened for public use in 1920. It offers a lovely boardwalk, the Meigs Point Nature Center with environmental programming for all ages, and camping access. *https:// hammonasset.org, 1288 Boston Post Rd*

★ ★ ★

REMEMBERING the *Amistad*

A unique episode in Connecticut's past is honored by a memorial at New Haven's City Hall (and in a 1997 movie version as well). In 1839 the Spanish schooner *Amistad* was taking enslaved Mende people from Havana to Puerto Principe, when the Mende on the ship revolted, killing the captain and attempting to sail back to Sierra Leone. Rather than return to Africa as he was ordered, the ship's navigator directed the *Amistad* north; on its capture by the US Navy off Long Island, the Mende were taken to New Haven to await trial for murder. The court found that the Mende were being illegally transported, and the Supreme Court upheld the decision on appeal in an important win for the cause of abolition. In 1842 the remaining Mende returned at last to Africa, their passage paid for by abolitionists.

© Romiana Lee / Shutterstock; Left: © fotoguy22 / Getty Images

★ ★ ★

SAILFEST

Summer is jammed with events in Connecticut, but Sailfest is perhaps the biggest of them, taking place annually in New London. Since 1977 tall ships have gathered at the Connecticut port, typically on the second weekend of July. Home to the Naval Submarine Base as well as the Coast Guard Academy, New London has a long nautical heritage that is celebrated at Sailfest. While the chance to see those stately sailing vessels of yore is the excuse for the party, the three-day event also includes live music shows, food vendors and the state's largest fireworks display.

KENT FALLS STATE PARK Given Connecticut's size, it makes sense that the state doesn't have parks on the scale of, say, Yellowstone. Its small ones, however, have their charm. Kent Falls, with its cascades tumbling into the Housatonic River, is in the pretty Litchfield Hills of northwestern Connecticut. Part of the southern Berkshires, it's a prime area to enjoy New England fall foliage. *www.ct.gov/deep/kentfalls, 462 Kent Cornwall Rd*

ARTS, HISTORY & CULTURE

GILLETTE CASTLE STATE PARK William Gillette was once one of the brightest stars of the theater world, and he spent much of the fortune he earned portraying Sherlock Holmes to commission a fabulous folly overlooking the Connecticut River in East Haddam. The 24-room 'castle' was built from 1914 to 1919 and combined technological advancements (a steel frame) and unique quirks (seaweed insulation). *www.ctvisit.com/listings/gillette-castle-state-park, 67 River Rd, East Haddam*

THE GLASS HOUSE Architect Philip Johnson's Glass House in New Canaan, constructed from 1948 to 1949, is one of modernism's iconic buildings. The simple structure was radical in its day – and still is now, more than a half century later. Tours sell out far in advance: you may want to reserve your Glass House tickets before you book your flights. *http://theglasshouse.org, 842 Ponus Ridge Rd*

GUILFORD Located on Long Island Sound, Guilford is one of Connecticut's oldest towns, settled in 1639 by a group of Puritans. The streets around its expansive town green are dotted with landmarked buildings from the 17th to 19th centuries, including Connecticut's oldest stone house. Built in the same year Guilford was founded, the house now holds the Henry Whitfield Museum. *www.ci.guilford.ct.us*

HARKNESS MEMORIAL STATE PARK The 'cottages' of Newport in Rhode Island may be better known, but Connecticut has Gilded Age mansions too, including Eolia,

From left: Fourth of July fireworks at Sailfest in New London; Old Saybrook; interior of Philip Johnson's Glass House in New Canaan. Previous page: A fishing boat at Mystic Seaport.

© Randy Duchaine / Alamy Stock Photo

constructed in Waterford from 1906 to 1907 for the Harkness family. The house was later complemented by gardens designed by Beatrix Jones Farrand. In 1950 the estate was donated to the state of Connecticut and opened to the public. *www.harkness.org, 275 Great Neck Rd*

MARK TWAIN HOUSE AND MUSEUM Samuel Clemens, aka Mark Twain, lived in Hartford from 1874 to 1891 and wrote *The Adventures of Tom Sawyer* and *Adventures of Huckleberry Finn* during that period. Twain was no starving writer, as becomes clear when you explore the opulent 25-room mansion. Next door, Harriet Beecher Stowe's home is now a museum dedicated to another 19th-century literary giant, the author of *Uncle Tom's Cabin*. *https://marktwainhouse.org, 351 Farmington Ave*

OLD SAYBROOK One of Connecticut's oldest towns, Old Saybrook was officially established in 1635 at the point where the Connecticut River pours into Long Island Sound. There was, however, an even earlier

settlement of Algonquin Nehantic Indians. Today day-trippers come to visit the beaches and to wander the streets lined with Colonial and Federal buildings, many now home to restaurants and boutiques. *www.oldsaybrookct.gov*

WADSWORTH ATHENEUM Connecticut's largest museum and the United States' oldest public art museum (founded in 1842) sits in its original castle-like structure in downtown Hartford, though it has expanded to include four later additions. The impressive collection of some 50,000 pieces includes old masters (Caravaggio, Tintoretto, Zurbarán) and leading modern and contemporary artists (Calder, Pollock, Kara Walker). *https://thewadsworth.org, 600 Main St*

YALE ART GALLERY AND YALE CENTER FOR BRITISH ART Two masterpieces by renowned architect Louis Kahn face each other in downtown New Haven. The Yale Art Gallery (Kahn designed one of its buildings) has collections that span

FUN FACT

'Yankee Doodle,' the state song, is believed to have been penned in derision by the British about Connecticut volunteers in the French and Indian War.

© f11photo / Shutterstock; Right: © jgorzynik / Shutterstock

GETTING THERE & AROUND

Connecticut is well-served by Metro-North out of Grand Central and Shore Line East trains, while I-95 hugs the coast. If you're planning to use I-84 or I-95 to enter the state from New York, budget plenty of time: these major arteries are clogged at rush hour and at many other unlikely times. Visitors can fly into NYC or use Hartford's Bradley International Airport, the main Connecticut air hub.

the centuries from ancient Greek art to contemporary works. Its sister museum boasts the largest collection of British art outside the United Kingdom, with drawings and paintings by artists including Hogarth, Constable, Reynolds and Turner. *https://artgallery.yale.edu, 1111 Chapel St; https://britishart.yale.edu, 1080 Chapel St*

YALE COLLEGE While Yale was founded in 1701, the college's many neo-Gothic buildings in New Haven were constructed from 1929 to 1936. If the gargoyles and leaded windows on campus are a little over the top, it is a remarkable attempt to bring a bit of Oxford across the Atlantic. Take a look inside the cathedral-like Sterling Memorial Library and the contemporary Beinecke Library, home to the university's rare book collection. By contrast, the home of the architecture school, Rudolph Hall is an early Brutalist building. *https://www.yale.edu*

FAMILY OUTINGS

LYMAN ORCHARDS Fall foliage season is prime apple picking time here. Lyman Orchards in Middlefield packages up all the family farm fun you could ask for in one place: a corn maze, pick-your-own apples and its signature extra-tall apple pies. *www.lymanorchards.com, 32 Reeds Gap Rd*

MYSTIC SEAPORT Mystic is an iconic Connecticut shorefront town, from its drawbridge to the Mystic Seaport Museum, which displays attractions focused on New England's maritime heritage. Visitors here can explore four vintage ships including the *Charles W Morgan*, the last surviving 19th-century wooden whaleship, and joint tickets provide access to the Mystic Aquarium. In summer, get out on the water on a steamship or sailboat tour. *Mystic Pizza* movie fans will want to try a slice at the nearby shop too. *https://mystic.org*

ITINERARY

Day 1
New Haven is a logical first stop. Wander to the New Haven Green, noteworthy for its three different churches side by side, and then up Chapel Street for a meal on this lively strip.

Day 2
Start the day visiting Yale University to soak up some of the collegiate atmosphere, leaving time for its two main museums, the Art Gallery and the Center for British Art. Proceed in the afternoon to Guilford, a lovely and historic shore town.

Day 3
Keep driving east along the coast, where you'll find more New England towns to explore. Madison and Old Saybrook are both filled with appealing restaurants and boutiques. You can get your toes wet at Hammonasset Beach State Park, then drive a little bit inland to Essex and the Griswold Inn for a late lunch or early dinner.

Day 4
Continue onward to Mystic and the Mystic Seaport Museum for a deep dive into New England's maritime culture. After Mystic you'll drive up to the state's capital, Hartford.

SUBMARINE FORCE LIBRARY & MUSEUM The archives of General Dynamics Electric Boat (which built most of the US Navy's submarines) were the basis of this unique historical museum in Groton, along the Thames River. While engineers will delight in the technical plans on display, many exhibits are kid friendly. The museum is home to the USS *Nautilus*, the first nuclear-powered submarine, which can be visited on self-guided tours. *www.ussnautilus.org, 1 Crystal Lake Rd*

From left: Yale's imposing facades; Mystic Seaport's *Charles W Morgan* museum ship.

DELAWARE

★ ★ ★ ★ ★ ★ ★ ★ ★ ★ ★ ★ ★ ★ ★ ★ ★ ★ ★ ★

POPULATION: 960,000 | **SIZE:** 1981 sq miles | **STATE CAPITAL:** Dover
LARGEST CITY: Wilmington | **WEBSITE:** www.visitdelaware.com

THE FIRST STATE TO RATIFY THE CONSTITUTION IS ALSO THE COUNTRY'S SECOND SMALLEST (after only Rhode Island), occupying the northeast third of the Delmarva Peninsula. Delaware's unusual Colonial history started with Swedish and Dutch settlements before the English took possession of it in 1664. While the state sits south of the Mason–Dixon Line, it straddled North and South. Though it was a slave state, the practice was never widespread and Delaware never seceded from the Union. After the Civil War, industrialization took hold in the northern part of the state – led by one of Delaware's most famous families, the du Ponts – while the southern end remained agricultural. It may be a small state, but Delaware offers a remarkable diversity of experiences. For visitors, its overlooked riches – historic sites and natural beauty – make the state an appealing gem.

© Bo Shen / Shutterstock

FOOD & DRINK

DELAWARE BAY OYSTERS In the 19th century, Delaware Bay oysters were sold to restaurants all along the Eastern Seaboard and even shipped to California. Today only a few operations harvest the bivalves, but the oysters are a favorite of connoisseurs, with distinct flavors depending on where in the bay they are harvested. Find them on the menus of the Henlopen City Oyster House in Rehoboth Beach and the Trolley Square Oyster House in Wilmington.

DOGFISH HEAD BREWERY TOUR Delaware may not be known for as robust a brewing tradition as other microbrew hubs across the country, but it boasts one of the best-known originators of the trend. Dogfish Head has developed a following among aficionados with its unusual approach to beer. Ales and lagers incorporate peach sugars, pumpkin and other unexpected ingredients while the Midas Touch attempts to recreate a beer from 2700 years ago. The Milton brewery offers 25-minute and one-hour tours that include tastings of several beers.
www.dogfish.com, 6 Cannery Village Center

LOCAL SEAFOOD A visit to Delaware must include trying some of the state's seafood: soft-shell crabs, oysters from Delaware Bay and fish fresh from the Atlantic. You'll find the local specialty soft-shell blue crabs during their May to September season, deep fried, grilled or sautéed at seafood restaurants in all of Delaware's beach towns. Feby's Fishery in Wilmington is a local, no-attitude favorite serving up crab cakes, oyster sandwiches, fish tacos and more.

NATURAL ESCAPES

BOMBAY HOOK NATIONAL WILDLIFE REFUGE Near the top of Delaware Bay and to the east of Dover by Whitehall Landing, the refuge is an increasingly rare area of salt marshes. Delaware Bay is an important stopping point for many migratory bird species, and birders can check off a number of varieties of ducks, geese, plovers and other species. Bring your binoculars!
www.fws.gov/refuge/Bombay_Hook

DELAWARE SEASHORE STATE PARK South of Rehoboth Beach, this state park is a barrier island stretching for six miles with Rehoboth Bay on one side and the Atlantic on the other. The bay's calm waters are ideal for windsurfing, while six trails can be explored on foot, by bike or on horseback. The park's Big Chill Beach Club serves casual fare and cocktails.
https://destateparks.com, 39415 Inlet Rd

ARTS, HISTORY & CULTURE

BIGGS MUSEUM OF AMERICAN ART This museum in Dover has 16 galleries dedicated to American fine and decorative arts. A number of leading American painters are represented, such as Gilbert Stuart, Albert Bierstadt and Childe Hassam, while its collections of Early American furniture and silver are among the most comprehensive anywhere.
www.biggsmuseum.org, 406 Federal St

HISTORIC ODESSA Today Odessa has a population of under 400, but it was once a booming Delaware port. When the railroad

★ ★ ★

FOLLOW *the* **UNDERGROUND RAILROAD**

With its unusual status as a slave state that held many Quakers and Methodists (often abolitionists), Delaware was an important Underground Railroad state. Thousands of former slaves arrived from nearby Maryland as they fled to the free states of the north. Some important stops on the route that you can visit today include the Friends meeting houses in both Camden and Wilmington. Woodburn (now the governor's mansion) was used to hide slaves and is rumored today to be haunted by the ghost of a slave trader, in fruitless pursuit of an escaped slave. In Odessa, the Corbit-Sharp House was a safe haven as was the courthouse in New Castle, which today houses a display recounting the story of the Underground Railroad in Delaware.

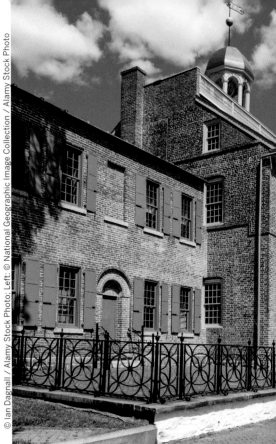

© Ian Dagnall / Alamy Stock Photo; Left: © National Geographic Image Collection / Alamy Stock Photo

---

★ ★ ★

GETTING THERE & AROUND

While Amtrak serves Wilmington and, less frequently, Newark, car is the best way around the state. Wilmington Airport is the state's largest, though visitors can fly into nearby Philadelphia and drive down. DART bus service runs throughout the state.

---

bypassed the town in 1855, it went into a slump, but that meant historic buildings survived, even if they were neglected. Today five have been restored and furnished with period pieces. Have lunch at Cantwell's Tavern in the Brick Hotel, from 1822. *www.historicodessa.org*

LEWES Sitting at the entrance of Delaware Bay, just north of Rehoboth Beach, Lewes was the site of the state's first European settlement, a Dutch trading post established in 1631. It would later be an important stop on the Underground Railroad. Today it's a charming seaside town. The Zwaanendael Museum (named after the Dutch settlement) covers the history of Delaware. *www.lewes.com*

NEMOURS MANSION AND GARDENS
Beginning with one gunpowder mill, the du Ponts amassed a fortune that placed them among the richest families in the country.

One product of that wealth is the 77-room Nemours Mansion and Gardens, built in Wilmington at the beginning of the 20th century. The house, in late-18th-century French style, is paired with the largest formal French gardens in America. *www.nemoursmansion.org, 850 Alapocas Dr*

NEW CASTLE
The history of New Castle, founded in 1651, is hard to sum up briefly: this city on the Delaware River changed hands a few times between the Dutch and the English and was an on-again, off-again Colonial capital. Its historic buildings owe their survival to the city's decline as a commercial center; today its enchanting, leafy streets are ideal for strolling. *https://newcastlecity.delaware.gov*

QUAKER HILL HISTORIC DISTRICT
In Colonial America, Delaware was governed by Pennsylvania at times, and some of the larger colony's Quaker

Left: On the Rehoboth boardwalk; historic New Castle; Dogfish Head Brewery's Steampunk Tree House. Previous page: Birds in Bombay Hook.

© James Nesterwitz / Alamy Stock Photo; Sean Orlando & Five Ton Crane Arts Collective

Day 1
Traveling the length of Delaware, you'll realize how surprisingly different its regions are. Start by visiting some of the du Pont estates like Winterthur or Nemours in Wilmington. You can spend the night in Wilmington (at the Hotel Du Pont if your budget allows, the city's legendary grande dame) or continue south to historic New Castle.

Day 2
The middle portion of the state offers something for every interest. The town of Odessa delights armchair historians: the town has felt lost in time ever since it was bypassed by the railroad. In Dover, the state capital, the Biggs Museum includes one of the country's premier collections of decorative arts. To the east of Dover, birders can watch for the 200 species that visit the Bombay Hook National Wildlife Refuge.

Day 3
The southern portion of the state is home to appealingly laid-back beach towns. You may not want to rush this part of your vacation, so extend this to four or five days if you want more time relaxing on the beaches here.

community settled in Wilmington. More than 150 buildings from three centuries are found in this historic residential neighborhood west of downtown. Among the most notable are the Friends Meeting House and elegant neo-Gothic and Italianate houses built by Quaker merchants. *http://quakerhillhistoric.org*

WINTERTHUR Another of the du Pont family's homes, Winterthur began as a modest house and expanded over time to become a 175-room mansion. Paintings by America's most important 18th- and 19th-century artists hang on the walls, exquisite examples of the decorative arts fill the rooms, and the gardens embody one of Henry Francis du Pont's passions – he graduated from Harvard with a degree in horticulture. Before or after visiting, make a pit stop at Buckley's Tavern, in an 1817 building. *www.winterthur.org, 5105 Kennett Pike*

FAMILY OUTINGS

FORT DELAWARE STATE PARK While Delaware was a slave state, it never joined the Confederacy. Fort Delaware, on the banks of the Delaware River, was crucial to the defense of Wilmington and Philadelphia, both located upstream. The fort also served as a prison during the Civil War. Now accessible by ferry, costumed volunteers transport visitors to 1864 at the height of the war. *https://destateparks.com*

REHOBOTH BEACH This popular beach town combines a charming historic district with lively restaurants (Back Porch Café, Espuma, Salt Air and others), making it a favorite destination of a variety of travelers. In addition to spending days by the seaside, kids will want to check out the Funland amusement park, which has 18 rides and a collection of old-time midway games. *www.cityofrehoboth.com*

DISTRICT of COLUMBIA

★ ★ ★ ★ ★ ★ ★ ★ ★ ★ ★ ★ ★ ★ ★ ★ ★ ★ ★

POPULATION: 702,000 | **SIZE:** 68 sq miles
WEBSITE: https://washington.org

WASHINGTON, DC WAS METICULOUSLY DESIGNED ON THE BANKS OF THE POTOMAC TO BE THE seat of the nation. The streets are broad, the architecture imposing, and the museums and monuments practically burst out of the seams of the National Mall – the dominant feature of DC for most visitors. A certain sterility hangs about the government offices of the capital, but on closer inspection the District of Columbia hosts a strikingly diverse population of multiethnic people across all socioeconomic strata, as evidenced by its colorful neighborhood crannies and delightfully distinct culinary offerings. A visit to Washington should undoubtedly include the classic homages to modern democracy and learning (it doesn't hurt that the memorials and Smithsonian outposts are all free), but don't miss out on its megawatt cultural output too.

© Doug Armand / Getty Images

FOOD & DRINK

HALF-SMOKE The main stock-in-trade at Ben's Chili Bowl, a DC institution, is half-smokes, DC's meatier, smokier version of the hot dog, and usually slathered with mustard, onions and the namesake chili. For nearly 60 years presidents, rock stars and Supreme Court justices have come to indulge at the humble diner, but despite the hype, Ben's remains a true neighborhood establishment. *http://benschilibowl.com*, 1213 U St NW

HISTORIC HOTEL BARS Experienced bartenders swirl martinis and manhattans for the suit-wearing crowd all across DC, but those in the know congregate in the city's historic, and discreet, hotel bars a stone's throw from the White House to transact their business. There's the POV Rooftop at the W, Round Robin at the Willard, and the St Regis bar. Nearby, enter luxe basement bar Off the Record through the Hay-Adams hotel lobby, built in 1928 on land that once held the homes of John Hay and Henry Adams.

THE SHAW Dupont Circle and Barracks Row off Capitol Hill, Adams Morgan and Logan Circle have all had their day as the must-eat destination in town (and continue to have a surplus of thriving restaurants), but it's the Shaw neighborhood that's center stage now, though with no shortage of contenders. Located in NW DC near Rhode Island Ave and 6th St, it's overflowing with in-demand eats. To name just one, Chef Jeremiah Langhorne at The Dabney earned a Michelin star for his updated mid-Atlantic cuisine.

NATURAL ESCAPES

ROCK CREEK PARK At 1700-plus acres, Rock Creek is twice the size of New York's Central Park and feels wilder. Terrific trails for hiking, biking and horseback riding extend the entire length, and the boundaries enclose Civil War forts, dense forest and wildflower-strewn fields. Rock Creek Park begins at the Potomac's east bank near Georgetown and extends to and beyond the northern city boundaries. *www.nps.gov/rocr, Glover Rd NW*

US NATIONAL ARBORETUM The greatest green space in Washington unfurls almost 450 acres of meadowland, sylvan theaters and a pastoral setting that feels almost like a bucolic American countryside. Highlights include the National Bonsai & Penjing Museum, the National Herb Garden and the otherworldly National Capitol Columns. It's operated by the US Department of Agriculture, and as such, functions as a major center of botanical research. *www.usna.usda.gov, R St NE*

ARTS, HISTORY & CULTURE

CAPITOL HILL City planner Pierre L'Enfant called it a pedestal waiting for a monument, and later designers provided what was lacking by placing the Capitol Dome atop the hill that rises above the city, presiding over the National Mall that stretches below. You're welcome to go inside the mighty, white-domed edifice and count the statues, ogle the frescoes and visit the chambers of the folks who run the country. *www.visitthecapitol.gov, 1st St NE & E Capitol St*

★ ★ ★

Mr Smithson's
GIFT

Surprisingly, the Smithsonian Institution began with James Smithson, a British scientist who never set foot in the USA, let alone Washington, DC. He died in 1829 with a provision in his will to found 'at Washington, under the name of the Smithsonian Institution, an establishment for the increase and diffusion of knowledge.' Actually, that was the backup plan. The money first went to his nephew Henry, but Henry died without heirs a few years after Smithson. So the 'institution' clause kicked in, and $508,318 arrived in Washington, DC for the task. But who was Smithson? The illegitimate son of the Duke of Northumberland, a mineralogist by trade and a shrewd investor, Smithson's motivations for bequeathing so much money to the USA, as opposed to his native Britain, remain a mystery.

© David Harmantas / Shutterstock; © Doug Armand / Getty Images

THE 51ST STATE?

★ ★ ★

For years, DC residents have paid billions in taxes but receive no representation in either house of Congress, despite having a population larger than two states (Vermont and Wyoming). It's no wonder that residents are proud of their license plates, which brandish the slogan 'Taxation Without Representation.' In November 2016, nearly 80% of DC voters approved a referendum for statehood. A few months later a bill called the Washington, DC Admission Act was introduced on Capitol Hill with a record-setting 116 cosponsors in the House (cosponsors are Congressional members who back the bill before it's officially proposed). For now, DC waits for its say in the bills passed within its bounds.

EMBASSY ROW Want to take a trip around the world? Stroll northwest along Massachusetts Ave from Dupont Circle (the actual traffic circle) and you pass more than 40 embassies housed in mansions that range from elegant to imposing to discreet. Tunisia, Chile, Turkmenistan, Togo, Haiti – flags flutter above heavy doors and mark the nations inside, while dark-windowed sedans ease out of driveways to ferry diplomats to and fro. The district has another 130 embassies sprinkled throughout it, but this is the main vein.

FORD'S THEATRE On April 14, 1865, John Wilkes Booth assassinated Abraham Lincoln here. Timed-entry tickets provide access to the site, which includes the theater itself, the basement museum displaying Booth's .44-caliber pistol, his muddy boot etc, and Petersen House across the street, where Lincoln died. Ford's Theatre still hosts shows as well, which together with the renowned John F Kennedy Center for the Performing Arts, National Theatre and Folger Theatre give

DC a notable theater scene. *www.fords.org, 511 10th St NW*

GEORGETOWN Just west of Dupont Circle, Georgetown is DC's most aristocratic neighborhood, home to elite university students, ivory-tower academics and diplomats. Luxury brand-name shops, dark pubs, snug cafes and upscale restaurants line the streets. Lovely parks and gardens color the edges, while sweet cycling trails roll out along the waterways.

LIBRARY OF CONGRESS
The largest library in the world, with 164 million books, manuscripts, maps, photos, films and other items, awes in both scope and design. The centerpiece is the 1897 Thomas Jefferson Building. Gawk at the Great Hall, done up in stained glass, marble and mosaics of mythical characters, then seek out the Gutenberg Bible (c 1455), Thomas Jefferson's round library and the reading room viewing area. Free tours of the building take place daily. *www.loc.gov, 10 First St SE*

From left: Ben's Chili Bowl; the main reading room at the Library of Congress; the Capitol Building. Previous page: The Library of Congress facade.

© Omar Chatriwala / Getty Images

LINCOLN MEMORIAL There's something extraordinary about climbing the steps of Abe Lincoln's neoclassical temple, staring up into his dignified eyes and reading about the 'new birth of freedom' in the Gettysburg Address chiseled beside him. Visitors here will stand where Martin Luther King Jr gave his 'Dream' speech and take in the sweeping view – it's a defining DC moment, sure to bring chills. *www.nps.gov/linc, 2 Lincoln Memorial Circle NW*

NATIONAL MUSEUM OF AFRICAN AMERICAN HISTORY AND CULTURE
This sensational Smithsonian museum, the newest, covers the diverse African American experience and how it helped shape the nation. Start downstairs in the sobering 'Slavery and Freedom' exhibition and work your way up to the community and culture galleries on the third and fourth floors, where African American achievements in sport, music, theater and visual arts are joyfully celebrated. The Contemplative Court provides respite during what can be an intense visit. While free, timed entry tickets are best reserved in advance. *www.nmaahc.si.edu, 1400 Constitution Ave NW*

POLITICS & PROSE BOOKSTORE
A much-loved DC literary hub, this independent bookstore carries an excellent selection of fiction and nonfiction, has knowledgeable staff and is fiercely supportive of local authors. It's known for hosting readings and book clubs, and it's the perfect place to buy that political biography or history book you've been meaning to brush up on. *www.politics-prose.com, 5015 Connecticut Ave NW*

SMITHSONIAN INSTITUTION
If America was a quirky grandfather, the Smithsonian Institution would be his attic. Rockets, dinosaurs, Rodin sculptures, Tibetan thangkas (silk paintings) – even the 45-carat Hope Diamond lights up a room here. The Smithsonian is actually a collection of 19 museums, including the National Gallery of Art and the Natural History Museum, and they're all free. Even

FUN FACT

It's said no structure higher than the Capitol Dome's 289ft is allowed, but is it true? Well, effectively. Restrictions from the 1899 Height of Buildings Act introduced regulations mostly focused on the width of the streets and safety concerns; a 1910 amendment restricted building heights further.

© Steven Heap / Getty Images; Right: © Sean Pavone / Shutterstock

★ ★ ★

GETTING THERE & AROUND

Most visitors arrive by air. The city has two airports: Dulles International Airport and the smaller Ronald Reagan Washington National Airport. Reagan is more convenient, as it's closer to the city and has a Metro stop. Baltimore's airport is a third, often cheaper option. It's connected to DC by commuter rail, though it's not handy if you're arriving at night. Stately Union Station receives Amtrak and bus service into the city. If you drive here, don't try to get around the city by car, as the Metro is the easiest way to get around. Capital Bikeshare is an option too.

the much beloved National Zoo is part of the Smithsonian! *www.si.edu*

TIDAL BASIN The 2-mile stroll around this constructed inlet incorporates the Franklin Delano Roosevelt, Martin Luther King Jr and Thomas Jefferson Memorials as well as the Floral Library. It's a lovely way to spend a couple of hours – just watch out for low-hanging tree branches near the FDR Memorial. During the National Cherry Blossom Festival, the city's annual spring rejuvenation, the basin bursts into a pink-and-white floral collage. Rent a paddleboat from the boathouse to get out on the water. The Tidal Basin also serves a practical purpose: flushing the adjacent Washington Channel via the Inlet and Outlet Bridges. *www.nps.gov/articles/dctidalbasin.htm*

VIETNAM VETERANS MEMORIAL
The opposite of DC's white, gleaming marble, this black, low-lying Vietnam

memorial cuts into the earth, just as the Vietnam War cut into the national psyche. The monument shows the names of the war's 58,000-plus casualties – listed in the order they died – along a dark, reflective wall. Seeing your own image among the names is meant to bring past and present together. It's uncannily effective. *www.nps.gov/vive/index.htm, 5 Henry Bacon Dr NW*

WASHINGTON MONUMENT Imbued with shadowy Masonic lore, this 555ft obelisk is DC's tallest structure. Workers set the pyramid on top in 1884 after stacking up some 36,000 blocks of granite and marble over the preceding 36 years. Its two-toned appearance comes from the gap in construction; after funding ran out during construction and the government took over, marble for the remaining two-thirds was sourced from a different quarry. A 70-second elevator ride whisks you to the observation deck at the top for DC's best

views. *www.nps.gov/wamo, 2 15th St NW*

WHITE HOUSE Thomas Jefferson groused it was big enough for two emperors, one Pope and the Grand Lama, but when you tour the White House you get the feeling – despite all the spectacle – that it really is just a house, where a family lives. Admittedly that family gets to hang out in Jefferson's green dining room and Lincoln's old office where his ghost supposedly now roams. Tours must be reserved well in advance. *www.whitehouse.gov, 1600 Pennsylvania Ave*

FAMILY OUTINGS

INTERNATIONAL SPY MUSEUM
One of DC's most popular museums, the International Spy Museum is flashy, over-the-top, and probably guilty of overly glamming up a life of intelligence-gathering. But who cares? The Spy

Museum feels like Q's lab. Check out James Bond's tricked-out Aston Martin, the KGB's lipstick pistol and more. *www.spymuseum. org, 700 L'Enfant Plaza SW*

NATIONAL AIR & SPACE MUSEUM
The legendary exhibits at this hugely popular Smithsonian museum include the Wright brothers' flyer, Chuck Yeager's Bell X-1, Charles Lindbergh's *Spirit of St Louis*, Howard Hughes' H-1 Racer and Amelia Earhart's shiny red plane. Children and adults alike love walking through the Skylab Orbital Workshop and viewing the incredible collection. Note that it's currently undergoing extensive updates to exhibits. *https://airandspace.si.edu, Independence Ave at 6th St SW*

From left: Washington Monument and reflecting pool; the National Air & Space Museum.

★

ITINERARY

Day 1
Enjoy the capital classics like the White House and Smithsonian museums on an epic hike through the National Mall. Take in a performance at one of DC's great theaters in the evening.

Day 2
Go deeper into neighborhood pockets like trendy Adams Morgan or posh Georgetown and dine at a Michelin-starred restaurant.

Day 3
Back to the monuments and the Smithsonian you go, making sure to pick up some extra museums and pay homage at the memorials you missed the first time. Make a stop at Ben's Chili Bowl too.

FLORIDA

★ ★

POPULATION: 21.3 million | **SIZE:** 65,755 sq miles | **STATE CAPITAL:** Tallahassee
LARGEST CITY: Jacksonville | **WEBSITE:** www.visitflorida.com

A HUNDRED WORLDS – FROM MAGIC KINGDOMS AND LATIN AMERICAN AND CARIBBEAN neighborhoods to mangrove islands, wild wetlands and artist colonies – are all contained within this flat peninsula. Some seek the hedonism of South Beach, spring break and Key West. Still more lose themselves within the phantasmagorical realms of Orlando's theme parks. Yet despite the best efforts of 21st-century humans, overwhelming portions of Florida remain untamed; alligators prowl the waterways, herons strut through ponds, manatees shelter in springs and sea turtles nest in the sand. Alongside this natural abundance is a unique culture. Florida is more culturally savvy than its resort reputation suggests. This state has a reputation for attracting eccentrics and idiosyncratic types from all over, and together they've generated an unstoppably active arts and culture scene.

© Smileus / Getty Images

FOOD & DRINK

CUBAN FOOD Miami's Cuban population makes itself known in myriad ways, but food is probably the standout. Grab a Cubano sandwich filled with ham, roasted pork, cheese, pickles and more to understand why, or try excellent black bean soup or fried yucca before moving on to heartier meat and seafood plates. Little Havana is filled with authentic restaurant options, but even South Beach has great Cuban food on offer.

KEY LIME PIE Florida produces some 80% of the citrus products in the US, and the tiny key limes of the Florida Keys are among the tastiest. Key lime pie, a concoction of key lime juice and condensed milk with a meringue topping, is a specialty of the house at restaurants across South Florida. The Key Largo Conch House's version is hard to beat, but you'd better conduct your own taste test.

KEY WEST BARS Key West has the most bars per capita in the country, with some legendary watering holes among the number. Raise a glass to Hemingway at the Green Parrot to start your night in these liquor-loving islands. The oldest bar in Key West – an island of bars – this rogues' cantina opened in the late-19th century and hasn't closed yet. Its ramshackle interior, complete with a parachute stretched across the ceiling, only adds to the atmosphere. Beyond bar décor, the crowds in Key West are colorful too, obviously out for a good time. With bars packed in close, it's possible to visit a good number, assuming you pace yourself.

ROCK SHRIMP Somewhere between a shrimp and a miniature lobster, rock shrimp are a Florida specialty. Rodney Thompson developed the rock-shrimp fishery off Cape Canaveral's coast in the early 1970s. The aim: to put local shrimp back on Canaveral's tables. Today Central Florida relishes in the specialty, and the local landmark Dixie Crossroads in Titusville continues to serve up seasonal shrimp, including sweet, blush-colored royal reds; succulent white shrimp; and melt-in-your-mouth, broiled rock shrimp.

TROPICAL FRUITS Florida doesn't just produce more oranges than anywhere else in the US; it also has a variety of unique tropical fruits that can often be bought roadside. Look for exotic, Florida-grown fruits you won't elsewhere – including black sapote, carambola (star fruit), sugar apples, longans and passion fruit. Local juices are fantastic through the state as well.

NATURAL ESCAPES

10,000 ISLANDS One of the best ways to experience the serenity of the Everglades is by paddling the network of waterways that skirt the western edge of the park. The 10,000 Islands, near Everglades City, consist of many (but not really 10,000) tiny islets that hug the southwestern-most border of Florida. *https://www.fws.gov/ refuge/ten_thousand_islands, Everglades Gulf Coast Visitor Center, 815 Oyster Bar Ln*

BISCAYNE NATIONAL PARK The park may not be far from Miami, but it feels like a world removed. Encompassing a vibrant swath of biologically rich coral reef near

★ ★ ★
MIAMI, OR MIAMI BEACH?

Miami and Miami Beach are actually two different municipalities with separate mayors. Even though a scant 10 miles separates one city from the other, culturally and ideologically it can feel like quite a bit more. Miami is rich with art and history, while across the causeway, Miami Beach is just...rich. The wealth here built beautiful art deco edifices, and Versace's influence still lingers among the new trendy restaurants and condos. The shared trait is the strong nightlife scene that unites both sides of the causeway.

© Justin Foulkes / Lonely Planet; Left: © Richard Ellis / Alamy Stock Photo

★ ★ ★

FANTASY FEST

Drive all the way to the southern end of the state, and the continental US, to visit Key West during the last week of October. That's when this island outpost of exiles, artists, eccentrics and those who generally live outside of the norm indulge their wildest, weirdest impulses during Fantasy Fest, the party when the Keys parade around at their Keys-iest. Expect lots of body paint, a fair bit of nudity, incredible floats, street music and theatrics, and more than a shake of bacchanalia. Unofficial patron saint Ernest Hemingway wouldn't have had it any other way.

Homestead, it teems with life – though you'll have to head out on a boat tour, or better yet don snorkel and mask, to see it firsthand. Manatees, dolphins and sea turtles are just a few inhabitants of this diverse ecosystem. *www.nps.gov/bisc, 9700 SW 328th St*

CAYO COSTA STATE PARK Accessible only by boat, Southwest Florida's Cayo Costa Island is almost entirely preserved as a 2500-acre state park. While its pale, ash-colored sand may not be as fine as that of other beaches, its idyllic solitude and bathtub-warm waters are without peer. Bring a snorkel and mask to help scour sandbars for shells and conchs. *www.floridastateparks.org/cayocosta*

EVERGLADES NATIONAL PARK One of America's great natural treasures, this vast, watery wilderness at the tip of Florida encompasses 1.5 million acres and three sub-parks. You can spy alligators basking in the noonday sun as herons stalk patiently through nearby waters in search of prey, go

kayaking amid tangled mangrove canals, or wade through murky, knee-high waters amid cypress domes on a rough-and-ready 'slough slog.' *www.nps.gov/ever*

FORT DE SOTO PARK With 1136 acres of unspoiled wilderness, St Petersburg's Fort De Soto is one of Florida's premier beach parks, where 7 miles of sand come together to form a tropical postcard. Of its two swimming areas, the long, silky stretch of North Beach is the best. *www.pinellascounty.org/park, 3500 Pinellas Bayway*

MERRITT ISLAND NATIONAL WILDLIFE REFUGE This unspoiled 140,000-acre refuge is one of the country's best birding spots, especially from October to May. More endangered and threatened species of wildlife inhabit the swamps, marshes and hardwood hammocks here than at any other site in the contiguous US. The best viewing is on Black Point Wildlife Drive. *www.fws.gov/merrittisland, Black Point Wildlife Dr, off FL-406*

From left: Fantasy Fest revelers; untouched Everglades National Park; ordering in Little Havana. Previous Page: Flamingos in the Everglades.

© Daniel Korzeniewski / Shutterstock

ST JOSEPH PENINSULA STATE PARK

This quilt of beach and pine forest, brackish bays and fuzzy salt marsh in Port St Joe is a fine slice of increasingly rare Gulf Coast wilderness. Visitors can walk wilderness trails and wander amid sugar-sand beaches that stretch for 2516 acres along grassy, undulating dunes. *www.floridastateparks.org/stjoseph, 8899 Cape San Blas Rd*

ARTS, HISTORY & CULTURE

APALACHICOLA Slow and mellow, shaded by live oaks and flush with historically preserved buildings sweating in the soft Gulf Coast sun, Apalachicola is one of the gulf's most appealing villages, boasting a plethora of nice restaurants, bars and bookstores, all threaded together by an attractive grid of walkable streets. It still has an active fishing industry and is a great seafood destination. *www.apalachicolabay.org*

CUBAOCHO MUSEUM & PERFORMING ARTS CENTER Jewel of Miami's Little Havana Art District, Cubaocho is renowned for its concerts, with excellent bands from across the Spanish-speaking world. The interior resembles an old Havana cigar bar, yet the walls are decked out in artwork that references both the classical past of Cuban art and its avant-garde future. The live entertainment is well worth a visit. *www.cubaocho.com, 1465 SW 8th St*

LITTLE HAVANA Miami comes alive in Little Havana; the most evocative reminder of Old Cuba is Máximo Gómez Park, or 'Domino Park,' where the sound of elderly men trash-talking over games of chess is harmonized with the quick clack-clack of slapping dominoes, the heavy smell of cigars and a sunrise-bright mural of the 1994 Summit of the Americas, surrounded by great Cuban restaurants.

MALLORY SQUARE Take all the energies, subcultures and oddities of life in the Florida Keys and focus them into one torchlit, family-friendly (but playfully edgy), sunset-enriched street party. Mallory

FUN FACT

South Florida is the only place in the world where both crocodiles and alligators can be found in the wild.

© Naughty Nut / Shutterstock; Left: © color and shape of underwater / Getty Images

★ ★ ★

MANATEE VIEWING CENTER

One of Florida's more surreal wildlife encounters is spotting manatees in the warm-water discharge canals of coal-fired power plants outside Tampa. Yet these placid mammals show up here so reliably from November through April that the Manatee Viewing Center in Apollo Beach is now a protected sanctuary. These gentle herbivores can live to 60 years and weigh between 800lb and 1200lb. Tarpon and sharks can be spotted as well, and an interactive stingray exhibit in a 10,000-gallon tank is a highlight.

Square in Key West is surely one of the greatest street shows on earth. It begins in the hours leading up to dusk, the sinking sun a signal to bring on the madness. *www.mallorysquare.com*

PÉREZ ART MUSEUM MIAMI The Pérez can claim fine rotating exhibits that concentrate on post-WWII international art, but just as impressive are its location and exterior. This art institution inaugurated Museum Park, a patch of land that oversees the broad blue swath of Biscayne Bay. Swiss architectural firm Herzog & de Meuron designed the structure, which integrates tropical foliage, glass and metal for a melding of tropical vitality and fresh modernism that is a nice architectural analogy for Miami itself. *www.pamm.org, 1103 Biscayne Blvd*

ROBBIE'S MARINA Located on Islamorada in the Florida Keys, this marina doubles as a flea market, tourist shop, sea pen for tarpons (massive fish) and jumping-off point for fishing expeditions,

all wrapped into one driftwood-laced compound. The best reason to visit is to hire a kayak for a peaceful paddle through nearby mangroves and lagoons. *https://robbies.com, Mile marker 77.5*

SALVADOR DALÍ MUSEUM The theatrical exterior of this institution in St Petersburg unfolds like a blueprint of what a modern art museum, or at least one devoted to the life, art and impact of Salvador Dalí, should be. Even those who dismiss his dripping clocks and curlicue moustache will be awed by the museum and its grand works, especially *The Hallucinogenic Toreador*. *www.thedali.org, 1 Dali Blvd*

WOLFSONIAN-FIU Visit this excellent design museum (part of Florida International University) in Miami Beach early in your stay to put the city's aesthetics into context. A stop here is vital to understanding the roots and shadings of local artistic movements. By chronicling the evolution of interior design in everyday life, the Wolfsonian reveals how these

From left: Manatees in Florida waters; the Kennedy Space Center; St Augustine's town square.

© Sean Pavone / Shutterstock

trends were manifested architecturally in South Beach's exterior deco, and from there, how they echoed across America. *www.wolfsonian.org, 1001 Washington Ave*

FAMILY OUTINGS

DISNEY'S ANIMAL KINGDOM Set apart from the rest of Walt Disney World both in miles and in tone, Animal Kingdom attempts to blend theme park and zoo, carnival and African safari, all stirred together with a healthy dose of Disney characters, storytelling and transformative magic. In Bay Lake near Orlando, it's the greenest, and most calm, of the Disney experiences. *www.disneyworld.disney. go.com, 2101 Osceola Pkwy*

KENNEDY SPACE CENTER Whether you're mildly interested in space or a die-hard sci-fi fan, a visit to the Space Center is awe-inspiring. To get a good overview, start at the Early Space Exploration exhibit, then progress to the 90-minute bus tour to the Apollo/Saturn V Center. Try to catch

a launch from the space coast if you can. *www.kennedyspacecenter.com, NASA Parkway, Merritt Island*

LEGOLAND With manageable crowds and lines, and no bells and whistles, this lakeside theme park in Winter Park maintains an old-school vibe – you don't have to plan like a general to enjoy a day here, and it's strikingly stress-free and relaxed. This is about fun (and yes, education) in a colorful and interactive environment. *http://florida.legoland.com, 1 Legoland Way*

PONCE DE LEON SPRINGS STATE PARK This park in Ponce de Leon features one of Florida's loveliest and least touristed springs. The spring has clear, almost luminescent waters, like something from a fairy tale, and is studded with knobby trees and surrounded by ladders for easy swimming access to the water, which is a constant 68°F. Interested in springs? Wakulla Springs, Rainbow Springs and Silver Springs are just a few of the other

★ ★ ★

ST AUGUSTINE

The oldest continuously inhabited colonial-era city within the continental US, St Augustine was founded in 1565 by Spanish conquistador Pedro Menéndez de Avilés. As such, it existed long before the British set sail for Jamestown. It's strongly identified with the mythic Fountain of Youth, commemorated in the city's aptly named Fountain of Youth Archaeological Park. Don't expect it to grant you immortality, though the huge number of retirees in the state would indicate that some of the belief in the state as a fount of youth remains to this day.

© Universal Orlando Resort; Left: © mariakraynova / Shutterstock

★ ★ ★

GETTING THERE & AROUND

Most travelers to Florida arrive by air, usually by flying into Orlando or Miami. For travelers who come by car or are road-tripping, I-95 runs from Georgia to South Florida; you can continue to the end of the US on the Overseas Highway (US-1) to Key West. A SunPass helps with the state's many tolls. Amtrak serves the state as well.

springs to visit throughout the state. *www.floridasprings.org, 2860 Ponce de Leon Springs Rd*

RINGLING MUSEUM COMPLEX The 66-acre winter estate of railroad, real-estate and circus baron John Ringling and his wife, Mable, is one of the Gulf Coast's premier attractions and incorporates their personal collection of artworks in what is now Florida's state art museum. Nearby, Ringling's Circus Museum documents his theatrical successes, while their lavish Venetian Gothic home and its attached gardens, the extravagantly named Cà d'Zan, reveals the impresario's extravagant tastes. Don't miss the PBS-produced film on Ringling's life, which is screened in the excellent Circus Museum. *www.ringling.org/circus-museum, 5401 Bay Shore Rd, Sarasota*

WIZARDING WORLD OF HARRY POTTER At this wildly popular Orlando spot, poke around among the cobbled streets and impossibly crooked buildings of Hogsmeade; munch on Cauldron Cakes; and mail a card via Owl Post, all in the shadow of Hogwarts Castle. Then check out the great rides. *www.universalorlando.com, Universal Orlando Resort, 6000 Universal Blvd*

From left: Sarasota's Ringling Museum; Wizarding World of Harry Potter.

ITINERARY

Days 1 & 2

Fly into Orlando, where
you have the pick of
several theme parks
to get lost in. The two
major parks are Universal
Studios and Walt Disney
World. The rough rule
of thumb is that Disney
is better for families
with smaller kids, while
Universal has more
thrill rides aimed at an
older audience. If you
go to Disney, don't miss
Animal Kingdom and
the spectacle of Epcot. In
Universal, lose yourself
at the Wizarding World
of Harry Potter. Try not
to leave Orlando without
popping into Legoland.

Day 3

Having finished with
Orlando's theme parks,
drive south to Merritt
Island National Wildlife
Refuge and live out your
astronaut dreams at the
Kennedy Space Center.

Days 4 & 5

On to Miami! Spend
your first day soaking up
the neon and art deco
architecture of Miami
Beach. On day 5, head
to Miami proper on the
mainland and prowl
around Little Havana and
artsy Wynwood.

Day 6

On your final day, head
from Miami into the un-
tamed Everglades, where
you'll come face-to-face
with Florida wilderness,
alligators and all.

GEORGIA

★ ★

POPULATION: 10.4 million | **SIZE:** 59,425 sq miles | **STATE CAPITAL:** Atlanta
WEBSITE: www.exploregeorgia.org

THE LARGEST STATE EAST OF THE MISSISSIPPI, EMBEDDED DEEP IN THE SOUTH, SULTRY GEORGIA surprises with a mix of rural and urban, forward-looking and traditional. But one thing is sure: you'll find southern hospitality and down-home cooking everywhere you go. Go hiking, white-water rafting, and wine tasting in the fabled Appalachians. Poke into small towns and cities, whether antebellum Athens and Macon, Augusta with its famous golf tournament, or sea-kissed Brunswick. Explore golden marshlands and empty barrier isles, with romantic Savannah providing an elegant touch. At the center of it all is the capital city of Atlanta, considered by some as the birthplace of the civil rights movement and today a progressive, alluring metropolis with edgy eateries and big-ticket attractions. As state native Ray Charles crooned: there are plenty of reasons to keep Georgia on your mind, y'all!

© Mel Myers / 500px

FOOD & DRINK

BRUNSWICK STEW Whether Brunswick stew originated in Georgia or Virginia is an ongoing debate, but in Georgia the dish dates back to 1898, and the 25-gallon pot in which it was stewed still stands on St Simons Island, commemorated by a plaque. The tomato-based stew of shredded pork (chicken in Virginia, and originally squirrel) and vegetables is celebrated every November at the annual Stewbilee in Brunswick, or stop by the Love Shack BBQ on Jekyll Island for a taste of the real thing, Georgia-style.

PEACHES As Georgia is the official Peach State, you can bet your last peach pit that its peaches are the sweetest, juiciest around, and they're used in everything from pies and ice cream to salsa and barbecue sauce. Dickey Farms in Musella is the state's oldest packinghouse, where you're guaranteed some of the best. If you can't make it to a farm, a farmers market will provide your peach fix; Atlanta State Farmers Market in Forest Park, near Atlanta, is a favorite. Not lucky enough to be here during the summer peach harvest, from May to August? Rest assured there are plenty of peach products to enjoy on sale year-round.

PONCE CITY MARKET Atlanta's famous food hall is where Atlantans go to find the latest foodie craze, offered by chefs ranging from James Beard Award winners to young restaurateurs in a variety of sit-down eateries and to-go stalls. But there's more than food in this mixed-use development, including a rooftop park, a Sunday artist market and the City Winery. *https://poncecitymarket.com, 675 Ponce de Leon Ave NE*

VIDALIA ONIONS Maybe they were a planting mistake back during the Great Depression, when Mose Coleman discovered his onions were strangely sweet rather than pungent and hot. But he had clearly stumbled upon something big, and Vidalia onions have since become treasured far and wide for their sweet, mild taste, to the point of becoming Georgia's official state vegetable in 1990. The secret to their unmatched taste? The real deals (as opposed to the fake Vidalias) are still hand planted and hand harvested. Look for them late April through August.

NATURAL ESCAPES

CUMBERLAND AND THE GOLDEN ISLES Fringed by golden marshes and laced with indigo waterways, the Lowcountry's sultry beauty shines on Cumberland Island and Golden Isles of Brunswick, St Simons, Sea, Little St Simons, Sapelo and Jekyll. Discover each island's unique character, whether you're wandering empty beaches, looking for wild horses, camping or staying at a super-luxe resort, or checking out the legacies of the Gilded Age elite. Cumberland and Sapelo are accessible by ferry only. *www.nps.gov/cuis, www.goldenisles.com*

OKEFENOKEE NATIONAL WILDLIFE REFUGE A vast, swampy expanse of moss-draped cypresses, mahogany-hued waters, water lilies, and alligators in southeast Georgia, Okefenokee is the East's largest

★ ★ ★

PEACHY GOOD

Franciscan monks introduced the area's first peaches on St Simons and Cumberland Islands, with the first commercial peaches being planted in the 17th century. Today the peach is Georgia's official state fruit, and in Atlanta, more than 55 streets are named Peachtree. Except... in that case, many believe the street names are references not to the sweet fruit but to a nearby Creek Nation settlement called Standing Pitch Tree.

Left: Jackson Street Bridge and Atlanta skyline.

© Stacy Funderburke / Shutterstock; Left: © karenfoleyphotography / Alamy Stock Photo

★ ★ ★

THE
Coca-Cola
LEGEND

Dr John S Pemberton, an Atlanta pharmacist, concocted a sweet syrup in May 1886, to be mixed with carbonated water. He sold it at a local pharmacy and the rest, as they say, is history. Pemberton's bookkeeper, Frank Robinson, thought up the name Coca-Cola – thinking 'the two Cs would look well in advertising' – while Pemberton himself penned the flowing script that remains its brand identity to this day. Sadly, Pemberton died in 1888 and never saw the extent of his success.

national wildlife refuge. It's a magical place for canoeing, kayaking, camping – and one of the nation's best spots for stargazing. Keep an eye out for carnivorous plants, including hooded pitcher plants and bladderworts (and watch out for water moccasins!). Outdoorspeople, note advance permits are required for camping. *www.fws.gov/refuge/okefenokee, 2700 Suwannee Canal Rd, Folkston*

PROVIDENCE CANYON STATE PARK
Painted a rainbow of oranges, pinks, reds and whites by the exposed rock, 16 gorges comprise the Little Grand Canyon, as it's called. Created thanks to erosion-causing farming techniques in the 19th century, today it's one of Georgia's natural wonders. Enjoy views from the rim or hike down to the bottom to spot fossils dating from a time when the ocean covered the region. *https://gastateparks. org/ProvidenceCanyon, 8930 Canyon Rd, Lumpkin*

SPRINGER MOUNTAIN
This 3780ft peak reigns as the southern terminus of the Appalachian Trail. If you're hard-core, this is where you start your 2181-mile trek to Maine. If you're not, enjoy either the 8.5-mile trail from Amicalola Falls State Park or the 2-mile round-trip from FS Road 42. Either way, you can send off the trekkers and get a taste of the experience. *www.blueridgemountains.com.*

TALLULAH GORGE STATE PARK
An early America mountain resort, Tallulah Gorge experienced a setback in the early 1900s with the building of a dam. Nevertheless, the 1200ft-deep Tallulah Gorge today retains enough waterfall-packed beauty to please most outdoorsy types. Hike the rim or climb down the 600-plus stairs of Hurricane Falls Trail, leading to six spectacular waterfalls, and don't miss L'Eau d'Or Falls. *https://gastateparks. org/Tallulahgorge, 338 Jane Hurt Yarn Rd, Tallulah Falls*

From left: A display at World of Coca-Cola in Atlanta; Okefenokee National Wildlife Refuge; Tallulah Gorge State Park; professional golfer Doug Ghim at the 2018 Masters Tournament.

© Andrew Redington / Getty Images: Left: Sean Pavone / Shutterstock

ARTS, HISTORY & CULTURE

ALLMAN BROTHERS BAND MUSEUM
Members of the Allman Brothers Band lived together in this 18-room, Tudor-style home in Macon between 1969 and 1973, no doubt drawn by its proximity to Capricorn Records, their recording studio. Today the Big House, as it was known, is filled with the world's largest collection of Allman Brothers memorabilia, including guitars, gold records and posters. *www.thebighousemuseum.com, 2321 Vineville Ave*

ANTEBELLUM TRAIL
The Old South is preserved in white-columned plantations, oak-shaded towns, and fascinating museums along this 100-mile pastoral route between Athens and Macon. Among the highlights are Heritage Hall, restored to antebellum elegance; Jarrell Plantation, an 1850s cotton plantation; and the Uncle Remus Museum, celebrating the Br'er Rabbit storyteller. Macon alone has 6000 historic homes and buildings in 14 historic neighborhoods. *https://antebellumtrail.org*

ATHENS
A beery, artsy and laid-back college town, Athens has an extremely popular football team (the University of Georgia Bulldogs, College Football Playoff National Championship runners-up in 2018), a world-famous music scene, a bona fide restaurant culture and surprisingly diverse nightlife. The university – UGA – drives the culture of Athens and ensures an ever-replenishing supply of young bar-hoppers and concert-goers, some of whom stick around long after graduation and become 'townies.' The pleasant, walkable downtown offers a plethora of funky choices for eating, drinking and shopping. *www.visitathensga.com*

AUGUSTA MUSEUM OF HISTORY
Some 12,000 years of regional history is explored at this downtown Augusta

★ ★ ★

The
MASTERS TOURNAMENT

The first week of every April, golf lovers around the world turn their gaze to Augusta National Golf Club's Masters Tournament. Co-founded by amateur champ Bobby Jones in 1934, this world-famous golf tournament – one of golf's four major championships – is known for its deep-rooted traditions, including the winner's green blazer, $1.50 pimento cheese sandwiches and azalea-sprinkled fairways. Another tradition? It's almost impossible to get tickets.

© Sean Pavone / Shutterstock; Left: © Jason Tench / Shutterstock

© Sean Pavone / Shutterstock; Left: © Jason Tench / Shutterstock

© Sean Pavone / Shutterstock; Left: © Jason Tench / Shutterstock

★ ★ ★

MUSIC IN THE 404

The South's largest city has a vibrant music scene. EDM pops off in downtown clubs, punk rages in Little Five Points, and Latin music rules outside the Perimeter. But hip-hop and R&B are Atlanta's claim to fame. This town gave the world Outkast, Ludacris, Jermaine Dupri, Lil Jon, 2 Chainz, CeeLo, Gucci Mane, TI, Usher... the list goes on. Trap, crunk and snap music would not exist without Atlanta.

museum, including an enormous tribute to the godfather of soul (and local son), James Brown. Other popular exhibits are a Victorian-era streetscape (complete with a steam engine) and, as Augusta is home to the Masters golf tournament, a whole section devoted to golf. *www.augustamuseum.org, 560 Reynolds St*

FORT PULASKI NATIONAL MONUMENT

A newly introduced rifled cannon breached one of Fort Pulaski's four corners during a Civil War battle in April 1862, putting an end once and for all to the strategic value of seemingly impenetrable brick fortifications. This national monument in Savannah tells the story of the battle and subsequent Confederate surrender, after which the fort was used as a POW prison. *www.nps.gov/fopu, US-80*

HELEN'S LITTLE BAVARIA
Gingerbread architecture, themed specialty shops and biergartens fill this charming, all-things-German village in the Blue Ridge Mountains of north Georgia. A marketing ploy thought up by town leaders back in the 1960s, Helen is today firmly rooted in German tradition, including a year-round slate of festivals ranging from Bavarian Nights of Summer to winter's Alpenfest to, naturally, the best Oktoberfest around. *www.helenga.org*

JIMMY CARTER NATIONAL HISTORIC SITE
Former President Jimmy Carter still lives in his hometown of Plains in southern Georgia. You can visit his campaign headquarters (in the train depot), tour his childhood farm and learn his story at the visitors center, housed in the town's high school. If it's Sunday, stop by the Maranatha Baptist Church, famed for his preaching from its pulpit. *www.nps.gov/jica, 300 N. Bond St*

MARTIN LUTHER KING JR NATIONAL HISTORICAL PARK
Celebrating the esteemed leader of the modern-day civil rights movement, this 35-acre national historical park in Atlanta centers on the historic Sweet Auburn neighborhood where Martin Luther King grew up. Explore

From left: Fort Pulaski; Forsyth Park fountain in Savannah; the tomb of Martin Luther King Jr.

REV. MARTIN LUTHER KING, JR.
1929 ~ 1968
"Free at last, Free at last, Thank God Almighty I'm Free at last."

© Erik Pendzich / Alamy Stock Photo

the home where he was born in 1929, Ebenezer Baptist Church (where he and his father pastored), exhibits at Freedom Hall, and King's gravesite and memorial. *www.nps.gov/malu, 450 Auburn Ave NE*

NATIONAL CENTER FOR CIVIL AND HUMAN RIGHTS Emotionally powerful, interactive displays share the story of the civil rights movement at this architecturally striking Atlanta museum. Among them are a segregated lunch counter replica, a photo of someone cleaning up MLK's blood, and a reconstruction of a Freedom Riders bus. Galleries are also devoted to global human rights and Martin Luther King Jr. *www.civilandhumanrights.org, 100 Ivan Allen Jr. Blvd NW*

OCMULGEE MOUNDS NATIONAL HISTORIC SITE This site tracks 17,000 years of the region's continuous habitation, to a time when the first indigenous peoples visited in search of Ice Age mammals. The national monument's centerpieces are its Early Mississippian ceremonial mounds,

built before 1000 CE. Trails wander through this 702-acre park in Macon, and a museum showcases thousands of artifacts excavated on-site. *www.nps.gov/ocmu, 1207 Emery Hwy*

SAVANNAH HISTORIC DISTRICT Oak-shaded squares, flowery gardens, 18th- and 19th-century mansions (many of which are museums) and striking war memorials fill Savannah's historic downtown. Highlights include the one-time home of Girl Scout founder Juliette Gordon Low; the Harper Fowlkes House, home to generations of the same family; and the 18th-century city market. Or simply linger on a park bench and soak it all in. *www.visitsavannah.com*

FAMILY OUTINGS

ANNA RUBY FALLS SCENIC AREA A dramatic duo of waterfalls dropping in tandem, this natural delight awaits in the heart of Chattahoochee National Forest, near the town of Helen. A paved, 0.4-mile path leads from the parking area to two

FUN FACT

Gainesville, Georgia, often considered the poultry capital of the world, passed a 1961 law making it illegal to eat fried chicken with a fork.

© Dejan Patic / Getty Images; Right: © Marilyn Nieves / Getty Images

★ ★ ★

GETTING THERE & AROUND

The main airport is Hartsfield-Jackson Atlanta International, one of the busiest in the US, while Savannah/Hilton Head's airport is a direct link to the coast. MARTA provides good public rail and bus transportation in the Atlanta Metro region. The state is crisscrossed by four major interstates: I-85, I-75, I-20 and I-95.

viewing decks. For those wanting a little more, the 4.6-mile Smith Creek Trail winds from the base of the falls into nearby Unicoi State Park. *www.fs.usda.gov, 3455 Anna Ruby Falls Rd, Helen*

AUGUSTA CANAL NATIONAL HERITAGE AREA

Augusta's role in the 19th-century Industrial Revolution is explored at this beautifully preserved canal-side destination. The Discovery Center, in the former Enterprise Textile Mill, tells the story through interactive exhibits. Then hop aboard a replica canal cargo boat for a narrated canal tour. Bikers, runners and anglers adore the tree-shaded towpath. *https://augustacanal.com, 1450 Greene St, #400*

CALLAWAY RESORT & GARDENS

Celebrated for its springtime azaleas, Callaway Gardens in Pine Mountain is a world-famous family resort with 14,000 acres of gardens. Ride bikes on the 10-mile Discovery Bike Trail, zip through the air at Treetop Adventures, enjoy a birds-of-prey show, or water-ski and wakeboard at Robin Lake Beach. *www.callawaygardens.com, 17800 US-27*

CENTENNIAL OLYMPIC PARK

Designed as a gathering spot for the 1996 Olympics in Atlanta, this 21-acre park is where Atlantans go to relax, play and rejuvenate. Cool off in the Fountain of Rings, which blasts choreographed jets of water into the air; enjoy weekly summer concerts; or picnic beneath the trees. Googie Burger, the park's only eatery, is a local favorite. *www.gwcca.org, 265 Park Ave West NW*

GEORGIA AQUARIUM

Tens of thousands of sea creatures representing several

thousand species reside in 10 million gallons of water, making this aquarium in Atlanta the world's largest. Here you'll find giant whale sharks, graceful manta rays, beluga whales, playful penguins, a living reef and more. Dolphins reveal their playful side in a spectacular dolphin extravaganza. *https://georgiaaquarium.org, 225 Baker St NW*

From left: Georgia Aquarium; Atlanta's Fountain of Rings in Centennial Olympic Park.

WORLD OF COCA-COLA This 92,000-sq-ft destination in downtown Atlanta celebrates everything Coca-Cola, including the rare chance to stand near the vault that holds the more than 125-year-old secret formula. You won't get the recipe, but you'll have lots of fun viewing nostalgic memorabilia, looking behind the scenes at the bottling process, and sampling a hundred-plus varieties of Coca-Colas from around the world. *www.worldofcoca-cola. com, 121 Baker St NW*

ITINERARY

Day 1
Start off in the heart of cosmopolitan Atlanta, home to Centennial Olympic Park, originally built for the 1996 Summer Olympics; the World of Coca-Cola; and the Georgia Aquarium. After lunch at Ponce City Market, learn about Atlanta's role in the civil rights movement at Martin Luther King Jr National Historical Park. For dinner, indulge in a world of international cuisine along Buford Highway.

Day 2
Experience a taste of the Old South along the 100-mile Antebellum Trail, starting in Athens. The route takes in a plethora of striking 19th-century houses, gardens and historic museums, so pick and choose which sites to visit since you should be in Macon by dinnertime. Some top recommended stops include the TRR Cobb House and Taylor-Grady House in Athens, Heritage Hall in Madison, the Uncle Remus Museum in Eatonton and the Jarrell Plantation in Juliette. Each town along the way has restaurants and shops to explore.

Day 3
Set off for historic Savannah. Take a free walking tour of the city's tree-shaded historic district, then tour one or more of the many historic homes, including the Mercer-Williams House, the birthplace of Flannery O'Connor, and the site of the founding of Girl Scouts of America. Don't overlook the chance to sit on a bench and watch the world go by (Forrest Gump didn't!).

Day 4
This morning, visit Wormsloe Historic Site, a former plantation with its famous tunnel of majestic oaks, near Savannah. In the afternoon, stop into Savannah's Bonaventure Cemetery, made famous by *Midnight in the Garden of Evil*, and filled with Southern ambiance.

Day 5
From Savannah, head south along the coast to the Golden Isles, where life slows down with beach strolling, kayaking and horseback riding. Splurge with a stay at the luxurious Cloisters on Sea Island and be sure to taste Brunswick stew at a local eatery.

Day 6
Stop at the Ocmulgee Mounds National Historic Site in Macon en route back to Atlanta.

HAWAII

★ ★

POPULATION: 1.43 million | **SIZE:** 10,931 sq miles | **STATE CAPITAL:** Honolulu
WEBSITE: www.gohawaii.com

IT'S EASY TO SEE WHY HAWAII HAS BECOME SYNONYMOUS WITH PARADISE. JUST LOOK AT ITS sugar-white beaches, technicolor coral reefs and volcanoes beckoning adventurous spirits. Sunrises and sunsets are so spectacular that they're cause for celebration all by themselves. Hiking paths cross ancient lava flows and weave down fluted *pali* (sea cliffs). Visitors can learn the ancient Hawaiian sport of 'wave sliding,' and then snorkel or dive with giant manta rays and sea turtles. On the Hawaiian Islands, the descendants of ancient Polynesians, European explorers, American missionaries and Asian plantation immigrants mix and mingle. Hawaii proudly maintains its own distinct identity apart from the US mainland. Spam, surfing, ukulele, hula, pidgin, aloha shirts – these are just some of the touchstones of everyday life, island style.

© mattpaul / Getty Images

FOOD & DRINK

FRESH FISH While spam is the hands-down favorite of the islands, freshly caught fish, preferably served with a tiki drink, is where Hawai'i shines. Mama's Fish House on Maui is one of the best examples, a South Seas dream. The fish is literally fresh off the boat – staff can even tell you who caught it. The eclectic building successfully integrates everything from driftwood to sugarcane. When the beachside tiki torches are lit at dinnertime, you'll swear you've entered a poster from *South Pacific*.

PLATE LUNCH A classic example of Hawai'i's ubiquitous plate lunch would be chunky layers of tender kālua pork, a dollop of creamy macaroni salad and two hearty scoops of white rice. Of course, the pork can be swapped for just about any other protein, maybe Korean-style *kalbi* (short ribs), Japanese *mochiko* (rice flour) batter-fried chicken or *furikake*-encrusted mahi-mahi. Health-conscious eaters can often substitute tossed greens and brown rice for the sides. A favorite breakfast combo is fried eggs with Portuguese sausage or Spam and, always, two scoops of rice.

STICKY WHITE RICE Sticky rice is more than a side dish in Hawai'i. It's a culinary building block, an integral partner in everyday meals. Without rice, spam musubi would just be a slice of canned meat. The *loco moco* (rice, fried egg and hamburger patty topped with gravy or other condiments) would be nothing more than an egg-covered hamburger. And without two scoops rice, the plate lunch would be just a ho-hum conversation between meat and macaroni salad. Even fish-heavy poké bowls require the white rice base to really sing. Just so you know, sticky white rice means exactly that. Not fluffy rice. Not wild rice. And definitely not instant.

NATURAL ESCAPES

DIAMOND HEAD A dramatic backdrop for Waikiki Beach, Diamond Head is one of the best-known landmarks in Hawai'i. Ancient Hawaiians called it Lē'ahi, and at its summit they built a *luakini heiau*, a temple dedicated to the war god Ku. Ever since 1825, when British sailors found calcite crystals sparkling in the sun on the beach, the sacred peak has been called Diamond Head. *http://dlnr.hawaii.gov/dsp/parks/oahu/ diamond-head-state-monument, O'ahu*

GARDEN OF THE GODS Weirdly shaped volcanic stones are strewn about this martian landscape; the multihued rocks and earth, with a palette from amber to rust to sienna, are stunning. It's utterly silent up here, and you can see up to four other islands across the white-capped waters. The colors change with the light – pastel in the early morning, rich hues in the late afternoon. Look for rocks oddly perched atop others. *Polihua Rd, Lana'i*

HALEAKALĀ NATIONAL PARK No trip to Maui is complete without visiting this national park, containing the mighty volcano that gave rise to East Maui. The volcano's crater measures a whopping 7 miles wide, 2 miles long and 2600ft deep; nearly as large as Manhattan. From its towering rim are dramatic views of its lunarlike surface. *www.nps.gov/hale, Maui*

★ ★ ★

SURFING

Ancient Hawaiians invented surfing, (calling it *he'e nalu*, or 'wave sliding'). In Hawaii today surfing is both its own sub-culture as well as a part of everyday island life. Hawaii's biggest waves roll in on the north shores of the islands from November through March. Summer swells, which break along the south shores, are smaller and more infrequent. With its overwhelming variety and sheer number of surf spots, O'ahu is where all the major pro surfing competitions happen; its North Shore is home to the Triple Crown of Surfing, which draws thousands of roadside spectators every November and December. All of the main islands have good, even great, surfing breaks. Surf lessons and board rentals can be found at just about every tourist beach that has rideable waves. As a newbie in the lineup, don't expect to get every wave that comes your way, but usually, if you give a wave, you'll get a wave in return.

Left and right: © Matt Munro / Lonely Planet

FUN FACT

Hawaii is the most isolated large population center on Earth, almost 2400 miles from California and about 4000 miles from Japan.

HANALEI BAY Well-known for being filmed in *The Descendants*, Hanalei Bay is easily Kaua'i's most famous beach and for good reason. Really one long beach that's divided into several sections with different names, there's something for almost everyone here: sunbathing, swimming, snorkeling and surfing. In summer the water is sometimes so calm it's hard to distinguish between sky and sea. *Kaua'i*

HĀPUNA BEACH Hāpuna Beach is a postcard snapshot of what a beach can be, world famous for its magnificent half-mile sweep of white powder sand and fabulously clear waters. In summer, waves are calm and allow good swimming, snorkeling and diving. When the surf's up in winter, bodyboarding is awesome. Sunsets here are like a smile from God. *http://dlnr.hawaii.gov/dsp/parks/hawaii/hapuna-beach-state-recreation-area, Hapuna Beach Rd, Hawai'i (The Big Island)*

HAWAI'I VOLCANOES NATIONAL PARK Even among Hawai'i's many wonders, this national park stands out. Its two active volcanoes testify to the ongoing birth of the islands: quiet Mauna Loa (13,679ft) sprawling above, its unassuming mass downplaying its height, and young Kīlauea (4091ft), one of the world's most active volcanoes, providing near-continual sources of awe. *www.nps.gov/havo, Hawai'i (The Big Island)*

KALAUPAPA NATIONAL HISTORICAL PARK The spectacularly beautiful Kalaupapa Peninsula is the remotest part of Hawai'i's most isolated island. The only way to reach this lush green peninsula edged with long, white-sand beaches, is on a twisting trail down the steep pali, the world's highest sea cliffs. This is one case where getting there truly is half the fun. *www.nps.gov/kala, Moloka'i*

KAMAKOU PRESERVE Hiking back through three million years of evolution is Kamakou's star attraction. This undisturbed Hawaiian montane bog is a miniature primeval forest of stunted trees, dwarf

From left: Waimea Canyon; Halema'uma'u Crater under the Milky Way in Volcanoes National Park; hiking on Kilauea Iki crater trail on Big Island. Previous page: Surfing Waimea Bay, Oahu.

© Maridav / Shutterstock

plants and lichens that make it feel like it's the dawn of time. Visit and you'll be rewarded with a fantastic view of majestic cliffs and the ocean beyond. *www.nature.org/en-us/get-involved/how-to-help/places-we-protect/kamakou, Moloka'i*

KEHENA BEACH If any place captures the vibe of wild Puna, on the island's east side, it's this beautiful black sand beach tucked beneath a cliff. Out here all walks of life – hippies, Hawaiians, gays, families, seniors, tourists – go about their own uninhibited way. Be prepared for nudity and *pakalolo* (marijuana) at this chill spot, though nobody minds if you don't participate. *Hwy 137, Mile 19, Hawai'i (The Big Island)*

MĀKAHA BEACH PARK This beautifully arcing beach invites you to spread out your towel and spend the day here. Except for on weekends and big surf days, you'll likely have the place to yourself. Snorkeling is good during the calmer summer months. Winter brings big swells that preclude swimming but which are beautiful to

photograph – or to surf, blissfully away from the Waikiki crowds. *84-369 Farrington Hwy, O'ahu*

PAPAHĀNAUMOKUĀKEA MARINE NATIONAL MONUMENT In a groundbreaking move, the Northwestern Hawaiian Islands became the US's first Marine National Monument in 2016. Encompassing 10 island clusters and almost 140,000 sq miles of ocean, Papahānaumokuākea Marine National Monument (PMNM) is the world's largest protected marine area and the US's first Unesco World Heritage Site designated for both natural and cultural reasons. *www.papahanaumokuakea.gov*

NĀPALI COAST WILDERNESS STATE PARK Roadless, pristine and hauntingly beautiful, this 16-mile-long stretch of stark cliffs, white-sand beaches, turquoise coves and gushing waterfalls links the island's northern and western shores. While fit trekkers tackle the exposed, undulating, slippery trail from

★ ★ ★
CHOOSE YOUR ADVENTURE

Wherever you travel around the Hawaiian Islands, fantastic beaches, friendly faces and ono grinds (good eats) are practically guaranteed, but every island has a unique flavor. Get swept up by the kinetic energy of the capital island, O'ahu. Hang loose on Maui, which offers a little something for everyone, but especially for beach bums. Gaze at the towering sea cliffs on ancient Kaua'i. Wonder at new land being birthed by volcanoes on the Big Island, Hawai'i's youngest isle. Escape to total resort luxury on Lana'i or learn to live life off the land on rural Moloka'i, where native Hawaiian traditions run strong.

© Pung / Shutterstock;Left: © Matt Munro / Lonely Planet

★ ★ ★

MAUNA KEA

It's breathless and breathtaking to be in the rarefied air of Mauna Kea, Hawai'i's highest mountain and most sacred spot. Once the sun goes down, the stars come out – and so do the telescopes. Mauna Kea is one of the world's best astronomical sites, and the clear skies make for good amateur stargazing as well. It hosts 13 major telescopes and counting, as part of the Mauna Kea Science Reserve. What you see through visitor telescopes, whether at the visitor center or on a tour, you won't soon forget. For a trophy experience, be here during a meteor shower. Local objections to the use of sacred land led to a protracted court battle over the proposed Thirty Meter Telescope, and astrotourists who come to witness the 'peak' achievements of science on the summit should keep in mind the importance of the ground underfoot.

Hā'ena to Kalalau Valley, it's also possible to experience the coastline by kayak, raft or catamaran. *http://dlnr.hawaii.gov/dsp/parks/kauai, Kaua'i*

TWO STEP Concealed within a (usually) placid bay is this snorkeling paradise, where the reef and marine life seem locked in a permanent contest to outdo each other with the gaudiest color palette. From above the water, your only indication of the action below is the presence of boats and crowds gathering at the titular two steps. *Hōnaunau Beach Rd, Hawai'i (The Big Island)*

WAIMEA CANYON STATE PARK This gargantuan chasm of ochre and blood-red lava rock is quite simply one of the world's natural wonders. At 10 miles long and over 3000ft deep, this gouge in the land is so spectacular it has been popularly nicknamed the 'Grand Canyon of the Pacific.' Flowing through the canyon is Waimea River, Kaua'i's longest river and a

great spot for adventures on the water. *http://dlnr.hawaii.gov/dsp/parks/kauai/waimea-canyon-state-park, Kaua'i*

ARTS, HISTORY & CULTURE

BERNICE PAUAHI BISHOP MUSEUM

Like Hawai'i's version of the Smithsonian Institute in Washington, DC, the Bishop Museum showcases a remarkable array of cultural and natural history exhibits. It is often ranked as the finest Polynesian anthropological museum in the world. Founded in 1889, it originally housed only Hawaiian and royal artifacts. These days it honors all of Polynesia. *www.bishopmuseum.org, 1525 Bernice St, Honolulu, O'ahu*

NATIVE BOOKS/NĀ MEA HAWAI'I So

much more than just a bookstore stocking Hawaiiana tomes, CDs and DVDs, this cultural gathering spot also sells beautiful silk-screened fabrics, koa wood bowls,

From left: Telescopes on Mauna Kea; The USS Arizona Memorial; a rack of vintage aloha shirts.

© Richard Newstead / Getty Images

Hawaiian quilts, fishhook jewelry and hula supplies. You can immerse yourself in local culture via classes; there is at least one each day. *www.nameahawaii.com, 1200 Ala Moana Blvd, Suite 270, Honolulu, O'ahu*

USS ARIZONA MEMORIAL One of the USA's most significant WWII sites, this somber monument commemorates the Pearl Harbor attack with an offshore shrine reachable by boat. The USS Arizona Memorial was built over the midsection of the sunken USS *Arizona*, with deliberate geometry to represent initial defeat, ultimate victory and eternal serenity. *www.nps.gov/valr, 1 Arizona Memorial Pl, Honolulu, O'ahu*

FAMILY OUTINGS

BIG BEACH This untouched beach is arguably the finest on Maui. In Hawaiian it's called Oneloa, literally 'Long Sand.' And indeed the golden sands stretch for the better part of a mile, the beach wide as they come. The waters are a beautiful turquoise. When they're calm you'll find kids boogie boarding; at other times, only experienced bodysurfers brave the waves. *Makena Rd, Maui*

'IMILOA ASTRONOMY CENTER OF HAWAI'I 'Imiloa, which means 'exploring new knowledge,' is a museum and planetarium complex with a twist: it juxtaposes modern astronomy on Mauna Kea with ancient Polynesian ocean voyaging. Rarely does a museum so wonderfully integrate history, mythology, anthropology and modern science. Located just outside of Hilo, it's the perfect museum to accompany a trip to the professional observatories on Mauna Kea's summit. *www.imiloahawaii.org, 600 'Imiloa Pl, Hilo, Hawai'i (The Big Island)*

HAWI Hawi (hah-vee) is a little slice of picturesque North Kohala that's been

★ ★ ★

HAWAIIAN SHIRTS

The textile mogul Alfred Shaheen made the Hawaiian shirt mainstream in the late 1940s. When you imagine classic aloha wear, you probably picture Shaheen's classic prints (Elvis wore them). His bold South Pacific styles and attention to detail defined quality aloha wear. They're collector's items now, but the aloha shirt is still an indispensable piece of island wear, even with Shaheen gone and his factory shuttered, as other companies carry on the tradition of the aloha shirt. It's all about the details. A quality aloha-shirt maker will attach the pockets and button panels to the shirt so the pattern is unbroken. If the tag says 'Made in Hawai'i,' odds are you're looking at something special.

The Silver Elephant

© Anita Sagastegui / Getty Images;
Right: © Matt Munro / Lonely Planet

★ ★ ★

GETTING THERE & AROUND

Hawaii is a competitive market for US domestic and international airfares, which vary tremendously by season, day of the week and demand. Competition is highest among airlines flying to Honolulu from major US mainland cities, especially between Hawaiian Airlines, Alaska Airlines and Virgin America. Travel between the islands is also by air.

shaped by mainlanders (and their money) into a bohemian enclave of cafes, locavore dining, galleries and artisan gifts, all within about two blocks, which is as big as this town gets. It's quite simply one of the nicest places in the islands to stop and smell the organic coffee. *Hawai'i (The Big Island)*

HANAPEPE Groovy young entrepreneurs have turned sleepy Hanapepe into the island's hippest, most creative spot. It's a town where quirky is cool. Most visitors turn up on Art Night, held on Fridays,

when the town's main drag is transformed by musicians and street vendors. *www. hanapepe.org, Kaua'i*

KOHALA MOUNTAIN ROAD Arguably the Big Island's best scenic drive, Kohala Mountain Rd (Hwy 250) affords stupendous views of the Kohala–Kona coastline and three majestic volcanic mountains: Mauna Kea, Mauna Loa and Hualālai. Start from Waimea, climb past an overlook, and then follow the spine of the peninsula through green pastures until you

finally descend to the sea.
Hawai'i (The Big Island)

THE ROAD TO HANA Spanning the northeast shore of Maui, the legendary Hana Hwy ribbons tightly between jungle valleys, towering cliffs, emerald mountain slopes, rugged coasts – and some serious hairpin turns. Along the way, 54 one-lane bridges mark nearly as many waterfalls, some tranquil and inviting, others so sheer they kiss you with spray as you drive past.
https://roadtohana.com, Maui

From left: A food truck at the weekly Hanapepe Art Night; the road to Hana.

ITINERARY

Day 1
Start on the capital island of O'ahu ('the Gathering Place') and, with a population of roughly a million, home to two-thirds of the Hawaiian population. Among the many sights around Honolulu on the southeast coast, don't miss the emotionally moving Pearl Harbor WWII memorials or the thriving Chinatown.

Day 2
Snorkel in Hanauma Bay in the morning and in the afternoon, hike to Honolulu's Manoa Falls after visiting the Lyon Arboretum. In the buzzing beach resort of Waikiki, you can end the day with a sunset catamaran 'booze cruise' and listen to live Hawaiian music at oceanfront bars.

Day 3
Drive up the Windward Coast, stopping at panoramic beaches and to hike into the misty Ko'olau Mountains. Keep going past the white-sand coves of Turtle Bay to end up on the North Shore, famous for its big-wave surfing in winter.

Day 4
Mosey over to Hawai'i, aka the Big Island. Yes, it's the largest of them, hence the name. For ocean adventures, go scuba diving or snorkeling at night with manta rays around Kailua-Kona and paddle a kayak to go snorkeling at cobalt-colored Kealakekua Bay. Down in Ka'u, hike to Green Sand Beach near windswept Ka Lae, the US's southernmost point.

Day 5
Next up, Hawai'i Volcanoes National Park, home of the world's longest-running volcanic eruption, offers alien-looking moonscapes for hiking, and glimpses of slowly flowing lava.

Days 6 & 7
Still on the Big Island, spend a night or two in Hilo and explore the beautiful Boiling Pots and Rainbow Falls. Take time to drive partway up Mauna Kea for stargazing after dark. After rolling up and down along the Hāmākua Coast, amble through the old sugar-plantation town of Honoka'a before dropping into ancient Waipi'o Valley. Giddyup through Waimea (aka Kamuela), a *paniolo* or Hawaiian cowboy town. In the quiet countryside of North Kohala, hike into Pololū Valley, circle around Mo'okini Heiau, then relax in the quaint and artsy town of Hawi to soak up some last Hawaiian vibes.

IDAHO

★ ★

POPULATION: 1.7 million | **SIZE:** 83,642 sq miles | **STATE CAPITAL:** Boise
WEBSITE: visitidaho.org

SHAPED LIKE A SKYWARD-POINTED PISTOL, IDAHO IS A TANTALIZING ENIGMA: GRITTY AND elegant, urban and wild, old and new. Its topography confines urban growth to a few fringe locations that swoop like a fishhook from the northern panhandle through Boise before snagging Yellowstone at the Wyoming border. It holds bountiful wilderness, jagged peaks, and churning white water that offset high desert plains and rolling agricultural swaths. The reaches of Idaho, from its forests and rivers to its skies, unconditionally offer access to a personal and undisturbed outdoor experience alongside glimpses of the roots of American history. What may surprise visitors here for the natural beauty is the resourceful and imaginative spirit bubbling in small towns and cities that dot the state. An authentic Idaho trip leaves room to roam; an exceptional one leaves dirt under the nails.

© Kris Wiktor / Shutterstock

FOOD & DRINK

BASQUE CUISINE Idaho is more diverse than its reputation might suggest. Boise is particularly notable for its Basque population, the largest outside Spain. Since beginning to settle in Idaho in the early 1800s, they have flavored downtown Boise's so-called Basque Block with paella, lamb grinders, chorizo and croquetas (a delicious fried treat). If you miss the annual Jaialdi (a cultural festival), make time to sample the regional specialties on offer here year-round. Idaho's unique Basque cuisine has evolved to merge traditional Basque flavors with American ingredients such as lamb.

FINGER STEAKS AND FRY SAUCE Scoff at these meat and potato plates to your own detriment. Strips of sirloin breaded and deep-fried, finger steaks are a veritable tradition in Idaho for a reason. Juicy inside, crispy outside, these tasty morsels usually come in a basket with hand-cut fries and fry sauce, a variant concoction of condiment ingredients, à la Idaho. Greasy-spoon joints like Trestle Brewing Company in Ferdinand and Boise's Westside Drive-In do them best.

POTATOES Yes, there is an Idaho Potato Museum. Yes, Idaho potatoes are an exceptionally delicious and abundant crop. You've probably had one; 13 billion pounds are harvested yearly. Whether you're sampling the top-tier french fries at Boise Fry Company (customizable by potato type) or trying an unconventional ice cream potato (don't worry; it only looks like a spud), the humble potato is indelibly and proudly linked to Idaho.

NATURAL ESCAPES

CRATERS OF THE MOON NATIONAL MONUMENT & PRESERVE This is a strange and ever-so-slightly-shifting landscape of hardened volcanic lava flow surrounded by diverse natural parkland. Descend into caves, climb cinder cones and learn Shoshone-Bannock Native American history through archaeological discoveries in the region. *www.nps.gov/crmo, US Hwy 20/26/93, midway between Arco and Carey*

PRIEST LAKE Unblemished by development, this 23,000-acre lake near Coolin ripples sky-blue reflections of the Selkirk Mountains. In addition to the usual lake activities, arborists will ogle 2000-year-old cedar trees (up to 12ft in diameter and 150ft tall) in the Roosevelt Grove of Ancient Cedars, and snow bums will groove on groomed Nordic tracks. *http://priestlake.org*

SHOSHONE FALLS Dubbed the Niagara Falls of the West, this natural waterfall near Twin Falls spans 900ft and cascades over 200 vertical feet. Peak flows are between April and July. Nearby Shoshone Falls Park offers photographic vantage points, a playground, grassy picnic areas and hiking, as well as boating and swimming opportunities. It's one of the West's most spectacular sights. *www.tfid.org, Shoshone Falls Ave*

WILD SALMON RIVER Originating in the waters of Redfish Lake (also the terminus of the longest Pacific sockeye salmon migration in North America), the Salmon

★ ★ ★

IDAHO... WINE?

Idaho grapes, competing with Oregon and Washington varietals, may ripen humbly, but with five science degrees between them, dynamic duo Karl and Coco Umiker of Clearwater Canyon Cellars are crushing it. Visit their Idaho Century Farm and Tasting Room in Lewiston during the fall and watch them literally crush it. From Coco: 'I think crush is my favorite time of year. We just throw ourselves into it and follow Mother Nature's lead...leaning into the awesome momentum of it all: weather, grape maturity and fermentation.' Renaissance Red wine, the 'friend-maker,' couples laid-back flavors with exceptional sophistication characteristic of its designers. Fourth-generation farmers reestablishing the region's wine-making history, Clearwater Canyon Cellars bottles the best of Idaho heritage, craft and ingenuity.

© Kris Wiktor / Alamy Stock Photo; Right: © Robert Crow / Shutterstock

★ ★ ★

GETTING
THERE &
AROUND

During multi-
layover flights
and lengthy drives,
be grateful that
your transport isn't
a dusty pioneer
wagon. Boise
International
Airport, Friedman
Memorial Airport
(Sun Valley) and
Spokane Inter-
national Airport
(Washington) are
the main hubs.

From left: Craters of the Moon National Monument; a peregrine falcon at World Center Birds of Prey.

River is styled the 'river of no return' for its swift flows and steep canyon walls. Situated in part next to the vast, rugged Sawtooth Wilderness, a trip on the Salmon River could be the American adventure of a lifetime. Observe 1.5 billion-year-old rock (the oldest dated in Idaho), rare and varied wildlife, and historical pioneer sites. *www.rivers.gov*

ARTS, HISTORY & CULTURE

BASQUE MUSEUM & CULTURAL CENTER
Sandwiched between the ethnic taverns, restaurants and bars of Boise is the Basque Museum & Cultural Center, a commendable effort to unveil the intricacies of Basque culture and how it was transposed 6000 miles west from the Pyrenees to Idaho. Language lessons in Euskara, one of Europe's oldest languages, are held here (check the schedule). *https://basquemuseum.eus, 611 W Grove St*

OLD PENITENTIARY & BOTANICAL GARDEN
In Boise, you can stand behind bars that confined hardened criminals of the Old West. Chilling stone and iron retain shadowy echoes of the pioneer past, but vibrant blooms color Idaho's modern history right next door. After tasting outlaw life, stroll the diverse plantings in the 12 gardens on-site. *https://idahobotanicalgarden.org, https://history.idaho.gov, Old Penitentiary Rd*

SILVER CITY
Witness a rare mining town largely untouched since the 1860s. Wander 70-plus structures including a hotel, schoolhouse, church, cemeteries and the birthplace of Idaho's first newspaper. In the backcountry of Owyhee County, Silver City Road closes for winter but reopens Memorial Day through November; 4WD recommended at all times. *www.historicsilvercityidaho.com, 20 miles off Hwy 78 south of Murphy*

FAMILY OUTINGS

BRUNEAU DUNES STATE PARK Climb and dune-sled in Bruneau at this 470ft phenomenon, the tallest single-standing sandhill in North America. Camp or stay in a cabin overnight and take advantage of the observatory's telescope collection and the pristine night sky. *https://parksandrecreation.idaho.gov, 27608 Bruneau Sand Dunes Rd*

ROUTE OF THE HIAWATHA This bike and hiking path is famous for St Paul Pass, a 1.66-mile, pitch-black tunnel connecting Montana and Idaho through the Bitterroot Mountains. Bike 15 miles from the East Portal trailhead to Pearson, descending through nine additional tunnels and crossing seven sky-high trestles. Shuttles are available for return transport. *www.ridethehiawatha.com, Lookout Pass Ski Area, I-90 exit 0*

SCHWEITZER MOUNTAIN
Schweitzer (named for the Swiss hermit who once lived there), in Sandpoint, offers 2900 acres of all-season terrain, plenty of character, and Stella, Idaho's only six-passenger high-speed chairlift, which carries visitors 1 mile in under six minutes toward wide-open mountaintop views of Lake Pend Oreille. *www.schweitzer.com, 10000 Schweitzer Mountain Rd*

WORLD CENTER BIRDS OF PREY
At this center in Boise, Fall Flights (September to November) display birds' natural athleticism and the staff's expert training. Hold on to your caps as hawks, owls and falcons show off what they do best: fly. Tour the Archives of Falconry library and outdoor and indoor exhibits to gain an appreciation for the conservation efforts here. *https://peregrinefund.org/visit, 5668 W Flying Hawk Ln*

ITINERARY

Day 1
Explore the Boise River Greenbelt, connecting pedestrians to cultural sites through the city: art, history, parks, zoo and gardens. Dine on the Basque Block.

Day 2
From desert to mountain, take the winding two-lane Payette River Scenic Byway to McCall. Raft or kayak along the Payette River or maneuver flatwater on Cascade or Payette Lake. In McCall, hike Ponderosa State Park.

Day 3
Unplug on the Wildlife Canyon Scenic Byway to Stanley, whichserves rugged peaks, crystalline lakes and wooded meadows. Don't forget to stargaze the brilliant nightscape of the Central Idaho Dark Sky Reserve.

Day 4
Past Galena Summit, Sun Valley offers outdoor opportunities with a distinctly decadent flavor. Intersperse a morning bike ride or fly-fishing with visits to boutiques and art galleries. Chairlift to the top of Baldy and catch afternoon rays over the Wood River Valley. Swing into night with live music at Sun Valley Pavilion or Whiskey Jacques'.

ILLINOIS

★ ★

POPULATION: 12.8 million | **SIZE:** 57,915 sq miles | **STATE CAPITAL:** Springfield
LARGEST CITY: Chicago | **WEBSITE:** www.enjoyillinois.com

WITH WORLD-CLASS ARCHITECTURE, MUSEUMS, RESTAURANTS AND AN ACTION-PACKED SLATE of events, Chicago is an urban explorer's paradise. Whether you're attending a baseball game at iconic Wrigley Field or a comedy show at the Second City, strolling the lakefront, touring the Chicago River by boat, or exploring some of the city's 77 distinctive neighborhoods, it's clear that America's third-largest city dominates the country's sixth-most populous state. But that doesn't mean the rest of Illinois should be overlooked. Small towns like Galena and Mt Carroll offer intimate charm, while midsize cities like Springfield and Champaign-Urbana offer plenty of culture and history in their own right. And some spectacular natural beauty blankets the Land of Lincoln, from the shores and beaches of Chicago's Lake Michigan to the rolling hills and bluffs of Shawnee National Forest near downstate Carbondale.

© Tim Bolle / 500px

FOOD & DRINK

CHICAGO FINE DINING Chicago isn't all deep-dish pizza and hot dogs with lavish toppings. There's a long legacy of experimental gourmet restaurants in the city, from the pioneering Charlie Trotter's (now defunct) to grande dames like Alinea and Oriole. Gastronomic creativity abounds throughout Chicago; former President Obama is a fan of the creations of chef Rick Bayless, owner of Mexican restaurants throughout the city from Frontera Grill to Topolobampo. Just be prepared to open your wallet for these luxe dinners.

CHICAGO-STYLE HOT DOGS Though no one's clear on the hot dog's origins, Chicagoans claim the wiener was invented at the 1893 World's Columbian Exposition. Whether or not this is true, Chicago certainly has one of the best regional variations of the ballpark favorite. Order one 'dragged through the garden' (peppers, tomato, onions, pickles, celery salt and mustard – no ketchup) at Hot Doug's or in the drive-through of Superdawg (complete with carhop service), open since 1948 in Chicago's Norwood Park neighborhood. The pure beef hot dog at Superdawg is served on a poppy seed bun and even comes in its own vintage-style cardboard box.

CRAFT BEERS While Chicago never established the brewing monoliths of midwestern neighbors Milwaukee and St Louis, its craft brewing scene kicked into overdrive in recent decades, and early standouts Goose Island and Revolution Brewing have been joined by a spate of inventive competitors. At the home of the University of Illinois, the twin cities of Champaign-Urbana see both students and locals flock to the popular Blind Pig brewery with tasty house-made ales and a charming brick patio. One of the best bars in the state, Fast Eddie's Bon Air, was originally built in the historic town of Alton by Anheuser-Busch (based across the river in St Louis) in 1921. Today it can still be counted on for affordable pub fare in a lively dive bar setting with a neon exterior; there's also live music seven nights a week.

DEEP-DISH PIZZA Eating deep-dish pizza is a must when visiting Chicago. It's impossible to miss it at the crowded tourist haunts downtown, but neighborhood favorite Pequod's, tucked away in the city's Lincoln Park area, makes for a more authentic experience. Mingle with locals over classic Chicago pan pizzas stuffed with cheese and ringed by Pequod's trademark caramelized crust.

HORSESHOE Springfield may be most famous as the home of Abe Lincoln, but the state capital's famed horseshoe dish may be just as revered. The open-faced sandwich consists of hamburger (unless you prefer other meats including chicken, bacon, sausage or walleye) on toasted bread, smothered in cheese and even fries.

ITALIAN BEEF SANDWICH No food invention is more of a Chicago classic than the Italian beef sandwich, consisting of thinly sliced, seasoned roast beef cooked in jus and served with peppers on an Italian roll. Al's Beef in Chicago's University Village has been serving the now-iconic local

★ ★ ★

PIZZA WARS

Like the age-old Chicago Cubs versus White Sox baseball rivalry, the type of pizza you order in Chicago can elicit strong emotions and allegiances. The city is most famous for deep-dish pizza, a thick, pie-like creation baked in a steel pan stuffed with large amounts of cheese and tomato sauce. Pizzeria Uno and Lou Malnati's are among the oldest and most iconic purveyors of this style of pizza, which often appeals to more of a tourist crowd. Most Chicagoans, however, prefer thin-crust pizza. So if you're looking to eat like a local, the cash-only environs of Vito & Nick's Pizzeria on Chicago's South Side is a top choice for experiencing the city's classic tavern-style pizza (thin-crust, square-cut) in a quaint neighborhood setting.

Freelance_Ghostwriting / Getty Images: Left: © Daniel Boczarski / Getty Images

★ ★ ★

FESTIVAL CITY, USA

Chicago is a festival-lover's mecca, with major summer festivals including Lollapalooza, Riot Fest, Pitchfork Music Festival, Chicago Blues Festival and Taste of Chicago. But you don't have to battle big crowds just to have a good time, as any weekend in summer is overflowing with smaller, more local neighborhood street festivals that can be just as much fun (often a lot cheaper), including Wicker Park Fest, Taste of Randolph Street, and Do Division Street Fest. For more local flavor there's even an Iditarod-style, costumed shopping-cart race, the Chiditarod, held every spring.

staple at a no-frills beef stand (literally; there are no chairs) since 1938. Order yours from the chain's cash-only original location. *1049 W Taylor Street.*

SOUTHERN ILLINOIS BARBECUE BBQ isn't just for the South – southern Illinois does a dry rub rib and pork in a Tennessee-style tomato sauce that you can't pass up. Downstate Illinois institution 17th St Barbecue in Murphysboro is serving up some of the finest barbecue in the nation, winning too many awards to count. Anything you order here is good, but the baby back ribs are the most famous item and should be enjoyed in full-rack fashion any day of the week. Down the road from Murphysboro, small southern Illinois towns Colp and Ina have their own barbecue offerings.

NATURAL ESCAPES

THE 606 This 2.7-mile urban hiking trail was created in 2015 on the site of an abandoned railway line that crosses

through several of Chicago's coolest neighborhoods, including Wicker Park. Today it is one of the best ways to see the interior of the city, as you can walk or bike the leafy pathway with plenty of stops for food and drink at local bars and restaurants located just off the trail. *www.the606.org*

CHICAGO LAKEFRONT TRAIL Few juxtapositions of tall buildings and shimmering water are more dramatic than those that can be enjoyed from Chicago's Lakefront Trail, an 18-mile scenic path along Lake Michigan that stretches through a number of Chicago neighborhoods and beaches. Walk, run or bike the paved trail and be sure to stop at Montrose Beach, where sand dunes, a bird sanctuary and a summer bar/music venue await. *www.choosechicago.com*

FOREST PRESERVES OF COOK COUNTY Encompassing more than 69,000 acres, this greenbelt surrounding Chicago is the largest forest preserve district in the US.

From left:Andrew McMahon In the Wilderness performs during Riot Fest 2015 at Douglas Park in Chicago; Shawnee National Forest; the view from the top of Willis Tower in Chicago; Previous page: the Chicago skyline

© Davide Giannuzzi / 500px

Taking in woodlands, wetlands, lakes and prairies, the massive expanse includes campsites, nature preserves, 300 miles of hiking trails and some of the best mountain-biking terrain in the state. *http://fpdcc.com*

SHAWNEE NATIONAL FOREST
Consisting of 280,000 acres of federal land sprawling across vast swaths of open space in southern Illinois, this stunning landscape of hills, canyons and springs is unlike anything else in the state. Popular destinations include Garden of the Gods Wilderness and Little Grand Canyon, with the nearby Shawnee Hills Wine Trail making for another fun excursion. *www.fs.usda.gov/shawnee, Herod*

STARVED ROCK STATE PARK One of the state's most popular natural retreats is famous for its canyons, bluffs and waterfalls, which you can explore via 13 miles of trails and 133 campsites dotted throughout this 2630-acre preserve on the Illinois River. Get out and roam the

surrounding historic communities of LaSalle and Ottawa, or book a room at the 1930s-era Starved Rock Lodge and have dinner under the stars on the lodge's back patio. *www.dnr.illinois.gov, 2668 E 875th Rd, Oglesby*

ARTS, HISTORY & CULTURE

ABRAHAM LINCOLN PRESIDENTIAL LIBRARY & MUSEUM Telling the life story of Illinois' most famous resident and 16th US president, Abraham Lincoln, this massive 200,000-sq-ft complex in Springfield houses a museum, library and archives, plus high-tech special effects including interactive displays, live actors and a replica of the White House circa 1861. Afterward, visit the Lincoln Tomb in Springfield's Oak Ridge Cemetery. *www2.illinois.gov/alplm, 212 N Sixth St*

ART INSTITUTE OF CHICAGO
Immortalized in the classic 1986 comedy *Ferris Bueller's Day Off*, Chicago's most well-known art museum is this national

FUN FACT
....

Willis Tower (formerly Sears Tower) was the tallest building in the Americas until One World Trade Center in New York City eclipsed it, but the Willis Tower roof stands 100ft higher than that of One WTC, which took the title based on its lofty spire.

© Charles Cook / Getty Images ·Left· © Jon Hicks / Getty Images

treasure housing nearly 300,000 works of fine art. The entrance to its historic downtown structure is guarded by two iconic bronze lions, standing watch over the priceless collections within. There's plenty to see, but don't miss the superb impressionist and post-impressionist paintings. *www.artic.edu, 111 S Michigan Ave*

CHICAGO MUSEUM CAMPUS Situated along Chicago's picturesque downtown lakefront, the city's Museum Campus is home to three world-class museums within a 57-acre museum park: the Field Museum of Natural History, Shedd Aquarium and Adler Planetarium. The campus also includes a professional football stadium, nature trails, a summer concert venue and a small public beach. *www.choosechicago. com, 1400 S Lake Shore Dr*

CHICAGO RIVERWALK The expanded downtown Chicago Riverwalk extends for more than a mile along the Chicago River and is bustling with bars, restaurants, art and a flurry of activity in the summer

months. One of the best ways to see the river is by boarding one of several tourist boats, preferably with drink in hand on a warm, sunny day. *www.chicagoriverwalk.us*

GALENA One of the most beautiful small towns in the Midwest is this serene, historic community near Illinois' western border with Iowa. Shop Galena's quaint cobblestone streets, paddle down the Galena River, ogle historic mansions including President Ulysses S Grant's former home or explore the rolling hills and vineyards outside town. Galena's historic DeSoto House Hotel is the state's oldest hotel. *www.visitgalena.org*

GREEN MILL COCKTAIL LOUNGE A slice of Chicago's infamous mobster history remains alive at this landmark North Side jazz club, once Al Capone's favorite bar during Prohibition. Opened in 1907, one of Chicago's oldest bars has made appearances in several films and is still one of America's premier jazz clubs, as well as a prime poetry slam venue. Shows can go

* * *

ASK A LOCAL

'With gorgeous hills and vast expanses of open space, southern Illinois is one of the most over-looked areas of the state. The Shawnee National Forest offers endless outdoor recreation, with the town of Carbondale making an excellent base for exploring it all.'

From left: The Field Museum on Chicago's Museum Campus; Chicago jazz legend Frank D'Rone performing on stage at Green Mill Cocktail Lounge; The Super Museum in Metropolis.

© Mark Reinstein / Getty Images

into the early morning hours. *http://greenmilljazz.com, 4802 N Broadway*

KRANNERT ART MUSEUM In Champaign, the second-largest general fine-art museum in the states houses more than 10,000 works of art from the 4th century BC to the present day on the campus of the University of Illinois at Urbana-Champaign. Signature pieces include *Marilyn*, Andy Warhol's Marilyn Monroe portrait. *https://kam.illinois.edu, 500 E Peabody Dr*

OAK PARK This suburb next door to Chicago spawned two famous sons: novelist Ernest Hemingway was born here, and architect Frank Lloyd Wright lived and worked here for 20 years. The town's main sights revolve around the two men. For Hemingway, a low-key museum and his birthplace provide an intriguing peek at his formative years. The Frank Lloyd Wright Home and Studio, where Wright developed the Prairie style, is the big draw, as are the many surrounding houses he designed for his neighbors. Ten of them cluster within

a mile along Forest and Chicago Avenues (though gawking must occur from the sidewalk since they're privately owned). *www.visitoakpark.com*

THE SECOND CITY Founded in 1959 in Chicago's Old Town neighborhood, this world-famous center for improv comedy has hosted dozens of legendary comics and actors over the years, from Bill Murray to Stephen Colbert. Today the influential theater performs a wide variety of improvisation and sketch comedy shows across several venues. Improv classes are also available. *www.secondcity.com, 1616 N Wells St*

WRIGLEY FIELD There are few better sports venues than the landmark Wrigley Field, opened on Chicago's North Side in 1914 and home to Major League Baseball's Chicago Cubs. Wrigley's outfield ivy and bleachers party scene are world-famous, but the park's newly added adjacent green space, Gallagher Way (which hosts concerts, events and games of catch),

★ ★ ★

FINDING SUPERMAN

Just in case you thought that the Superman-themed Super Museum in the small southern Illinois town of Metropolis wasn't quirky enough, stop by in June for the town's four-day Superman Celebration, an annual festival dedicated to all things Superman. There's even a 12ft, 2-ton Superman statue outside the museum.

© Jing lowdive Li / Shutterstock; Right: elesi / Shutterstock

★ ★ ★

GETTING THERE & AROUND

O'Hare International Airport is the main Chicago hub, while Midway International Airport is a more relaxed alternative. Chicago is well served with public transit options including extensive city subway, the elevated 'L' and bus lines, with Metra rail lines serving most suburbs and Amtrak lines extending further out to midsize Illinois cities like Peoria and Springfield. Caution: Chicago drivers are often aggressive, but taxis and ride-sharing services in the city are plentiful.

makes an experience that's just as enjoyable as a game. Plus, you can visit now without fear of the Curse of the Billy Goat (look it up and be amazed); it was broken by the Cubs' 2016 World Series win. *www.mlb.com/cubs, 1060 W Addison St*

FAMILY OUTINGS

CAHOKIA MOUNDS STATE HISTORIC
SITE The largest pre-Columbian Native American settlement north of Mexico and Illinois' only Unesco World Heritage Site can be found in this 22-acre park, which showcases these flat-topped mounds, dated to AD 1200. Imagine what life was like before the iPhone as you explore the hallowed grounds, which also include a Stonehenge-style 'Woodhenge' made of wooden posts. *https://cahokiamounds.org, Collinsville (near East St Louis)*

CHICAGO RIVER BOAT CRUISE AND
NAVY PIER Multiple companies run Chicago architecture tours by boat down

the Chicago River, some going into Lake Michigan; all offer a great chance to take in Chicago skyline highlights. Boats usually depart from Michigan Avenue Bridge or Navy Pier; if the latter, spend some time in Navy Pier before or after the trip. The half-mile-long pier is one of the city's most-visited attractions, sporting a 196ft Ferris wheel and other (pricey) carnival rides, an Imax theater, a beer garden and more. Locals groan over Navy Pier's commercialization, but its lakefront view and cool breezes can't be beat. *https://navypier.org*

GREAT RIVER ROAD Extending more than 2000 miles along the Mississippi River from Minnesota to Louisiana, some of the most scenic stretches of the Great River Road (actually a series of roads) can be found in Illinois, hugging the state's western boundary. Enjoy unobstructed views of nature while visiting charming small towns like Quincy and Alton as the road curls by bluff-strewn scenery

and forgotten towns with real-deal Main Streets. As you slip under wind-beaten cliffs, keep an eye out for Elsah, a hidden hamlet of 19th-century stone cottages, wood buggy shops and farmhouses.
http://greatriverroad-illinois.org

From left: Great River Road outside Galena; Navy Pier.

MILLENNIUM PARK
The city's showpiece is a trove of free and arty sights. It includes Jay Pritzker Pavilion, Frank Gehry's swooping silver band shell, which hosts free weekly concerts in summer; Anish Kapoor's beloved silvery sculpture *Cloud Gate*, aka the 'Bean'; and Jaume Plensa's *Crown Fountain*, an interactive video installation/fountain. The McCormick Tribune Ice Rink fills with skaters in winter, and alfresco diners in summer. The hidden Lurie Garden blooms with prairie flowers and tranquility, Gehry-designed BP Bridge spans Columbus Dr with great skyline views, and the Nichols Bridgeway arches from the park to the Art Institute's 3rd-floor sculpture terrace.
www.millenniumpark.org

ITINERARY

Day 1
Explore downtown Chicago by admiring world-renowned architecture, investigating the wealth of museums and cultural attractions, and getting on the Chicago River with a boat cruise. Grab dinner in the bustling River North district before taking in drinks at Cindy's on the rooftop of the Chicago Athletic Association Hotel overlooking Millennium Park and Lake Michigan.

Day 2
Get out into the 'real' Chicago by exploring some of the city's 77 unique neighborhoods. Take in a Cubs game at iconic Wrigley Field in Wrigleyville, walk the trendy Wicker Park neighborhood around North and Milwaukee Avenues, or explore President Barack Obama's former neighborhood of Hyde Park on the South Side. Make your way back downtown to enjoy an urban hike at Northerly Island or a quiet walk on the Ohio Street Beach. Spend the evening checking out the nightlife in Chicago's hip Logan Square neighborhood.

Day 3
Leave Chicago and make your way west to the charming, historic town of Galena near the Mississippi River and the Iowa border, where you can take trolley tours to see the bluffs and mansions or explore the quaint shops and restaurants that line the town's cobblestone streets. Stroll the scenic Galena River Trail and spend the night at the historic DeSoto House Hotel.

Day 4
Get up early for a journey south down the scenic Great River Road, which hugs Illinois' western border along the Mississippi River. Grab lunch at the biker-friendly Poopy's Pub n' Grub in Savanna (closed Mon–Wed) before exploring the nearby New England–style town of Mt Carroll. Conclude your day in Springfield, the state capital.

Day 5
In Springfield, history awaits at every turn. To start, grab a classic horseshoe breakfast at Charlie Parker's Diner and then spend the day enjoying presidential sights at the Abraham Lincoln Presidential Library and Museum. Save time to explore the Illinois State Capitol; visitors often rub the statue's nose for good luck at the Lincoln Tomb.

INDIANA

★ ★

POPULATION: 6.7 million | **SIZE:** 36,418 sq miles | **STATE CAPITAL:** Indianapolis
WEBSITE: https://visitindiana.com

'THERE'S MORE THAN CORN IN INDIANA' IS A PHRASE YOU MIGHT FIND HARD TO AVOID IN YOUR travels across the country's 38th-largest state. The sentiment rings true immediately in the friendly city of Indianapolis, the state's compact and tidy capital, which is home to the Indy 500, the NCAA's headquarters, and the largest number of US war memorials outside of Washington, DC. The Hoosier State is also home to several major college campuses including the University of Notre Dame, Purdue University and Indiana University, the last of which is in the funky, artist-friendly city of Bloomington. Along the way you'll want to explore Amish communities, sand dunes, the Indiana Wine Trail perched along the scenic Ohio River, the most distinctive collection of modern architecture in the country and a vast expanse of wilderness in Hoosier National Forest.

© Sam Gwinn / Shutterstock

FOOD & DRINK

PORK TENDERLOIN SANDWICH Like much of the Midwest, the Hoosier State loves its pork. The finest expression of this affection is the pork tenderloin sandwich, a deep-fried slab of pork loin on a bun, the edges of the meat far overhanging the bun. Devour one in your car at the Mug-n-Bun drive-in near the Indianapolis Motor Speedway (and don't tell nearby Iowa, also devoted to the classic pork tenderloin sandwich, that this listing went to Indiana).

ST ELMO STEAK HOUSE This longtime Indianapolis institution is nationally acclaimed for its steaks and world renowned for its shrimp cocktail, one of Indiana's most classic and popular dishes. Order yours with a variety of steaks and chops, lobster tails or king crab and shrimp linguine in an old-school tavern-style space that hasn't changed much since 1902. *https://stelmos.com, 127 S. Illinois St*

SUGAR PIE Going to Indiana and not ordering a sugar pie would be like... well...going to Indiana and not ordering a sugar pie. Correcting such an egregious oversight should be easy; there's even a beloved Zionsville mainstay named after the dessert. My Sugar Pie offers a wide range of handmade pies in addition to their signature sugar cream Hoosier pie.

NATURAL ESCAPES

HOOSIER NATIONAL FOREST If you really want to get away from it all, this more than 200,000-acre national forest of hills and wilderness sprawls out to parts of nine southern Indiana counties and surrounds Larry Bird's hometown of French Lick. Hike some of the forest's 266 miles of trails and then kick back to watch the sunset along Patoka Lake. *www.fs.fed.us*

INDIANA DUNES NATIONAL PARK The newest National Park, the unique landscape of this popular park in Chesterton along Lake Michigan in northwest Indiana draws a good number of visitors from Chicago, but it remains a tranquil oasis of almost 25 miles of undeveloped beach marked by trails and sand dunes up to 200ft high. Climb the dunes or just spread out a blanket and relax in the sand. Next door is Indiana Dunes State Park. *www.nps.gov/indu/ index.htm, 1215 N State Road 49, Porter*

ARTS, HISTORY & CULTURE

BLOOMINGTON Home of Indiana University, Bloomington has charm to spare with its funky shops, ethnic restaurants, the large Tibetan Mongolian Buddhist Cultural Center and abundant nearby nature at locations like Brown County State Park and Lake Monroe (where singer John Mellencamp maintains a home). Explore Bloomington's B-Line outdoor urban trail, and for a more traditional college experience, a basketball game at the university's Assembly Hall is a must. *https://bloomington.in.gov*

COLUMBUS This unique town of 44,000, the 'Athens on the Prairie,' is famous for its modernist architecture, public art and historic landmarks that appear almost everywhere you look. Tour more

★ ★ ★

Divine
INTERVENTION

Polish monks built a series of trippy, fluorescent shrines to make the Grotto of the Blessed Virgin Mary at the Carmelite monastery hiding in suburban Munster. First came 250 tons of sponge rock that the friars used for the grotto's dark, twisting, three-story caverns. Then came the bright-hued bits of rose quartz, blue fluorite and other minerals that glimmer in starry designs from the walls. The real eye-popper, though, is the Fluorescent Altar. Flip the light switch, and the stones around Mary's statue jolt to life.

Pictured left: View from Hickory Ridge Fire Tower in Hoosier National Forest.

© gnagel / Getty Images; Right: © Action Sports Photography / Shutterstock

★ ★ ★

GETTING THERE & AROUND

Indiana, the 'Crossroads of America,' has more miles of interstate per sq mile than any other US state. Public transit is available in larger cities like Indianapolis, and rail lines serve many of the midsize towns, but travel by car is most common. Indianapolis International Airport is the state's main hub.

than 70 architectural wonders around town, including churches, a courthouse, sculptures and private homes. Stop by the lively downtown district for an array of bars and restaurants. *https://columbus.in.us*

FORT WAYNE MUSEUM OF ART
This museum is known across the state for its collection of visual arts from the 19th century to the present, specializing in showcasing artists from diverse backgrounds. It also hosts the annual Chalk Walk street painting event, held in conjunction with Fort Wayne's Three Rivers Festival every July.
www.fwmoa.org, 311 E. Main St

INDIANA MEDICAL HISTORY MUSEUM
When you think 'horror movie asylum,' this century-old state psychiatric hospital is exactly what you envision. Guided tours roam the former pathology lab, from the cold-slabbed autopsy room to the eerie

specimen room filled with brains in jars, and exhibits on early psychiatric medical research. *www.imhm.org, 3045 W Vermont St, closed Sundays to Tuesdays*

SOLDIERS & SAILORS MONUMENT
Did you known Indianapolis is home to the most US war memorials outside of Washington, DC? Its most famous is the landmark Soldiers & Sailors Monument, recognized as an iconic image of the city. Learn about the Hoosiers who served in wars throughout US history while you peruse artworks and get a good glimpse of Indianapolis from the monument's observation level.
https://in.gov, 1 Monument Circle

FAMILY OUTINGS

AMISH COUNTRY One of the largest Amish communities in the US is near the backroads of northern Indiana around the

towns of Middlebury and Shipshewana, where horse-drawn buggies, quilt gardens, and quaint shops and galleries offer a step back in time. Rent a bike to explore the 16-mile Pumpkinvine Nature Trail and cap your day with a home-cooked Amish feast at Das Dutchman Essenhaus. *www.amishcountry.org*

CHILDREN'S MUSEUM OF INDIANAPOLIS

The world's largest kids' museum is a crowd favorite that sprawls over five floors holding dinosaurs aplenty and a 43ft sculpture by Dale Chihuly that teaches tykes to blow glass (virtually!). The Sports Legend Experience expansion complements the NCAA Hall of Champions in downtown Indy. Families can shoot hoops, be inspired by the stories of famous sports legends or work together on a pit-stop challenge, and more. *www.childrensmuseum.org, 3000 N Meridian St*

INDIANAPOLIS MOTOR SPEEDWAY MUSEUM Located on the grounds of the speedway, home of the world-famous Indianapolis 500 auto race, this museum features several Indy 500–winning cars as well as a large selection of more general motorsport and consumer autos that take you on a high-octane journey through American automotive history. *https://indyracingmuseum.org, 4790 W. 16th St*

SANTA CLAUS It's Christmas year-round in the quirky little southern Indiana town of Santa Claus, where every year the local post office replies to letters to Santa from all over the world. With local attractions named Santa's Candy Castle, the Santa Claus Museum and Santa's Stables, you have a pretty good idea of what to expect here. For dinner? St Nick's Restaurant at Santa's Lodge, naturally. *https://santaclausind.org*

ITINERARY

Day 1
Start your journey exploring Indianapolis' downtown with a stop at the Soldiers & Sailors Monument, where you can get a nice city view from its observation deck before moving on to explore the Indiana Statehouse and Indiana State Museum. Get a look at the NCAA Hall of Champions (the collegiate sports governing body is located here). Grab dinner and spend the evening exploring downtown along Massachusetts Avenue.

Day 2
Head to Bloomington, a youthful and vibrant college town south of Indianapolis. Once there you can roam Bloomington by bike on the B-Line Trail, explore the leafy campus of Indiana University, or tour the peaceful grounds of Bloomington's Tibetan Mongolian Buddhist Cultural Center.

Day 3
Drive past the scenic rolling hills of Brown County State Park on your way to tour the modernist architectural gems of Columbus, filled with buildings from some of the top architects in the world.

From left: Eero Saarinen's North Christian Church in Columbus; the Indy 500.

IOWA

★ ★

POPULATION: 3.1 million | **SIZE:** 56,273 sq miles | **STATE CAPITAL:** Des Moines
WEBSITE: www.traveliowa.com

THERE'S MORE TO IOWA THAN THE STEREOTYPICAL BUTTER SCULPTURES, tractor pulls, presidential caucuses and fried foods on a stick that the name most often conjures. Des Moines boasts a diverse food and cultural scene, and Iowa City is a thriving college town and Unesco City of Literature, while Sioux City is rich in Native American history. Beyond the larger towns, explore the heart of Iowa by touring the covered bridges of Madison County, visiting offbeat religious communes or hand-feeding bison on a local farm. There's also an abundance of nature and plenty of open space besides farmland to explore all across the state. The towering bluffs on the Mississippi River and the soaring Loess Hills lining the Missouri River bookend the rolling farmland of this bucolic state. In the middle you'll find the commune dwellers of the Amana Colonies, and plenty of picture-perfect rural towns.

© Felix Mizioznikov / Shutterstock

FOOD & DRINK

CORN DOGS A summer dominated by the Iowa State Fair produces a strong following for its most addictive treats, and the cornmeal-coated and fried corn dog has the staying power to be in demand year-round. (Not all Iowa food comes deep-fried on a stick, of course; upscale restaurant Proof in Des Moines has 10-course gourmet tasting menus.)

LOOSE MEAT SANDWICH Ground beef. On a bun. No sauce. No ketchup. No nothin'. You don't get any more midwestern than the famed Iowa loose meat sandwich, aka a tavern sandwich, aka a Maid-Rite sandwich. Try one at any location of Maid-Rite, a local chain that claims to have invented this sandwich in 1926, or at Canteen Lunch in the Alley in Ottumwa, operating since 1927.

SWEET CORN ON THE COB Iowa produces almost 2 billion bushels of corn each year, and though much of it gets used for industrial purposes, there's plenty of fresh sweet corn on the cob to go around in summer. Grilled and buttered, and served with some salt, it's a simple taste of Iowa heaven.

NATURAL ESCAPES

BACKBONE STATE PARK Iowa's oldest state park is also one of its most beautiful, with plenty of outdoor recreation opportunities including camping, canoeing, beach volleyball, rock climbing and trout fishing. The heavily wooded area of rocky terrain and forested bluffs in Dundee is most well known for its steep ridge, nicknamed the Devil's Backbone, and a popular hike along the Backbone Trail. *www.iowadnr.gov, 1347 129th St*

DUNNINGS SPRING PARK When you think of Iowa, you don't necessarily think of waterfalls. But one visit to the small of town of Decorah in northern Iowa will change all that, thanks to the town's proximity to the two waterfall locations of Dunnings Spring Park and nearby Malanaphy Springs. While here, take time to explore the cool reaches of the Dunnings Springs ice caves as well. *www.visitdecorah.com/business/dunning-springs-park, Ice Cave Rd*

MINES OF SPAIN RECREATION AREA Wildlife from wild turkeys and white-tailed deer to rarer species like bobcats and bald eagles are on display at this diverse state park near Dubuque that features 15 miles of hiking trails, 4 miles of ski trails, and a bird and butterfly garden. Check out the scenic bluffs and overlooks or launch your canoe into Catfish Creek. *www.minesofspain.org, 8991 Bellevue Heights Rd*

ARTS, HISTORY & CULTURE

BRIDGES OF MADISON COUNTY Madison County is a postcard-perfect representation of the quintessential Iowa landscape, particularly the iconic covered bridges made famous in the 1995 film (and 1992 novel) *The Bridges of Madison County*. Explore all six of the picturesque bridges as well as nearby vineyards, breweries and cideries. The town of Winterset is the hub of most tourist activity in the area, particularly around the

★ ★ ★

FAIR GAME

The quintessential cultural represen-tation of the state, the long-running Iowa State Fair began in 1854 and has been held every year on the Iowa State Fairground since 1856. One of the largest and most well-known state fairs in America takes place over 11 days in August, encompassing more than 450 acres filled with campsites, live music stages and over 200 vendors selling food. You can taste all types of fried items on a stick, from pork chops to Oreos. Among the events are rooster crowing contests, cow chip (dried cow dung) throwing and carnival rides; the butter cow sculp-ture is a highlight of any state fair experience.

Left: Iowa's iconic farmland.

© VDB Photos / Shutterstock

Des Moines has the state's main air hub, and although bus and rail lines do exist, the car is king in this predominantly rural state. I-80, America's second-longest highway, runs east–west through the whole state, often with long stretches of empty space between towns. Beware of snow and ice conditions when driving in winter.

courthouse square. *www.madisoncounty.com/the-covered-bridges*

IOWA CITY The youthful, artsy vibe here is courtesy of the University of Iowa campus, home to good art and natural history museums. It spills across both sides of the Iowa River (which has lovely walks on the banks); to the east it mingles with the charming downtown. In summer, when the student-to-townie ratio evens out, the city mellows somewhat. The school's writing programs are renowned, and Iowa City was named a Unesco City of Literature in 2008. For a sharp parody of the town and school, read Jane Smiley's novel *Moo*. *www.icgov.org*

JOHN WAYNE BIRTHPLACE & MUSEUM
As the world's only museum dedicated to legendary Hollywood actor John Wayne, this 6100-sq-ft museum in his Iowa hometown of Winterset features a movie theater and an array of John Wayne artifacts including original movie posters, film wardrobes, scripts, contracts, letters and even one of the Duke's custom cars. *www.johnwaynebirthplace.museum, 205 S John Wayne Dr*

LEWIS & CLARK INTERPRETIVE CENTER
Located in Sioux City near the banks of the Missouri River along Iowa's western border, this 20,000-sq-ft cultural complex brings history to life with a 14ft *Spirit of Discovery* sculpture of famous explorers Lewis and Clark plus traditional Native American games, exhibits, art galleries and DVD presentations. *www.siouxcitylcic.com, 900 Larsen Park Rd*

PAPPAJOHN SCULPTURE PARK
This expansive outdoor sculpture museum (unrelated to Papa John's Pizza) occupies

© Kyle Kephart / Shutterstock

ITINERARY

Day 1
The Iowa State Capitol building makes a good opener as you start your day exploring Des Moines; every detail at this bling-heavy space seems to try to outdo the next. Join a free tour and you can climb halfway up the dome. followed by an intake of art at the Des Moines Art Center and Pappajohn Sculpture Park. Stroll the cool shops in the walkable East Village neighborhood before stopping for a drink in the bustling Court District downtown. If you're here in spring, an Iowa Cubs minor league baseball game is not to be missed.

Days 2 & 3
A couple hours' drive east along I-80 will bring you to Iowa City, a fun college town that is also a Unesco City of Literature. After exploring the compact downtown and its charming pedestrian mall, drop into Prairie Lights Bookstore in the evening. The next day head out to the villages of the Amana Colonies, founded in the mid-1800s by Inspirationists, for a craft-filled side of offbeat local history.

From left: Grilled sweet corn on the cob; a Madison County bridge.

a 4-acre portion of downtown Des Moines real estate within the city's larger Western Gateway Park. It features 29 works of art donated by the Pappajohn family and valued at $40 million. Stroll the well-manicured grounds with your camera ready. *www.desmoinesartcenter.org, 1330 Grand Ave*

FAMILY OUTINGS

AMANA COLONIES Originally established as religious communes in the 1800s, this quaint community of seven villages stretches along a 17-mile loop about halfway between Iowa City and Cedar Rapids. It's reminiscent of Amish Country (although the villages embrace tourism and technology), and handcrafted arts and goods are the name of the game. The area also offers several festivals and a historical museum. *www.amanacolonies.com*

HAWKEYE BUFFALO RANCH
There's more than corn at this family farm in Fredericksburg. You can hand-feed the small herd of bison on wagon rides during public tours. The 500-acre farm dating back to 1854 also offers Native American history, wildlife viewing and, at the on-site store, buffalo meat. *www.hawkeyebuffalo.com, 3034 Pembroke Ave*

SPOOK CAVE & CAMPGROUND The cave at the base of the 90ft bluff here is only accessible by boat, but don't let that deter you from boarding a canoe and exploring the always 47°F environs of Spook Cave via tourist boat tour. Camp near a trout stream and waterfall on this family-friendly site in McGregor, with cabins and golf cart rentals also available. It's open for relaxing stays May through October. *http://spookcave. com, 13299 Spook Cave Rd*

KANSAS

★ ★

POPULATION: 2.9 million | **SIZE:** 82,278 sq miles | **STATE CAPITAL:** Topeka
LARGEST CITY: Wichita | **WEBSITE:** www.travelks.com

OFTEN CONSIDERED A PLACE TO TRAVEL THROUGH BUT NOT *TO*, KANSAS HAS NO INTEREST IN competing for the hurried passerby. Kansas' classic two-lane highways are perfect for road trips, as you're waved along by human-height grass stalks. In the Flint Hills, stand on one of the last pieces of delicate native prairie. Witness the power of nature in the badlands of the West, or yes, maybe even in the dark, ominously swirling clouds of a tornado taking shape in the all-expansive sky. Kansas' towns are authentic charmers, from thriving Main Street Americana in Lawrence to untamed outsider art in Lucas. Step into the past in Wichita's living history museum or experience cowboy culture in Dodge City. And make time to chow down: Kansas City's slow-cooked barbecue is second to none, and family-style comfort food brings diners to the Amish town of Yoder. Is it that surprising that Dorothy couldn't wait to get home?

© KSwinicki / Shutterstock

FOOD & DRINK

BREADBASKET PLENTY Kansas doesn't grow so much of the country's grains for nothing, and it has the overflowing breadbasket to show for it. Whether you visit the annual National Festival of Breads in Manhattan, Kansas, home of the Kansas Wheat Innovation Center, or sample sunflower-topped bread from award-winning WheatFields Bakery in Lawrence, your time in Kansas will be surrounded by plentiful wheat in all its forms.

HOME COOKING Kansas-style home cooking bears a passing resemblance to the vittles of the South, but the Sunflower State is still heavily influenced by the 1850s-era recipe books of German and Russian immigrants, the first white settlers in the territory. The Brookville Hotel in Abilene has been serving fried chicken since 1915. A menu won't be provided: get ready for family-style sides of creamed corn, fresh biscuits and a heaping helping of nostalgia. Carriage Crossing in Yoder, population 200 and home to the state's largest Amish community, is famous for its plate-size cinnamon rolls, which you'll want to dip in chili, a classic Kansas combo (trust us!).

KANSAS CITY BARBECUE In Kansas City, barbecue is an art form – ask locals to name their favorite spot, and you won't hear the same answer twice. Dripping with a tangy, molasses-sweet, tomato-based sauce with just a touch of spice, this tender, lovingly smoked meat will leave its mark (most likely on your sticky fingers or dribbled onto your shirt). Don't miss the KC favorite of burnt ends, the small, tougher shreds of brisket once considered scraps and given away for free until restaurant owners realized how much diners loved them. Joe's Kansas City Bar-B-Que, inside a working gas station, is an unmissable stop on your personal quest to find the city's best.

SUDS & SPIRITS FROM THE SOIL Kansas' native flavors come through most boldly in its homegrown booze. Wichita has an ever-increasing number of microbreweries, but when Free State Brewing Company opened in Lawrence in 1989, it was the first legal brewery in Kansas in more than 100 years, after temperance supporter Carrie Nation traveled the state smashing up saloons with a hatchet. Liquor aficionados wrangling for something harder should look west to Boot Hill Distillery in Dodge City. This farmer-owned company uses a 'soil-to-sip' ethos to keep Kansas' grains closer to home by developing its own whiskeys, vodka and gin. It also revives Old West cowboy cures such as Prickly Ash Bitters, an aperitif once sold as an indigestion antidote.

NATURAL ESCAPES

MONUMENT ROCKS Rising mirage-like out of the flat landscape 25 miles south of Oakley, the 70ft-tall Monument Rocks are a huge reminder that the High Plains were once covered by an ancient inland sea. As the water dried up, the elements started eating away at the seabed, exposing deposits of chalky limestone and shale. *www.kansastravel.org/monumentrocks. htm, off US-83*

★ ★ ★

Wichita's
RIVERFEST

The Arkansas River (it's pronounced 'our Kansas' river here, not ar-kan-saw like the state) cuts through the heart of Wichita, and is at the center of the city's nine-day Riverfest. Held in late May into early June, a festival highlight is the Cardboard Regatta: teams must build a water-worthy vessel in just 90 minutes using only cardboard, duct tape, pool noodles and a box cutter. Elsewhere, the action has a particularly Middle America flavor, with a funnel-cake eating contest and displays of armored storm-chasing vehicles. Entry to the festival is by purchasing a button; these are something of a local collector's item. The festival mascot is Admiral Windwagon Smith, who is said to have cruised across the Kansas prairie in a covered wagon rigged with a sail.

Left: *The Keeper of the Plains* statue in Wichita at the fork of the Arkansas River, a sculpture by Blackbear Bosin.

© Rawpixel.com / Shutterstock: Left: © ilumus photography / Alamy Stock Photo

© Sharon Day / Shutterstock

★ ★ ★

GETTING THERE & AROUND

Kansas' biggest airport, in Wichita, has a handful of domestic flights, but most visitors arrive from Kansas City, Missouri. A car is essential to get around the open roads of this sparsely populated state. Greyhound bus services and a single Amtrak train line pass through, but departure times of these usually once-daily services are inconvenient.

TALLGRASS PRAIRIE NATIONAL PRESERVE This 11,000-acre preserve near Strong City is home to one of the final remaining stretches of virgin tallgrass in the entire country. Thanks to its rocky, thin soil, this patch of prairie was spared the fate of its surroundings, which were gleefully overturned by plows and grazed by cattle. After a 140-year absence, a free-roaming herd of American bison were reintroduced in 2009, and peaceful trails crisscross the grasslands, where stalks that can grow 10ft tall sway in the nearly constant breeze. Get there via the rolling Flint Hills Scenic Byway. *www.nps.gov/tapr, 2480B Kansas 177*

ARTS, HISTORY & CULTURE

ALLEN FIELDHOUSE For several months of the year, you'll find residents of the progressive college town of Lawrence making a pilgrimage to Allen Fieldhouse to worship the town's patron saint, James Naismith, who invented basketball at the turn of the 20th century. Dress in your best crimson and blue to catch the Jayhawks at the loudest arena in college basketball. *https://kuathletics.com, 1651 Naismith Dr*

BROWN V BOARD OF EDUCATION NATIONAL HISTORIC SITE Inside a once-segregated elementary school in Topeka, this museum honors the African American parents who took their case all the way to the Supreme Court in 1951 to end segregation in public schools. The site's powerfully moving collection covers the verdict, the slow path to change and the wider civil rights movement. *www.nps.gov/brvb, 1515 SE Monroe St*

GARDEN OF EDEN Tiny Lucas (pop. 390) is a magnet for eccentric grassroots artists, a trend that may have started with Civil War veteran Samuel Dinsmoor, who constructed a 'log cabin' from limestone and christened it the Garden of Eden. He spent his life sculpting more than 200 haunting concrete figures. When Dinsmoor

died in 1932, he wanted his body to be on display, and his moth-eaten remains are still on view. *www.garden-of-eden-lucas-kansas.com, 305 E. 2nd St*

MID-AMERICA ALL-INDIAN CENTER
Guarded by Native American artist Blackbear Bosin's 44ft *Keeper of the Plains* statue, this museum in Wichita is the only in the state to preserve the rich history of the area's Native peoples, through collections of art and artifacts as well as a traditional Wichita-style grass lodge. *www.theindiancenter.org, 650 N. Seneca St*

FAMILY OUTINGS

BEAUMONT HOTEL Since the 1940s, the main street of blink-and-you'll-miss-it Beaumont (pop. 50) has moonlighted as an aircraft landing strip, originally used by ranchers checking on their cattle and now by local pilots looking for weekend brunch. On the second Saturday of the month from April to October, the Beaumont Hotel hosts a monthly fly-in, welcoming as many as 70 people who arrive by airplane. Aviators taxi down Main Street to the hotel and hop out to enjoy the 'pilot's breakfast' of double eggs, bacon and pancakes. *http://beaumonthotelks.com, 11651 SE Main St*

DODGE CITY AREA Wild West visions come to life in Dodge City, whether at the Santa Fe Trail Tracks outside town or at Boot Hill Museum on Front Street. The museum preserves the history of this one-time stop on the wagon trail and later cattle town; most of the original buildings of Front Street were torn down in 20th-century urban renewal efforts. The town is one of many places in Kansas that keep the past alive; an hour northeast, Fort Larned National Historic Site is a remarkably well-preserved fort in a lovely setting. It's well worth the trip to learn about the turbulent history of the Indian Wars era. The Santa Fe Trail passed right in front of the fort. *www.dodgecity.org*

KANSAS COSMOSPHERE & SPACE CENTER A contender for the most unexpected attraction in Kansas, the Cosmosphere in Hutchinson documents the race into space through 13,000 captivating artifacts, from a restored WWII German V-2 missile to a flight-ready backup Sputnik and moon rocks collected by Neil Armstrong and Buzz Aldrin during the Apollo 11 mission. It's worth a detour. *https://cosmo.org, 1100 N. Plum St*

OLD COWTOWN MUSEUM Step into the dusty streets of 1870s Wichita at this open-air museum that brings history to life with in-character reenactors, farm animals and authentic architecture, all set on a site near the endpoint of the Chisholm Trail. Grab a refreshing sarsaparilla soda (it's like an old-fashioned root beer) and watch a gunfight erupt in the streets as if you're on an Old West film set (you actually are!). *www.oldcowtown.org, 1865 Museum Blvd*

ITINERARY

Day 1
After rolling yourself out of Kansas City's famous barbecue restaurants, head an hour south to Lawrence, an adorable college town with a rocking music scene, an unshakable basketball passion, and Kansas' first post-Prohibition brewery.

Day 2
Get an early start and drive to Topeka's domed Kansas Statehouse which rises 16ft higher than the US Capitol. Catch your breath from walking the 296 steps up into the dome at the Brown v Board of Education National Historic Site, honoring the 1951 Supreme Court case that ended segregation in public schools. Then take the Flint Hills National Scenic Byway to the Tallgrass Prairie National Preserve and roam on the range with a herd of bison before heading to Wichita for the night.

Day 3
In Wichita, stop at the Old Cowtown Museum and the Mid-America All-Indian Center. Or day-trip to Hutchinson and Yoder for space-race relics and Amish cinnamon buns.

From left: Kansas City-style BBQ pork ribs; Monument Rocks; Flint Hills' tallgrass prairie.

KENTUCKY

★ ★

POPULATION: 4.5 million | **SIZE:** 40,409 sq miles | **STATE CAPITAL:** Frankfort
LARGEST CITY: Louisville | **WEBSITE:** www.kentuckytourism.com

NEITHER TOTALLY SOUTHERN NOR TOTALLY MIDWESTERN, KENTUCKY HAS A CULTURE ALL ITS own. There's the highbrow: million-dollar racehorses, top-notch theater, exquisite Gilded Age mansions, bourbons that auction for more than cars. And there's the wild, country side: hot rods, fried chicken, beer-fueled bluegrass pickin' on summer nights. Indulge in both. Kentucky's cities are underrated delights. Tour Louisville's picturesque historic district, all red brick and stamped tin and stained glass. Sip cocktails in arty speakeasies and eat at world-renowned farm-to-table restaurants. Visit the gorgeous Kentucky State Capitol building in diminutive, bashful Frankfort. Then get out into the countryside. Visitors flock here to see the world's largest cave, marvel at bizarre natural arches, climb the sandstone crags and swim in fast-flowing rivers. And, oh yeah, the grass really is blue.

© Lottie Davies / Lonely Planet

FOOD & DRINK

BOURBON TRAIL Spend a weekend or a week making a pilgrimage to the distilleries that produce almost all the world's silky, smoky, mellow oak-aged bourbon. Among others, explore the barrel-shaped tasting room at Heaven Hill in Bardstown, the Spanish Mission–style buildings of Four Roses in Lawrenceburg and the veritable bourbon theme park at Maker's Mark in Loretto, where you can stamp your own bottle with a red wax seal. *https://kybourbontrail.com*

FRIED CHICKEN You can't visit the Bluegrass State without trying Kentucky fried chicken. No, not that Kentucky Fried Chicken – though KFC was founded here, in the eastern Kentucky town of Corbin, and you can have a meal at the Harland Sanders Cafe and Museum on the site of the first kitchen where Sanders developed his recipe. All southern states have their own version, but locals sing the praises of the fried chicken at Brown Bag Burgers and Bangie's Cafe in the middle-of-nowhere burg of Henderson.

KENTUCKY HOT BROWNS Live it up like it's 1928 at the storied downtown Louisville Brown Hotel, the perfect place to savor a mint julep (a sweet bourbon and mint cocktail associated with Kentucky Derby season). If you get hungry, tuck into a Hot Brown, an open-faced turkey and bacon sandwich topped with Mornay sauce, invented here to satisfy hungry Roaring Twenties partiers and iconic ever since. *www.brownhotel.com, 335 W. Broadway*

NATURAL ESCAPES

DANIEL BOONE NATIONAL FOREST More than 700,000 acres of rugged ravines and gravity-defying sandstone arches cover much of the Appalachian foothills of eastern Kentucky. Within the forest is the Red River Gorge, whose sandstone cliffs draw rock climbers from around the globe. But you don't have to be a climber to appreciate the natural arches, wild rivers, waterfalls, wildflower-spangled hillsides and miles of hiking trails. Check out gravity-defying Gray's Arch, accessible by a 4-mile loop trail. *www.fs.usda.gov/dbnf*

LAND BETWEEN THE LAKES On the border of Tennessee and Kentucky, the narrow strip of land between two lakes has been turned into a vast family recreation area, with swimming, boating, fishing, hiking and a recreated 1850s farm. The highlight is a 700-acre grazing prairie for elk and bison; see the lumbering land mammals by driving tour along a loop road. *www.landbetweenthelakes.us*

MAMMOTH CAVE NATIONAL PARK The world's longest cave system has been used by humans since prehistory – for mineral gathering, for a tuberculosis hospital, even as a church. Choose from an array of ranger-guided tours, from sedate strolls amid the alien rock formations to wriggling-on-your-belly-in-the-dirt adventures. On the surface, you can hike, mountain bike or go horseback riding through the dappled old-growth forest. Mammoth Cave is near Cave City. *www.nps.gov/maca*

★ ★ ★

KENTUCKY DERBY FESTIVAL

It's easy to partake in Derby spirit, as the Kentucky Derby Festival starts two weeks before the actual race in May, with hot-air balloons, concerts, charity dinners, golf tournaments, fireworks and more. But seeing the Derby, or at least seeing it at Churchill Downs, is much trickier. Real seats sell out years in advance, and often to people with titles like viscount in front of their names. But you can buy a general access ticket into the teeming party scene in the infield and paddock area, though don't expect to see, like, actual horses. Going to a Derby watching at an area joint may be your best bet to actually view the so-called 'greatest two minutes in sports.'

© Shackleford Photography / Shutterstock; Left: © Thomas Carr / Shutterstock

★ ★ ★

KENTUCKY BOURBON

Bourbon whiskey has been distilled in Kentucky since the late 1700s, brought over by waves of Scots settlers. It takes its names from Bourbon County, from whose port barrels of the liquor were sent down the Ohio River. Authentic straight bourbon must be at least 51% corn and aged in a charred white-oak barrel for at least two years. The longer the aging, the more complex the flavors become, the wood leaching whiffs of vanilla, resin and caramel. The very best aged bourbons can sell for thousands of dollars a bottle, causing auction frenzies and even thefts – in 2013, 222 bottles of the legendary Pappy Van Winkle's Family Reserve 20 Year went missing from the Buffalo Trace distillery in Frankfort.

ARTS, CULTURE & HISTORY

ABBEY OF GETHSEMANI Tucked away in central Kentucky, you'll find the ascetically beautiful Abbey of Gethsemani, a Trappist monastery where monks live in prayer and silence. Book a spiritual retreat or come for a day visit of the 1500 acres of wooded grounds; it's near Bardstown. Or just pop in to the gift shop for some monk-made fudge or bourbon fruitcake.
www.monks.org, 3642 Monks Rd, Trappist

CHURCHILL DOWNS It all happens here in Louisville on the first Saturday in May – the hats, the seersucker suits, the bourbon cocktails and, of course, the horse race. Home to the Kentucky Derby since 1875, Churchill Downs is perhaps the most famous track in the world. From April through November a few bucks will get you seats to watch warm-ups and minor races.
www.churchilldowns.com, 700 Central Ave

FRANKFORT Kentucky's diminutive capital (pop. 26,000) makes for an amiable afternoon of historic sightseeing. There's the Beaux Arts–style capitol building, and across the river is the bluff-top Frankfort Cemetery, final resting place of iconic frontiersman Daniel Boone. Fuel up with a pimento-cheese burger or a fried chicken platter at 1940s-era Cliffside Diner.
www.visitfrankfort.com

HEADLEY-WHITNEY MUSEUM In the heart of Bluegrass Country in Lexington, this marvelously eccentric decorative arts museum is the private collection of Old Hollywood jewelry designer George Headley. Highlights include dollhouse mansions crafted by socialite Marylou Whitney, a three-car garage turned into a shell-covered grotto, and Headley's own bibelots – precious metal and gem trinkets that serve no purpose other than to dazzle.
www.headley-whitney.org, 443 Old Frankfort Pike

KENTUCKY ARTISAN CENTER Handicrafts enthusiasts shouldn't miss this 25,000-sq-ft center, right off I-75 in

From left: Bourbon barrels at Woodford Reserve distillery in Versailles; Shaker Village; the stalactites at Mammoth Cave.

© Zack Frank / Shutterstock

Berea, where artisans demonstrate and sell their wares to passing road-trippers and serious collectors alike. On display are traditional regional crafts like quilts, baskets and beeswax candles, as well as modern jewelry, blown glass and textile art. Look too for bourbon-infused chocolates, cakes and BBQ sauces.
www.kentuckyartisancenter.ky.gov, 200 Artisan Way

MARY TODD LINCOLN HOUSE Poor Mary Todd Lincoln had already lost three of her four children before her husband was shot in front of her in Ford's Theatre in Washington, DC. Visit where she lived in happier times, her tidy brick childhood home in Lexington, now a museum of her life. Many of the antiques in the home are original Todd family pieces.
www.mtlhouse.org, 578 W. Main St

OLD LOUISVILLE Imagine yourself as a captain of industry during Louisville's Victorian heyday while you stroll through this supremely elegant neighborhood of

Italianate mansions and brick town houses. One highlight is St James Court, with aristocratic homes surrounding a park lit with gas lamps. Another is Millionaire's Row, a stretch of 3rd Street lined with some of the most lavish mansions.
http://oldlouisville.org

MUHAMMAD ALI CENTER Born Cassius Clay, the trailblazing boxer nicknamed the Louisville Lip is the city's most famous son. At the center, explore the tribulations Ali experienced growing up with racism and segregation and learn about his most famous fights, all illustrated with multimedia exhibits. Temporary exhibitions on subjects close to Ali's heart – barrier-busting athletes, international Muslim culture – shine.
https://alicenter.com, 144 N 6th St

SHAKER VILLAGE AT PLEASANT HILL During the group's early 1800s heyday, some 500 Shakers lived a communal lifestyle of craft, pacifism and ecstatic dancing (hence the name 'Shaker') on this

FUN FACT

Although Kentucky is bourbon's home, about a fifth of the state's 120 counties are completely dry, meaning no liquor sales allowed.

© James R. Martin / Shutterstock

★ ★ ★

GETTING THERE & AROUND

The state's largest airport is the Cincinnati/Northern Kentucky Airport in the town of Hebron, just across from Ohio. Louisville has a reasonably sized airport too, while Lexington's airport is smaller and more regional. Amtrak only serves the fringes of the state, though Greyhound buses go most everywhere. Drivers looking to get off the interstate will find numerous scenic byways to explore, from Woodlands Trace to the Country Music Highway. Public transit options are mostly limited.

patch of rolling hillside in Harrodsburg, near Lexington. Unfortunately the strict celibacy rules led to rather rapid extinction of the community. Visit this restored village to discover the Shakers' unusual history. *https://shakervillageky.org, 3501 Lexington Rd*

SPEED ART MUSEUM Built in 1927 and made over to the tune of $60 million between 2012 and 2016, Kentucky's most important art museum is a beautiful juxtaposition of classic and contemporary. Architectural highlights are Spencer Finch's (of National September 11 Memorial & Museum fame) Grand Atrium, walled with fretted glass designed to reflect light away from the precious art, and Thai architect Kulapat Yantrasast's striking stacked concrete exterior. The museum is on the University of Louisville campus but unaffiliated with the school. *www.speedmuseum.org, 2035 S 3rd St*

FAMILY OUTINGS

KENTUCKY HORSE PARK Watch sleek Arabians, fuzzy little Shetland ponies and exotic Marwaris trot past during the daily Parade of Breeds at this working horse farm and equine theme park in Lexington. You can also take a trail ride, watch horses being bathed and groomed, and learn about equine history at the Smithsonian-affiliated International Museum of the Horse. In the middle of Bluegrass Country, these once-wild woodlands and meadows have been a center of horse breeding for almost 250 years. The region's natural limestone deposits – you'll see limestone bluffs rise majestically from out of nowhere

© Lottie Davies / Lonely Planet

ITINERARY

Day 1
Spend your first day in Lou-ah-vuhl: spectate at the early morning Thoroughbred warm-ups at Churchill Downs, visit the Muhammad Ali Center or the Louisville Slugger Museum (or both!), walk through Old Louisville past rambling 19th-century mansions, try a Hot Brown on a barstool at the glittering Brown Hotel, and sip bourbon in the evening.

Day 2
Aim for two major distilleries on the Bourbon Trail: Buffalo Trace in Frankfort and Woodford Reserve in Versailles (pronounced 'ver-sales'). Buffalo Trace is the country's oldest continuously operating distillery, while Woodford Reserve still uses old-school copper pots. If you've got time, pop into Frankfort to see the handsome capitol building.

Day 3
Save your last day for Lexington. You could spend a few hours to over a half day at the Kentucky Horse Park, or visit Shaker Village.

– are said to produce especially nutritious grass. No wonder Lexington is called the Horse Capital of the World. *https:// kyhorsepark.com, 4089 Iron Works Pkwy*

LOUISVILLE SLUGGER MUSEUM Take a left at the 120ft baseball bat and you'll be at this wonderful family-friendly museum and factory dedicated to the iconic wooden baseball bats produced in Louisville since 1884. Tour the plant, check out the hall of baseball memorabilia and swing a replica Babe Ruth Slugger in the batting cage. *www.sluggermuseum.com, 800 W. Main St*

NATIONAL CORVETTE MUSEUM The legendary American muscle car has been produced in Bowling Green since 1981. Come see 80 different models set against period backgrounds. Wildest is the display

of eight cars swallowed by a sinkhole that opened up in the middle of the museum in 2014 – some are restored, others totally crushed. Be sure to book ahead to reserve tours of the nearby factory. *www.corvettemuseum.org, 350 Corvette Dr*

WAVERLY HILLS SANATORIUM Towering over Louisville like a mad king's castle, the abandoned Waverly Hills Sanatorium once housed victims of an early-20th-century tuberculosis epidemic. When patients died, workers dumped their bodies down a chute into the basement. No wonder the place is said to be one of America's most haunted buildings. Reserve ahead of time to search for spooks with a nighttime ghost-hunting tour; the genuinely fearless can even spend the night. *www.therealwaverlyhills.com, 4400 Paralee Ln, Mar–Aug, weekends only*

From left: Kentucky Horse Park; musicians playing traditional bluegrass tunes at the Bill Monroe Homeplace, Rosine.

LOUISIANA

★ ★

POPULATION: 4.7 million | **SIZE:** 52,378 sq miles | **STATE CAPITAL:** Baton Rouge
LARGEST CITY: New Orleans | **WEBSITE:** www.louisianatravel.com

LOUISIANA RUNS DEEP AND COMPLEX: A FRENCH COLONY TURNED SPANISH PROTECTORATE turned reluctant American purchase; a southern fringe of swampland, bayou and alligators dissolving into the Gulf of Mexico; and a northern patchwork prairie of heartland farm country. Everywhere, the population is tied together by a firm, unshakable appreciation for the good things in life: food and music. New Orleans, its first city, lives and dies by these qualities, and its restaurants and music halls are second to none. This is at once the most European, the most African and most Caribbean city in the country. Everywhere in the state, people indulge in an intense joie de vivre, a keen pleasure in life. We're not dropping French for fun, by the way; while the language is not a cultural component of North Louisiana, near I-10 and below it is a generation removed from the household – if it has been removed at all.

© Kris Davidson / Lonely Planet

FOOD & DRINK

BEIGNETS Not so much a dessert as a round-the-clock breakfast specialty, beignets are flat squares of dough flash-fried to a golden, puffy glory, dusted liberally with powdered (confectioner's or icing) sugar and served scorching hot. Café du Monde in New Orleans is the gold standard, but options are plentiful.

CRAWFISH The humble crawfish is served a million ways across Louisiana: in pies, as étouffée, over french fries – the list goes on. But there's one preparation not to miss. A Louisiana crawfish boil is something special: a mini-festival of sorts that unites friends and family over good music, beer and, most important of all, tables of fresh-boiled crawfish. While the best boils tend to take place in someone's backyard, you can't go wrong finding crawfish in Breaux Bridge, the self-proclaimed Crawfish Capital of the World, which hosts its annual Crawfish Festival in May.

GUMBO Perhaps no dish in Louisiana has a name-brand recognition like gumbo. Like many other items on the local menu here, gumbo is a one-pot wonder with a million variations. Typically served over rice, the dish includes a roux (a simple base of flour and oil or butter, stirred until a desired color takes hold) and filé powder (dried sassafras), which is used as a thickening agent. Past that, the sky's the limit in terms of gumbo's diversity – anything can go in the pot. In the prairies you'll find meatier gumbos, while seafood dominates on the coast. This synthesis of diverse ingredients is a major reason the dish is often used as a culinary analogy for the state's demographics.

JAMBALAYA This spicy mix of rice, veggies and meat can include just about any combination of fowl, shellfish or meat, but usually includes ham, hence the name (derived from the French jambon or the Spanish jamón). It's the perfect representation of Louisiana's diverse history. Stuff yourself for cheap at Coop's Place in NOLA's French Quarter.

MUFFULETTA In the late 1800s, more Italian immigrants were moving to New Orleans than any other city (yes, that includes New York City). Among them was Salvatore Lupo, a Sicilian who owned Central Grocery. Lupo would see Italian workers come in and order meat, olives, anchovies and cheese for lunch. The large plates were hard to eat on the go, so one fateful day in 1906, Lupo decided to combine them in a sandwich of meat, cheese and an olive/anchovy tapenade, served on a sesame seed–studded bun, which came to be known as the muffuletta. It's still popular today.

PO'BOYS What's in a name? Legend has it the po'boy was first served to striking streetcar workers as a way to show solidarity. Don't be fooled by those who tell you it's just a sandwich: the po'boy elevates the sandwich to something special by dint of its bread (not as hard as a baguette, not as soft as a sub – the consistency is both firm and yielding) and its ingredients, which include options like slow-cooked roast beef with gravy, fried seafood or whatever else you please.

★ ★ ★

LOUISIANA CEMETERIES

The distinctive cemeteries of New Orleans result from the shallow water table, which made it necessary to inter the remains of early Creoles in aboveground tombs, many in a distinctive Greek Revival style. The oldest of a trio of burial grounds, St Louis Cemetery No 1 is a spooky top sight in New Orleans and great for tapping into the history of the Big Easy. Among the tombs you'll spot is 'Voodoo Queen' Marie Laveau's. Rumors said that Laveau would grant wishes if a visitor drew an X on her tomb, spun three times and knocked. Alas, a vandal (maybe a Laveau devotee wishing to provide space for more wishes) covered the tomb in pink latex paint. Since then, cemetery visitation has been limited to relatives of those buried there and those on approved tours, though other unique cemeteries around town are open to all, from Lafayette Cemetery No 1 to Metairie.

© Darrell Miller / 500px; Left: © Sandra O'Claire / Getty Images

★ ★ ★
MARDI GRAS

In February or early March, Mardi Gras (Fat Tuesday) marks the finale of the Carnival season and is the ribald precursor to the fasting of Lent. Expect parades, floats, insane costumes and absolute madcap revelry. The first New Orleans float appeared in 1857 when a group of wealthy and secretive Anglos, calling themselves the Mistick Krewe of Comus, paraded through town on floats lit by flambeaux (torches). In the ensuing years, new parade clubs formed, and they too dubbed themselves 'krewes' – an intentional misspelling of 'crews.' Today more than 50 parades wind through New Orleans during Carnival season. Floats celebrate a theme chosen by the krewe and spotlight history, mythology or modern cultural touchstones.

SAZERAC Cocktail culture began in NoLa, and the Sazerac in particular comes up in city lore. Considered to be America's first cocktail, it dates all the way back to 1838, when apothecary Antoine Peychaud mixed brandy, his signature bitters and sugar in an absinthe-coated glass for the first time. Today an updated Sazerac is available in just about any New Orleans bar, but the most classic place to get one is the elegant, wood-paneled Sazerac Bar in the Roosevelt Hotel. Yes, you'll pay more here, but the art deco atmosphere is worth it.

NATURAL ESCAPES

BARATARIA PRESERVE This section of the Jean Lafitte National Historical Park and Preserve near Marrero provides the easiest access to the dense atmospheric swamplands that ring New Orleans. The 8 miles of boardwalk trails are a stunning way to tread lightly through the fecund, thriving swamp, home to alligators, tree frogs and hundreds of species of birds. *www.nps.gov/jela, 6588 Barataria Blvd*

LAKE MARTIN Near Breaux Bridge, this lake – a mossy green dollop surrounded by thin trees and cypress trunks – serves as a wonderful, easily accessible introduction to bayou landscapes. A few walking paths take visitors over the mirror-reflection sheen of the swamp, while overhead thousands of great and cattle egrets and blue herons perch in haughty indifference. *www.louisianatravel.com/paddle/trail/lake-martin, Lake Martin Rd*

ARTS, HISTORY & CULTURE

CONGO SQUARE At this spot in modern Louis Armstrong Park in New Orleans, slaves practiced the cultural traditions of the continent they were exiled from for one day a week. This laid the groundwork of a distinctly New Orleanian link to Africa, and much of the city's iconic food and music was built on its foundation. The park was host to the first-ever jazz fest and continues to pay tribute to NoLa's legacy of black jazz born from this unique cultural heritage. *701 N. Rampart St*

From left: Krewe of Zulu on Mardi Gras; a Louisiana crawfish boil; brass band on Frenchman Street in New Orleans. Previous page: Floating cabin in Atchafalaya Basin near Henderson.

© The Washington Post / Getty Images

FRENCHMEN STREET In New Orleans' Faubourg Marigny, this is where you'll find bars and clubs arrayed side by side for several city blocks in one of the best concentrations of live-music venues in the country. Out-of-towners flood the street every weekend, so it gets crowded, but between the music and local outdoor arts markets, Frenchmen is absolutely a ton of fun.

LAURA PLANTATION This popular plantation tour in Vacherie, near New Orleans, teases out the distinctions between Creoles, Anglos, and free and enslaved African Americans via meticulous research. Laura is fascinating because it was a Creole mansion, founded and maintained by a continental European–descended elite. The cultural and architectural distinctions between this and other plantations are obvious and striking. *www.lauraplantation.com, 2247 Hwy 18*

RW NORTON ART GALLERY Set amid 40 acres of lovingly manicured gardens, the

Norton is a wonderful museum, especially for a midsize city like Shreveport. It's airy, spacious and full of fascinating works spanning some four millennia of history, including an impressive collection of work by the American painters Frederic Remington and Charles M Russell. *www.rwnaf.org, 4747 Creswell Ave*

ST JOSEPH'S DAY In New Orleans, March 19 and its nearest Sunday (aka Super Sunday) bring 'tribes' of Mardi Gras Indians – African Americans dressed in highly stylized Native American regalia – out into the streets in all their feathered, drumming glory. It's a hypnotic showcase of pageant and spectacle. The parade usually begins around noon at AL Davis Park in Central City.

WHITNEY PLANTATION The Whitney in Wallace, west of New Orleans, is the first plantation in the state to focus its tours on slavery, and in doing so they've flipped the script on plantation tours. Whereas before the story told was primarily that of the 'big house,' here the emphasis is given to the

FUN FACT

Thanks to its French heritage, Louisiana is the only state in the country to adhere to a civil law system, as opposed to the common law used in the other 49 states.

★

© Kristi Blokhin / Shutterstock; Right: © Kris Davidson / Lonely Planet

GETTING THERE & AROUND

Three main interstates cut across Louisiana: I-10 runs from Florida to Texas; I-49 runs from Lafayette up to Shreveport; and I-20 runs east–west, from Mississippi to Texas. The major point of air access is New Orleans, though there are airports in Baton Rouge, Lafayette and Shreveport. Amtrak runs to New Orleans and Lafayette.

hundreds who died to keep the residents of the big house comfortable. There's a museum on-site that you can self-tour, but admission to the plantation is by 1½-hour guided tour only; it's worth doing. *www.whitneyplantation.com, 5099 Hwy 18*

FAMILY OUTINGS

ABITA SPRINGS MYSTERY HOUSE

With its stuffed alligator-dog-monster, psychedelic art, paint-by-numbers paintings, River Road dioramas and comb collection, as far as roadside attractions go, the Mystery House in Abita Springs is Queen of the Weirdos. Totally bizarre and yet somehow perfectly 'offbeat,' this museum is home to Buford the Bassigator, the Aliens vs Airstream 'crash site,' the

House of Shards and lots of remarkably random exhibits and displays that are equal parts peculiar and compelling. *www. abitamysteryhouse.com, 22275 Hwy 36*

AUDUBON LOUISIANA NATURE PARK

At this nature center in New Orleans, kids (and their parents) can learn about the wetlands and forests of South Louisiana. A 4000-sq-ft interpretive center has displays on swamp flora and fauna, while several trails (ranging from 0.3- to 1.3-mile loops), both boardwalk and dirt, meander through lush Louisiana forest and wetland ecosystems. *https://audubonnatureinstitute. org/nature-center, 11000 Lake Forest Blvd*

CITY PARK Live oaks, Spanish moss and lazy bayous frame this masterpiece of

ITINERARY

Day 1
Wake up in New Orleans to a beignet breakfast, then take a stroll around the streets of the French Quarter as they wake up (or shake off last night). Wander through Jackson Square and stroll along the Mississippi. In the evening catch some music on Frenchmen Street and the surrounding Faubourg Marigny.

Day 2
Take a streetcar ride through New Orleans' lush, tree-lined Garden District, then wander around the stately mansions of Uptown. A po'boy is essential.

Day 3
Head west from New Orleans and make sure to engage with this state's long history of slavery at the Whitney Planta-tion. As you head west into Acadiana in Cajun Country, you'll cross over the Atchafalaya Basin, a primeval swamp that resembles something out of Jurassic Park.

Days 4 & 5
Spend your next few days dining on crawfish in Breaux Bridge, exploring the bayou landscape in Lake Martin, and getting some barn dancing on in small Cajun towns.

From left: Live oak in Audubon Park; St Charles Streetcar in New Orleans.

urban planning. Three miles long and 1 mile wide, dotted with gardens, waterways and bridges and home to the captivating New Orleans Museum of Art, City Park is bigger than Central Park in NYC; it's New Orleans' prettiest green space. Inside the park are the fantastical statuary of small theme park Storyland. *https://neworleanscitypark.com, Esplanade Ave and City Park Ave,*

SECOND LINES These are New Orleans' neighborhood parades, especially those put on by the city's African American Social Aid and Pleasure (S&P) Clubs through the Tremé-Lafitte neighborhood. S&P members deck themselves out in flash suits, hats and shoes, and carry decorated umbrellas and fans. This snazzy crowd, accompanied by a band pumping music,

step in a kind of syncopated marching dance. Marching behind it is the Second Line: the crowds that join in, stopping for drinks and food along the way. The parades are not the easiest thing to find, but check out 90.7FM WWOZ's Takin' It to the Streets section for listings. *www.wwoz.org*

ST CHARLES STREETCAR Riders love the charms of the St Charles Streetcar, which plies the world's oldest continuously operating street railway system, and it's understandable why. It travels through the New Orleans CBD and Garden District and into Uptown/Riverbend; great for moving around the city, it has its own merit as a draw. The transit authority offers an all-day ticket option that gives you unlimited rides for a full 24 hours. *www.norta.com*

MAINE

★ ★

POPULATION: 1.3 million | **SIZE:** 35,385 sq miles | **STATE CAPITAL:** Augusta
LARGEST CITY: Portland | **WEBSITE:** https://visitmaine.com

THE EASTERN SEABOARD OF THE US, PARTICULARLY NEW ENGLAND, IS OFTEN THOUGHT OF AS A manicured, developed place, more well-tended garden than untamed, rugged wilderness. This cliché is blown away in Maine by a salty wind lashing off the Atlantic Ocean over granite sea cliffs that look as raw as the oysters plucked from a cold-water estuary. Maine is heart-meltingly beautiful, and for all of its reputation as a summer resort area, it is still a land of deep, dark forests and pebble beaches whipped by ocean winds. You'll also find small towns aplenty, where older generations of lumber workers and fisherfolk increasingly share space with young families who are seeking fresh air and open space. Places like Bangor and Portland are filled with more restaurants, bars and culture than you'd expect given their compact size, but even in these cities, there's a distinctive small-town vibe.

© mandritoiu / Shutterstock

FOOD & DRINK

BLUEBERRY PIE Maine does lip-smacking blueberry pies for a reason. Out of every 100 US lowbush berries, 99 come from Maine, and a blueberry pie makes a fine way to use the 89 million pounds of juicy morsels the state grows each year (the classic children's picture book *Blueberries for Sal* was set in Maine for a reason). A slab of wild blueberry pie likely will follow your dinner at the local lobster shack, so forgo that last claw to save room.

LOBSTER These clawed crustaceans are the symbol of Maine, whose rocky coastal towns are still very much dependent on the fishing industry. Eat them the way they're meant to be eaten – freshly boiled and served with a dip of hot clarified butter. Harraseeket Lunch & Lobster in South Freeport has been serving them straight from the sea since 1970, but it's impossible to choose just one venue for relishing lobster, whether in the shell or on a lobster roll. Just don't forget your bib!

PORTLAND FOOD SCENE In recent years the vibrant city of Portland has become one of the East Coast's must-visit foodie cities, with a farm-to-fork philosophy that's the envy of New England. Above everything, Portland is a seafood Valhalla. But the city is much more than that. It was ahead of the craft-beer bell curve in New England: the state's pioneer, DL Geary, began brewing in 1983 as the first post-Prohibition brewery east of the Mississippi, and opened its first brewpub in 1986. And the city's food heroes are permanently mindful of shrinking the distance between product and plate.

NATURAL ESCAPES

ACADIA NATIONAL PARK The only national park in New England, Mt Desert Island's Acadia offers unrivaled coastal beauty and activities for both leisurely hikers and adrenaline junkies. The summit of Cadillac Mountain is touted as the first spot in the US to see the sunrise. On clear days the glassy waters of 176-acre Jordan Pond reflect the image of Penobscot Mountain like a mirror. Adorable Bar Harbor is the perfect base. *www.nps.gov/acad*

BAXTER STATE PARK Set in the remote forests of northern Maine, Baxter centers on Mt Katahdin (5267ft), Maine's tallest mountain and the northern terminus of the 2190-mile Appalachian Trail. This vast 209,000-acre park is maintained in a wilderness state: no paved roads, no electricity and no running water (bring your own or plan on purifying stream water). There's a good chance you'll see moose, deer and black bears. *https://baxterstatepark.org*

CAMDEN HILLS STATE PARK With more than 30 miles of trails, this densely forested park in Camden is a choice place to take in the Midcoast's magic. A favorite hike is the 45-minute (0.5 mile) climb up 780ft Mt Battie, which offers exquisite views over island-dotted Penobscot Bay. Short on time or energy? You can also drive to the summit via the Mt Battie Auto Road. *www.maine.gov/camdenhills, 280 Belfast Rd/US-1*

★ ★ ★

LIGHTHOUSES

Maine has almost 60 active lighthouses along its coast; visitors are sure to have favorites. Portland is graced by a handful of handsome lights, including the 1875 Portland Breakwater Light with its Corinthian columns. Dubbed the Bug Light because of its tiny size, it sits in a small park in South Portland with a panoramic view of downtown across the harbor. Rockland Breakwater Lighthouse is a sweet light sitting atop a brick house, with a sweeping view of town from its vantage point almost a mile into the harbor. Nubble Light, a white lighthouse and Victorian lighthouse-keeper's cottage just off the tip of Cape Neddick, provides one of Maine's best photo ops.

Left: Pemaquid Point Lighthouse Park on the coast of Bristol.

© LindaRaymondPhotography / Getty Images

★ ★ ★

GETTING THERE & AROUND

Many travelers fly into Portland, but domestic travelers often take Amtrak; the Downeaster makes daily trips between Boston and Portland. Except for the Maine Turnpike (I-95 and I-495) and part of I-295, Maine has no fast, limited-access highways. Roads along the coast flood with traffic during the summer tourist season.

FORT WILLIAMS PARK Just 4 miles southeast of Portland on Cape Elizabeth, 90-acre Fort Williams Park is worth visiting simply for its land and sea panoramas and picnic possibilities. Stroll around the ruins of the fort, a late-19th-century artillery base, to check out the WWII bunkers and gun emplacements dotting the rolling lawn. *www.capeelizabeth.com/visitors/ attractions/fort_williams_park/home.html, 1000 Shore Rd*

ARTS, CULTURE & HISTORY

BOWDOIN COLLEGE MUSEUM OF ART Set in a 19th-century building with a dramatic glass entrance pavilion, this campus art museum in Brunswick is small but impressive. The 20,000-piece collection is particularly strong in the works of 19th- and 20th-century European and American painters, including Mary Cassatt, Andrew Wyeth, Winslow Homer and Rockwell Kent. Look out for some surprising antiquities too. *www.bowdoin. edu/art-museum, 9400 College St*

FARNSWORTH ART MUSEUM One of the country's best small regional art museums, the Farnsworth in coastal Rockland houses a collection spanning 200 years of American art. Artists who have lived or worked in Maine are the museum's strength – look for works by the Wyeth family (Andrew, NC and Jamie), Edward Hopper, Louise Nevelson, Rockwell Kent and Robert Indiana. *www.farnsworthmuseum.org, 16 Museum St*

MONHEGAN ISLAND There are no TVs, no cars, no bars and no shopping on Monhegan, and the weather is unpredictable and often foggy. But this tiny chunk of rock is a refuge. With its isolated vistas of dramatic granite cliffs, gnarled maritime forest and lush floral meadows, the island has been attracting artists since the 19th century. To this day, Monhegan residents and visitors who visit on the Port Clyde ferry are drawn to plain living, traditional village life and peaceful contemplation. It's classic Maine, austere and serene. *http://monheganwelcome.com*

© wbritten / Getty Images

ROOSEVELT COTTAGE The highlight of a trip to Campobello Island is a visit to the 34-room 'cottage' where Franklin and Eleanor Roosevelt spent many fine summers. The house has been little altered since 1920 and has original wallpaper, furnishings, artwork and other memorabilia – like the piano where the family would gather over songs in the evening (which happened sometime after the 5pm martini hour, a ritual to which Franklin was rather devoted). *www.nps.gov/roca*

FAMILY OUTINGS

KENNEBUNKS The towns of Kennebunk and Kennebunkport comprise the Kennebunks. Kennebunk is a modest town largely centered on US-1, with few tourist attractions beyond its lovely beaches. Just across the river, proudly Waspy Kennebunkport crawls with visitors. The epicenter of activity is Dock Square, lined with cafes, art galleries and upscale boutiques selling preppy goods (whale-print shorts, anyone?). Drive down Ocean

Avenue to gawk at the grand mansions and hotels overlooking the surf, including the massive compound that belonged to the late George HW Bush.
www.visitthekennebunks.com

LL BEAN FLAGSHIP STORE A 10ft-tall Bean Boot sits outside the flagship LL Bean store. The wildly popular LL Bean (famously open 24/7 year-round) is still the core of Freeport and one of the most popular tourist attractions in Maine. It's part store and part outdoor-themed amusement park, with an archery range, an indoor trout pond and coffee shops.
www.llbean.com, 95 Main St

MARGINAL WAY Tracing the 'margin' of the sea, Ogunquit's famed mile-long footpath winds above the crashing gray waves, taking in grand sea vistas, rocky coves and some impressive real estate too. The neatly paved path, fine for children and slow walkers, is dotted with benches. It starts south of Beach Street at Shore Road and ends near Perkins Cove.

ITINERARY

Day 1
Spend your first day in Portland, popping into the city's museums, dining on fresh seafood at any number of great restaurants and taking in Portland's 2.1 mile Eastern Promenade.

Day 2
Take a ferry from Portland to cycle around Peaks Island, getting a good taste of the sea air.

Day 3
Drive north, making sure to have lunch in Brunswick, where you can check out excellent museums on the campus of Bowdoin College. Finish the day in Boothbay Harbor. Make sure to take some hikes in the woods and go out on an old wooden sailing boat (and have a lobster roll too).

Day 4
Stop into the charming small towns that dot the Midcoast, including Camden, Rockland and Rockport, all with a wealth of good restaurants and wonderful waterfronts.

Days 5 & 6
End your trip at Acadia National Park, a gorgeous sweep of towering, ocher-hued sea cliffs and thick copses of dark woods; the bustling yet quaint town of Bar Harbor makes a good base.

From left: Lobster roll; Monhegan Island.

MARYLAND

★ ★ ★ ★ ★ ★ ★ ★ ★ ★ ★ ★ ★ ★ ★ ★ ★ ★ ★ ★

POPULATION: 6 million | **SIZE:** 12,407 sq miles | **STATE CAPITAL:** Annapolis
LARGEST CITY: Baltimore | **WEBSITE:** www.visitmaryland.org

THE NICKNAME AMERICA IN MINIATURE PERFECTLY CAPTURES MARYLAND: THIS SMALL STATE possesses everything from the Appalachian Mountains to white-sand beaches. A blend of northern street smarts and southern down-home appeal gives this border state an appealing identity crisis. Its main city, Baltimore, is a port town with some great cultural cred; rolling fields are showcased on the Horses and Hounds Scenic Byway; the Eastern Shore jumbles art-and-antiques-minded city escapees and working fisherfolk; and Frederick offers history with fine dining and access to nearby vineyards, frequented by DC office workers. Yet it all somehow works. Scrumptious blue crabs bind everything together, but the real glue of the state is its most prominent geographic feature: the Chesapeake Bay, the largest estuary in the country, an invaluable source of wildlife and sheer natural beauty.

© Sean Pavone / Alamy Stock Photo

FOOD & DRINK

BLUE CRAB The Chesapeake Bay is known country-wide for its sweet-fleshed blue crabs, and savory crab cakes and crab feasts of mounded steamed crab are the locals' way to partake of the bounty. Faidley's Seafood stall in Baltimore's Lexington Market makes them right, with lump crabmeat and homemade tartar sauce on the side. Prefer steamed crabs? Cantler's Riverside Inn in Annapolis is one of the best crab shacks in the state, where crab has been elevated to an art form: eating here is a hands-on, messy endeavor, normally accompanied by corn on the cob and ice-cold beer. Cantler's can be approached by road or boat (a waterfront location is a crab-house industry standard).

NATURAL ESCAPES

ASSATEAGUE ISLAND NATIONAL SEASHORE A low-key barrier island just 8 miles south of Ocean City at the end of Route 611, Assateague is a place to relax. In the Maryland section of the national seashore, you can cycle along a 4-mile road, hike nature trails, paddle a kayak, check out the exhibits at the visitors center in Berlin and spot the island's famed herd of wild horses. *www.nps.gov/asis, 7206 National Seashore Ln*

BLACKWATER NATIONAL WILDLIFE REFUGE This enormous expanse of marsh and pine forest near Cambridge contains a third of Maryland's wetland habitat, a key Atlantic Flyway migratory sanctuary. Thousands upon thousands of birds call the refuge home or stop here on their migratory routes. Driving or cycling the paved 4.5-mile wildlife drive is perhaps the seminal wildlife experience on the entire Eastern Shore. *www.fws.gov/refuge/blackwater, 2145 Key Wallace Dr*

CALVERT CLIFFS Skinny Calvert County scratches at the Chesapeake Bay and the Patuxent River in a landscape of low-lying forests, estuarine marshes and placid waters outlined by the 10- to 20-million-year-old Calvert Cliffs. These burnt-umber pillars stretch along the coast for some 24 miles and form the seminal landscape feature of Calvert Cliffs State Park in Lusby, where they front the water and a pebbly, honey-color-sand beach scattered with driftwood and drying beds of kelp. *http://dnr.maryland.gov/publiclands, 9500 HG Trueman Rd*

PATAPSCO VALLEY STATE PARK The Patapsco River Valley is the defining geographic feature of the region, running through central Maryland to the Chesapeake Bay. Gorgeous Patapsco Valley State Park – one of the oldest in the state – runs for 32 miles near Ellicott City and encompasses a whopping 170 miles of trails, especially prized by mountain bikers. *http://dnr.maryland.gov/publiclands, 8020 Baltimore National Pike*

SWALLOW FALLS STATE PARK One of the most rugged, spectacular parks in the state is set near Deep Creek Lake in the far western part of the state. Hickory and hemlock trees hug the Youghiogheny River, which cuts a white line through wet slate gorges. A 1.25-mile hiking trail loops past

Mix it up in Mount Vernon
The Gilded Age lives on in this exclusive corner of town, about a mile up North Charles from the Inner Harbor. It all started with a Revolutionary War hero, John Eager Howard, whose family donated land for the tall, stately Washington Monument's Doric marble column.

Fawn over Fell's Point
This historic neighborhood was founded in 1730 as a shipping hub; one-of-a-kind boutiques, bars, restaurants and nightclubs occupy the neighborhood's colonial-era homes, set along cobbled streets.

Happening Hampden
The heart of funky Hampden is 36th St, a boulevard that's simply called 'The Avenue.' Some cinema buffs may be familiar with the area, which featured in many John Waters films (the iconic film director is a Baltimore native; hence *Hairspray*).

© Jon Bilous / Shutterstock.Left: © Andrea Izzotti / Shutterstock

★ ★ ★

FREDERICK

Central Frederick is, well, perfect. Its historic, walkable center of redbrick row houses is filled with an appealing array of restaurants and shops. The active arts community is anchored by the excellent Weinberg Center for the Arts. Meandering Carroll Creek runs through it all, flanked by a lovely park with art and gardens. Unlike other communities in the region with historic districts, this is a midsize city, an important commuter base for thousands of federal government employees and a biotechnology hub in its own right. For travelers, Frederick makes a great central base for exploring Brunswick, Mt Airy and the region's Civil War battlefields.

several waterfalls, including the 53ft-high Muddy Creek Falls, the highest in the state. *https://dnr.maryland.gov/publiclands/ Pages/western/swallowfalls.aspx, 2470 Maple Glade Rd, Oakland*

ARTS, CULTURE & HISTORY

AMERICAN VISIONARY ART MUSEUM

Housing a jaw-dropping collection of self-taught (or 'outsider') art, AVAM in Baltimore is a celebration of unbridled creativity utterly free of arts-scene pretension. Across two buildings and two sculpture parks, you'll find broken-mirror collages, homemade robots and flying apparatuses, elaborate sculptural works made of needlepoint, and gigantic model ships painstakingly created from matchsticks. *www.avam.org, 800 Key Hwy*

ANTIETAM NATIONAL BATTLEFIELD

The site of the bloodiest day in American history is now, ironically, supremely peaceful, quiet and haunting. This Civil War battle in Sharpsburg in 1862 left more than 23,000 dead, wounded or missing – more casualties than America had suffered in all its previous wars combined. Check out the exhibits in the visitors center and then take a reflective walk or drive on the grounds. *www.nps.gov/anti, 5831 Dunker Church Rd*

CHESAPEAKE & OHIO CANAL NATIONAL HISTORICAL PARK A

marvel of engineering, the C&O Canal was designed to stretch alongside the Potomac River from the Chesapeake Bay to the Ohio River. Construction on the canal went from 1828 to 1850, when it was stopped in Cumberland by the Appalachian Mountains. The C&O's protected 184.5-mile corridor includes a 12ft-wide towpath, now a hiking and bicycling trail, along the entire course of the canal from Cumberland to Georgetown in Washington, DC. The Cumberland Visitor Center has displays on the importance of river trade in US history. *www.nps.gov/choh*

FORT MCHENRY On September 13 and
14, 1814, this star-shaped fort successfully

From left: Frederick historic homes; Antietam Battlefield; wild ponies at Assateague Island. Previous page: The United States Naval Academy Chapel dome in Annapolis on the Chesapeake.

© JackVandenHeuvel / Getty Images

repelled a British navy attack during the Battle of Baltimore in the War of 1812. After a long night of bombs bursting in the air, shipbound prisoner Francis Scott Key saw, 'by the dawn's early light,' the tattered American flag still waving. Inspired, he penned 'The Star-Spangled Banner,' which was set to the tune of a popular drinking song. *www.nps.gov/fomc, 2400 E. Fort Ave*

HARRIET TUBMAN UNDERGROUND RAILROAD NATIONAL HISTORICAL PARK Maryland native Harriet Tubman, 'the Moses of her people,' led enslaved African Americans to freedom on the Underground Railroad, a pipeline for slaves escaping north. This historical center in Church Creek on the Eastern Shore takes a deep dive into her story, and links to the Harriet Tubman Underground Railroad Byway. *www.nps.gov/hatu, 4068 Golden Hill Rd*

HISTORIC SHIPS Ship lovers can tour four historic ships in downtown Baltimore: a Coast Guard cutter that saw action in

Pearl Harbor, a 1930 lightship, a submarine active in WWII and the USS *Constellation* – one of the last sail-powered warships built (in 1797) by the US Navy. You can opt for a two- or four-vessel admission ticket. If you only see two, include the four-deck USS *Constellation*, which spotlights the stories of past crew members. *www.historicships.org, 301 E. Pratt St*

US NAVAL ACADEMY The undergraduate college of the US Navy in Annapolis is one of the most selective universities in America. Come for the formation weekdays at 12:05pm sharp, when 4000 students conduct a 20-minute display of raw, enchanting precision. Naval history buffs can get nautically nostalgic in the well-done Naval Academy Museum. *www.usnabsd. com/for-visitors, 52 King George St*

WALTERS ART MUSEUM In Baltimore the eclectic collections of the Walters (free admission) span more than 55 centuries, from ancient to contemporary, with top-notch displays of Asian treasures, rare

FUN FACT

Baltimore's NFL franchise is the namesake of local author Edgar Allan Poe's poem 'The Raven.'

★

©Panoramic Images / Getty Images: Left: ©Philip Rink Jr. / Alamy Stock Photo

★ ★ ★

GETTING THERE & AROUND

The largest airport in the state is Baltimore/Washington International Thurgood Marshall Airport, but any airport in and around Washington, DC, can be a potential good point of entry. Amtrak stops at Pennsylvania Station in Baltimore on various routes and in downtown Cumberland on the daily Capitol Limited run. For points in Western Maryland and along the Eastern Shore, a car is necessary.

and ornate manuscripts and books, and a comprehensive French paintings collection. The magnificent Chamber of Wonders recreates the library of an imagined 17th-century scholar, one with a taste for the exotic. *www.thewalters.org, 600 N Charles St*

WARD MUSEUM OF WILDFOWL ART

This museum in Salisbury is built around a little-known but fascinating art form, highly emblematic of Maryland's quieter Eastern Shore. It celebrates brothers Stephen and LT Ward, who spent a lifetime carving waterfowl decoys that are wonderful in their realism and attention to detail. The Ward Museum exhibits the works of the Wards, as well as decoy art from around the world. *www.wardmuseum.org, 909 S. Schumaker Dr*

FAMILY OUTINGS

GREAT FALLS TAVERN VISITOR CENTER
Opened as a tavern in 1831, this visitors center in Potomac sits beside the Potomac River and the C&O Canal towpath. From here you can walk to the Great Falls Overlook, a little over a half mile away, for a stunning view of the falls. *www.nps.gov/choh, 11710 MacArthur Blvd*

HISTORIC ST MARY'S CITY
In the 1600s St Mary's City was a busy port and served as the state's first Colonial capital. Today the spot is a living-history museum romantically positioned among the surrounding forests, fields and farmlands along the St Mary's River. The reconstructed buildings and costumed

ITINERARY

Days 1 & 2
Start in Baltimore, where you can easily spend two days wandering around the Inner Harbor and the city's handsome row houses, bouncing between the National Aquarium and fantastic museums like the American Visionary Art Museum, BMA and Walters Art Museum. If you're looking for a night out, you can find a raucous scene in Fell's Point, or indulge in watering holes that range from hipster to posh on Charles Street near Penn Station.

Day 3
Head to Annapolis for abundant seafood, where sailboats creak in the harbor and naval cadets can be seen jogging along the historic streets.

Day 4
Drive east over the Chesapeake Bay Bridge to the Eastern Shore, which for centuries was almost entirely isolated from the burgeoning population centers of the East Coast. Here small towns mix antiques and artiness with working watermen, independent harvesters of the state's many commercial fisheries.

From left: The Ocean City Boardwalk; Oriole Park at Camden Yards.

docents really make the past feel relevant. Given the lack of crowds here, HSMC feels more colonial than similar places like Colonial Williamsburg. *https://hsmcdigshistory.org, 18751 Hogaboom Ln*

NATIONAL AQUARIUM Standing seven stories high and capped by a glass pyramid, this beloved and impressive institution on Baltimore's Inner Harbor houses almost 20,000 creatures, from amphibians to dolphins and puffer fish. There's a rooftop rainforest, multistory shark tank and a recreation of an Indo-Pacific reef (all at a hefty admission cost). *www.aqua.org, 501 E Pratt St*

OCEAN CITY Two words describe OC from June through August: party central. This is an American seaside resort in its wildest glory, a steaming hybrid of tacky and fun. Yet this Eastern Shore retreat has provided generations of family entertainment too. Grab some funnel cake and a gaudy T-shirt, then relax. The center of action is the 2.5-mile-long boardwalk, stretching from the inlet to 27th Street. *https://oceancitymd.gov/oc*

ORIOLE PARK AT CAMDEN YARDS There may be bigger, brasher ballparks in the US, but few can match Baltimore's Camden Yards for its classic redbrick beauty. Baseball's appeal at least partly lies in its slow pace and nostalgia, and you get a sense of both at this influential grande dame of a ballpark, opened in 1992. *www.orioles.com, 333 W Camden St*

MASSACHUSETTS

★ ★

POPULATION: 6.9 million | **SIZE:** 10,565 sq miles | **STATE CAPITAL:** Boston
WEBSITE: www.massvacation.com

PLYMOUTH WASN'T THE FIRST EUROPEAN SETTLEMENT IN AMERICA – THAT'S FLORIDA'S ST Augustine – but it, and Massachusetts, are indelibly associated with the country's earliest days. It was here that the Pilgrims set up their colonies, here that the first university (Harvard) was founded, here that the American Revolution began. To visit Massachusetts is to engage with that history, from the 17th-century buildings of Boston's Freedom Trail to the witch trial sights of Salem and the tradition-bound fishing towns of the coast. But Massachusetts is way more than history. Boston is a cosmopolitan city of universities, cutting-edge tech companies, a thriving music scene and excellent cuisine. Move westward into the Berkshires and you'll find arty little mountain towns, primo hiking and destination restaurants. And don't forget the Cape Cod coast, its sandy beaches a favorite of New Englanders.

© HDnrg / Shutterstock

FOOD & DRINK

CLAM CHOWDER Creamy New England clam chowder, made hearty with potatoes, crushed oyster crackers and chewy chunks of local clam, kept the colonists warm through the bitter Massachusetts winters. It hasn't gone out of favor since then.

NORTH END Boston's historic Little Italy district may have only a fraction of the Italians it did a century ago, but it still has one of the highest concentrations of excellent Italian restaurants in the country. Come for cannoli and crackly, cream-filled sfogliatelle at old-school bakeries, slurp up handmade tagliatelle, gorge on thin-crust pizza and dig the nostalgic, brick-and-cobblestone atmosphere. *www.northendboston.com*

OYSTERS With plump, creamy oysters from Wellfleet and firm, briny-sweet ones from Barnstable (to name just two), Massachusetts has first-class aquaculture. No wonder that Boston's oldest restaurant is Union Oyster House, just off the Freedom Trail and serving up shellfish since 1826. Start with a dozen oysters at any oyster house in the state and you won't be sorry.

QUINCY MARKET This 19th-century granite and redbrick food hall is a classic and fun lunch stop for anyone wandering the Boston waterfront. Look for clam chowder bread bowls, gyros and meatball-topped pizza slices. If it's warm enough, take your food outside to watch jugglers and other touts work the cobblestones. *www.quincy-market.com, 4 S. Market St*

NATURAL ESCAPES

BASH BISH FALLS A short but steep hike through cool deciduous forest and across mossy, boulder-strewn creeks takes you to this fetching double waterfall, the highest in the state, near Mt Washington. It's a primo spot for picnicking, photography or landscape painting, but don't swim in the notoriously dangerous pool. There's excellent hiking amid the northern hardwoods of surrounding Mt Washington State Forest. *www.mass.gov, Falls Rd*

CAPE COD NATIONAL SEASHORE The iconic seashore extends some 40 miles around the curve of the Outer Cape and encompasses the Atlantic shoreline from Orleans all the way to Provincetown. Under the auspices of the National Park Service, the area is a treasure trove of unspoiled beaches, dunes, salt marshes, nature trails and forests. Thanks to the backing of President John F Kennedy, this landscape was set aside for preservation in the 1960s, just before a building boom hit the rest of Cape Cod, where the Kennedy family had a home. Access to the park sights is easy: everything of interest is on or just off US-6. The year-round Salt Pond Visitor Center in Eastham is the place to start. *www.nps.gov/caco*

MT AUBURN CEMETERY Bostonians used to picnic at this 1831 'garden cemetery' in Cambridge, and while food is no longer allowed, you're still encouraged to explore the tranquil, leafy grounds. Walk the miles of loop trails; bird-watch in the woodlands, glades and ponds; photograph the stately monuments; and

★ ★ ★

WHAT TO EAT IN THE BAY STATE

With the state's long maritime history, it's no wonder so much Massachusetts food is seafood crazy. Before New England clam chowder there was cod, once a staple of the local fisheries but now almost vanished from state waters; striped bass is a tasty alternative. For sides, Boston is so famous for its baked beans it got the nickname Beantown. Dessert could be Boston cream pie (a yellow cake stuffed with custard and topped with chocolate) or anything with cranberries, which grow rampant in the state's coastal bogs. Boston is particularly fond of its donuts too. And although you can get a warm chocolate chip cookie anywhere, they were invented at Massachusetts' famed Toll House Inn in 1938 (sadly now burned down).

Left: Old North Church in Boston, launch point for Paul Revere's ride, and the oldest surviving church in the city.

© Steve Dunwell / Getty Images; Left: © Roman Debree / Shutterstock

★ ★ ★

FALL RIVER

Fall River, close to the border with Rhode Island, is one of the most densely Portuguese American cities in the country. Almost half of the population claims Luso American heritage, some of around 320,000 Massachusetts residents to do so. Three distinct waves of immigration, including one caused by volcanic eruptions in the Portuguese Azores during the 1950s, have led to a thriving Portuguese food scene in small Fall River, with restaurants like Sagres and Estoril serving up *caldo verde* (kale soup with Portuguese chorizo) and killer *pastéis de nata* (egg-custard tarts) in all the local bakeries.

climb Washington Tower for panoramic views of Boston and Cambridge. *https:// mountauburn.org, 580 Mt Auburn St*

MT GREYLOCK Climb the state's highest peak (3491ft) for 100-mile panoramic views of the Berkshires and the Taconic Mountains. Ascend through a jagged ravine and an ancient boreal forest, and continue past the Appalachian Trail junction to the summit. It's a perfectly doable day hike for the moderately fit, but it's more fun to stay at Arts and Crafts–style Bascom Lodge, built by the Civilian Conservation Corps (CCC) during the Depression. *www.bascomlodge.net, N. Adams Rd*

PLUM ISLAND With 9 miles of wide, wild beaches, this barrier island near Newburyport is a delicious spot for swimming, sunbathing and generally getting away from it all. Climb the lighthouse and kayak or go birding in the marsh (the island is 75% nature sanctuary), then cross the causeway back to Newburyport for a lobster roll dinner and

comfy night at a B&B. *www.newburyport.com/plum-island-beach*

WALDEN POND Henry David Thoreau came to this Concord lake to 'live deliberately' in a self-built cabin. His resulting 1854 memoir, *Walden; Or, Life in the Woods*, still resonates with those seeking a simpler life. Today Bostonians come here to escape the summer heat, swimming in the pond's cold, deep waters and hiking its perimeter. A cairn marks the cabin site. *www.mass.gov/locations/walden-pond-state-reservation, 915 Walden St*

ARTS, HISTORY & CULTURE

AFRICAN AMERICAN HERITAGE TRAIL OF MARTHA'S VINEYARD The ritzy summer isle of Martha's Vineyard has been drawing well-heeled African Americans to vacation here for more than a century, including luminaries like Dr Martin Luther King Jr and Jackie Robinson. Visit the 27 sites of the African American Heritage

From left: Traditional Portuguese pastry Pastéis de Nata, a Fall River classic; sunset at Walden Pond in Concord; the Old State House in Boston, a stop on the Freedom Trail.

© joe daniel price / Getty Images

Trail to follow their path, from historic cemeteries to the gingerbread-trimmed homes of Oak Bluffs to the Inkwell beach, the swimming hole of choice for summering families then and now. *https://mvafricanamericanheritagetrail.org*

BRATTLE BOOK SHOP Bibliophiles, weep with joy! The Brattle, with its three stories of used and rare books, is the place to find that first edition you've been searching eBay for. A Boston institution since 1825, it's stuffed with a quarter million books, maps, postcards and prints. Spend a happy afternoon browsing the third-floor collectibles or the cheapie outdoor sale lot. *www.brattlebookshop.com, 9 West St*

BRIMFIELD ANTIQUE SHOW The largest outdoor antiques fair in North America is spread over a mile of US-20 near Sturbridge. Collectors, interior designers and prop directors flock here for antique furniture, architectural salvage items and more (headless mannequins! Vintage medical tools! Creepy clown paintings!).

There are three annual shows, in May, July and September, but plenty of venues in nearby Sturbridge are open year-round too. *www.brimfieldshow.com*

FENWAY PARK For Red Sox fanatics, Fenway is a true shrine. Opened in 1912 in Boston, it has seen luminaries from Babe Ruth to Ted Williams to David Ortiz step up to its plate. When the Sox CEO proposed a new stadium in 1999, fans lost their minds; the plan was abandoned. Catch a home game to see history in action. *www.redsox.com, 4 Yawkey Way*

FREEDOM TRAIL Spend a full day getting your historical bearings by walking this 2.5-mile trail through 16 of Boston's most important historical sites, from the Boston Common through several 17th-century burying grounds (pay your respects to Samuel Adams and John Hancock) to Faneuil Hall (aka 'the cradle of liberty'), the Paul Revere House and the monument commemorating the Battle of Bunker Hill. *www.thefreedomtrail.org*

FUN FACT

Lake Chargo-ggagoggm-anchaug-gagoggcha-ubunagun gamaugg, in the town of Webster, is the longest place-name in America.

© Douglas Mason / courtesy of MASS MoCA; Left: © harpazo_hope / Getty Images

★ ★ ★

HALLOWEEN IN SALEM

In a strange, paranoid year between 1692 and 1693, the Puritan settlers of Salem executed 20 'witches,' women and men accused of trafficking with Satan himself. The infamous episode has given modern-day Salem a notorious reputation as a mecca for secular fans and occult believers of spooky stories alike. Come Halloween time, the town goes all out, with ghost tours, horror movie nights, haunted houses and a Grand Parade, capping off with the October 31 crowning of a King and Queen of Halloween.

HARVARD UNIVERSITY In cool Cambridge near Boston, America's oldest university (established 1636) is worth exploring. Start in Harvard Square, with its bohemian-gone-corporate vibe, then head into Harvard Yard to see redbrick buildings that predate the founding of the nation. Rub the foot of the John Harvard statue for good luck (but know that students pee on it at night). Join a free public tour or go solo, and check out the top-notch Harvard Art Museums if you have time. *www.harvard.edu*

ISABELLA STEWART GARDNER MUSEUM For our money, this quirky museum in Boston, the personal collection of a Gilded Age philanthropist, is one of the coolest art experiences around. Set in a Venetian-style palazzo with a greenhouse courtyard, it's got room after room of Old Master paintings, Gothic tapestries and Japanese screens. It's free on your birthday or if your name is Isabella. It was also the site (in 1990) of one of the most daring art heists in recent memory, with a haul that included three Rembrandts, a Vermeer, a Manet, and Degas sketches; the empty painting frames are still on display as the museum continues to search for clues. *www.gardnermuseum.org, 25 Evans Way*

KRIPALU CENTER Walk into Stockbridge's famed Berkshires yoga center a knotted stress ball and float out a picture of New Age serenity. Open since the early 1980s, Kripalu offers customizable multiday retreats of yoga, meditation, labyrinth walks, saunas and massages, with delicious (organic, naturally) meals and classily spartan accommodations. Prepare to disconnect: no phones or TVs here. *https://kripalu.org, 57 Interlaken Rd*

MAPPARIUM It doesn't make many Top 10 Must-Do lists, but you'll be hard-

From left: Salem's graveyard; MASS MoCA in the Berkshires; two fishing trawlers tied up at dockside in Gloucester, Cape Ann.

© genekrebs / Getty Images

pressed to find a more memorable sight in Boston than this three-story walk-in stained-glass globe within the Mary Baker Eddy Library. Walk across a glass bridge to gaze at the world inside out. The globe was built in 1935, so expect some defunct countries (hello Czechoslovakia and South Rhodesia!). *www.marybakereddylibrary.org, 200 Massachusetts Ave*

MASS MOCA North Adams' defunct Sprague Electric Company has been transformed into this monumental modern art museum and performance center, with several dozen buildings spread over 13 acres. You'll find 19 galleries of contemporary art – expect immersive light-and-sound experiences and massive kinetic sculptures – and regular theater, music and avant-garde dance performances. Little ones can go wild with art materials at the Kidspace. *https://massmoca.org, 87 Marshall St*

MUSEUM OF FINE ARTS Since 1876 the Museum of Fine Arts has been Boston's premier venue for art. Nowadays the museum's holdings encompass all eras, from the ancient world to contemporary times, and all areas of the globe, making it truly encyclopedic in scope. Most recently the museum has added gorgeous new wings dedicated to the Art of the Americas and to contemporary art, contributing to Boston's emergence as an art center in the 21st century. *www.mfa.org, 465 Huntington Ave*

NANTUCKET Once a whaling port, Nantucket now attracts politicians, celebrities and CEOs (think Bill Clinton and Warren Buffet) who appreciate the discretion to be found in the small island's cedar-shingled cottages and cobblestone lanes. Catch the ferry over from New Bedford or the Cape to visit the whaling museum and amble streets lined with churches and boutiques, and smell the salt

★ ★ ★

CAPE ANN COAST

Cape Ann is the anti-Cape Cod, still rough-and-tumble, and towns like Rockport, Essex and Manchester-by-the-Sea retain their fishing village charm. Settled in 1623 by English fisherfolk, Gloucester is one of New England's oldest towns. This port has made its living from fishing for almost 400 years, and inspired books and films such as Rudyard Kipling's *Captains Courageous* and Sebastian Junger's *The Perfect Storm*. You can't miss the fishing boats, festooned with nets and tied to the wharves or in the harbor, seagulls hovering above. It's a great place to take a whale-watching tour. Vibrant Rocky Neck Art Colony is across the harbor in East Gloucester.

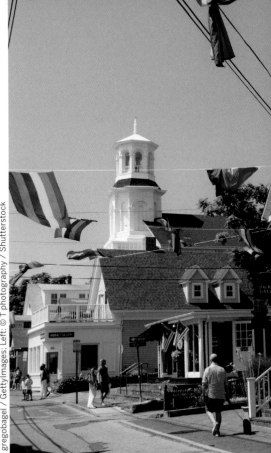

© gregobagel / GettyImages; Left: © T photography / Shutterstock

★ ★ ★

Tanglewood
MUSIC FESTIVAL

Each summer, the Boston Symphony Orchestra has a residency at this rural Berkshires estate in Lenox. The orchestra's holiday is now occasion for a season-long festival, with musicians of all genres – from classical to jazz to pop – playing on the property's lawns and concert halls. It's an event both cultured and casual, with Boston Brahmins showing up in jeans to eat caviar and cheese in the grass before performances.

and summer roses in the air. *www.nantucket-ma.gov*

NORTHAMPTON The very picture of the charming New England college town, Northampton is home to prestigious, all-female Smith College. Visit the college's art museum and Victorian conservatory before heading downtown for some progressive pub grub (tempeh burger, anyone?) and a wander of the boutiques, bookshops and historic churches. Catch some live neo-folk music, then take your pick of postcard-worthy B&Bs. *www.visitnorthampton.net*

PEABODY ESSEX MUSEUM The collection of the nation's oldest continuously operating museum, in historic Salem, was founded on the art and decorative objects brought from the Far East by Salem merchants and traders. Wander from the 1825 East India Marine

Hall to the contemporary Moshe Safdie–built addition, admiring striking highlights like the Yin Yu Tang House, a reconstructed Qing Dynasty home. *www.pem.org, Essex St and New Liberty St*

PLIMOTH PLANTATION In Plymouth, tour a recreation of the hardscrabble settlement of the Pilgrims who came on the *Mayflower* and landed here in 1620. Kids will dig costumed interpreters spinning and making candles in the English Village, while craft aficionados can watch artisans weave and throw pottery. Get the corrective Native American perspective at the Wampanoag Homesite (hint: it wasn't all pumpkin pie and friendship). *www.plimoth.org, off MA-3A*

PROVINCETOWN Head to the tip of Cape Cod to this gay beach mecca, attracting LGBTQ (and plenty of other) travelers for

From left: World-famous cellist Yo-Yo Ma at Ozawa Hall, Tanglewood Music Festival; rainbow flags fly in Provincetown; historical reenactors at Old Sturbridge Village.

© Carol Ann Mossa / Getty Images

generations with chilled-out (and some clothing-optional) beaches, excellent art galleries, a renowned theater scene and bars offering tea dances and drag shows. August means Carnival, an all-out celebration of LGBTQ life with a parade, costume ball, dance parties and art shows. *https://provincetowntourismoffice.org*

FAMILY OUTINGS

THE AMAZING WORLD OF DR SEUSS
The country's first (and only) museum dedicated to beloved children's author and Springfield native Theodore Geisel (aka Dr Seuss) opened in Springfield in 2017. Kids can clamber over statues of Horton and the Cat in the Hat or 'draw' on the walls, while adults can peruse exhibits about Geisel's life, including his childhood bedroom and collection of 117 bow ties.
www.seussinspringfield.org, 21 Edwards St

MINUTE MAN NATIONAL HISTORICAL PARK
Come here to trace the route that British troops followed to Concord in 1775 in the kickoff to the American Revolution. The visitors center at the eastern end of the park shows an informative multimedia presentation depicting Paul Revere's ride and the ensuing battles. Within the park, which spans the small colonial towns of Lexington, Lincoln and Concord, Battle Road is a 5-mile wooded trail that connects the historic sites related to the battles – from Meriam's Corner, where gunfire erupted while British soldiers were retreating, to the Paul Revere capture site.
www.nps.gov/mima, 3113 Marrett Rd

NEW BEDFORD WHALING MUSEUM
The centerpiece of New Bedford's historic district, this excellent, hands-on museum remembers the town's heyday as a whaling port. The museum occupies

⋆ ⋆ ⋆

THE BIG E

The Eastern States Exposition is a massive state fair for all six New England states, running for 17 days each fall in West Springfield. This is classic Americana at its finest: livestock shows, petting zoos, creaky rides, quilting demos, darts games with cheapo stuffed animal prizes. And food, of course: snacks representing each state include Maine's whoopie pies (a doughnut-sized cake-cookie hybrid), Rhode Island's clam cakes and New Hampshire's maple cotton candy.

© Betty Wiley / Getty Images; Right: © Megapress / Alamy Stock Photo

★ ★ ★

GETTING
THERE &
AROUND

Boston's Logan International Airport is a major national and international hub. Boston is well-connected with other major cities, especially in the Northeast, by Amtrak, and buses run regularly to the cities and towns of central and western Mass. If you're headed to Martha's Vineyard or Nantucket, the ferry's the way to go (ferries also serve Provincetown from Boston). Whether you land at Logan or alight from Amtrak, plan on going car-less in Boston: it's a notorious pain-in-the-you-know-what for drivers, and public transportation is excellent.

seven buildings between William and Union Streets. A 66ft skeleton of a blue whale and a smaller skeleton of a sperm whale welcome you at the entrance. To learn what whaling was all about, you need only tramp the decks of the Lagoda, a fully rigged, half-size replica of an actual whaling bark. *www.whalingmuseum.org, 18 Johnny Cake Hill*

OLD STURBRIDGE VILLAGE Historic buildings have been moved to this site in Sturbridge to recreate a New England town from the 1830s, with 40 restored structures filled with antiques. Rather than labeled exhibits, this museum has costumed interpreters who answer visitor questions. The country store displays products brought by sailing ships, while crafters and artisans use authentic tools and materials; the livestock has even been back-bred to match the animals that lived on New England farms in the 19th century. *www.osv.org, 1 Old Sturbridge Village Rd*

PUBLIC GARDEN A ride in the Swan Boats in this Victorian-era park's pond has been making childhood memories in Boston since 1877. The bronze statues of the mallard family from the much-loved children's book *Make Way for Ducklings* is another must-stop for kiddos. Adults will enjoy meandering along pathways lined with beech trees, elms and stately oaks. *www.swanboats.com, 4 Charles St, boat rides mid-April–mid-September*

WELLFLEET DRIVE-IN Catch the double feature on a balmy Cape Cod summer evening in Wellfleet at this delightful 1957 drive-in, a vanishing breed. Tune your radio to FM 89.3 or use the old-school mono speakers to get sound. If the movie's getting slow, walk out to the Dairy Bar for a soft-serve cone or play a round of mini-golf on the adjacent court. It's summery perfection. *www.wellfleetcinemas.com/drive-in-theatre, off US-6*

ITINERARY

Day 1
Take your first day to explore Boston's history: walk the Freedom Trail from Boston Common to the Bunker Hill Monument, stopping for a meander through the Public Garden and a clam chowder lunch at Quincy Market. For dinner, hit the Italian enclave of the North End for handmade pasta and a cannoli (or three) at Mike's Pastry.

Day 2
Check out the quirkier, artier side of Boston, with a visit to the sui generis Isabella Stewart Gardner Museum and a walk through the bizarre three-story glass globe of the Mapparium. If it's baseball season, score a seat at iconic Fenway Park and prepare to cheer along with the Red Sox Nation until the blood vessels in your face burst.

Day 3
Sip coffee with the punks in Cambridge's Harvard Square, then tour the venerable Harvard campus, whose museums could easily take up the whole day. If you've got time and the weather's nice, take the half-hour stroll down Brattle Street to Mt Auburn Cemetery for a wander amid the gracious monuments and stately hardwoods.

Day 4
Head west into the hilly Berkshires to see Massachusetts' arty, agrarian side. Spend an afternoon in the absurdly charming college town of Northampton or, if you've got kids in tow, stop to say hi to the Lorax at the Amazing World of Dr Seuss in Springfield. In summer, the Boston Symphony Orchestra is in residence in Lenox.

Day 5
Cut northwest to spend the following day at MASS MoCa, a sprawling contemporary art museum in a defunct factory complex in North Adams in the Berkshires. If you've got the energy for a quick jaunt up nearby Mt Greylock, go for it.

From left: Race Point Lighthouse on Cape Cod; Boston Public Garden's swan boats.

MICHIGAN

★ ★

POPULATION: 10 million | **SIZE:** 96,716 sq miles | **STATE CAPITAL:** Lansing
LARGEST CITY: Detroit | **WEBSITE:** www.michigan.org

THERE'S MORE TO MICHIGAN THAN THE MOTOR CITY HERITAGE OF CAR MANUFACTURING. With the nation's longest freshwater coastline, more than 100 public beaches, and 19 million acres of forest, the state is an outdoor enthusiast's dreamscape. It has more than 100 state parks and recreation areas in addition to the second-highest number of ski resorts in America. Detroit is in the midst of an arts-led renaissance, Grand Rapids is one of America's leading craft beer meccas, and Ann Arbor is home to the largest football stadium in the country. That's not even counting the array of charming small towns from the beaches of Saugatuck to the scenic shores of Traverse City, or the state's Upper Peninsula, blanketed in serene, forested wilderness. There are a variety of island escapes in Michigan, from the remote wilderness of Isle Royale National Park to tourist-friendly, car-free Mackinac Island.

© StevenSchremp / Getty Images

FOOD & DRINK

BEER CITY ALE TRAIL Get a taste of the booming Grand Rapids beer scene along the Beer City Ale Trail, where you can sample ales from more than 80 breweries in Grand Rapids and nearby communities. Founders Brewing Company is the most iconic local stop on the trail, but leave time to explore new favorites dotted throughout one of America's premier craft beer centers. Use the Brewsader app to unlock deals and perks. *www.experiencegr.com/things-to-do/beer-city/beer-tour*

CHERRY PIE They say you don't get any more American than apple pie, but Michiganders would beg to disagree. The midwestern state produces some 70% of America's tart cherries, which go beautifully inside a flaky piecrust. Grab a slice at Crane's Pie Pantry in the lakeshore town of Fennville.

CONEY DOG The 'coney' – a hot dog smothered with chili and onions – is a Detroit specialty. When the craving strikes (and it will), competing versions all have their claim to be the top, but whichever you choose, this hearty variation on a hot dog carries the essence of Detroit flavor.

LAKE MICHIGAN SHORE WINE TRAIL Explore the tranquil beachfront communities of southwest Michigan, with stops at more than 20 local wineries along the Lake Michigan Shore Wine Trail, which extends more than 70 miles from New Buffalo to Saugatuck. Along the way, check out classic beach towns like St Joseph and be sure to save time to relax at laid-back Warren Dunes State Park. *www.miwinetrail.com*

TRAVERSE CITY FOOD SCENE Food markets, breweries, wineries, farm-to-fork cuisine and cherries in abundance make dining in small Traverse City, the 'Cherry Capital,' unique. Sample wood-fired pizza, seven-course meals and even cherry-dusted tortillas for your meals in this foodie destination.

ZINGERMAN'S DELICATESSEN Michigan's Jewish community has made the state a hotbed of corned beef on rye, and the quintessential version comes from one of the most famous sandwich shops in America, this Midwest institution in a small historic building in Ann Arbor. Started as a nondescript Jewish deli in 1982, today Zingerman's makes a wide range of foods including breads and cheeses, but its claim to fame remains the remarkable deli sandwiches. Though it's on the expensive side, this institution is worth it. *www.zingermansdeli.com, 422 Detroit St*

NATURAL ESCAPES

BELLE ISLE PARK The largest city-owned island park in the US, this nearly 1000-acre public park just minutes from downtown Detroit is the ultimate urban retreat. Situated in the middle of the Detroit River, which separates Michigan from Canada, the leafy enclave features an aquarium, conservatory, nature center, golf course, maritime museum, swimming beach and yacht club. *www.belleisleconservancy.org, bridge access at E Jefferson Ave and E Grand Blvd*

★ ★ ★

SIBLING RIVALRY

Few food rivalries in America are as intense as the long-simmering feud between two next-door restaurants in downtown Detroit. Both serve the signature Coney Island hot dog (or coney dog), a Detroit invention that consists of a hot dog topped with chili sauce, chopped onions and yellow mustard. American Coney Island was opened by Greek immigrant Gust Keros in 1917, followed a few years later by Lafayette Coney Island, which was opened by Gust's brother Bill (reportedly after a falling out with his brother) right next door using a slightly different hot dog and chili. Detroiters remain fiercely loyal to one restaurant or the other, but never both. Lafayette is smaller and more dive-y, while American is larger and has more of a traditional diner feel. Judge for yourself.

© Viktor Posnov / Getty Images; Left: © Monica Wells / Alamy Stock Photo

ISLE ROYALE NATIONAL PARK This remote wilderness in Lake Superior is closer to Thunder Bay, Canada, than Michigan, but its isolated location is one of its chief assets. One of the least-visited US national parks is a serene and solitary location with few modern amenities but abundant wildlife including wolves and moose. One of the best places in America to view the northern lights, the park, sadly, is closed in winter. *www.nps.gov/isro*

PICTURED ROCKS NATIONAL LAKESHORE This national treasure at the tip of Michigan's Upper Peninsula is a secluded paradise of colorful rock formations and sandstone cliffs that create caves, arches and stunning vistas across 42 miles of Lake Superior shoreline. The best way to explore the coastline is by kayak or boat in summer, with snowmobiling and ice-fishing opportunities available in winter. *www.nps.gov/piro*

PORCUPINE MOUNTAINS WILDERNESS STATE PARK Michigan's seemingly endless bounty of natural beauty continues in this off-the-beaten-path wilderness in Michigan's Upper Peninsula, where small mountains sprawled out across vast virgin wilderness reveal spectacular fall foliage and myriad small inland lakes, including the popular Lake of the Clouds. Caution: bears are common in 'the Porkies.' *www.michigan.gov/dnr*

SLEEPING BEAR DUNES NATIONAL LAKESHORE One of the most gorgeous natural locations in the country is this northwest Michigan gem encompassing miles of scenic forests, beaches, sand dunes, bluffs and inland lakes. Among the wealth of outdoor activities are dune climbing, fishing, cross-country skiing and island camping. Spectacular sunsets await. *www.nps.gov/slbe*

ARTS, HISTORY & CULTURE

BAKER'S KEYBOARD LOUNGE This Detroit institution is one of the world's oldest jazz clubs, operating since 1934 in

---

★ ★ ★

WELCOME TO HELL

The small, unincorporated community of Hell, about 15 miles from Ann Arbor, makes the most of its unusual name with local attractions that include the Hell Hole Bar & Diner. Amorous travelers can get married at Hell's Chapel of Love and, for around $100, anyone can become mayor of the town for a day.

From left: The *Thinker* bronze sculpture by Auguste Rodin in front of the Detroit Institute of Arts; Pictured Rocks National Lakeshore; Sleeping Bear Dunes National Lakeshore. Previous page: Rock Harbor Lighthouse in Isle Royale National Park.

© James Schaedig / Alamy Stock Photo

old-school environs with live music almost nightly (it's closed Mondays); note the curved bar made to look like piano keys. In addition to the Detroit-style jazz, local history and interesting characters, the club serves up killer soul food dishes like catfish or liver and gizzards. *www.theofficialbakerskeyboardlounge.com, 20510 Livernois Ave*

DETROIT INSTITUTE OF ARTS With one of the top art collections in the US, this historic museum encompasses more than 658,000 sq ft, including an 1150-seat auditorium, a 380-seat lecture/recital hall and an art reference library. At its heart are the Detroit Industry Murals, whose twenty-seven panels were executed by Diego Rivera. The museum is in Detroit's Cultural Center Historic District, which also includes the Detroit Public Library. *http://dia.org, 5200 Woodward Ave*

MBAD AFRICAN BEAD MUSEUM AND OUTDOOR INSTALLATIONS One of several funky outdoor art installations popping up across Detroit, the colorful street project presents 18 installations on grounds stretching nearly a city block; there are also a few indoor spaces. This one-of-a-kind space dedicated to African culture includes a sculpture garden, a variety of African beads and materials, and an 'African language wall.' The Heidelberg Project is another block-spanning art installation, with polka-dotted streets, houses covered in Technicolor paint blobs, and strange doll sculptures in yards. *mbad.org, 6559 Grand River Ave; www. heidelberg.org, 3600 block of Heidelberg St*

MOTOWN MUSEUM For an intimate look at Detroit's cultural heritage, a trip to the city's Motown Museum is a must. Located in a historic home on West Grand Boulevard that served as Motown Records' original studio, a tour of 'Hitsville USA' exposes the fascinating history behind the legendary label. The museum is currently raising funds for a massive $50 million expansion. *www.motownmuseum.org, 2648 W Grand Blvd*

FUN FACT

Mackinac Bridge crosses 5 miles over the Straits of Mackinac; its exposed span means that the bridge sometimes closes due to extreme weather.

© Walter Bibikow / Getty Images; Right: © Aubrie Pick / Lonely Planet

★ ★ ★

GETTING THERE & AROUND

You'll have little trouble reaching most of Michigan's cities by public transit or Amtrak rail, but to truly experience all the state has to offer, a car is a must. In addition, some of Michigan's more remote island attractions are only accessible by boat or ferry. Detroit Metropolitan Airport is the state's main hub.

SAUGATUCK & DOUGLAS The arts-heavy southwest Michigan beachfront community of Saugatuck showcases one of the Midwest's most beautiful beaches (Oval Beach) in addition to an unrelentingly cute downtown packed with more than a dozen small art galleries. Peruse fine art in Saugatuck and the adjacent community of Douglas to discover why this gay-friendly area is called the Art Coast of Michigan. *www.saugatuck.com*

FAMILY OUTINGS

BOYNE MOUNTAIN RESORT Did you know Michigan is home to more ski resorts than any US state besides New York? One of the premier resorts in the Midwest is northern Michigan's expansive Boyne Mountain, which features more than 115 ski runs across a vast terrain in Boyne Falls. The year-round resort complex also includes 10 golf courses, zip-lining and Michigan's largest indoor water park. *http://boyne.com, 1 Boyne Mountain Rd*

DINOSAUR GARDENS Tucked away in Ossineke, in a secluded stretch of northeast Michigan near the western shore of Lake Huron, hides this delightfully weird 25-acre 'prehistoric zoo,' where life-size, hand-sculpted replicas of dinosaurs and cave men and women come to life across 26 Instagram-worthy exhibits. There's even a dinosaur-themed mini-golf course. *http://dinosaurgardensllc.com, 11160 US-23 S*

THE HENRY FORD There's more than just a few Model T antique autos at this museum in Dearborn dedicated to auto

maker Henry Ford, one of Detroit's most famous sons. America's largest indoor/outdoor museum sprawls across 250 acres that also include President Kennedy's limo, the Rosa Parks bus from Montgomery, and the Wright Brothers' workshop, as well as a digital projection theater and live factory demos. *www.thehenryford.org, 20900 Oakwood Blvd*

MACKINAC ISLAND Take a step back in time to this car-free island nestled in the Straits of Mackinac between the northern tip of Michigan's 'mitt' and the Upper Peninsula. Biking and riding in a horse-drawn carriage are the chief modes of transport for exploring the island's fort and tourist-friendly village, distinguished by charming historic Colonial and Victorian architecture. *www.mackinacisland.org*

From left: The Grand Hotel on Mackinac Island; a rest stop while cycling on the Leelanau Peninsula wine trail near Traverse City.

ITINERARY

Day 1
Spend the day exploring Detroit by visiting a trio of museums: the Motown Museum, Detroit Institute of Arts, and The Henry Ford in nearby Dearborn. Check out the ongoing artistic revitalization of the city at offbeat installations like the MBAD African Bead Museum, then roam the scenic grounds of Belle Isle Park. At night, catch a live jazz performance at Baker's Keyboard Lounge.

Day 2
Grab a Coney dog from Lafayette Coney Island and head west to the idyllic beach community of Saugatuck, stopping en route to explore the beautiful college town of Ann Arbor, where a trip to the university's Big House (the largest stadium in the US) is a must.

Day 3
From Saugatuck, make your way to Grand Rapids with a quick stop to check out the beautiful, Dutch-inspired village of Holland. Once there, sample brews in this craft beer city.

Day 4
Head north from Grand Rapids to the endlessly scenic town of Traverse City and northern Michigan's surrounding Leelanau Peninsula to explore Sleeping Bear Dunes National Lakeshore.

MINNESOTA

★ ★ ★ ★ ★ ★ ★ ★ ★ ★ ★ ★ ★ ★ ★ ★ ★ ★

POPULATION: 5.6 million | **SIZE:** 86,943 sq miles | **CAPITAL:** St Paul
LARGEST CITY: Minneapolis | **WEBSITE:** www.exploreminnesota.com

LONG THE HEARTLAND OF AMERICAN FRIENDLINESS (THOSE TRADEMARK 'HELLOS' WITH rounded o's), Minnesota is the anchor of the Midwest. The Land of 10,000 Lakes (true story!) actually has over 11,000, in typically modest fashion. Intrepid outdoors folk can wet their paddles in the Boundary Waters, where nighttime brings a blanket of stars and the lullaby of wolf howls. Those wanting to get further off the beaten path can journey to Voyageurs National Park, where there's more water than roadway. If that all seems too far-flung, stick to the Twin Cities of Minneapolis and St Paul, where you can't swing a moose without hitting something cool or cultural. And for those looking for middle ground – a cross between the big city and big woods – the dramatic, freighter-filled port of Duluth beckons.

© JB Manning / Shutterstock

FOOD & DRINK

JUCY LUCY If lutefisk is a bridge too far and you aren't inclined to go ice fishing and catch your own fresh walleye (the state fish), the jucy lucy may be more your speed. This calorific burger features the innovation of cheese within the burger patty itself, rather than melted on top. When winters are as cold as they are in Minnesota, you have to invent your own ways of getting through the season.

LUTEFISK Though it's definitely an acquired taste, this aged, lye-soaked whitefish dish is iconic in Minnesota, a state with a strong Scandinavian heritage. Buy a gelatinous slice at Ingebretsen's Scandinavian Gifts in Minneapolis, and hold your nose!

SOMALI FOOD Minneapolis is the center of the largest Somali diaspora in the country, and it's a great place to dive into the cuisine (watch out for the ever-present banana on the table, to be eaten with the meal). Meat spiced with turmeric, coriander and cumin is usually served alongside rice or a flatbread called sabayad, with influences from Turkish, Italian, Arab and East African food all in the mix. Safari is considered the top choice for luxe Somali food in the city, but if you're feeling adventurous, stop into the nearest hole-in-the-wall.

NATURAL ESCAPES

BOUNDARY WATERS Legendarily remote and pristine, the Boundary Waters Canoe Area Wilderness (BWCAW) is one of the world's premier paddling regions. More than 1000 lakes and streams speckle the piney, 1.1 million-acre expanse within the Superior National Forest. Nature lovers make the pilgrimage to this remote northeastern part of the state for the 1500 miles of canoe routes, rich wildlife and sweeping solitude. If you're willing to dig in and canoe for a while, it'll just be you and the moose, bears, wolves and loons that roam the landscape.
www.fs.usda.gov/detail/superior

HIGHWAY 61 This highway in northeastern Minnesota conjures up a headful of images. Local boy Bob Dylan mythologized it in his angry 1965 album *Highway 61 Revisited*. It's the fabled Blues Highway, clasping the Mississippi River en route to New Orleans. Here, the road evokes red-tinged cliffs and forested beaches as it follows Lake Superior's shoreline. The best part? The drive on the old shore road after Two Harbors is a glorious strip of pavement going all the way to the Canadian border. *www.superiorbyways.com*

ITASCA STATE PARK While Minnesota is deservedly famous for its bountiful lakes, which serve as the backdrop to countless childhood vacations, it's also notable as the birthplace of the mighty Mississippi River. In local highlight Itasca State Park, you can walk across the tiny headwaters of the Mississippi itself before it sets out on its 2522-mile journey to the Gulf of Mexico, which is pretty wild. Wade in the knee-deep flow and hop over a couple of stepping stones, then boast you strode over the Father of Waters. *www.dnr.state.mn.us, off Hwy 71 N Park Rapids*

★ ★ ★
TWINSIES?

Just what makes Minneapolis and St Paul twin cities, anyway? The cities are independent municipalities, though they are governed by the same seven-county Metropolitan Council, and they each have a distinct feel. According to the Minnesota Historical Society, the nickname originally referred to Minneapolis and a settlement across the Mississippi River named St Anthony's Falls. When the two growing towns merged in 1872, the nearby state capital, a mere 7.5 miles downriver on the Mississippi, took over the shared title.

Pictured left: Boundary Waters Canoe Area.

© Barcroft Media / Getty Images; Left: ©Panoramic Images / Getty Images

★ ★ ★

DYLAN IN DULUTH

While the Iron Range town of Hibbing is the spot most associated with Bob Dylan, he was actually born in Duluth. You'll see brown-and-white signs on Superior Street and London Road for Bob Dylan Way, pointing out places associated with the legend, like the armory where he saw Buddy Holly in concert and decided to become a musician. But you're on your own to find Dylan's birthplace, up a hill a few blocks northeast of downtown. Dylan lived on the top floor until age six, when his family moved inland to Hibbing. It's a private residence (and unmarked), so all you can do is stare from the street.

SPLIT ROCK LIGHTHOUSE

STATE PARK This is rightly the most visited spot on the entire North Shore. The lighthouse itself is a state historic site with a separate admission fee. Guided tours are available (they depart hourly), or you can explore on your own. If you don't mind stairs, say 170 or so each way, tramp down the cliff to the beach for incredible views of the lighthouse and surrounding shore. The lighthouse was built after a whopping storm in November 1905 battered 29 ships in the area. Modern navigation equipment rendered it obsolete by 1969. No matter. It remains one of the most picture-perfect structures you'll come across. *www.dnr. state.mn.us, 3755 Split Rock Lighthouse Rd*

VOYAGEURS NATIONAL PARK In the

17th century, French-Canadian fur traders, or voyageurs, began exploring the Great Lakes and northern rivers by canoe. Voyageurs National Park covers part of their customary waterway, which became the border between the US and Canada. It's all about water up here. Most of the park is accessible only by foot or motorboat – the waters are mostly too wide and too rough for canoeing. Getting a houseboat is all the rage. *www.dvnpmn.com*

ARTS, HISTORY & CULTURE

GRAND PORTAGE NATIONAL

MONUMENT Located beside the Canadian border in northeastern Minnesota, this site in Grand Portage is where the early voyageurs had to carry their canoes around the Pigeon River rapids. It was the center of a far-flung trading empire, and the reconstructed 1788 trading post and Ojibwe village are worth seeing. *www.nps.gov/grpo, 170 Mile Creek Rd*

MARY TYLER MOORE STATUE The

Mary Tyler Moore Show put Minneapolis on the pop-culture map in the 1970s, reminding American viewers that there were hip, progressive cities beyond the country's coasts. The spot where the titular character threw her hat in the air during the show's opening sequence is now

From left: Downtown Duluth, boyhood home of Bob Dylan; Voyageurs National Park; Mall of America.

© James Kirkikis / Shutterstock

marked by a great, cheesy statue depicting our girl doing just that. *505 Nicollet Mall*

MINNEAPOLIS' NORTH LOOP Sprouting out just beyond the downtown high-rises, the North Loop was a busy industrial area and railroad depot until it fell into disrepair in the 1960s. In the '80s it became a cornerstone of the Twin Cities' alternative arts scene (Prince's club Glam Slam was here). Today it's home to some of the most coveted food and retail in town while still keeping a certain unpolished quality to its gentrification. *https://northloop.org, Washington Ave N*

PAISLEY PARK After Prince died in 2016, his family opened his 65,000-sq-ft home in Chanhassen, near Minneapolis, to the public for tours. Fans have been streaming to the mod, boxy white mansion ever since. It's a must-see if you're a devotee of the Purple One. The general walk-through takes 70 minutes and covers Prince's recording studios, concert hall, rehearsal rooms, wardrobe, instruments and

more. Tickets are available online and in advance only, and more expensive VIP and nighttime tours are also offered. *https:// officialpaisleypark.com, 7801 Audubon Rd*

ST PAUL CURLING CLUB For those uninitiated in northern ways, curling is a winter sport that involves sliding a hubcap-sized 'puck' (called a curling rock or stone) down the ice toward a bull's-eye. The friendly folks here in St Paul don't mind if you stop in to watch the action. Heck, they might invite you to share a ridiculously cheap microbrew from the upstairs bar. *https://stpaulcurlingclub.org, 470 Selby Ave*

WALKER ART CENTER A first-class art center in Minneapolis, the Walker has a strong permanent collection of 20th-century art and photography, including big-name US painters and great US pop art, and regular exhibits. On weekly late summer evenings, the museum hosts free movies and music across the pedestrian bridge in Loring Park. *https://walkerart.org, 725 Vineland Place*

FUN FACT

Bloomington's Mall of America is 4.87 million sq ft and could fit seven Yankee Stadiums inside it. Surprisingly, it's only the fifth largest shopping mall in the country by retail space!

© Oksana Tysovska / Shutterstock; Right: © photo.ua / Shutterstock

★ ★ ★

GETTING THERE & AROUND

Minneapolis–St Paul airport is by far the biggest in the state. Duluth, Bemidji and International Falls have smaller commercial facilities. Amtrak's Empire Builder train stops at several Minnesota cities, including St Paul and Red Wing. Minnesota has eight border crossings to Canada, with the busiest at International Falls and Grand Portage. In winter, 4WD is necessary.

WEISMAN ART MUSEUM The Weisman, which occupies a swooping silver structure by architect Frank Gehry, is a University of Minnesota (and Minneapolis) highlight. The airy main galleries hold cool collections of 20th-century American art, ceramics, Korean furniture and works on paper. Perched over the Mississippi River, it's a commanding sight. *https://wam.umn.edu, 333 E. River Rd*

FAMILY OUTINGS

LUTSEN MOUNTAINS Lutsen, in the state's northeast, is more than just any ski resort – it's the biggest alpine ski area in the Midwest. It bustles in winter when skiers and snowboarders pile in for the 95 runs on four mountains. In summer, visitors come for the aerial gondola to the top of Moose Mountain. The Superior Hiking Trail cuts through, and you can take it plus a spur for the 4.5-mile trek back down the mountain. *www.lutsen.com*

MALL OF AMERICA Welcome to Bloomington and the USA's largest shopping center. Yes, it's just a mall, filled with the usual stores, movie theaters and eateries. But there's also a wedding chapel inside. And an 18-hole mini-golf course. And a zip line. And an amusement park with 27 rides, including a couple of scream-inducing roller coasters. To walk through will cost you nothing, but you can buy a one-day, unlimited-ride wristband or pay

Day 1
Discover the enormity of the Twin Cities with laps around bustling Minneapolis and quieter St Paul, and dine on delicious Somali food. Check out the University of Minneapolis campus on the Mississippi River and visit the Weisman Art Museum, designed by Frank Gehry.

Day 2
Spend the morning shopping and cafe hopping in Minneapolis' North Loop, then start your journey northward, choosing any one of the state's myriad lakes as your destination.

Day 3
Minnesota lakes are for relaxing. Activities on water are the draw (canoeing or ice-fishing sound good, depending on the season).

Day 4
Drive on MN 61 from Duluth to Grand Portage (this route was Dylan's Hwy 61) with a stop at Split Rock Lighthouse as you drive toward the pine-studded wilderness of some of America's most pristine forests along the Canadian border.

for rides individually. The state's largest aquarium, Sea Life Minnesota, is in the mall too. *www.mallofamerica.com, off I-494*

MINNEAPOLIS SCULPTURE GARDEN
This 19-acre green space is a true gem, studded with contemporary works such as the oft-photographed *Spoonbridge and Cherry* by Claes Oldenburg and Coosje van Bruggen, sits beside the equally noatble Walker Art Center. The Cowles Conservatory, abloom with exotic hothouse flowers, is also on the grounds. In summer a trippy mini-golf course amid the sculptures adds to the fun. It all makes for a visit you won't soon forget. *https://walkerart.org/visit/garden, 725 Vineland Pl*

SPAM MUSEUM
An entire museum in Austin is devoted to the peculiar canned meat. It educates on how the blue tins have fed armies, become a Hawaiian food staple and inspired legions of haiku writers. What's more, you can chat to the staff (aka 'spambassadors'), indulge in free samples and try your hand at canning the sweet pork magic. *www.spam.com, 101 3rd Ave NE*

WORLD'S LARGEST BALL OF TWINE
OK, so there are three other Midwest twine balls also claiming to be the largest, but the town of Darwin maintains it has the 'Largest Built by One Person': Francis A Johnson wrapped the 17,400lb whopper on his farm over the course of 29 years. Gawk at it in the town gazebo. *1st St*

From left: Fall colors in the Lutsen Mountains; downtown Minneapolis.

MISSISSIPPI

★ ★ ★ ★ ★ ★ ★ ★ ★ ★ ★ ★ ★ ★ ★ ★ ★ ★ ★

POPULATION: 3 million | **SIZE:** 48,430 sq miles | **STATE CAPITAL:** Jackson
WEBSITE: https://visitmississippi.org

THE STATE NAMED FOR THE MOST VITAL WATERWAY IN NORTH AMERICA FEATURES PALATIAL mansions and rural poverty; haunted cotton flats and lush hill country; honey-dipped sand on the coast and serene farmland in the north. Oft mythologized and misunderstood, this is the source of some of the rawest history – and music – in the country. That legacy is most evident in Mississippi Delta country. A long, low land of silent cotton plots bending under a severe sky, the Delta is a place of surreal, Gothic extremes. Here, in a hierarchical society of great manors and enforced servitude, songs of labor and love became the blues and then American rock 'n' roll. Don't miss Jackson, which has a surprisingly funky arts-cum-hipster presence, or Oxford, a lively student town with a vibrant culinary scene. Meanwhile, the Mississippi River unfurls down the state's western border, carrying the nation's history on its waters.

© Franz Marc Frei / Getty Images

FOOD & DRINK

CATFISH This riverside state is crazy for catfish, the bewhiskered bottom-feeders that prowl local waterways (neighboring Arkansas shares the same predilection). Outside the town of Oxford, Taylor Grocery, a dive-y little haunt in an old dry-goods store, is a cult favorite for its fried, grilled or blackened catfish platters.

COURTHOUSE SQUARE DINING Oxford's Courthouse Square has dining and bar options to satisfy students and literary pilgrims alike. Mississippi culinary icon John Currence dominates the culinary scene around Oxford, and beautiful City Grocery on the Square is one of his finest restaurants.

HOT TAMALES Though their origin is shrouded in mystery, hot tamales are a staple of the Delta region. Were they a contribution by migrant laborers from Mexico, or did they evolve from the seasoned meal eaten by African Americans in the state? Whatever their genesis, hot tamales are all over the Delta. Scott's Hot Tamales in Greenville is one of the originals, and devotees can follow the Hot Tamale Trail or attend the annual Delta Hot Tamale Festival, held in October. You'll bust your stomach way before you bust your wallet.

NATURAL ESCAPES

GULF ISLANDS NATIONAL SEASHORE
This maze of wetlands, beaches and barrier islands, which stretches from Cat Island, Mississippi to Fort Island Beach, Florida, is replete with migrating birds, scrubby dunes and empty white-sand beaches, plus an attractive quilt of marsh islands and flatwater horizons. Beyond the mainland areas, three offshore islands are open to camping, but you'll need to charter a boat to get there. *www.nps.gov/guis*

TISHOMINGO STATE PARK Named for a Chickasaw chief, this park in Tishomingo offers camping among the evocative, moss-covered sandstone cliffs and rock formations, fern gullies and waterfalls of Bear Creek Canyon. It's a special oasis, once utilized by the Chickasaw and their Paleo-Indian ancestors. *www.mdwfp.com, mile 304.5, Natchez Trace Pkwy*

ARTS, HISTORY & CULTURE

BB KING MUSEUM AND DELTA INTERPRETIVE CENTER While ostensibly dedicated to legendary bluesman BB King, this museum in Indianola tackles life in the Delta as a whole. It's filled with interactive displays, artifacts and video exhibits, effectively communicating the history and legacy of the blues while shedding light on the soul of the Delta. *https://bbkingmuseum.org, 400 2nd St*

DELTA BLUES MUSEUM A small but well-presented collection of memorabilia is on display at this Clarksdale museum. The shrine to Delta legend Muddy Waters includes the actual cabin where the musician grew up. Walls full of local art exhibits help round out the display. The museum, in the epicenter of the blues world occasionally hosts live music shows at night that are well worth seeing. *www.deltabluesmuseum.org, 1 Blues Alley*

★ ★ ★

NATCHEZ TRACE

Originally a Native American trading route, the Natchez Trace Parkway was built in the 1930s by the Civilian Conservation Corps and is administered by the National Park Service; its end points are outside Nashville, Tennessee, and in namesake Natchez. The two-lane road, which is closed to semitrucks, is a tranquil drive. If you're short on time but still want to take in the parkway's natural offerings in Mississippi, detour to mile 122 for Canton's Cypress Swamp on the Pearl River. The wide-trunked tupelo and cypress trees stick out from the dark water like legs in a pool, reflected in the glass-like surface of the water. It's not uncommon to spot reptiles, including alligators sunning themselves on the riverbanks. View this eerie beauty from the wooden boardwalk that winds through the swamp for just under a mile.

Left: Rowan Oak in Oxford, home of William Faulkner.

★ ★ ★

DELTA BLUES

The Mississippi Delta is the birth-place of the blues, the progenitor of all modern American pop music. While New Orleans jazz gave the world improvisation and syncopated rhythms, the blues demonstrated the sheer sonic utility of a guitar and simple yet power-ful lyricism. Such a genre of music could only arise under a unique set of physical and cultural circum-stances, borne out of the land and a specific time. Few American places are as iconic as the Mississippi Delta, a land of low horizons, stark landscapes of cotton fields and river shacks, and an economy built first on slavery and then on tenant farming. African Americans inevitably occupied the bottom rung of the social ladder, but they utilized a guitar heritage and call-and-response lyrics learned in the fields to forge a style of music that has never lost its raw potency.

EMMETT TILL INTERPRETIVE CENTER
The trial of the murderers of 14-year old Emmet Till, a young African American who was kidnapped and killed in Money, Mississippi in 1955, helped galvanize the 20th-century civil rights movement. This museum in Sumner, located in the courthouse where the trial occurred (two white men were found not guilty; they later said they had killed Till), is primarily a storytelling experience. There is a focus on reconciliation and community healing, and the overall experience of visiting is immensely powerful.
www.emmett-till.org, 120 N Court St

HIGHWAY 61 This is the Blues Highway, ribboning south out of Memphis to Vicksburg past cotton fields and floodplains. Stop at the crossroads of Highways 61 and 49 in Clarksdale, supposedly the intersection where the great blues musician Robert Johnson made his mythical deal with the Devil, immortalized in his tune 'Cross Road Blues.' Now all of the implied fear and dark

mysticism of the space is taken up by a gloriously tacky guitar sculpture. (For what it's worth, few historians agree where the actual crossroads is located.)

OHR-O'KEEFE MUSEUM OF ART In Biloxi, this funky, Frank Gehry–designed museum campus celebrates the enormous, eccentric ceramic output of master potter and Biloxi native George Ohr. Other exhibits concentrate on the creative culture of the entire Mississippi Gulf Coast. (Word to the wise: the O'Keefe in the museum's name refers to a generous donor family, rather than to artist Georgia O'Keeffe.)
www.georgeohr.org, 386 Beach Blvd

RED'S The Delta town of Clarksdale is inextricably bound up with the blues, and Red's is among the best (and one of the few remaining) juke joints going. A tourist-heavy crowd packs in amid neon-red mood lighting and soulful music. For now, Red runs the bar, knows the acts and slings a cold beer when you need one.
395 Sunflower Ave

© Peek Creative Collective / Shutterstock; Left: © James Kirkikis / Shutterstock

From left: The legendary crossroads at the intersection of US Routes 49 and 61 in Clarksdale; Red's juke joint in Clarksdale; Square Books in literary Oxford.

© Kirkikis / Getty Images

ROWAN OAK Literary pilgrims head to the 1840s home of William Faulkner, tucked away in a dark grove of woods in Oxford, to see what may reasonably be dubbed, to use the author's own elegant words, his 'postage stamp of native soil.' He purchased the Greek Revival house in 1930 and lived there until his death in 1962. Afterwards, take a walk through the surrounding forest, one of his inspirations. *www.rowanoak.com, Old Taylor Rd*

SMITH ROBERTSON MUSEUM In Jackson, Mississippi's first public school for African American children is the alma mater of Richard Wright, author of the classic memoir *Black Boy* and many other works. Exhibits at the on-site museum offer insight into the pain and perseverance associated with the African American legacy in Mississippi, and into Wright's own searing race consciousness. *www.jacksonms.gov, 528 Bloom St*

SQUARE BOOKS The University of Mississippi (Ole Miss) is renowned for its excellent writing program. Square Books, one of the South's great independent bookstores, is the epicenter of Oxford's lively literary scene and a frequent stop for traveling authors. A cafe and balcony are upstairs, and of course there's an immense section devoted to Faulkner. *www.squarebooks.com, 160 Courthouse Sq*

TUTWILER TRACKS Tutwiler in the Delta is where the blues began its migration from oral tradition to popular art form. Here, WC Handy, the 'Father of the Blues,' first heard a sharecropper moan his 12-bar prayer while the two waited for a train in 1903. The meeting is immortalized by a lonely, faded mural that feels a thousand years old. *100 Bruister St*

VICKSBURG NATIONAL MILITARY PARK Vicksburg controlled access to the Mississippi River during the Civil War, and its seizure by Union troops in 1863 was one of the turning points of the war. A driving tour passes historic markers explaining battle scenarios and key events from the

FUN FACT

The name of the state comes from the Ojibwe words Misi zipi, or 'Great River.'

© MilesbeforeIsleep / Shutterstock; Right: © Rush Jagoe / Lonely Planet

city's siege. Cycling is a fantastic way to tour the park. *www.nps.gov/vick, 3201 Clay St*

WALTER ANDERSON MUSEUM OF ART

A consummate artist and lover of Gulf Coast nature, Walter Anderson pursued his lifework of being, in his own words, one of 'those who have brought nature and art together into one thing.' The beachside shack where he lived on Horn Island was painted in mind-blowing murals, which you'll see at this Ocean Springs museum of his paintings, drawings, and more. *www.walterandersonmuseum.org, 510 Washington St*

FAMILY OUTINGS

BAY ST LOUIS Charming Bay St Louis near NASA's Stennis Space Center (close by the Louisiana border) has a slightly more countercultural cast than you might expect in Mississippi. Yoga studios, antiques stores and galleries cluster on Main Street. Avoid the underwhelming beach on the Gulf Coast and opt to browse the charming local small businesses. *www.baystlouis-ms.gov*

EMERALD MOUND The grassy ruins of a Native American city, including the second-largest pre-Columbian earthworks in the US, can be found just outside Natchez. Using stone tools, indigenous peoples graded this 8-acre mountain into a flat-topped pyramid. There are shady, creekside picnic spots here, and an almost eerie sense of stillness. *www.nps.gov/natr, Natchez Trace Pkwy mile 10.3*

NATCHEZ TRACE PARKWAY You should plan at least part of your trip in Mississippi around driving one of the oldest roads in North America: the Natchez Trace. This 444-mile trail from Natchez, Mississippi to Nashville, Tennessee, follows a natural ridgeline that traverses a wide panoply of southern landscapes: thick, dark forests; soggy wetlands; gentle hill country; and long swaths of farmland. *www.nps.gov/natr*

★ ★ ★

GETTING THERE & AROUND

Jackson is the main point of air access, but its airport is pretty small. There are three routes most folks take when traveling through Mississippi by car. Both I-55 and Highway 61 run north–south from the state's north-ern to southern borders; Highway 61 goes through the Delta, and I-55 flows in and out of Jackson.

ITINERARY

Day 1
Explore Vicksburg National Military Park from your starting point in Jackson, where you can have a good southern meal and a mixed drink in the Fondren neighborhood. It's easy to have a good time in Jackson.

Day 2
Head up to the glorious Natchez Trace Parkway en route to Oxford, home of Rowan Oak, the pretty campus of Ole Miss and the iconic Square.

Day 3
Pay tribute to Clarksdale and Highway 61, where you should visit the Delta Blues Museum and catch a show at Red's, one of the last remaining traditional juke joints (blues clubs) in the region. Try to find hot tamales to sample while you're in the area.

Day 4
Turn to the Mississippi Delta before heading back towards Jackson. Make sure to visit the Emmett Till Interpretive Center in Sumner and the BB King Museum in Indianola; both provide insight into the region's racial history, while the BB King Museum grounds visitors in the blues.

From left: The bridge over the Tennessee River on the Natchez Trace Parkway; a wooden shack in Clarksdale.

MISSOURI

★ ★

POPULATION: 6.1 million | **SIZE:** 69,715 sq miles | **STATE CAPITAL:** Jefferson City
LARGEST CITY: Kansas City | **WEBSITE:** www.visitmo.com

SPREADING WITH EASE ACROSS THE GREAT PLAINS, THIS IS A PLACE OF LORE AND LEGEND.
The most populated state in the Plains, Missouri likes to mix things up, serving visitors ample portions of both sophisticated city life and down-home country sights. St Louis and Kansas City are the region's most interesting cities, and each is a destination in its own right. However, with more forest and less farmland than neighboring states, Missouri also cradles plenty of wild places and wide-open spaces, most notably among the undulating green hills of the Ozark Mountains. The winding valleys in the Ozarks invite adventurous exploration or just some laid-back meandering behind the steering wheel. Maybe you'll find an adventure worthy of Hannibal native Mark Twain as you wander the state. Certainly you'll find some of the best barbecue in the country.

© joe daniel price / Getty Images

FOOD & DRINK

BREWERY BONANZA Missouri is overflowing with drafts. One of the world's largest beer plants, the historic Anheuser-Busch Brewery in St Louis, gives marketing-driven tours where you can view the bottling plant and Clydesdale horses. In Kansas City, craft beer fans are in their element at Boulevard, the Midwest's largest specialty brewer. There's a huge range of home brews on tap in the 2nd-floor beer hall, or check out experimental specials, such as whiskey-barrel stout or black-currant sour ale.

GOOEY BUTTER CAKE First dreamed up in St Louis, this flat cake with a chewy crust is just what its name promises: make sure to split your slice with a friend, as rich is an understatement. Missouri Baking Company, operating in St Louis since 1924, has an almond-flavored version for maximum decadence.

KANSAS CITY BARBECUE Kansas City is one of the country's great barbecue hubs, with slow-smoked pork, beef and chicken smothered in sweet-tangy red sauce. True locals know to order the 'burnt ends' – the charred, deeply savory ends of the brisket. The ones at Arthur Bryant's Barbeque, LC's Bar-B-Q and Gates BBQ are all heavenly.

TOASTED RAVIOLI 'Toasted' is a misnomer – these ravioli bites are breaded and then deep-fried before being served alongside marinara sauce. Restaurants in The Hill, St Louis' Italian district, are a good bet for sampling this original appetizer found throughout the city.

NATURAL ESCAPES

ELEPHANT ROCKS STATE PARK With a little imagination (read: squinting), the hefty pink granite boulders that steal the show in this state park look like a train of circus elephants. Located in southeastern Missouri near Belleview, the park is a geologist's dream, formed from 1.5-billion-year-old granite. The mile-long, accessible Braille Trail loop is a great introduction to the terrain, and kids love clambering up and over the rocks. *https://mostateparks.com, MO-21*

FOREST PARK St Louis moves effortlessly from urban to the outdoors at this enormous 1371-acre spread, the setting of the 1904 St Louis World's Fair. Far more than a park, it brings together forest, lakes, streams, nature trails, tennis courts and golf courses, besides a zoo, a planetarium and an outstanding art museum that includes the 2013 David Chipperfield–designed East Building. Forest Park is even 528 acres bigger than New York's Central Park! *www.forestparkforever.org, Lindell Blvd, Kingshighway Blvd and I-64*

JOHNSON'S SHUT-INS STATE PARK Welcome to Mother Nature's water park! Looking up to the St Francois Mountains, lushly wooded Johnson's Shut-Ins State Park in Middlebrook is where the East Fork of the Black River swirls through canyon-like gorges (known as shut-ins). The swimming here is a real blast, with natural chutes and falls, and bottle-green pools to plunge into that are a cooling delight on hot summer days. *https://mostateparks.com, 148 Taum Sauk Trail*

★ ★ ★

MISSOURI
Music

At opposite ends of the state, St Louis and Kansas City each have a unique musical sound. If there's a soundtrack that underpins everyday life in St Louis, it's the lyrical syrup of Mississippi blues. In contrast, St Louis blues music is notable for its heavy use of the piano, and it was St Louis' rollicking music halls that rocketed the likes of Chuck Berry, Miles Davis and Ike and Tina Turner to global stardom. The Kansas City jazz scene flourished in the early 1930s under political boss Tom Pendergast's Prohibition-era tenure, when he allowed alcohol to flow freely. At its peak, Kansas City had more than 100 nightclubs, dance halls and vaudeville houses swinging to the beat (and booze). Native son Charlie Parker rode the wave to an explosively successful style of bebop. You can still see jazz on a nightly basis at The Majestic Restaurant and elsewhere in town.

© Russell_Images / Shutterstock; Left: © larrybraunphotography.com / Getty Images

© Russell_Images / Shutterstock; Left: © larrybraunphotography.com / Getty Images

★ ★ ★

STE GENEVIÈVE

Petite Ste Geneviève on the Mississippi River waves the flag as Missouri's oldest town, founded by the French. It's worth a detour (60 miles south of St Louis) for a spin of the historic center's attractively preserved 18th- and 19th-century buildings, many of which are now B&Bs or gift shops. From here, you can follow the Route du Vin Wine Trail out of town to visit its wineries, mostly small, family-run operations, for a tasting.

MARK TWAIN NATIONAL FOREST
Named after that intrepid, itinerant Missouri hero Mark Twain, this vast forest unfurls over 1.5 million acres from the Ozarks to the prairies. Spring-fed streams and rivers twist through oak and pine woods that are overlooked by bluffs. Kayaking, hiking and camping in the more remote reaches, you might get lucky and spot wildlife from roadrunners to bald eagles, wild turkeys and black bears. *www.fs.usda.gov/mtnf*

OZARK NATIONAL SCENIC RIVERWAYS
Unraveling across southern Missouri, the Ozarks are a gloriously off-the-radar corner of the state, with thickly wooded hills, lakes, waterfalls, caves and rich birdlife. Protecting the Current and Jacks Forks Rivers, the national park is best explored by canoe, kayak or inflatable tube; on foot; or by horseback. You can also camp overnight. There are ranger-led tours in summer, and keen hikers can hook onto the 350-mile Ozark Trail. *www.nps.gov/ozar*

PRAIRIE STATE PARK
For a true flavor of the Great Plains as they once were, strap on hiking boots and head over to this state park in southwestern Missouri. Here you can wander among tall prairie grasses, ablaze in spring with wildflowers like fire-red Indian paintbrush. Big skies (star-spangled at night), herds of resident bison and elk to spot, hiking trails and back-to-nature camping are the major draws. *https://mostateparks.com, 128 NW 150th Ln, Mindenmines*

ARTS, HISTORY & CULTURE

GATEWAY ARCH NATIONAL PARK
Rising like a silver rainbow above the Mississippi River, the Gateway Arch is St Louis' most eye-catching icon. This 630ft landmark in stainless steel is the world's tallest arch and the highest man-made monument in the US. It's now the shimmering centerpiece of its own recently designated (2018) national park, and since 1965 the arch has symbolized St Louis' historical

From left: Ste Geneviève; cascade in the Ozarks; the *American Eagle* paddle wheel riverboat docks in Hannibal, hometown of Mark Twain. Previous page: The Gateway Arch designed by Eero Saarinen and St Louis skyline beyond.

© Brian S / Shutterstock

role as the Gateway to the West. *www.nps.gov/jeff, 11 N 4th St*

MARK TWAIN BOYHOOD HOME & MUSEUM Along the banks of the Mississippi, the town of Hannibal is where you'll find Mark Twain's white-clapboard childhood home and a museum crammed with memorabilia – from first editions to the Norman Rockwell oil paintings created for special editions of *The Adventures of Tom Sawyer* and *Adventures of Huckleberry Finn*. The museum offers great insight into how Twain's childhood buddies became some of America's best-loved fictional characters. *www.marktwainmuseum.org, 120 N Main St*

MUTUAL MUSICIANS FOUNDATION In the Historic Jazz District of Kansas City (also home to worthwhile museums), this former union hall for African American musicians has jumped to after-hours jam sessions since 1930. Famous veteran musicians gig with young hotshots. A little

bar serves cheap drinks in plastic cups. There's no cover charge, but a donation is suggested. *mutualmusiciansfoundation.org, 1823 Highland Ave*

NATIONAL BLUES MUSEUM Click into the groove of rhythm and blues over the ages at this flashy museum in St Louis, which spotlights home-grown talent like Chuck Berry while also making a strong case for the genre's influences on modern rock, folk, R&B and more with interactive exhibits. Check the website for details on Thursday evening jam sessions, and Howlin' Friday and Soulful Sunday live music sessions. *www.nationalbluesmuseum.org, 615 Washington Av*

NELSON-ATKINS MUSEUM OF ART Giant badminton shuttlecocks (the building represents the net) surround this encyclopedic museum in Kansas City. Glass cubes filter light into the subterranean galleries, which take a spectacular romp through an expansive,

FUN FACT

Missouri was named after a tribe of Sioux Indians called the Missouria, or Missouri. The name means 'he of the big canoe.'

© LanaG / Shutterstock; Right: © Serhii Chrucky / Alamy Stock Photo

★ ★ ★

GETTING THERE & AROUND

St Louis has the largest airport in the Great Plains. There are daily Amtrak trains to cities like Chicago, Kansas City and Dallas, plus regular Greyhound buses. Car rental is recommended for reaching more remote places: public transport is almost nonexistent in the Ozarks, for example.

high-caliber collection of European paintings, contemporary photography, Japanese porcelain, Chinese ceramics and more. Standouts include Henry Moore works in the sculpture garden and art masterpieces of the Rembrandt, Caravaggio and Monet ilk. Entry is free. *www.nelson-atkins.org, 4525 Oak St*

TRUMAN PRESIDENTIAL MUSEUM & LIBRARY
History fiends should factor in a visit to this museum and library in Independence, topping a hill overlooking Kansas City. Among the thousands of artifacts is the famous 'The Buck Stops Here!' sign, from the man who led the US through one of its most tumultuous eras in the aftermath of WWII. The museum provides a vivid snapshot of America in the late 1940s and early 1950s. *www.trumanlibrary.org, 500 W. US-24*

FAMILY OUTINGS

CITY MUSEUM
The brainchild of sculptor Bob Cassilly, this delightful and downright bizarre fun house in a cavernous old shoe factory is the highlight of any visit to St Louis. Run, jump and explore exhibits made from salvaged objects, including tunnels, a life-size fiberglass whale and a 10-story slide. The summer-only rooftop Ferris wheel offers sky-high views of the city. *www.citymuseum.org, 701 N 15th St*

KATY TRAIL STATE PARK
You might not be able to manage it all in one bite, but this rail-to-trail path runs 240 miles across Missouri, between Clinton and Machens, along what was once the Missouri–Kansas–Texas Railroad. Largely hugging the banks of the Missouri River, it's a family favorite for its easygoing, largely flat trails

ITINERARY

Day 1
Launch your trip in St Louis. The Gateway Arch is mandatory; afterward, churn up the Big Muddy with a spin on a replica of a classic 19th-century paddle steamer.

Day 2
Get a culture fix at one of the big-hitter museums: the City Museum, St Louis Art Museum, or National Blues Museum. By night, head up to Italian American neighborhood The Hill for St Louis–style pizza and frozen custard; then head over to Blueberry Hill, where Chuck Berry rocked the basement bar until the day he died.

Days 3 & 4
You could swing north along the Mississippi to the low-key, rather quaint midwestern town of Hannibal to visit Mark Twain's boyhood home. After that, make your way west, taking in the superb art museums, restaurants and bars of Kansas City. Alternatively, devote a couple of days to explore the offbeat Ozarks in southern Missouri, with forests, lakes, hills and rivers great for touring the backcountry.

that can be explored on foot, by bike or on horseback. *https://mostateparks.com*

MERAMEC CAVERNS The family-mobbed Meramec Caverns in Stanton is as interesting for its Civil War history and hokey charm as for the stalactites. Yet these are no minor attraction; this cavern system is the largest in the Ozarks, extending for 4.6 miles and helping to give Missouri its nickname: The Cave State. *https://americascave.com, I-44, exit 230*

SILVER DOLLAR CITY Winging you back to the 1880s, this huge theme park in Branson sits scenically at Indian Point on Table Rock Lake in the Ozarks. Besides one of the deepest limestone caves in the state, Marvel Cave, there's plenty of whizzy fun, with attractions from the Time Traveler (the world's fastest and steepest spinning roller coaster) to white-water rafts. *www.silverdollarcity.com, 399 Silver Dollar City Pkwy*

ST JOSEPH Right by the border with Kansas, St Joseph was a key piece of movements west in the 19th century. The city's Pony Express National Museum marks the short-lived service that began here in 1860 at the start of a 2000-mile journey to California, before the Civil War and Western Union telegraph expansion doomed the effort. Just a few blocks from where the horses once departed, Patee House Museum showcases St Joseph's rich history with exhibits full of 19th-century memorabilia, and the Jesse James Home Museum nearby marks where the infamous outlaw Jesse James was killed by Bob Ford. The fateful bullet hole is still in the wall. *https://stjomo.com*

From left: The imaginative play areas of the City Museum in St. Louis; an old rail bridge along the Katy Trail.

MONTANA

★ ★

POPULATION: 1 million | **SIZE:** 147,040 sq miles | **STATE CAPITAL:** Helena
LARGEST CITY: Billings | **WEBSITE:** www.visitmt.com

MONTANA IS ENORMOUS. THE FOURTH-LARGEST STATE, IT IS ROUGHLY THE SIZE OF JAPAN, yet is home to only 1 million people. It's not just the sky that's big; everything in Montana is larger than life. The mountains seem just a touch taller, the valleys feel a smidge wider and the lakes are a bit longer than in other mountain states. The people who live here have known this for a while, and are perfectly happy to let everyone else flock to Colorado while they ski the legendary 'cold smoke' powder, fish blue-ribbon trout streams, and live quiet and peaceful lives surrounded by a gazillion microbreweries. Of course, they don't mind if you come to explore the state's hidden treasures, but they'd rather you didn't stay too long. And, please don't tell your friends about it. Whether you are in the badlands in the east or the Rockies in the west, your eye can travel to the horizon without any settlements in sight.

© Feng Wei Photography / Getty Images

FOOD & DRINK

BISON Also known as buffalo, bison once roamed from the Gulf of Mexico to Alaska. Relentless hunting, as well as the introduction of diseases from cattle, nearly wiped them out – the population plummeted from a peak of some 60 million to only 541 animals in 1889. Today bison have rebounded to around 500,000, and you can order bison steaks and burgers at restaurants around Montana. Aleworks in Bozeman serves bison burgers and patty melts, while the Hummingbird Cafe in Butte is a local favorite for bison burgers.

HUCKLEBERRY PIE Black huckleberries, which only grow at high altitudes in Idaho, Montana and the Pacific Northwest, are a rare treat. The berries are not grown commercially, and the best way to enjoy their tart bite is to seek out a bakery or restaurant serving local huckleberry pie. Leave room for dessert at the Glacier Highland restaurant in West Glacier, famous for its pies. At Loula's in Whitefish, you can choose from pure huckleberry pie or ones that pair the fruit with blackberries, cherries, peaches or raspberries.

NATURAL ESCAPES

BEARTOOTH HIGHWAY Along its 69 miles, the Beartooth Highway is one of the country's most scenic drives. It runs between Red Lodge and Cooke City, both in Montana, but dips into Wyoming for a portion of the route. The highway has countless switchbacks and hairpin turns, and stunning views of the peaks of the Rockies. It is open only from May to October.

BIG SKY RESORT With the Rocky Mountains running through Montana, it's an under-the-radar ski destination that's home to the country's second-largest ski area, Big Sky. There are 34 lifts and almost 5850 acres of skiable terrain here, a (for now) secret haven for powder lovers. In the summer, visitors can enjoy the 18-hole golf course and opportunities to hike, mountain bike, or zip-line. *https://bigskyresort.com*

GLACIER NATIONAL PARK Few parks can compete with Glacier when it comes to sheer grandeur. Running along the Canadian border, the more than 1500-sq-mile park includes six peaks over 10,000 feet high and more than 700 lakes. Logan Pass on the Going-to-the-Sun Road crosses the Continental Divide for incredible views, including some wildlife spotting; grizzly bears, moose and Canadian lynx have managed to survive the centuries here largely undisturbed. Grinnell Glacier is a must-see highlight. *www.nps.gov/glac*

HOT SPRINGS The geothermal activity that fuels the geysers of Yellowstone is also responsible for Montana's many hot springs. If you want to take a long soak in a natural mineral bath (we certainly recommend it), you have literally dozens to choose from. Norris Hot Springs is a popular low-key and affordable option. *https://norrishotsprings.com, 42 MT-84, Norris*

THE MISSOURI RIVER Draining one-sixth of the US, the Missouri River invites exploration by raft, canoe or kayak on many stretches, though the most popular is between Great Falls and Fort Peck Lake.

★ ★ ★

CROW FAIR

The largest Native American event in Montana and one of the largest powwows anywhere in the country takes place in Crow Agency every August. The event celebrated its centennial in 2018 and is still going strong. Over four days, parades, dances and rodeo celebrate the history and culture of the Crow people. Don't worry that you will feel like you are intruding. Around 50,000 people attend as spectators annually, and Crow participants are happy to explain Crow food, dress and other aspects of their culture to interested (and respectful) outsiders.

Left: Highline Trail in Glacier National Park.

★ ★ ★

GETTING THERE & AROUND

Montana's busiest airport is in Bozeman, where many visitors opt to start their Yellowstone adventure. Billings and Missoula also have well-connected airports. Bus routes tend not to deviate much from the I-90 corridor. Amtrak's Empire Builder line is an excellent option to access northern Montana and Glacier National Park. Check conditions for the latest road hazards and issues before setting out.

Many outfitters offer trips on the river ranging from half-day ones to weeklong excursions, and fly fishers will find plenty to cheer about. You'll pass through dramatic canyons as you explore the West as Lewis and Clark did.

YELLOWSTONE NATIONAL PARK The country's first national park straddles three states: Idaho, Montana and Wyoming. At almost 3500 sq miles, the park is enormous, with many geysers (the most famous is Old Faithful) and countless trails. The bison roaming the valley floors are spectacular, though the reintroduction of bison, and wolves, has come with some controversy. Nearby Bozeman is a popular starting point for exploring Yellowstone. *www.nps.gov/yell*

ARTS, HISTORY & CULTURE

BUTTE-ANACONDA HISTORIC DISTRICT Today Butte is home to some 36,000 residents, but in the late 19th century (it was established in 1864), it was the biggest city between the Mississippi and the West Coast thanks to its copper mines, with nearby Anaconda and Walkerville sharing in the wealth. The Butte-Anaconda Historic District is the country's largest historic district, with 6000 landmarked properties from mining buildings to owners' mansions and more modest workers' housing. *http://butte-anacondanhld.blogspot.com*

C M RUSSELL MUSEUM Artist Charlie M Russell (1864–1926), who also went by 'Kid,' captured the cowboys and Native Americans of the West in some 2000 oil paintings and bronze sculptures. The museum in Great Falls includes Russell's house, his log cabin studio and newer gallery spaces, housing works by Russell and his contemporaries. *https://cmrussell.org, 400 13th St N*

LITTLE BIGHORN BATTLEFIELD NATIONAL MONUMENT An hour's drive east of Billings, Little Bighorn Battlefield is the site of General George Custer's famous Last Stand. On June 25 and 26, 1876, 700 US cavalry troops led by Custer faced off against Lakota, Northern Cheyenne and Arapaho warriors. The cavalry was defeated, with at least 263 fatalities including Custer. A 4.5-mile road tours the battlefield, and Custer National Cemetery is nearby. *www.nps.gov/libi*

TIPPET RISE ART CENTER This center between Billings and Bozeman sits on a 10,000-acre working sheep ranch. Its founders were inspired by sculpture parks like New York's Storm King, and Tippet Rise is home to works by Alexander Calder, Mark di Suvero and others. It also hosts performances of classical music in an unforgettable setting; the concert series runs from May to October. *https://tippetrise.org, 96 S Grove Creek Rd, Fishtail*

Beartooth Portal, **a work by Spanish architects Antón García-Abril and Débora Mesa, known together as Ensamble Studio, at the Tippet Rise Art Center near Fishtail.**

FAMILY OUTINGS

BANNACK STATE PARK Montana is dotted with ghost towns – mining settlements that arose from nothing and whose populations plummeted as soon as nearby deposits were exhausted. Bannack in southwestern Montana is one of the earliest of them and among the best preserved. Once a town of 3000, it was established in 1862 and even served as the territorial capital for a period. *http://bannack.org, 4200 Bannack Rd*

LEWIS AND CLARK NATIONAL HISTORIC TRAIL INTERPRETIVE CENTER On a bluff overlooking the Missouri River, this interpretive center in Great Falls brings to life the epic 1804–1806 journey of Meriwether Lewis and William Clark from St Louis to the Pacific Ocean. Films and interactive, kid-friendly exhibits tell the tale of the beginning of the westward expansion of the US. *www.visitmt.com, 4201 Giant Springs Rd*

ITINERARY

Day 1
Start in Montana's largest city, Billings, with a visit to the state's most famous historic site, the Little Bighorn Battlefield, and the Tippet Rise Art Center. A bison burger for dinner will supply you with the energy needed for a week exploring some of the country's very finest National Parks.

Day 2
Go south to the Beartooth Highway for a drive that meanders among soaring peaks and by alpine lakes. The highway ends not far from an entrance to Yellowstone National Park. Spend today exploring the trails and geysers of Yellowstone, keeping your eyes open for bison (easy to spot) and wolves (more elusive). Around two million people visit the park each summer, but many of those are there simply to see Old Faithful.

Day 3
Take in Yellowstone for a second day. There are endless opportunities to commune with nature if you venture a little deeper into the park.

Days 4 and 5
Set aside at least two days enjoying life at a dude ranch, exploring trails on horseback and dining on bison burgers and local

trout. The ranches range tremendously from true working facilities that offer opportunities to assist with game drives to others that are closer to western-inspired resorts. You can search for one that suits your style at www.duderanch.org.

Day 6
Today you'll drive north toward Canada and Glacier National Park, but make it a leisurely trip with time for stops in Helena (the state capital), Butte and other towns. In Butte, the country's largest historic district includes the stately homes of mine owners and the more modest ones of the men who worked the mines. The Berkeley Pit is a giant, now water-filled hole that is a dramatic reminder of the destruction wrought by mining operations.

Day 7
Spend today exploring Glacier National Park, which sits on the Canadian border. The park contains six peaks over 10,000ft and countless lakes. It's part of a network of parks on both sides of the border that has helped ensure that the area's endemic species, like Canadian lynx and grizzly bears, have not only survived but thrived.

© Nature Picture Library / Alamy Stock Photo

N E B R A S K A

★ ★

POPULATION: 1.9 million | **SIZE:** 77,358 sq miles | **STATE CAPITAL:** Lincoln
LARGEST CITY: Omaha | **WEBSITE:** https://visitnebraska.com

LOCATED IN THE HEART OF AMERICA'S GREAT PLAINS, THE CORNHUSKER STATE HAS A BEAUTIFUL and dramatic topography consisting of vast prairies, mystical sand dunes and the breathtaking rock formations of its panhandle. Dive into western history at the Scotts Bluff National Monument, a key stopping point on the famous Oregon Trail. Enjoy a thick-cut Omaha steak from one of this city's famed steak houses, which serve Grade A meat from cows raised on the sandhills and fed Nebraska-grown corn. Float down the mighty Missouri River and don't skip the famous Nebraska State Fair. Also be sure to attend a Native American powwow to experience the rich history of Nebraska's indigenous populations, including the Omaha, Missouria, Ponca, Pawnee, Otoe and Sioux nations. With its haunting natural beauty, charming cities and amiable down-home flavor, this friendly state is 'Nebraska Nice'.

FOOD & DRINK

BIEROCK & ROLL A little-known fact about Nebraska is that its central region was settled by the Volga Germans who emigrated from Russia in the 1800s. They brought bierocks with them, soft, lightly sweetened bread pockets filled with ground beef, onions, cabbage and sometimes cheese. Bierocks can be found anywhere from a roadside stand to local bakeries, and also go by the name runza. Sehnert's Bakery in McCook serves a fantastic version, and they're also the star of the show at Nebraska chain Runza.

KOOL-AID Surprised that Nebraska's state soft drink is...Kool-Aid? Don't be! Invented by Edwin Perkins in the town of Hastings, this is a born-and-bred Nebraska original. Perkins originally focused on shipping his beverages by mail, but glass breakage led him to create the Kool-Aid powder concentrate in 1927. The rest is history.

OMAHA STEAK Nothing says Nebraska like a bone-in rib-eye steak straight from one of this state's healthy, corn-fed cows, which are the pride of state. Though vegan and vegetarian offerings are growing, steaks are served in almost every restaurant, from small-town steak houses to grand joints in Lincoln and Omaha. In Lincoln, try Lazlo's Brewery & Grill, where meats are grilled over a hickory-wood fire to create an unparalleled flame-grilled taste. Drover, one of the best steak houses in Omaha, drenches its meats in a homemade whiskey marinade before grilling them. The marinade recipe is over 40 years old!

SWEET NEBRASKA CORN Nebraska's nickname is the Cornhusker State, due to its crop of some of the sweetest, most delicious corn in the world. Every summer, corn stands appear like magic on the street. Feast on local delicacies such as corn pone, corn pudding and even corn ice cream! The corn bread from Big Mama's Kitchen in Omaha is a must-try.

NATURAL ESCAPES

MISSOURI NATIONAL RECREATIONAL RIVER This winding recreational park set along the Missouri River as it cuts between Nebraska and South Dakota features exceptional outdoor opportunities as well as a historical link to the Lewis and Clark Expedition, which traveled this way. Named after Nebraska's Ponca tribe, Ponca State Park in the eastern section of the river has exceptional views of the surrounding landscape. The Missouri River winds along the glacier-carved bluffs, making this an ideal launching spot for kayaks and canoes. To the west, Niobrara State Park plays host to the Poncas' annual powwow. *www.nps.gov/mnrr*

SANDHILLS The largest dune formation in the Western Hemisphere, Nebraska's sandhills cover just over 25% of the state, at 19,000 sq miles (the size is comparable to West Virginia). The undulating prairie on these grass-stabilized sand dunes stretches over the Ogallala Aquifer; dotted with lakes, this is the largest wetland in the US and a key component of the Central Flyway for migratory birds. Unlike other dune landscapes around the world, these are almost completely stabilized

★ ★ ★

CRANE CRAZE

Held every March, Audubon's Nebraska Crane Festival celebrates the state's legacy as home to 80% of the world's population of migratory sand-hill cranes. These unique birds make an annual stopover in the water-rich sandhills as they travel from their warm-weather winter homes to Siberia, Alaska and Canada, where they migrate to give birth to their chicks every year. This festival celebrates their pit stop in Nebraska with family-friendly events, environmental talks and plenty of bird-watching!

Left: Riding at Gracie Creek Ranch in the Nebraska Sandhills.

GETTING THERE & AROUND

The best way to enjoy this long, open stretch of America is to take smaller highways, such as US-30 instead of I-80, the main interstate. To reach the stunning Black Hills, take I-20 or the long, lonesome, beautiful US-2. The two main airports are Eppley Airfield in Omaha and Lincoln Airport.

by vegetation and are fertile ground for beef cattle. Arthur Bowring Sandhills Ranch State Historical Park in Merriman preserves a turn-of-the-20th-century working cattle ranch on the sandhills, while the Valentine National Wildlife Refuge is a good introduction to this unique ecosystem. Further south, the Sandhills Journey Scenic Byway beckons.

ARTS, HISTORY & CULTURE

CARHENGE For a one-of-a-kind pit stop, be sure to check out this replica of Stonehenge made out of, yes, cars. Built by Jim Reinders in Alliance and dedicated at the 1987 summer solstice, it's the only spot in the world where you can get your fix of

both Druid culture and car culture. *http://carhenge.com, 2151 County Rd 59*

DURHAM MUSEUM Located in the gorgeous Union Station building in Omaha, this art deco masterpiece houses some of the finest art and artifacts from the city's rich history. Multiple galleries showcase its expansive permanent collection, including a great model train exhibit, and recreations of structures such as a classic Nebraska general store from the 1800s are on view. *https://durhammuseum.org, 801 S 10th St*

JOSLYN ART MUSEUM This Omaha museum's 1931 building is one of the best examples of art deco architecture in America (and admission is free!). Enjoy

From left: © marekuliasz / Shutterstock; © Zack Frank / Shutterstock

the outdoor sculpture garden, or attend a lecture in the stunning 1000-seat auditorium. *www.joslyn.org, 2200 Dodge St*

MUSEUM OF NEBRASKA HISTORY

Housing over 125,000 artifacts from Nebraska history, this museum in Lincoln brings the amazing story of Nebraska's statehood to life. Patrons can learn about Nebraskan life before it officially became a state; the museum also explores the unique moments that gave Nebraska its identity. Even better, admission is free. *https://history.nebraska.gov/museum, 131 Centennial Mall N*

UNION PACIFIC RAILROAD MUSEUM

Across the Missouri River from Omaha in downtown Council Bluffs, Iowa, this gem is devoted to the history of the famous Union Pacific Railroad. Union Pacific is the largest railroad system in America after the BNSF Railway; it operates over 32,100 miles in 23 states. This is a must-see. *www.uprrmuseum.org, 200 Pearl St*

FAMILY OUTINGS

HENRY DOORLY ZOO This family-friendly zoo and aquarium in Omaha is a wonderful adventure for all ages and a standout in its class, not just in Nebraska but in the US. A short list of the many impressive exhibits includes the Asian Highlands, African Grasslands, Hubbard Gorilla Valley, Owen Sea Lion Pavilion, Berniece Grewcock Butterfly and Insect Pavilion, and many more! *www.omahazoo.com, 3701 S 10th St*

OMAHA CHILDREN'S MUSEUM For travelers with children, this is the perfect stop for family fun and entertainment. With a variety of permanent exhibitions as well as daily programming in areas such as science and creative arts, this museum in Omaha has great options for visitors traveling in all seasons. *www.ocm.com, 500 S 20th St*

SCOTTS BLUFF NATIONAL MONUMENT Visitors who grew up on the early computer game *The Oregon Trail* will thrill to this national monument in Gering, which commemorates one of the main landmarks along the Oregon Trail, the route taken by wagoners heading west. Set 800ft over the North Platte River, the 3000 acres of this national monument surrounding Scotts Bluff are where the route through Mitchell Path was trod by generations of Native Americans and pioneers. Nearby Chimney Rock, another iconic natural formation in the region, was also the site of a Pony Express station. *www.nps.gov/scbl, 190276 Old Oregon Trail, Gering*

ITINERARY

Day 1
Start your adventure in Omaha, the state's largest city (and base of investor extraordinaire Warren Buffet). Follow lunch with a visit to the Joslyn Art Museum. Stroll the beautiful outdoor sculpture garden and end the day with a laid-back dinner of local specialty, runzas.

Day 2
Check out the Henry Doorly Zoo and take a trip across the Missouri River to the nearby Iowa town of Council Bluffs for the Union Pacific Railroad Museum, an important historical landmark only a 10-minute drive away. Head back to Omaha for a steak dinner.

Day 3
Drive out to Lincoln via the Eugene T Mahoney State Park, a convenient stop on the way to Lincoln that has hiking trails, a treetop ropes course, rock climbing and more. Then visit the Museum of Nebraska History to learn all about the moments that shaped Nebraska's past.

Day 4
Explore the Sandhills region as you follow in the path of the Oregon Trail toward Scotts Bluff National Monument.

From left: Carhenge; Scotts Bluff National Monument.

NEVADA

★ ★

POPULATION: 3 million | **SIZE:** 110,567 sq miles | **STATE CAPITAL:** Carson City
LARGEST CITY: Las Vegas | **WEBSITE:** https://travelnevada.com

OUT IN THE DUSTY, ROASTING-HOT DESERTS OF THE SOUTHWEST, NEVADA CONJURES UP SOME of the wildest images in the States – both with the razzmatazz of its parties and glitzy shows (we need only say 'Vegas, baby') and the eerie, vast, spellbinding wilderness beyond, where arid plains run to the snowcapped peaks of the Sierra Nevada. In this state of contrasts, you'll find Mormon churches and casinos in happy coexistence. Lonely roads (including America's loneliest) lead to forgotten ghost towns rooted in pioneering legend and to middle-of-nowhere valleys where UFOs are often rumored. Weird? You bet. Wonderful? Most certainly, from the playas of the Black Rock Desert to the expanses of the Great Basin to the dry-as-a-bone Death Valley. This state is for daredevils, opportunists, dreamers, and outdoors lovers. Entertainment-seekers will have their fill as well.

© Gary Yeowell / Getty Images

FOOD & DRINK

MEXICAN FOOD Nevada's population of three million is 30% Latino, with the dining options to prove it. The Downtown Container Park in Vegas includes some great taco trucks, but going even further afield into the everyday neighborhoods of Las Vegas is where you'll find the most authentic eateries (favorite Jefe's is in a gas station in the northwest of the city).

MICROBREWING One reason to detour to Carson City and Reno is to stop by their independent, retro-cool microbreweries and delicious brewpubs. Carson's Shoetree Brewing is the brainchild of two beer-mad brothers, Jeff and Paul Young. Go for a tasting or try specials like root beer stout (brewed with sassafras, licorice root and spearmint), mocha porter (with coffee and chocolate) and cherry-infused sour ale. In Reno the renovated East 4th Street warehouses turn out tipples with distinction at The Depot Craft Brewery and Under the Rose Brewing.

PINE NUTS Native Americans have been harvesting these sweet, buttery little nuts for 10,000 years. You can join in the harvesting tradition at Great Basin National Park each fall, when the single-leaf piñon offers up its bounty. They're perfect for making pesto or pignoli cookies.

STEAK AND EGGS Casino workers and late-night gamblers alike delight in the cheap plates of 'steggs' available early in the Vegas morning hours from 24-hr diners like the Ellis Island Cafe. Not into slumming it? Richly upholstered half-moon booths,

domed lights and impeccably polite waiters set the super-stylish tone at Joe Vicari's Andiamo Steakhouse, perfect for high rollers looking for their steak plate fix.

VEGAS FINE DINING The acclaimed Joël Robuchon led the pack in the French culinary invasion of the Strip, and was promptly followed by other top chefs from the world over. Robuchon's plush, chandelier-lit dining rooms, with midnight-blue walls and velvet banquettes, feel like a dinner party at a 1930s Paris mansion. Meanwhile, Nobu has Vegas outposts for high-end sushi, and celebrity chef offerings pop up like mushrooms (or truffles, in this instance). Complex seasonal tasting menus at high-end Vegas restaurants promise the meal of a lifetime – and they often deliver.

NATURAL ESCAPES

CATHEDRAL GORGE STATE PARK
Sidling up to the Utah border in eastern Nevada near Panaca, this park enchants with its spectacular cathedral-like spires, starkly eroded bentonite clay cliffs and slot canyons in buff pinks and rust reds. The result of volcanic activity millions of years ago, the formations are best explored on the 4-mile ridge trail. Keep an eye out for wildlife including cottontail rabbits, gophers, hummingbirds and roadrunners. *http://parks.nv.gov*

DEATH VALLEY NATIONAL PARK
Straddling the Nevada–California border, the very name of this national park near Beatty recalls all that is harsh, hot and hellish – a punishing, barren and lifeless

---

★ ★ ★

America's Loneliest Road:
HIGHWAY 50

Cutting across the heart of Nevada, Highway 50 (US-50) links Carson City in the west to Great Basin National Park in the east, and is better known by its nickname, The Loneliest Road in America. Barren, brown desert hills collide with big blue skies on the asphalt. The highway goes on forever, crossing solitary terrain, with towns few and far between, and the only sounds are the whisper of wind or the rattle-and-hum of a truck engine. Once part of the Lincoln Highway, Highway 50 follows the route of the Overland Stagecoach, the Pony Express and the first telegraph line to link the coasts.

Left: Cathedral Gorge State Park.

© encrier / Getty Images; Left: © lukas bischoff / Alamy Stock Photo

© encrier / Getty Images; Left: © lukas bischoff / Alamy Stock Photo

★ ★ ★

Burning MAN

For a week in August, 'Burners' from around the world flock to the Black Rock Desert to build the temporary Black Rock City for the Burning Man festival, only to tear it all down again at the end. In between, peace, love, music, art, nudity, drugs, sex and frivolity rule in a safe space where attendees uphold the principles of the festival and Silicon Valley types descend in a flurry. When it's over, 'leave no trace.'

place. It's the hottest, driest and lowest national park in the US. Look more closely, though, and you'll also find singing sand dunes, water-sculpted canyons, boulders moving across the desert floor, extinct volcanic craters, palm-shaded oases and endemic wildlife. *www.nps.gov/deva*

GREAT BASIN NATIONAL PARK Wheeler Peak, Nevada's highest mountain, rising abruptly from the desert to 13,063ft, is the icing on the cake of this uncrowded national park near Baker and the Nevada–Utah border. Hiking trails take in glacial lakes, high mountains, limestone caves and gnarly 4000-year-old bristlecone pine trees. Or tick off some of the highlights on the 12-mile Scenic Drive. The night skies are some of America's darkest. *www.nps.gov/grba*

RED ROCK CANYON NATIONAL CONSERVATION AREA Vegas is right nearby but feels a world away from the bare, rugged, starkly eroded Red Rock Canyon. Shaped by extreme tectonic forces

some 65 million years ago, the canyon's 3000ft red rock escarpment rises sharply from the valley floor. A 13-mile, one-way scenic loop drive offers arresting views of the canyon's most striking features. Hiking trails and rock-climbing routes radiate from roadside parking areas. *www. redrockcanyonlv.org, 1000 Scenic Loop Dr*

TULE SPRINGS FOSSIL BEDS NATIONAL MONUMENT Up to some 20,000 years ago, Las Vegas was filled with lush vegetation and freshwater lakes that supported now-extinct creatures like Columbian mammoths, giant ground sloths and North American lions. Their fossils were laid down along the now-dry northern edge of the valley, where the national monument was eventually established. Paleontology fans are free to wander about with a camera. *www.nps.gov/tusk, northeast of US-95*

VALLEY OF FIRE STATE PARK A breath of fresh desert air after the madness of Vegas, this astounding showcase of southwestern

From left: A scene from Burning Man; Red Rock Canyon National Conservation Area; the famous Las Vegas sign.

© Chris Hepburn / Getty Images

desert scenery in Overton wows you with 40,000 acres of rippling red Aztec sandstone, petrified trees, slot canyons and ancient Native American petroglyphs at Atlatl Rock. Wind and water worked together to carve out the psychedelic landscape here over millions of years. *http://parks.nv.gov, 29450 Valley of Fire Hwy*

ARTS, HISTORY & CULTURE

HOOVER DAM Towering above the Black Canyon of the Colorado River on the Nevada–Arizona border, the Hoover Dam elicits gasps of wonder as it emerges from the stark landscape. At the height of the Depression, thousands migrated here and worked in excruciating conditions in 120°F heat to build this massive 726ft-high, art deco-style dam, completed ahead of schedule and under budget in 1936. Ninety-six workers lost their lives building the iconic art deco-styled structure. Visitors continue to ooh and ahh over their impressive handiwork. *www.usbr.gov/lc/hooverdam, near Boulder City*

MOB MUSEUM Taking a detour down a dark alley into Las Vegas' underworld, the museum lifts a lid on the gangster culture in Sin City and elsewhere. Housed in a historic federal courthouse where mobsters sat for FBI hearings in 1950–51, the museum's exhibits whisk you from the birth of the mob to the forbidden spirits and flappers in Prohibition-era underground speakeasies. *https://themobmuseum.org, 300 Stewart Ave*

NEON MUSEUM 'Neon never dies' could be the tagline of this kooky open-air Vegas museum. In the Neon Boneyard, glittering vintage neon signs – Las Vegas' original art form – spend their retirement. Kick off at the visitors center inside the salvaged La Concha Motel lobby, a mid-century icon designed by African American architect Paul Revere Williams. Book tours ahead – they're most spectacular at night, when the colors and designs overwhelm the eye. *www.neonmuseum.org, 770 N Las Vegas Blvd*

FUN FACT

Death Valley is officially the hottest place on earth. In July 1913, temps at Furnace Creek nudged 134°F, the highest ever recorded.

© MedFaiFotograf / Shutterstock; Left: © Paul Lemke / Getty Images

★ ★ ★

WHERE GHOSTS LIVE

Nevada is home to more than 600 ghost towns – all echoes of once-thriving communities. The queen of these is Rhyolite. Founded in 1905 and abandoned a decade later after its gold petered out, it's an eerie and atmospheric place with decaying original buildings, including a railroad depot and the Bottle House, a house made from 50,000 beer bottles. More intact is Berlin, within Berlin-Ichthyosaur State Park. This former mining town reached its height in 1908, and its tiny cabins still hold original furniture. North of Wells is Metropolis, a one-of-a-kind ghost town intended to be a wheat harvesting settlement. The unpredictable climate put those plans to rest, however, and it was deserted in the 1940s – though ruins of its school, hotel and a cemetery still remain.

NEVADA MUSEUM OF ART Evoking the geological formations of the Black Rock Desert north of town, this architecturally striking behemoth harbors Reno's prized art museum. A floating staircase leads to galleries showcasing temporary exhibits and broad-ranging collections on the American West and contemporary landscape photography. For killer views of the Sierra Nevada, head up to the Sky Room area's rooftop penthouse and patio. *www.nevadaart.org, 160 W. Liberty St*

NATIONAL AUTOMOBILE MUSEUM This hands-on museum in Reno steps things up a gear with its enormous collection of classic cars spanning over a century of automobile history. Here you can view one-of-a-kind vehicles, including James Dean's 1949 Mercury from *Rebel Without a Cause*, Elvis Presley's 1973 Cadillac Eldorado, and John Wayne's 1953 Chevrolet Corvette. Exhibits showcase all kinds of souped-up and fabulously retro rides. *www.automuseum.org, 10 S. Lake St*

O Alluding to the French word for water (*eau*), this stunning aquatic-themed Cirque du Soleil show on Vegas' Strip is a dramatic feat of imagination and engineering, with lithe acrobats, synchronized swimmers, divers and special effects on a custom-built stage. As such, it is insanely popular, so you'll be lucky to snag tickets – and you'll pay full price for them. Thankfully there's no shortage of other Cirque du Soleil show options if it's fully booked. *www.bellagio.com, Bellagio, 3600 S. Las Vegas Blvd*

VIRGINIA CITY The discovery of the Comstock Lode in 1859 sparked a silver bonanza in this mountain town near Reno. During the 1860s gold rush, Virginia City was a high-flying, rip-roaring Wild West boomtown. Journalist Samuel Clemens, alias Mark Twain, spent time here during its heyday, describing his mining life in *Roughing It*. Far from the lights of Las Vegas, the National Historic Landmark District here has a main street of Victorian buildings, wooden sidewalks and some

From left: A crumbling building at Rhyolite, an abandoned town near Death Valley; Hoover Dam; Highway 375.

© Nebs / Shutterstock

hokey but fun museums.
https://visitvirginiacitynv.com

WESTERN FOLKLIFE CENTER
Would-be cowboys and cowgirls should head on over to the redbrick Pioneer Hotel in Elko, a remote town with Wild West spirit. Here you'll find a gallery with art and history exhibits, videos of ranch life, and events from gigs to dances. In late January it hosts the Cowboy Poetry Gathering, with performances and workshops zooming in on the likes of spit cooking and rawhide braiding. *www.westernfolklife.org, 501 Railroad St*

FAMILY OUTINGS

THE DISCOVERY Learn through play at this interactive museum in downtown Reno, covering science, technology, art and math in its themed galleries. There are labs with fun experiments, discovery corners with brainteasers, art rooms, an 'Under the Stars' natural history area, a jungle

gym modeling Nevada's water cycle, and a climb-and-crawl space for tots. *https://nvdm.org, 490 S Center St*

LEHMAN CAVES This cave in Great Basin National Park near Baker has the wow factor, eliciting wonder with its staggeringly ornate depths. Visits on guided tours reveal veritable curtains of stalagmites and stalactites, and there are intricate limestone formations like columns, draperies, popcorn, flowstone, soda straws and rare shields to admire. Bring a jacket; it gets cold down here! *www.nps.gov/grba, 5500 NV-488*

SAND HARBOR, LAKE TAHOE Making a splash on the Nevada–California border, Lake Tahoe shimmers in cobalt blue, emerald and turquoise, rimmed by cedars and pines and backdropped by the snowcapped Sierra Nevada range. Families are in their element at Sand Harbor, near Incline Village, with rocky coves, beaches and shallow water for swimming and

★ ★ ★

Aliens
AND
Earthlings

Highway 375 (NV-375) is dubbed the Extraterrestrial Highway both for its huge number of UFO sightings and because it intersects US-93 near top-secret Area 51, part of Nellis Air Force Base, rumored a holding area for captured UFOs. It's a desolate stretch that some people find unnerving, and you'll be grateful when you see signs of earthling life in the remote town of Rachel, self-proclaimed UFO Capital of the World. Here you can stop for refreshments and alien-themed souvenirs, and spend the night (if you dare) at the Little A'Le'Inn.

©Jon Hicks / Getty Images; Right: © Alexander Davidovich / Shutterstock

★ ★ ★

GETTING THERE & AROUND

McCarran International Airport in Las Vegas is the main gateway to the region. Reno-Tahoe International Airport is another option. Greyhound runs long-distance buses in the state, but if you want to explore Nevada's remoter regions, you're going to need to rent a car.

snorkeling, boating and relaxation. *http://parks.nv.gov, 2005 NV-28*

SHARK REEF AQUARIUM In Vegas extravagant attractions in casino lobbies are par for the course, and kids will have a blast at Mandalay Bay's whopping aquarium, with walk-through tunnels for gawping at 2000 submarine beasties, such as green turtles, frilly lionfish and 15 species of sharks. Highlights include a 1.3 million-gallon shipwreck exhibition and hands-on touch pools. Diver caretakers and naturalists are available to chat as you wander around. Better (and more

extravagant) still, pay to go scuba diving yourself. *www.sharkreef.com, 3950 Las Vegas Blvd S*

THE STRATOSPHERE Kids of all ages will beg you to take them to this 1149ft-high tapered tripod tower. Besides unrivaled views of Las Vegas from the viewing decks and Top of the World revolving restaurant, it has the nation's highest thrill rides, including Big Shot, pinballing you into the air at 45mph, the X-Scream roller coaster and the heart-stopping SkyJump bungee drop (for ages 14 and up). Only in Vegas could an amusement ride veer over the edge of a

Days 1 & 2
Begin in Las Vegas, that
city of spangles, gambles
and theme-park-like
hotels. Between slot
machines, roller coasters
and Cirque du Soleil
spectacles, allow time for
attractions like the Neon
Museum. In the evening,
reserve tables ahead for
showstopper restaurants.
(You can stay based in
Vegas for your next few
days of excursions.)

Day 3
Go west from Vegas to
Red Rock Canyon, hiking
out for views across the
rugged, rusty rockscapes.
Time permitting, you
could drive north to the
Tule Springs Fossil Beds,
where Columbian
mammoths once roamed.

Day 4
Head east to Lake Mead
and the mind-blowing
Hoover Dam and the
Valley of Fire, with slot
canyons, petrified trees
and petroglyphs.

Day 5
Head west toward Califor-
nia to the hottest, driest
place in the US, Death
Valley National Park.

Day 6
Finish in Reno, city of
roulette wheels and rapid
waters, where sights like
the National Automobile
Museum beckon.

**From left: The Las
Vegas Strip; Lake
Tahoe.**

skyrise roof. *www.stratospherehotel.com,
2000 S Las Vegas Blvd*

THE STRIP Take the ideals of freedom
and abundance to their extremes, and
what happens is The Strip (a section
of S. Las Vegas Boulevard). It is Vegas'
entertainment central, the epicenter
in a vortex of limitless potential, where
almost anything goes and time becomes
elastic. It's not all about gambling here,
though that's the heartbeat of the casinos;
to distract and entertain, the Bellagio's
fountains awe, Paris Las Vegas has its own
Eiffel Tower, New York-New York offers
a roller coaster, and the Venetian has
gondola rides. The commitment to theme
is a wonder, and merely taking in each
casino's intricate interior world is a great
way to spend time.

TRUCKEE RIVER WHITEWATER PARK
Mere steps from the Reno casinos, this
park has class II and III rapids that are
gentle enough for kids riding inner tubes,
yet sufficiently challenging for professional
freestyle kayakers. Two courses wrap
around Wingfield Park, a small river
island. Outfitters offer kayak trips and
lessons. *www.reno.gov, 1 E 1st St*

NEW HAMPSHIRE

★ ★ ★ ★ ★ ★ ★ ★ ★ ★ ★ ★ ★ ★ ★ ★ ★ ★ ★ ★

POPULATION: 1.3 million | **SIZE:** 9349 sq miles | **STATE CAPITAL:** Concord
LARGEST CITY: Manchester | **WEBSITE:** www.visitnh.gov

NEW HAMPSHIRE'S CITIZENS HAVE LONG VIEWED THEMSELVES AS EMBODYING A CERTAIN STOIC New England tradition. The slogan 'Live Free or Die', credited to Revolutionary War hero (and native son) General John Stark, is inscribed on the state's license plates and taken to heart. Residents are – and this is admittedly a stereotype – contrarians in flannel. Only 1.3 million people live here, and its largest city, Manchester, is home to just over 100,000 residents. Jewel-box colonial settlements like Portsmouth set a sophisticated tone, while historical allure and small-town culture live on in pristine villages like Keene and Peterborough. Jagged mountains, serene valleys and island-dotted lakes fill every corner, and the whole rugged state begs for exploration, whether kayaking the hidden coves of the Lakes Region or trekking the upper peaks surrounding Mt Washington.

© DenisTangneyJr / Getty Images

FOOD & DRINK

APPLE CIDER DOUGHNUTS These treats are typically only available for a short period, during apple-picking season, though during that time you'll find them at farm stands and bakeries throughout the state. Some places selling especially tasty apple cider doughnuts include the Carter Hill Orchard in Concord, the Chichester Country Store and the Meadow Ledge Farm in Loudon.

MAPLE SUNDAES Ice-cream sundaes topped with maple syrup (and often made with maple ice cream too) showcase one of New Hampshire's signature products. Polly's Pancake Parlor in Sugar Hill uses Maple Hurricane Sauce, made by boiling apples in syrup, on their sundaes. Bishop's Homemade Ice Cream in Littleton also serves this New Hampshire dessert.

NATURAL ESCAPES

BRETTON WOODS While Bretton Woods is New Hampshire's largest ski area, skiers used to peaks out west should keep their expectations in check: there are only 10 lifts and 454 acres of skiable terrain. On the plus side, the enormous Nordic area has 62 miles of trails for cross-country skiers and snowshoers, and even 7 miles of dog-friendly trails. *www.brettonwoods.com, 99 Ski Area Rd*

FRANCONIA NOTCH STATE PARK For centuries this park in the White Mountains was the home of the Old Man in the Mountain, a series of cliffs that formed what looked like the profile of a man. The iconic landmark collapsed in 2003 due to natural fissures, but visitors still come to explore a magnificent mountain pass that includes the stunning Flume Gorge and an aerial tramway. *www.nhstateparks.org, Flume Gorge, Daniel Webster Hwy, Lincoln*

MONADNOCK STATE PARK Visible from 50 miles in any direction, the commanding 3165ft peak of Mt Monadnock is southwestern New Hampshire's spiritual vortex. The surrounding state park in Jaffrey is an outdoor wonderland, complete with a visitors center, a camp store, 12 miles of ungroomed cross-country ski trails and over 40 miles of hiking trails, about 10 miles of which reach the summit. The 3.9-mile White Dot & White Cross loop is a popular hiking route to the top. *www.nhstateparks.org, 169 Pool Rd*

SACO RIVER The Saco River, which is south of Mt Washington and flows into Maine, is ideal for first-time canoers. The water is 3ft deep, the rapids aren't too scary, and sandy beaches line its banks. The Saco River Canoe Company in Conway will teach you the basics and get you out on the water. *www.sacocanoerental.com, 558 White Mountain Hwy*

WHITE MOUNTAIN NATIONAL FOREST This forest, New Hampshire's largest wilderness area, straddles the New Hampshire–Maine border. It includes Mt Washington, the tallest peak in the Northeast at 6288ft, some 1200 miles of trails for hikers (including a storied section of the Appalachian Trail) and, in the winter, 400 miles of snowmobile trails. *www.fs.fed.us*

★ ★ ★

THE COG RAILWAY

Built in 1869 the Mt Washington Cog Railway in the White Mountains is one of New Hampshire's most popular attractions. It's an enjoyable way to reach and explore the summit of the Northeast's highest mountain; the railway uses both vintage coal-fired steam and eco-friendly bio-diesel engines. One great argument in its favor? Mt Washington is one of the deadliest summit attempts for hikers in the US. Taking the railway to the 6288ft-high summit may have less cred, but it avoids the rapid shifts in microclimate that can be so dangerously disorienting on the mountain. For those who want to drive, the Mt Washington Auto Road has twists and turns to please the most thrill-seeking motorist. At top is the Mt Washington Observatory Weather Discovery Center.

Left: The covered bridge in Stark.

© Dan Lewis / Shutterstock; Right: © Dan Logan / Shutterstock

★ ★ ★

GETTING THERE & AROUND

Manchester-Boston Regional Airport is the state's largest and offers direct flights to a dozen North American cities. The smaller Lebanon Municipal Airport and Portsmouth International Airport serve Hanover and Portsmouth. The nearby Portland airport, in Maine, is a major hub and offers additional flight options. Car is the best way around the state, though there are some regional bus lines. The Blue Star (or New Hampshire) Turnpike along the seacoast, Everett (or Central) Turnpike (I-93) and Spaulding Turnpike (NH 16) are toll roads. Insurance rules differ here; drivers take care.

ARTS, HISTORY & CULTURE

SAINT-GAUDENS NATIONAL HISTORIC SITE One of the most acclaimed sculptors of the 19th century, Augustus Saint-Gaudens spent many summers in Cornish. Today his home and its extensive grounds are a National Historic Site which houses around 100 of his works. *www.nps.gov/saga, 139 Saint Gaudens Rd*

DARTMOUTH COLLEGE This Ivy League college in Hanover has a postcard-perfect campus just off the Connecticut River, with Georgian-style buildings around the Dartmouth Green and imposing, hushed libraries. Founded in 1769 to educate Native Americans and train Congregationalist ministers, most of the buildings date from the 19th century or later. The college's Hood Museum of Art has an encyclopedic collection, with works from around the world, while the Baker-Berry Library contains José Clemente Orozco's monumental mural cycle *The Epic of American Civilization*, painted by the Mexican artist from 1932 to 1934. *https://home.dartmouth.edu, 6 E Wheelock St*

EXETER Located in southeastern New Hampshire, halfway between Boston and Portland, Maine, Exeter is one of New Hampshire's most picturesque and historic towns. It was briefly the capital of the colony and then state of New Hampshire, a period covered by the American Independence Museum. The Folsom Tavern, where George Washington once slept, has been restored and is part of the museum. *www.exeternh.gov*

ROBERT FROST FARM While poet Robert Frost was born in San Francisco, he is most associated with New England where he spent most of his life and which inspired his pastoral vision. From 1900 to 1911, he lived with his family on this farm in Derry, in southern New Hampshire. In addition to

Day 1
Although New Hampshire has only a thin strip of coastline on the Atlantic, much of the state's population is concentrated in this southeastern corner. Start here and explore Exeter, one of the state's most appealing coastal towns, before heading on to Portsmouth, where you can visit the Strawbery Banke Museum, a recreated historic village that portrays life over the last three centuries. Especially during summer, Portsmouth's waterfront and restaurants are bustling.

Day 2
Immerse yourself in the lives of two cultural giants with visits to the Robert Frost Farm in Derry and the house of Augustus Saint-Gaudens in Cornish. The town of Cornish is also home to one of the state's iconic covered bridges.

Day 3
Spend the morning at Dartmouth College before driving back east to Franconia Notch State Park or the White Mountain National Forest, whose crown jewel is the 6288ft summit of Mt Washington. There's almost no bad time of the year to take in the state's natural beauty and outdoors.

From left: Dartmouth College; the Cog Railway.

providing a glimpse of the poet's world, the museum hosts readings and other literary events. *www.robertfrostfarm.org, 122 Rockingham Rd*

STARK BRIDGE Covered bridges are not unique to New England, but the region is known for its picturesque bounty, built by hand and weathered by the seasons. The bridge in Stark is one of New Hampshire's most beautiful, constructed in 1862; it was threatened with demolition in the 1950s before an outcry saved it. The state publishes an online guide to all 54 bridges. *www.nh.gov/nhdhr/bridges*

FAMILY OUTINGS

CANTERBURY SHAKER VILLAGE At this living-history museum with almost 30 restored and reconstructed Shaker buildings, you can explore the Shaker heritage in Canterbury, which dates to 1792. Interpreters demonstrate the Shakers' daily lives, artisans create Shaker crafts, and walking trails invite pond-side strolls. For more than two centuries the Shakers' abundant gardens have been turning out vegetables, medicinal herbs and bountiful flowers the organic way. You could easily spend half a day on the 700-acre site. A store sells Shaker-inspired handicrafts, and there's a farm stand and a restaurant serving the kind of food grandma used to make. *www.shakers.org, 288 Shaker Rd*

STRAWBERY BANKE MUSEUM This 10-acre 'historic village' in downtown Portsmouth lets you step back in time as you explore 37 restored buildings and talk with costumed interpreters. The museum also has a series of highly unique gardens that span the centuries, including a Colonial garden, one that might have been created by a Ukrainian immigrant, and a 1943 wartime Victory garden. *www.strawberybanke.org, 14 Hancock St*

NEW JERSEY

★ ★

POPULATION: 8.9 million | **SIZE:** 8722 sq miles | **STATE CAPITAL:** Trenton
LARGEST CITY: Newark | **WEBSITE:** www.visitnj.org

NEW JERSEY SUFFERS A BAD RAP – IT'S THE BUTT OF TOO MANY UNFAIR JOKES, AND THE SUCCESS of the MTV series *Jersey Shore* did the state no favors. There is more, however, to New Jersey than its shopping malls and highway network. Its fertile farmland grows some of the country's best corn and tomatoes, and more than 50 resort towns along the Atlantic Coast offer 127 miles of beautiful beaches. The shore towns run the gamut from funky Asbury Park to stately Cape May. Inland, much of early US history played out here, given the state's location sandwiched between Philadelphia and New York City. Travelers will find overlooked gems like the Princeton University Art Museum and Newark Museum. And, yes, there is some wilderness to be found even in the most densely populated state in the country, such as the isolated Pine Barrens and the Delaware Water Gap.

© Car Culture / Getty Images

FOOD & DRINK

ASIAN FAVORITES With New Jersey's large Asian community concentrated on the west bank of the Hudson, noodles and dumplings are local specialties. Mitsuwa in Edgewater is an enormous Japanese emporium where you can stock up on straight-from-Japan products while the food court inside has stalls serving tempura, ramen bowls and treats both savory and sweet. The population of Palisades Park is 65% Korean and many excellent Korean restaurants are found by Broad Avenue.

DINERS New Jersey is the land of diners, which dot its highways and main streets. A visit to New Jersey should include a meal at one; Tops Diner in East Newark is a good choice. From French toast and waffles to burgers and shakes, you'll find American comfort food favorites in an appealingly retro 1920s–style building. The Vincentown Diner, another local favorite with a Greek twist, is famous for its Mile-High Meatloaf.

SALTWATER TAFFY For many people, chewy pastel-colored saltwater taffy is the flavor of summer. Some stores in New Jersey shore towns have been selling the candy since the 19th century – often producing it on-site. Taffy also makes a great souvenir of your New Jersey trip. Check out Shriver's in Ocean City, James Candy Company in Atlantic City and Ocean City, and Seaside Heights' Berkeley Candy.

TOP DOGS New Jersey has some unique regional variations on the hot dog that frankfurter fans will want to sneak out.

Rutt's Hut in Clifton is the home of the 'ripper,' a deep-fried hot dog. (When the sausages are fried, the casings rip open, hence the name.) Jimmy Buff's in West Orange serves 'Italian hot dogs,' one or two sausages served in an Italian pizza bread roll with grilled peppers and onions.

NATURAL ESCAPES

BENJAMIN T BYRNE STATE FOREST
Over 37,000 acres of peaceful state forest beckon in the New Jersey Pine Barrens between Philadelphia and the Jersey Shore. The trails here pass through the hardwood and Atlantic white cedar swamps, pitch pine lowlands and upland pine and oak forests, which visitors have almost to themselves. Visit the nearby Whitesbog Village after hiking the forest to see one of New Jersey's first cranberry bogs, and the place where the highbush blueberry was cultivated. Nature trails wind through the property.
www.state.nj.us/dep/parksandforests, Hwy Rte 72 E, Woodland Township

DELAWARE WATER GAP Much of New Jersey is developed, either as cities or suburbia, but there are still some corners of wilderness to be found. The Delaware Water Gap National Recreation Area includes the 'gap' created by the Delaware River. On its west bank are Pennsylvania's Blue Mountains and on its east, New Jersey's Kittatinny Ridge.
www.nps.gov/dewa/index.htm

SANDY HOOK GATEWAY NATIONAL RECREATION AREA Once a military base, Fort Hancock has been folded into

★ ★ ★

New Jersey's
OWN MONSTER

New Jersey's NHL ice hockey team gets its name, the Devils, from the state's legendary monster. The devil is said to live in the Pine Barrens in the south of the state and is typically described as having the hooves of a goat and bat-like wings. Some have speculated that reported sightings of the animal, which date back to the 18th century, may have been caused by confusion with sandhill cranes, seen from a distance on dark nights. Merchants in Camden, New Jersey, and the Philadelphia Zoo have both offered rewards, yet to be collected, for the live capture of a devil. Keep your eyes peeled around the Pine Barrens. You may be able to cash in and more than cover the cost of your New Jersey vacation.

Left: The Bendix Diner in Hasbrouck Heights.

© Richard T. Nowitz / Getty Images; Left: © Tom Mendola / Getty Images

★ ★ ★

ASK A LOCAL

'The Great Falls, northwest of downtown Paterson, is one of New Jersey's best sights. The roar of the Passaic River falling 77ft drowns out the noise of the city, and through the mist, visitors can see the now abandoned mills. Paterson was America's first planned industrial city and its mills and factories produced silk hats, guns and locomotives for the new nation. The mills are being converted into residences and a museum, and after visiting the falls you can experience Paterson's diversity by dining at its Latin American, Caribbean and Middle Eastern restaurants.'
– *Bruce Harris, mayor of Chatham, New Jersey*

the Gateway National Recreation Area, which spans across the water to Staten Island and Jamaica Bay. Here you'll find the nation's oldest lighthouse, excellent birding in a holly forest, outstanding views of Manhattan's skyline on clear days, beautiful white dunes, and even a nude beach alongside a gay beach (Area G). Best of all, you can get here via a ferry from Lower Manhattan in a cool and salty 45 minutes. Bring your bike along for the ride, and you can enjoy the paved bike paths through the dunes and pedal on to the nearby towns of Atlantic Highlands and Highlands. *www.nps.gov/gate/index.htm, 128 S Hartshorne Dr, Highlands*

ARTS, HISTORY & CULTURE

GROUNDS FOR SCULPTURE Located on 42 acres that were once part of the New Jersey State Fairgrounds in Trenton, Grounds for Sculpture is home to 270 sculptures from dozens of leading artists, scattered around a landscaped park. The former fairground buildings host temporary exhibitions. *www.groundsforsculpture.org, 80 Sculptors Way, Hamilton*

LAMBERTVILLE Set on the Delaware and Raritan Canal, Lambertville rose and fell with the canal. In the 19th century, merchants built elegant townhouses here, but after commerce moved to the highways, Lambertville fell into a slump. Now its homes are once again coveted and are being lovingly restored, and the town is still approached through a striking covered bridge linking it to quaint New Hope, Pennsylvania. With its many antique shops and inviting restaurants, Lambertville is best explored on foot. *www.lambertvillenj.org*

LIBERTY STATE PARK Even if you aren't making the journey to New York's Ellis Island and the Statue of Liberty – ferries to both depart from the park – you can take in postcard views of the Manhattan skyline from here. The Liberty Science Center, located in the park, has kid-friendly interactive exhibits like the pitch-black

From left: The Great Falls in Paterson; Victorian homes and hotels line Cape May; Thomas Edison's laboratory in West Orange.

© Helen89 / Shutterstock

Touch Tunnel and the musical Dream Machine. *https://lsc.org*

MUSEUM OF AMERICAN GLASS With its sandy soil, the pine barrens of southern New Jersey have been a center of glass manufacturing for over two centuries; silica, commonly found in sand, is an essential component of glass. Many of the objects on display at this museum in the WheatonArts and Cultural Center were originally created in the area and include items from glass caskets to the world's largest glass bottle. The museum is open from April to December, and there is also a glassblowing facility. *www.wheatonarts.org, 1501 Glasstown Rd, Millville*

NEWARK MUSEUM The state's largest museum is located in several different buildings, including its original 1920s home and the neighboring YWCA, renovated by architect Michael Graves after it was acquired by the museum. Its permanent collection includes some of the most important works by 19th- and 20th-century

American painters and also, surprisingly, a world-class selection of Tibetan art. *www.newarkmuseum.org, 49 Washington St*

OLD BARRACKS MUSEUM Given its location in the middle of the mid-Atlantic, New Jersey was the crossroads of the Revolutionary War, and Trenton's Old Barracks Museum is the only surviving British barracks in North America. Among the artifacts it houses is the Pine Tree flag, believed to be the oldest American flag. Costumed interpreters bring colonial America to life for visitors. *www.barracks. org, 101 Barrack St, Trenton*

PRINCETON Ivy League Princeton University is the fourth-oldest institution of higher learning in the United States, and any tour of its 500-acre campus should include Nassau Hall, the country's capitol for six months in 1783. It also boasts a first-class art museum. A charming (if rather well-heeled) college town, downtown Princeton's upscale shops and restaurants

FUN FACT

While New Jersey has much to brag about, its 7 malls in a 25-sq-mile radius is a hard to beat stat.

© MyLoupe / Getty Images

Newark International Airport serves North Jersey, while Shore visitors can fly into Philly. Though many NJ folks love their cars (and the NJ Turnpike, completed in 1951, was dubbed 'the greatest highway of all'), transport options are plentiful. The PATH train connects lower Manhattan to Hoboken, Jersey City and Newark. NJTransit operates buses and trains around the state, including buses to NYC's Port Authority and trains to Penn Station, NYC.

are centered around Palmer Square. *www.visitprinceton.org*

THOMAS EDISON NATIONAL HISTORIC PARK
Thomas Alva Edison has been described as 'America's greatest inventor,' with a list of accomplishments that includes the light bulb, the motion-picture camera, and advances in areas from the telegraph to the electrical grid systems. In all, he filed 2332 patents in his lifetime. The National Historic Park includes his laboratory and his stately home, Glenmont. *www.nps.gov/edis/index.htm, 211 Main St, West Orange*

FAMILY OUTINGS

ATLANTIC CITY
Atlantic City may be best known for its casinos, and bets still fly here. It is also, however, a family destination with a boardwalk lined with stores selling

saltwater taffy and souvenirs, 'rolling chairs' carrying tourists, the Steel Pier amusement park (which dates from 1898), an aquarium and an IMAX theater. *www.atlanticcitynj.com*

CAPE MAY
America's oldest seaside resort sits at the southern end of the Jersey Shore. While other towns have similar fudge and taffy shops, Cape May's many Victorian buildings, with their gingerbread details painted in colorful hues, set it apart. Even if you don't stay there, drop by Congress Hall, an enormous hotel which first opened in 1816 (the current building dates from 1879). *www.capemaycity.com*

FIELD STATION: DINOSAURS
This attraction near Fort Lee includes 32 animatronic dinosaurs located throughout an outdoor campus. It's not quite Jurassic Park, but for a kid with a vivid imagination it

© jvphoto.ca / Shutterstock

★

ITINERARY

Day 1
Assuming you will be visiting the state in summer, start on the coast at Sandy Hook or funkier Asbury Park.

Day 2
Spend the day driving south, with stops at other shore towns like Long Beach, on a barrier island hugging the coast, or Atlantic City and visit the casinos or the historic boardwalk. End the day in Cape May; with one of the largest historic districts in the state, it's a well-preserved Victorian seaside town.

Day 3
Enjoy the morning in Cape May before heading to Trenton with visits to some of the capital's historic sites like the Old Barracks Museum and the stately capitol; built in 1790, it's one of the US's oldest statehouses. Continue north to Lambertville, where 19th-century merchants' homes now house restaurants and boutiques (you can also hop over the border to charming New Hope, in Pennsylvania).

Day 4
Today visit Princeton, an upscale college town with a historic university. In Morristown, explore one of General Washington's winter headquarters.

From left: Wildwood; Sandy Hook.

can pass for one. The Paleontologists' Lab and the park's staff attempt to elevate the amusement park experience by including some educational aspects to visits to this unique New Jersey attraction. *www.fieldstationdinosaurs.com, Overpeck County Park, Leonia*

LUCY THE ELEPHANT Lucy is a survivor. This six-story elephant-shaped building was erected in 1881 to promote real estate sales near Atlantic City. While other novelty attractions have been demolished over the years, Lucy has the distinction of being the oldest such building in America. Visitors can climb through the building and ascend to her howdah with its views of Margate. *www.lucytheelephant.org, 9200 Atlantic Avenue*

WHIPPANY RAILWAY MUSEUM This museum is worth a detour even if it is a somewhat odd hodgepodge of items saved from destruction, including the Whippany station itself and various train crossing gates and signs. Its vintage engines and other cars come from various railroads, mostly from the Northeast. The museum also runs excursion trains on the old Morris County Central Railroad tracks several times a year, to the delight of passengers. *www.whippanyrailwaymuseum.net, 1 Railroad Plaza*

WILDWOOD Where Cape May is a celebration of a Victorian version of a seaside resort, its neighbor to the north, Wildwood, is a funkier 1950s/60s one. Many of the neon signs of motels still bring a glow to the community every night, while the amusement park on its boardwalk makes it a draw for families, including day-trippers from other Jersey Shore communities. *http://njwildwood.com*

NEW MEXICO

★ ★

POPULATION: 2.1 million | **SIZE:** 121,697 sq miles | **STATE CAPITAL:** Santa Fe
LARGEST CITY: Albuquerque | **WEBSITE:** www.newmexico.org

WHEN YOU ASK WHY SOMEONE MOVED TO NEW MEXICO, YOU'LL HEAR ANSWERS LIKE 'the magical light' or 'the smell of piñon pines at dawn.' There's just something about the Land of Enchantment that's, well, enchanting. It's the endless vistas of sagebrush in the high desert. It's the wildflower-spangled alpine meadows in the Sangre de Cristo Mountains, where snow still frosts the peaks even in summer. It's the dusty smell of roasting chiles (New Mexico spells its red and green peppers with an *e*) in the air each fall. And it's the culture, a singular mix of Native and European – Ancestral Puebloan dwellings inhabited for centuries, Spanish colonial churches, flea markets hawking tamales and turquoise, quirky spa towns offering crystal massages. And, oh yes, the food: hot sopapillas with honey, green chile cheeseburgers, and steaming piñon coffee mean your taste buds will be in heaven.

© Justin Foulkes / Lonely Planet

FOOD & DRINK

CARNE ADOVADA The New Mexican twist of this delicious braised pork is in the marinade of rich red chile (adovada means 'marinated' in Spanish). The pork is stewed in chile until it's falling apart, then served with warm, buttered flour tortillas. Sample it while in the village of Chimayó, famous for its red chile.

GREEN CHILE CHICKEN ENCHILADAS You'd be hard-pressed to come up with a more popular New Mexican dish than this. Corn tortillas layered with chicken, cheese and the state favorite green chile are stacked (not rolled as in Tex-Mex cooking) and baked. Try it at Duran Central Pharmacy, a hidden restaurant in the back of a historic downtown Albuquerque pharmacy.

MAIZE Cultivated in New Mexico for centuries, maize (or corn) has long been the staple ingredient used by Native American Pueblo cooks. In addition to yellow and white, more colorful varieties of corn, including red and blue, are used to make tortillas, and blue corn tortilla chips are a common starter on many restaurant tables here. Posole is common also; boiled maize is cooked for hours with pork shoulder, red chile and garlic, making a kind of corn-like, porky stew that's impossible to resist. Posole is traditionally eaten with tamales on New Mexican Christmas tables.

SOPAPILLA You may see this name used for some fry breads in parts of Latin America, but New Mexican sopapillas are distinct. Rectangular fluffy, crispy dough fried in oil, sopapillas accompany every New Mexican meal and can be used to mop up leftover chile. More popularly, they're drizzled in honey and eaten, hot and crispy, as a dessert.

NATURAL ESCAPES

CARLSBAD CAVERNS NATIONAL PARK Descend beneath the sunny Chihuahuan Desert into this vast and chilly cave system. You'll gawk at the Big Room, the size of 11 football fields, shiver over the Bottomless Pit and marvel at formations resembling coral, pearls and angels. In summer, watch 400,000 bats emerge from the cave's mouth at sunset. *www.nps.gov/cave*

CHACO CULTURE NATIONAL HISTORICAL PARK The Ancestral Puebloan people began building around this remote canyon more than 1000 years ago, making Chaco one of the oldest ruins in the US. Come to see their ancient handiwork, hike the mesas and contemplate the stars – the area is a certified International Dark Sky Park, meaning the Milky Way glows here like you've probably never seen. *www.nps.gov/chcu*

WHITE SANDS NATIONAL MONUMENT Close your eyes and you can almost hear the ocean at this fantastical inland dune field, with its 275 sq miles of white gypsum sand glittering in the pitiless New Mexico sun. Picnic, hike or rent a saucer and 'sled' down the sand. Don't miss the otherworldly sunrise and sunset, when the skies turn a Martian orange and the sand glows pink. *www.nps.gov/whsa*

★ ★ ★

Albuquerque
INTERNATIONAL BALLOON
Fiesta

Each October some 500 hot-air balloons take to Albuquerque's skies like a flock of strange birds. The largest balloon festival in the world, the Fiesta has been an annual event since 1972. Find balloon races, rides, launches of penguin-, cacti- and Darth Vader-shaped balloons, and a general atmosphere of music- and burrito-fueled merriment. Don't miss the after-dark launches of glowing balloons, which look like the landing of an alien sky armada.

Left: The 1583ft peak of Shiprock rising up in Navajo Nation.

© LizCoughlan / Shutterstock; Left: © Steve Snowden / Getty Images

★ ★ ★

BREAKING BAD

Over its run from 2008 to 2013, TV series *Breaking Bad* became a cult hit, helped by the vast blue skies and sweeping desert scenes that gave the show its iconic atmosphere. Creator and writer Vince Gilligan said that over the course of the show, the city of Albuquerque became an integral character on the show. These beautiful, stark and sometimes lonely vistas have drawn fans to the Duke City in search of Heisenberg's hometown. If you're looking to discover Walter White's city, there are lots of ways to tour Albuquerque (including some wonderful tour companies focused on the show), but it's just as easy to find your own way. The most recognizable of the *Breaking Bad* locations are situated in the Northeast Heights, including Walter White's house and the A1 Car Wash. Just don't throw pizza on the roof.

ARTS, HISTORY & CULTURE

BANDELIER NATIONAL MONUMENT

Climb wooden ladders to explore cave homes carved from the cliffs by the Ancestral Puebloans, who lived in the Jemez Mountains near Santa Fe a millennium ago. See their kivas (ceremonial buildings), paintings and petroglyphs, hike the canyonlands (or snowshoe, in winter) and watch out for black bears and coyotes. Summer weekends bring illuminating demonstrations of Pueblo pottery making, bread baking, drumming and dances. *www.nps.gov/band, Los Alamos*

EL SANTUARIO DE CHIMAYÓ Thousands

of pilgrims journey annually to this 1816 chapel in Chimayó to partake of the allegedly healing earth from its floor – some eat the dirt, but it's recommended that you save it in a special tin instead. Inside the church's adobe walls are dark wood beams and a hand-painted altar; a side room is hung with emotional testimonials of prayers answered. The chapel is a link to an earlier period of Spanish rule and Puebloan worship. *www.holychimayo.us, 15 Santuario Dr*

GILA CLIFF DWELLINGS NATIONAL

MONUMENT These remarkable 13th-century cliff dwellings were only occupied by a small Mogollon group of 30 to 80 people for some 20 years. It's unclear why the dwellings, perfectly situated in six alcoves (some of which are enormous), were suddenly abandoned, but the buildings remain relatively intact. It's a long and winding road from Silver City (average time two hours), but pictographs, hot springs, endless hiking opportunities and superb vistas combine to make it a must. *www.nps.gov/gicl, NM-15*

GEORGIA O'KEEFFE MUSEUM New

Mexico's most iconic artist, O'Keeffe began spending time here in the 1920s, taking inspiration from the state's striped mesas and lonely vistas. She eventually settled near Santa Fe, where she died at 98. This adobe building in Santa Fe has the

From left: The Octopus Car Wash (location of the A1 Car Wash in *Breaking Bad*) in Albequerque; El Santuario de Chimayó; interactive art exhibit inside Meow Wolf: House of Eternal Return.

© Kate Russell / courtesy of Meow Wolf

largest collection of her work anywhere, though many of O'Keeffe's most famous paintings are in museums elsewhere, and the museum can also arrange tours of her former home in nearby Abiquiú. *www.okeeffemuseum.org, 217 Johnson St*

INDIAN PUEBLO CULTURAL CENTER
Run by New Mexico's 19 pueblos (Native communities), this Albuquerque museum is a crucial introduction to Native life and history. See displays on food, beliefs, music and dress – past exhibits have covered topics from state-run Native schools to moccasin making. Then lunch on Pueblo-inspired cuisine (elk with corn porridge, fry-bread tacos) at the site's cafe. *www.indianpueblo.org, 2401 12th St NW*

LOS ALAMOS This placid high desert town outside Santa Fe birthed one of humanity's darkest inventions, the atomic bomb – the Manhattan Project was conducted here in utter secrecy. Today the area is still dominated by scientists from the Los Alamos National Laboratory; visit to learn about the history of their research at the local Bradbury Science Museum, which includes sobering life-size models of the Little Boy and Fat Man A-bombs. *www.lanl.gov/museum, 1350 Central Ave*

MEOW WOLF: HOUSE OF ETERNAL RETURN
Fantasy writer George RR Martin bought this 20,000-sq-ft bowling alley in Santa Fe and turned it over to the Meow Wolf art collective, who transformed the space into a mind-blowing immersive exhibit centering on the mystery of a disappeared family. Explore their house and trip into other dimensions of neon-glowing forests and mad scientists. The site has a concert venue as well. *https:// meowwolf.com/santa-fe, 1352 Rufina Circle*

SANTA FE'S CANYON ROAD This former Puebloan footpath is now the center of Santa Fe's ritzy southwestern art scene, with some 100 galleries in flower-draped adobe houses. You'll find everything from Native carvings to contemporary paintings, as well as some of the best food in the city.

FUN FACT

New Mexico has an official state question: 'Red or green?' This refers to which variety of chile sauce you'd like on your food. Answer 'Christmas,' and you'll get both.

© Justin Foulkes / Lonely Planet; Left: © Johnny Haglund / Getty Images

★ ★ ★

NUCLEAR TOURISM

New Mexico is indelibly linked to the most powerful weapon humans ever invented, the nuclear bomb. WWII's Manhattan Project was conducted at Los Alamos National Lab, and the bomb was tested down south at the White Sands Missile Range. Visit the range's Trinity Test Site on twice-yearly open days and check out the trinitite, a glassy green material created when the bomb liquidated the sand with its hellfire. In Albuquerque, hit the informative National Museum of Nuclear Science and History, where you'll learn about uranium, the secret history of Los Alamos, and its lasting legacy in modern-day nuclear medicine.

Feed your appetite at 19th-century El Farol. *http://visitcanyonroad.com*

SANTA FE INDIAN MARKET In late August, 150,000 people descend on Santa Fe's historic plaza to buy work by more than 1100 Native artists from across America. The market has been going on since the 1920s and is strictly regulated: find everything from high-quality turquoise jewelry to tribal weavings to traditional pottery to contemporary paintings. There are also dance performances, fashion shows, galas and more around this annual event. *www.swaia.org*

SANTA FE OPERA Built to resemble a ship sailing on the high desert sea, the Santa Fe Opera is stunning enough to be worth a visit even from those averse to opera. Its summer season draws culturati from far and wide, who tailgate with splendid picnics of champagne and salmon before performances of *La Bohème* or *Aida*. *www.santafeopera.org, 301 Opera Dr*

TAOS Almost everything in this perfect little postcard of a northern New Mexico town is a worthy attraction, from the excellent museums (the Millicent Rogers Museum is a standout) to the well-curated art galleries to the impeccable restaurants. Just wandering around the adobe streets is splendid too, with the highly skiable Taos Mountains looming in the background, including the peak of Wheeler Mountain. Don't miss the still-inhabited 1000-year-old Native homes of Taos Pueblo. *https://taos.org*

TEN THOUSAND WAVES Transport yourself to the mountains of Hokkaido at this exceptional, luxurious Santa Fe spa, designed like a Japanese onsen (hot spring resort). Entry buys an afternoon lounging in an outdoor hot tub amid the piñons and junipers; clothing is optional. Afterward, splurge on a massage or just scrub down with complimentary hinoki (Japanese cypress) soap. *https://tenthousandwaves. com, 21 Ten Thousand Wave Way*

From left: The remains of Jumbo nuclear bomb at Trinity Site where the world's first atomic explosion test took place on July 16, 1945; pueblos near Taos; a display of red hatch chiles.

© Justin Foulkes / Lonely Planet

FAMILY OUTINGS

CUMBRES & TOLTEC SCENIC RAILWAY

From late May through much of October, you can weave along the border of New Mexico and Colorado on the nation's highest and longest steam railway. The train rises slowly from ranchland through aspen forest and into the jagged Rockies before chugging across the 10,015ft Cumbres Pass. Head to the historic train's outdoor gondola car to sniff the cool mountain air as you descend into Colorado. *https://cumbrestoltec.com, from Chama, NM to Antonito, CO*

LAS VEGAS This original Las Vegas was founded seventy years before its now much better known namesake, and quickly became a haven for outlaws. Legendary Wild West characters like Doc Holliday and Jesse James drank and rumbled in this once-booming railroad town. Admire the photogenic old bordellos, look for ghosts in the allegedly haunted Railway Depot,

take a dip in the nearby hot springs and bed down at the gilded 1882 Plaza Hotel (the 'Belle of the Southwest'), a favorite of Teddy Roosevelt and his Rough Riders. *www.lasvegasnm.gov*

ROSWELL The city of Roswell, infamous as the site of a supposed crash landing by a UFO in the 1940s, happily trades on its alien mythos. Even the city streetlights are painted with 'alien' eyes. The delectably kitschy local International UFO Museum & Research Center explores the Roswell Incident through old newspaper clippings, alien autopsy 'reports' and flying saucer dioramas. *www.roswell-nm.gov*

SANDIA PEAK TRAMWAY The longest aerial tram in the US climbs 2.7 miles from the desert floor in the northeast corner of Albuquerque to the summit of 10,378ft Sandia Crest. The views are spectacular at any time, though sunsets are particularly brilliant. The complex at the top has hiking trails that lead off through the woods;

★ ★ ★

HATCH CHILE FESTIVAL

Chile is essential to the New Mexican identity – red or green chile sauce (or 'Christmas,' the mix of both) tops everything from burgers to eggs to pizza, and ristras (dried chile wreaths) decorate porches across the state. In late summer the air smells sweet and smoky as vendors set up wire drum roasters in empty lots and outdoor farmers markets for locals to bring their bounty for roasting. Celebrate the beloved crop at this September festival in the chile-growing town of Hatch, with cooking demos, carnival games and the crowning of the Chile Queen.

© Westend61 / Getty Images; Right: © Coast-to-Coast / Getty Images

there's also a small ski area. You can also hike down (or up). *www.sandiapeak.com, 30 Tramway Rd NE*

SANTA ROSA BLUE HOLE Just off Route 66 in Santa Rosa is a sapphire-blue artesian well with such perfect visibility it draws divers from hundreds of miles to explore its 70ft depths. It's also a dream of a swimming hole, for those brave (or hot) enough to cannonball into its 62°F waters. There's a recreational lake nearby. *http://santarosabluehole.com, 1085 Blue Hole Rd*

TRUTH OR CONSEQUENCES Once called Hot Springs, T or C (as locals know it) renamed itself on a dare from a 1950s radio show of the same name. That out-there spirit still pervades this charmingly ramshackle desert spa town, where you can bathe in local mineral water, get a reiki massage, have your tarot cards read or pick out a new healing crystal. The Hot Springs Bathhouse and Commercial Historic District features the legacy of the town's bathhouses, and there's no shortage of hot spring establishments to choose from in the area. *www.sierracountynewmexico.info/ truth-or-consequences*

VERY LARGE ARRAY In the absolute middle of nowhere, west of Socorro on the Plains of San Agustin, you'll find 27 immense radio antennae trained toward the sky. Astronomers use the array to peek at distant planets, observe black holes and – yes – listen for noises from far-off civilizations. Run by the National Radio Astronomy Observatory, you can wander around yourself or geek out with a guided tour on first and third Saturdays (no reservations required). Check road conditions in advance. *www.vla.nrao.edu*

★ ★ ★

GETTING THERE & AROUND

The Albuquerque International Sun-port, New Mexico's only major airport, is conveniently located near the middle of the state off I-40. Amtrak trains link Albuquerque with Chicago and LA on its Southwest Chief route. You'll need a car to get most places.

ITINERARY

Days 1, 2 & 3

Founded by the Spanish in 1610, Santa Fe is the oldest state capital in America and the best place to base yourself to explore northern New Mexico. Explore the city's adobe art galleries on Canyon Road, the tree-shaded Spanish-style central plaza, and the world-class restaurants and museums. Be sure to take a couple of half-day trips too – wind through the gold-and-green desert and tiny Native pueblos on the High Road to Taos, explore nuclear history in Los Alamos, hike amid the millennium-old ruins at Bandelier National Monument or scoop up some healing dirt at El Santuario de Chimayó.

Day 4

Get up early in Santa Fe and hit up the hot spring spas in quirky Truth or Consequences on your way to the wild inland dunes of White Sands National Monument. Rent a plastic disk for sand sledding, and don't forget your SPF 100!

Day 5

Spend the last day at the massive chambers of Carlsbad Caverns National Park or saying hi to the little green men at Roswell.

From left: Radio antennaes at the Very Large Array; Sandia Peak Tramway.

NEW YORK

★ ★ ★ ★ ★ ★ ★ ★ ★ ★ ★ ★ ★ ★ ★ ★ ★

POPULATION: 19.6 million | **SIZE:** 54,555 sq miles | **CAPITAL:** Albany
LARGEST CITY: New York | **WEBSITE:** www.iloveny.com

NO PLACE ON THE PLANET DOES BIG-CITY CHARM QUITE LIKE GOTHAM, AND FOR MOST, A TRIP TO the Empire State starts and finishes with its iconically diverse and thriving metropolis, bustling with museums, restaurants, and energy. However, if you travel only to the five boroughs there's a considerable amount you're missing out on. 'Upstate' New York – generally accepted as anywhere north of the NYC metro area – shouldn't be neglected either. The Hudson River acts as an escape route from the city, leading eager sojourners north. From capital city Albany, the Erie Canal cuts west to Lake Erie, passing spectacular Niagara Falls and resurgent Buffalo and Rochester along the way. In the northeast you'll find the St Lawrence River and its thousands of islands, as well as the Adirondack and Catskill Mountains. Head to the middle of the state and you'll be ensconced in the serene Finger Lakes.

© Tetra Images / Getty Images

FOOD & DRINK

BAGELS Fresh, toothsome bagels fuel New York's mornings and have made its kosher delis a veritable institution. Tell the bagelmonger your preference of bagel, then choose from a sprawling counter of cream cheeses and other sandwich fillings. For a classic, opt for scallion cream cheese with lox (salmon), capers, tomato and red onion. Ess-a-Bagel is one of the old standbys, but it's hard to go wrong.

ETHNIC FOOD Don't restrict yourself only to pizza and bagels. Get bibimbap or Korean fried chicken in midtown's Koreatown (mostly centered on 32nd street, near Macy's) before heading out to a karaoke bar on the second floor of a midtown high-rise. The Astoria neighborhood has some of the best Greek food this side of Athens; few restaurants are quite as revered as Taverna Kyclades but many contenders offer seafood, moussaka and conviviality-establishing wines. In another part of Queens, Little Tibet could be the nickname for all of Jackson Heights, where traditionally Indian shops and restaurants are slowly giving way to entrepreneurs peddling momos (dumplings) from the Himalayas, both Tibet and Nepal.

FINE DINING From the dining rooms of Per Se, Masa, Gramercy Tavern, Eleven Madison Park, Le Bernardin and endless others, New York's celebrity chefs – a roster including David Chang, Enrique Olvera and Daniel Boulud to name a few – continue to redefine notions of the great New York restaurant. Whatever you choose, settle in for an eye-popping multicourse feast lasting at least three hours; fine dining in New York's top restaurants is serious, if delicious (and costly) business. Further upstate, there's locavore heaven Blue Hill at Stone Barns in Tarrytown. Be sure to book around two months in advance and note the dress code: typically this is jackets and ties preferred for gentlemen, and shorts not permitted.

FINGER LAKES WINERIES With its cool climate and short growing season, the Finger Lakes region is similar to Germany's Rhine valley, and is similarly strong in off-dry whites such as riesling. More than 120 wineries make it tempting to spend several days sipping. It pays to pack a picnic lunch; not every winery does food, and a lot of the little towns along the way have limited options. *www.fingerlakeswinecountry.com*

FLUSHING CHINATOWN Downtown Flushing in Queens can feel like the Times Square of a city a world away from NYC. Immigrants from all over Asia, primarily Chinese and Korean, make up this neighborhood bursting at the seams with markets and restaurants filled with delicious and cheap delicacies. Off Main Street, the Golden Shopping Mall's basement food court is an ideal spot to find fantastic hawker-style grub. Don't be intimidated by the lack of English menus: most stalls have at least one English speaker, and regulars are usually happy to point out personal favorites, from Lanzhou hand-pulled noodles to spicy pig ears.

HARLEM SOUL Jump aboard the A train to 125th Street for the feasts on offer in

---

★ ★ ★

FOUR HUBS OF
New York City's
STREET ART

Welling Court, Astoria
The best spot in Queens for graffiti peeping, promising over 130 murals that bring together a host of talent from legendary taggers to new-found artists.

Greenpoint, Brooklyn
Tucked into Brooklyn's northern edges along the G train, Greenpoint feels refreshingly intact with un-gentrified warehouses providing plenty of brick canvases.

The Bushwick Collective
Start your east-of-Williamsburg adventure along St Nicholas Avenue where over 50 murals (and counting) add a needed splash of color to the gritty Bushwick vibe.

Hunts Point, Bronx
The playground for Tats Cru, a coterie of noted taggers, is well worth the trek to the Bronx for a walk along over 200ft of wall art.

© Beverly Logan /Getty Images : Left: © DenisTangneyJr / Getty Images

★ ★ ★

A SECRET SYMPHONY

On Your Morning Commute

Imagine turning the drudgery of negotiating cease-less traffic on your way to work into a concert, with the instrument the very road you're driving on. For commuters in the know near Pough-keepsie, about an hour north of New York City, tuning into 95.3FM as they pass over the Mid-Hudson Bridge and its adjacent parks lets them listen to an original piece of music by composer Joseph Bertolozzi, who used the heady mix of materials on the bridge itself as his auditory palette of clanks and bonks. There are free listening booths stationed through the riverside area as well for pedes-trians who also want to enjoy the music. The result will cure even the meanest case of the Mondays.

historic Harlem. Amy Ruth's on 116th St delivers many crowd-pleasers, including a smothered pork chop with fried eggs and grits, along with its much loved 'Rev Al Sharpton,' a vast plate of fried chicken and waffles. Tucked discreetly in a workaday shop row on Lenox Ave, Sylvia's is Harlem's most famous soul food address. Also on Lenox, you'll find the best-dressed crowd at the uber-trendy Red Rooster, a hotspot run by Ethiopian-Swedish chef Marcus Samuelsson.

PIZZA Whether it's lunchtime or closing time, a big greasy slice of New York-style pizza, folded sideways, is true New York food. You don't get more classic than Joe's in Greenwich Village. For a hipster update on brick-oven pizza, head to Roberta's in Bushwick. The classic margherita is sublimely simple; more adventurous palates can opt for the seasonal hits like the 'speckenwolf' (mozzarella, speck, crimini and onion). But a lowly dollar slice has its own appeal as a meal-on-the-go that powers New Yorkers of all stripes.

VEGAN AND VEGETARIAN At long last, NYC has vegan and vegetarian options to compete with the West Coast. Even the most meat-heavy four-star restaurants are figuring out the lure of the legume; from the market-inspired le potager section on the menu of Café Boulud to abcV by Jean-Georges Vongerichten. Vegans have much to celebrate with the arrival of excellent eateries serving up guilt-free goodness all around town: Michelin-starred Nix, Modern Love out in Williamsburg, James Beard–nominated Amanda Cohen's Dirt Candy, and the elegant Blossom in Manhattan. Other icons include Candle Cafe and the Harlem soul food gem Seasoned Vegan.

NATURAL ESCAPES

FINGER LAKES GORGES AND WATERFALLS This region spurred the phrase 'Ithaca is Gorges' for a reason. Stunning hikes abound, whether at Watkins Glen State Park off Seneca Lake, winding under and over waterfalls, or at Taughannock Falls near Ulysses, where

From left: The Mid-Hudson Bridge in Poughkeepsie; New York bagels at a food stall; The waterfall canyon at Watkins Glen State Park. Previous page: Aerial view of the Statue of Liberty.

© Ultima_Gaina / Getty Images

you can view the cascade from a lookout above, or hike down the easy Gorge Trail to the base of the falls (the Rim Trail is a little more difficult but worth it for the views). Remember your swimsuit if you're headed to Buttermilk Falls outside Ithaca during summer and take a dip in the natural pool at its base after completing your hike. (In winter, the trails become icy.) *https://parks. ny.gov/regions/finger-lakes/default.aspx*

FIRE ISLAND NATIONAL SEASHORE
Federally protected, this barrier island offers sand dunes, forests, clean beaches, camping, hiking trails and nightife across 15 hamlets and two villages. The scenery ranges from car-free areas of summer mansions and packed nightclubs to stretches of sand with nothing but pitched tents and deer. Most of the island is accessible only by ferry and is free of cars – regulars haul their belongings on little wagons instead. *www.nps.gov/fiis*

MOHONK PRESERVE Some 8000
acres of land held in private trust make up the Mohonk Preserve, just off the Appalachian Trail and home to some of the best rock climbing on the East Coast. Over 80,000 climbers each year scale the cliffs of Shawangunk Ridge, or the Gunks; come on your own or with an outfitter. Catering to everyone from total newbies to those looking to learn advanced skills, High Xposure Adventures is one of many outfitters to operate a variety of rock climbing programs in the Gunks. Access to the Gunks is via the West Trapps Trailhead outside New Paltz. *www.mohonkpreserve. org, 3197 Rte 44-55, New Paltz*

ARTS, HISTORY & CULTURE

BETHEL WOODS CENTER FOR THE ARTS
Sixty miles southwest of Woodstock is the location of Max Yasgur's Catskills farm, where the famed 1969 Woodstock Music & Art Fair took place. Bethel Woods Center for the Arts, as it's now called, has an outdoor amphitheater that is still used for summer concerts by major-league artists and an evocative museum with exhibits

FUN FACT

George Washington was declared Commander in Chief at NYC's Federal Hall at the first United States Congress in 1789.

© Sylvain Sonnet / Getty Images ; Left: © Atlantide Phototravel / Getty Images

★ ★ ★

New York's OVERLOOKED Vacationland

An hour by subway from midtown Manhattan, Coney Island was once New York's most popular beachside amusement area. After decades in the doldrums, revitalization has brought the summer crowds back for Nathan's Famous hot dogs, roller coasters, minor-league baseball games and strolls down the boardwalk. Directly to the east along the board-walk is Brighton Beach, dubbed 'Little Odessa' for its large population of Ukrainian and Russian families. Running under the elevated subway tracks, the always bustling main drag is lined with vibrant Slavic shops, restaurants and cafes.

that burst with the music and images that made Woodstock such a cultural force. *www.bethelwoodscenter.org, 200 Hurd Rd*

BOLDT CASTLE This Gothic gem, a replica of a German castle, was (partly) built by tycoon hotelier George C Boldt in the late 19th century. In 1904, however, midway through construction, Boldt's wife died suddenly, and the project was abandoned. Since 1977 the Thousand Islands Bridge Authority has spent millions restoring the place to something of its planned grandeur. *www.boldtcastle.com, Heart Island*

BROADWAY & TIMES SQUARE Sizzling lights, electrifying energy: this is the New York of the world's imagination. Stretching from 40th St to 54th St, between Sixth and Eighth Aves, Broadway is where romance, betrayal, murder and triumph come with dazzling costumes and stirring scores. The district's undisputed star is bright, blinding Times Square. More than the junction of two avenues, this is America in concentrate – an intense, intoxicating rush of Hollywood

billboards, shimmering cola signs, and buffed topless cowboys. Same-day discounted tickets to the shows on- and off-Broadway are available from the TKTS booth right in the middle of it all.

DIA:BEACON The 300,000 sq ft of a former Nabisco box printing factory beside the Hudson River is now a storehouse for a series of stunning monumental works by the likes of Richard Serra, Dan Flavin, Louise Bourgeois and Gerhard Richter. The permanent collection is complemented by temporary shows of large-scale sculptures and installations, making this a must-see for contemporary art fans. It's an easy day trip from NYC by Metro-North. *www.diaart.org, 3 Beekman St*

HERBERT F JOHNSON MUSEUM OF ART IM Pei's brutalist building looms like a giant concrete robot above the ornate neo-Gothic surrounds of Cornell's campus. Inside you'll find an eclectic collection ranging from medieval wood carvings to modern masters and an extensive

From left: The entrance of Coney Island's Luna Park; the High Line; Sackets Harbor Battlefield at sunset.

© Phillip Bourquin / Getty Images

collection of Asian art. If nothing else, it's worth a visit if only for the panoramic views of Ithaca and Cayuga Lake from the top floor galleries. *www.museum.cornell.edu, 114 Central Ave, Ithaca*

THE HIGH LINE A resounding triumph of urban renewal (and its attendant issues around gentrification), the High Line is New York's proudest testament to its continuous effort to transform the scarred vestiges of the city's industrial past into eye-pleasing spaces. Once an unsightly elevated train track that snaked between slaughterhouses and low-end domestic dwellings, the High Line is today an unfurled emerald necklace of park space that mixes sculpture installations with an intricate landscape of native plants. At the High Line's southern terminus sits the new Whitney Museum of American Art, and the park itself feels like an extended work of creative energy. *www.thehighline.org*

HUDSON VALLEY ESCAPES Hudson, Saugerties, Kingston, Beacon: the towns of the Hudson Valley exert a magnetic pull as the polar opposite of their teeming neighbor down the river. Once the capital of New York state, then an industrial hub that eventually went bust, Kingston is in transition as it looks to shed its past and metamorphose into an exciting city, while the other hamlets are finding new life as alternatives to the big city. All are filled with lively restaurants, galleries and coffee shops teeming with hip upstate residents and curious New York City visitors. *www.hudsonriver.com*

MARTIN HOUSE This ambitious 15,000-sq-ft house, completed in 1905, was designed by Frank Lloyd Wright for his friend and patron Darwin D Martin. Representing Wright's Prairie House ideal, this Buffalo architectural highlight located in regal Parkside consists of six interconnected buildings, each meticulously restored inside and out. Two tour options offer different levels of detail on this elaborate project (book online). *www.martinhouse.org, 125 Jewett Pkwy*

★ ★ ★

WAR OF 1812 *Battlefield*

North of Oswego is the pretty village of Sackets Harbor alongside Lake Ontario. Here, the historic Sackets Harbor Battlefield holds many events during the summer season, the main one being the War of 1812 Living History Weekend, usually at the end of July, when the battle is staged by locals in uniforms. You can practically smell the cannon smoke as old shooters are wheeled around to take aim at the retreating redcoats. At other times of year, the grounds with their heritage buildings make for an attractive place to take a stroll along the lake shoreline.

© Busara / Shutterstock; Left: © The Alexander Liberman Trust, Photograph by Jerry L. Thompspon

Inspiration **FOR THE** *Constitution*

Before the arrival of European colonists, several Native American tribes, including the Mohawk, Oneida, Onondaga, Mahican, Seneca and Cayuga, made their homes in what we now call New York state. Around the 15th century, a powerful alliance of five tribes joined what would come to be called the Iroquois Confederacy. The self-described 'League of Peace' controlled most of the land and trading in the area, and when British, Dutch and French colonists began to pour into the state, they quickly realized the importance of their relationship with the confederacy. Some historians believe that the United States Constitution may have been influenced by the tenets of the Iroquois Confederacy.

METROPOLITAN MUSEUM OF ART The Met is the crown jewel of Fifth Avenue's Museum Mile, which also boasts The Frick, Guggenheim, Neue Galerie, Cooper Hewitt Design Museum, Museum of the City of New York, and El Museo del Barrio. The Met's collection of over two million great works spans the world, from the chiseled sculptures of ancient Greece to the evocative tribal carvings of Papua New Guinea. The Renaissance galleries are packed with Old World masters, while the 2000-year-old Temple of Dendur fires the imagination. Uptown is the connected medieval museum, The Cloisters. *https:// metmuseum.org, 1000 Fifth Ave, New York*

MOMA Among the greatest hoarders of modern masterpieces on earth, NYC's Museum of Modern Art (MoMA) is a cultural promised land. It's here that you'll see Van Gogh's *The Starry Night*, Cézanne's *The Bather*, Picasso's *Les Demoiselles d'Avignon*, Pollock's *One: Number 31* and Warhol's *Campbell's Soup Cans*. Just make sure you leave time for

Chagall, Dix, Rothko, de Kooning and Haring, a free film screening, a glass of vino in the Sculpture Garden, and a fine-dining feast at its lauded in-house restaurant, the Modern. *www.moma.org, 11 W 53rd St*

NATIONAL SEPTEMBER 11 MEMORIAL & MUSEUM Rising from the ashes of Ground Zero, the National September 11 Memorial & Museum is a beautiful, dignified response to the city's darkest chapter. Where the Twin Towers once soared, two reflecting pools now weep dark, elegant waterfalls. Framing them are the names of those who lost their lives on September 11, 2001 and in the 1993 WTC bombing. Deep below lies the Memorial Museum, a powerful, poignant exploration of these catastrophic events. *www.911memorial.org, 180 Greenwich St*

NEW YORK STATE MUSEUM Set on Empire State Plaza across from the New York State Capitol building, there are exhibits here on everything from New York's original Native American residents,

© Achim Thomae / Getty Images

From left: Storm King Art Center; T-Rex skeleton at the American Museum of Natural History; 1WTC reflecting in the pool of the 9/11 memorial.

its architectural and engineering marvels and more. A large chunk is dedicated to the history of New York City. The section on 9/11, including a damaged fire truck and debris from the site, is very moving. Don't miss riding the gorgeous antique carousel on the fourth floor. *www.nysm.nysed.gov, 222 Madison Ave, Albany*

STATUE OF LIBERTY & ELLIS ISLAND

Since its unveiling in 1886, Lady Liberty has welcomed millions of immigrants sailing into New York Harbor in the hope of a better life. It now welcomes millions of tourists, many of whom head up to her crown for one of New York City's finest skyline and water views. Close by lies Ellis Island, the gateway for over 12 million new arrivals between 1892 and 1954. These days it's home to a moving museum, paying tribute to these immigrants and their indelible courage. *www.nps.gov/stli*

STORM KING ART CENTER

This 500-acre sculpture park, established in 1960, has works by the likes of Barbara Hepworth, Alexander Calder, Andy Goldsworthy and Isamu Noguchi. All have been carefully sited across the grassy estate's natural breaks and curves. Open seasonally, it's an ideal way to experience each season but winter. *www.stormking. org, 1 Museum Rd, New Windsor*

FAMILY OUTINGS

AMERICAN MUSEUM OF NATURAL HISTORY

Founded in 1869, these classic halls contain a veritable wonderland of more than 30 million artifacts – including towering dinosaur skeletons – as well as the Rose Center for Earth and Space, with its cutting-edge planetarium. From October through May, the museum is home to the Butterfly Conservatory, a glasshouse featuring 500-plus butterflies from all over the world that will flutter about and land on your outstretched arm. *www.amnh.org, Central Park W at 79th St, New York*

BROOKLYN BRIDGE PARK

This 85-acre park is one of Brooklyn's best-loved

★ ★ ★

ERIE CANAL

Few feats of engineering in history have matched the scale, scope and eventual influence of the Erie Canal. First proposed in the 1780s and finished in 1825, the 363-mile-long canal connects Lake Erie and Lake Ontario with the Hudson River, from where ships can continue on to New York Bay and the Atlantic Ocean. The canal was a massive factor in not only New York's rise in economic power and influence, but also that of the US. After completion, the course of the canal was altered several times, with the version we can see today finally completed in 1918. Although the route is different, the effect is similar: an incredible man-made river that flows right through the heart of the state, connecting cities hundreds of miles inland to the ocean.

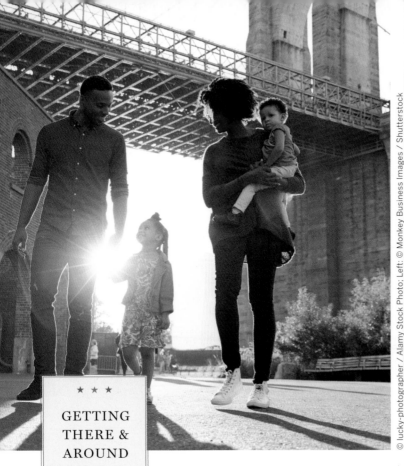

© lucky-photographer / Alamy Stock Photo; Left: © Monkey Business Images / Shutterstock

★ ★ ★

GETTING THERE & AROUND

Three major airports, JFK, LaGuardia (both in Queens) and Newark (in New Jersey), serve New York City and its surroundings with international arrivals. Major regional airports include ones in the Buffalo Niagara region, Rochester and Albany. Amtrak has train services across the state and into Canada, crossing the border at Niagara Falls, while Metro-North runs up the Hudson. Don't bother driving in NYC. Long Island has rail service also, via the LIRR.

attractions. Wrapping around a bend on the East River, it runs 1.3 miles from the far side of the Manhattan Bridge in Dumbo to the west end of Atlantic Ave in Brooklyn Heights. It has revitalized a once-barren stretch of shoreline, turning abandoned piers into a beautiful park with jaw-dropping views of Manhattan. Its pièce de résistance (apart from the stunning views of the 1883 Brooklyn Bridge, a Gothic Revival masterpiece) might be the refurbished Jane's Carousel, built in 1922 and housed in a glass encasement. *www.brooklynbridgepark.org*

EMPIRE STATE BUILDING The striking art-deco skyscraper may no longer be New York's tallest building, but it remains one of its most recognizable icons. The ESB has appeared in dozens of films and still provides one of the best views in town, particularly around sunset when the twinkling lights of the city switch on. The

beloved landmark hasn't stopped turning heads, especially with the addition of LED lights that create more than 16 million color combos. *www.esbnyc.com, 20 W 34th St*

FREDERICK LAW OLMSTED AND CALVERT VAUX PARKS The design duo of Olmsted & Vaux created the dual gems of Manhattan's Central Park and Brooklyn's Prospect Park. Designed as a leisure space for all New Yorkers regardless of color, class or creed, they're oases from the insanity: the lush lawns, cool forests, flowering gardens, glassy bodies of water and meandering, wooded paths provide the dose of serene nature that New Yorkers crave.

GOVERNORS ISLAND Off-limits to the public for 200 years, this former military outpost is now one of New York's most popular seasonal playgrounds. Each summer, free ferries on weekend mornings make the seven-minute trip

from Lower Manhattan and downtown Brooklyn to the 172-acre oasis. With bikes for rent and food trucks on-site, it's great for an entire day's exploring. Historic spots include Fort Jay, fortified in 1776 in a failed attempt to prevent the British from invading Manhattan; Colonel's Row, lovely 19th-century brick officers' quarters; and Castle Williams, a 19th-century fort later converted to a military penitentiary. There's also Hammock Grove (complete with 50 hammocks). *www.govisland.com*

LAKE GEORGE Lake George covers 45 sq miles of the Adirondacks and attracts thousands of visitors to its shores every summer for swimming, boating and just sitting and staring at its shimmering waters in admiration. The town of Lake George is a major tourist center with arcades, weekly fireworks in July and August, and paddleboat rides. It's a chaotic good time for those looking to dive headfirst into summer-by-the-lake culture. Charming nearby towns abound, such as upscale Bolton Landing, cozy Glens Falls and bucolic Warrensburg. *www.visitlakegeorge.com*

MONTAUK At the tip of Long Island's South Fork, you'll find the mellow town of Montauk, aka 'The End,' and the famous surfing beach Ditch Plains. With the surfers have come affluent hipsters and boho-chic hotels, but the area is still far less of a scene than the Hamptons. Covering the eastern tip of the South Fork is Montauk Point State Park, with its impressive lighthouse, dating from 1796 and the fourth-oldest active lighthouse in the country. Montauk Point State Park is a great place for windswept walks. *https://parks.ny.gov/parks/61/hunting.aspx*

NIAGARA FALLS One of the first things that will come to most people's minds when they think about New York is Niagara Falls, located on the northwestern border with Canada. The Niagara River feeds 3160 tons of water per second over the 167ft craggy cliff face that gives the falls its unreal presentation. The falls have long been a tourist destination known the world round and it is still a popular honeymoon spot. *www.niagarafallsstatepark.com*

SARATOGA SPRINGS The effervescent water that gives Saratoga Springs its name has been thought to have healing properties since the land was inhabited by the Mahican Native Americans. Shortly after Europeans forged permanent settlements in the area, the healing springs made the town of Saratoga Springs a full-fledged tourist destination. People came not just to soak in the mineral-rich spring water, but also to visit the gambling houses that sprung up after the popularity of the now famous Saratoga Race Course. *www.saratoga.com*

ITINERARY

Day 1
You're going to need several days in NYC to hit the classics and dip into the local scene. Start with the landmarks like Central Park and the Museum Mile, then work your way down the island (Manhattan, that is) until you reach the 9/11 Memorial.

Day 2
Carbo-load your way around town gorging on pizza and bagels, then burn off the extra calories with walks around the shops of Soho and the stately brownstones of the West Village.

Day 3
Dive deep into Brooklyn, taking in reclaimed green spaces, emerging neighborhoods and creative quarters dripping with graffiti.

Days 4 & 5
Follow the Hudson River upstate and find constellations of artist enclaves and quaint inns. Dia:Beacon or Storm King add a jolt of visual inspiration.

Days 6 & 7
Head west through the Finger Lakes and try some of America's best white wines after walks through stunning gorges.

From left: Brooklyn Bridge Park; Niagara Falls.

NORTH CAROLINA

★ ★ ★ ★ ★ ★ ★ ★ ★ ★ ★ ★ ★ ★ ★ ★ ★ ★ ★ ★

POPULATION: 10.4 million | **SIZE:** 53,819 sq miles | **STATE CAPITAL:** Raleigh
LARGEST CITY: Charlotte | **WEBSITE:** www.visitnc.com

'NORTH CACKALACKY,' AS IT'S KNOWN 'ROUND HERE, IS EQUAL PARTS SOUTHERN HOSPITALITY and American innovation. One of the original 13 colonies, North Carolina blends the best of traditional Americana with a thriving university and high-tech scene centered on the dynamic cities of Raleigh, Charlotte and Wilmington. While the innovative central Piedmont district sees the majority of the state's industry – banking in Charlotte; universities, medicine and research in the Triangle – the most stunning natural beauty hugs the farther reaches. In the west, Asheville and the Blue Ridge Mountains are a scenic forested paradise, especially along the Blue Ridge Parkway as it wends toward the Great Smoky Mountains in fall leaf-peeping season. To the east, the coast and Outer Banks islands' white sand beaches are home to rental cottages, nesting sea turtles, lighthouses and seafood shacks.

© Allison Jehlicka / Shutterstock

FOOD & DRINK

BISCUITS If it's Southern, it's atop a biscuit: fried chicken, country ham, you name it. At Asheville's Biscuit Head, there's even a jam bar with homemade preserves (sweet potato chai caramel, anyone?) and a gravy flight with three options, including espresso gravy.

CHEERWINE While Pepsi was born in North Carolina and has spread its wings far afield, the Salisbury-based Cheerwine has kept it local. Bubbly with a hint of cherry, it was created in 1917 as a response to WWI sugar shortages by the same family that owns the company today. Not only does 'the nectar of North Carolina' get served alongside the state's iconic barbecue – it's an ingredient in some sauces as well.

PULLED PORK BBQ Originally from Caribbean slave roots, barbecue is now synonymous with Southern cooking. In North Carolina, the Lexington/Eastern Carolina pulled pork rivalry almost rivals Duke/UNC basketball (almost). Eastern North Carolinians – bless their hearts – use vinegar-based barbecue, but in Lexington, they add the unholy spot of ketchup (say it ain't so!). You'll have to sample both styles to pick your favorite.

NATURAL ESCAPES

BLUE RIDGE PARKWAY Think of the 469-mile Blue Ridge Parkway as the world's best hiking trail for cars. Work began in the post–Depression 1930s, when the New Deal put able-bodied men to work building this link between Shenandoah and Great Smoky Mountains National Parks. They created a real beaut; the Parkway's winding road hugs waterfalls and oak-covered rolling mountains. At milepost 382 (six miles east of downtown Asheville), stop at the superb Folk Art Center, a mix of art gallery and store that's wholly dedicated to Southern craftsmanship. *www.blueridgeparkway.org*

CAPE HATTERAS NATIONAL SEASHORE Cape Hatteras Seashore in the Outer Banks is home to a delicate ecosystem, including salt marshes and sea turtles, which hatch on the beach in summer. Its beaches and lighthouses are attractions in their own right too. In 1999, to avoid encroaching sea erosion, engineers spent years moving the Cape Hatteras Lighthouse, the tallest brick lighthouse in the United States, in a process detailed fully in the lighthouse's museum. *www.nps.gov/caha*

DUPONT STATE FOREST With 10,000 acres, over 80 miles of trails, six waterfalls, and one covered bridge, this park drips with scenery year-round. However, gorgeousness goes into overdrive in late spring when the blue ghost fireflies light up the park (late May/early June) and in fall, when the waterfalls are gently bathed in the red-orange glow of the surrounding forest. *www.ncforestservice.gov/Contacts/dsf.htm, 89 Buck Forest Rd, Cedar Mountain*

GREAT SMOKY MOUNTAINS NATIONAL PARK The sun-dappled forests of the Great Smoky Mountains are a four-season wonderland. This breathtaking range in the

---

★ ★ ★

NORTH CAROLINA BREWERIES

With a 300-strong brewery industry (the most per capita in the South), North Carolina was the obvious choice for Sierra Nevada's second brewery. The castle-like homage to beer opened in 2014 near Asheville with a restaurant, tap room and guided tours. To find the heart of NC's smaller breweries, check out:

Jack of the Wood, Asheville: Celtic beer gods meet NC mountains.
Wedge Brewery Co, Asheville: Food trucks along with beer in the River Arts District.
Sugar Creek Brewing Company, Charlotte: Belgian-inspired beer and kitchen.
Fullsteam Brewery, Durham: Downtown hipsters, families and cornhole.
Mother Earth Brewing, Kinston: 100% solar-powered taproom.
Raleigh Beer Garden, Raleigh: World's largest selection of draft beer.

© karenfoleyphotography/ Getty Images; Left: © Matt Munro / Lonely Planet

ASHEVILLE MUSIC

In Asheville, music is fuel for the city, integrated into all aspects of local culture. Here in Western North Carolina, surrounded by the Blue Ridge Mountains, nearly 30 music venues service Asheville's artsy community. 'Music is everywhere,' according to Jessica Tomasin, studio manager at Asheville's Echo Mountain Recording, located inside a repurposed 1926 Methodist church building, which has recorded albums from artists including The Avett Brothers, Band of Horses, The War on Drugs, and more. 'For a town as small as we are, the amount of talent and resources we have here is pretty incredible. People come here for music.' Buskers on the street know it, and create a warm community for visitors and musicians. Outside downtown, the music flows into the River Arts District.

Appalachians is split between neighboring Tennessee, but has ample attractions in both states. Log cabins built by early settlers nestle in the fertile forest valleys alongside one-room schoolhouses, stream-fed gristmills and single-steeple churches. The park has preserved many of these vestiges of the past, which make up one of the largest collections of log buildings in the nation. They make a mesmerizing addition to this World Heritage Site that harbors more biodiversity than any other national park in the country, alongside significant doses of Americana. *www.nps.gov/grsm/index.htm*

JOCKEY'S RIDGE No wonder the Wright Brothers chose nearby Kitty Hawk in which to test their flights; the winds around this sand dune – the largest on the East Coast – can get fierce. But the wind is precisely what makes these rolling ridges look like a sculpture from nature. Bring a kite to experience the wind that lifted the Flyer. *www.friendsofjockeysridge.org, 300 W Carolista Dr, Nags Head*

ARTS, HISTORY & CULTURE

BATTLESHIP *NORTH CAROLINA* This 45,000-ton megaship earned 15 battle stars in the Pacific Theater in WWII before it was decommissioned in 1947 and came to rest in charming Wilmington just over the Cape Fear Bridge. Sights include the bake shop and galley, the print shop, the engine room, the powder magazine and the communications center. Note that there are several steep stairways leading to lower decks. *www.battleshipnc.com, 1 Battleship Rd*

BILTMORE ESTATE George Vanderbilt fell in love with the area's gently rolling mountains as a young man in the late 1880s, and most of the hundreds of workers who arrived to build his 250-room French chateau – the largest private home ever built in the United States – stayed thereafter, creating the artsy scene Asheville is still known for. Tours will awe the most hard-to-impress visitor. *www.biltmore.com, 1 Lodge St, Asheville*

From left: Bluegrass musicians on the street in Asheville; Jockey's Ridge; Biltmore Estate. Previous page: A beach in Corrolla, part of the Outer Banks.

© ZakZeinert / Shutterstock

BLUE RIDGE MUSIC TRAIL Traditional American music has grown like the ubiquitous kudzu vines through the Appalachian region of Western North Carolina over the last two centuries: bluegrass, blues, Cherokee dance, gospel, square dancing. Bring a fiddle or banjo (or your ears will do fine) and join in one of the region's many jam sessions.
www.blueridgemusicnc.com

HISTORIC STAGVILLE PLANTATION
Exceptional in prioritizing the 1000 or so 'enslaved persons' who worked here above the families that claimed their ownership, Stagville Plantation ranks among North Carolina's most important historic sites. What survives today, 10 miles north of downtown Durham, is just a fragment of the huge plantation where the state's largest enslaved population lived in scattered groups. The fascinating guided tours drive in convoy to an emotive cluster of slave homes, along with a massive barn, a mile from the main house.
www.stagville.org, 5828 Old Oxford Hwy

INTERNATIONAL CIVIL RIGHTS MUSEUM
On February 1, 1960, four young African American university students staged a sit-in at the Woolworth's 'whites only' lunch counter, helping launch the nation's groundbreaking civil rights movement against Jim Crow. The stirring museum is housed in that selfsame Woolworth's and details the history of fighting racial oppression in Greensboro and the US.
www.sitinmovement.org,
134 S Elm St, Greensboro

MUSEUM OF THE CHEROKEE INDIAN
This remarkable modern museum traces Cherokee history from their Paleo-Indian roots onwards. Its villain is the perfidious Andrew Jackson, who made his name fighting alongside the Cherokee, but as president condemned them to the heartbreak of the Trail of Tears from the south to the Oklahoma territory. One fascinating section follows the progress through 18th-century London of a Cherokee delegation that sailed to England in 1762.
www.cherokeemuseum.org, 589 Tsali Blvd

FUN FACT

The waters off the Outer Banks became known as 'The Graveyard of the Atlantic' after causing over 1000 shipwrecks amidst its sandbars and strong currents.

© LEE SNIDER PHOTO IMAGES / Shutterstock; Right: © Lance King / Getty Images

Charlotte (CLT) is North Carolina's main international airport; Raleigh–Durham's RDU is a respectable second. Trains crisscross central NC, but driving is the main mode of transport within the state. North Carolina is surprisingly wide west to east; driving across takes about eight to nine hours.

NORTH CAROLINA MUSEUM OF ART

This superb museum stands 6 miles west of downtown Raleigh. Ranging far and wide, from ancient Egypt to modern Africa, its permanent collection includes works credited to Giotto and Botticelli – albeit with 'assistance' – and even a 17th-century 'Golf Player' etched by Rembrandt. The museum also holds a gallery celebrating alumni of the pioneering Black Mountain College near Asheville, including Robert Rauschenberg. *https://ncartmuseum.org, 2110 Blue Ridge Rd*

OLD SALEM Moravian settlers came to the Winston-Salem region in the 1760s. The religious sect from central Czechia created a bustling city center, with craftsmen a school (still operating) and taverns. Dine on traditional fare or learn how to bake bread in the 18th-century style. Delicate Moravian cookies are a must! *www.oldsalem.org, 900 Old Salem Rd, Winston-Salem*

VOLLIS SIMPSON WHIRLIGIG PARK

Burning Man meets Eastern Carolina tobacco country here at this folk art extravaganza. Vollis Simpson was a former machinery repairman, WWII vet and self-taught engineer who started building giant metal whirligigs in his 60s. Come to the sculpture park at sunset when lighting illuminates his trippy outsider creations, some as high as several stories tall; it's free and open daily. *www.wilsonwhirligigpark.org, 301 Goldsboro St S, Wilson*

ITINERARY

Day 1
Start in Charlotte, then head to the nearby DuPont State Forest for fireflies, leaves or waterfalls.

Day 2
Mosey up the Blue Ridge Parkway, stopping at the Folk Art Center to watch demonstrations and pick up regional arts and crafts. Stretch your legs on a hike on the Parkway's majestic natural beauty – climb Mt Mitchell, check out Linville Falls or Gorge. Spend the night in Asheville under the gaze of the Blue Ridge Parkway's Mt Pisgah, hitting up local breweries.

Day 3
After a biscuit breakfast, head east, stopping in Lexington for barbecue. Spend the evening in the Raleigh–Durham Triangle, center of the state's enormous foodie/farm-to-table culture (and another substantial craft brew scene).

Days 4 & 5
Spend the last two days touring the Cape Hatteras Seashore and Lighthouse, hang gliding at Jockey's Ridge, or ferrying to Ocracoke Island.

From left: The C Winkler Bakery in Old Salem, built in 1800; fans at a Duke basketball game.

FAMILY OUTINGS

CAMERON INDOOR STADIUM North Carolina has been known to, ahem, enjoy its college basketball. Duke undergrads vying for tickets (Cameron Crazies) set up camp for weeks, or sometimes months, at a time in 'Krzyzewskiville' (named after much-beloved Coach Krzyzewski). An adjacent Duke basketball museum details the passion for this pastime. *www.goduke.com, 115 Whitford Dr, Durham*

DUKE LEMUR CENTER Fly to Madagascar or stop by Durham for two hours: your choice to see the world's largest two homes to these ethereal-looking primates. The reservations-only guided tour takes you through outdoor enclosures and an indoor sanctuary, and also supports the 200+ lemurs and their primatologists. *https://lemur.duke.edu, 3705 Erwin Rd, Durham*

OCRACOKE ISLAND Filled with beloved beaches and Blackbeard history, the most chill (and remote) Outer Banks island is a one- to two-hour ferry ride from civilization. It's where Blackbeard fought his last battle, and he's believed to have been buried here. Even the language has taken its time; the local 'Ocracoke Brogue' dates to Elizabethan English. With a speed limit of 20mph, why not rent one of the ubiquitous golf carts or bikes to get around? *www.visitocracokenc.com*

NORTH DAKOTA

★ ★

POPULATION: 755,393 | **SIZE:** 70,762 sq miles | **STATE CAPITAL:** Bismarck
LARGEST CITY: Fargo | **WEBSITE:** www.ndtourism.com

NORTH DAKOTA IS IDEAL FOR ADVENTURERS SEEKING TO GET OFF THE BEATEN PATH. Located in the Great Plains, it is considered the least visited of all 50 states. This is a place to get lost on remote two-lane routes and to appreciate the raw land's beauty. And don't forget to pause to marvel at the meadowlarks' songs. Fields of grain stretch beyond every horizon in magnificently desolate North Dakota, broken up by oil boomtowns in the west. From bison to bobcats, you can view abundant wildlife in its natural habitat at Theodore Roosevelt National Park where prairie meets the badlands. Afterward, a road trip to the Fort Union Trading Post will take you back in time, immersing you in the state's long Native American history. Drive east to find Fargo: a fur-trading post, frontier town, quick-divorce capital and haven for folks in the Federal Witness Protection Program.

© Zak Zeinert / Shutterstock

FOOD & DRINK

BISON Bison are so important to North Dakota culture they're featured on the state quarter. They're also mighty tasty. The Woodhouse in Bismarck serves up juicy bison burgers in a retro setting, and Fargo's Mezzaluna is equally renowned for its bison meatloaf. Bison turns up on menus throughout the state, so you can sample it prepared every way there is.

KUCHEN Thanks to recipes passed down by generations of German immigrants, North Dakota has (almost) as many kuchen varieties as it does bison. Fruit fillings and custard tops come accompanied by a scoop of ice cream for a decadent, nostalgic treat. Charlie's Main Street Cafe in Minot has some of the best in the state, though Kroll's and the Cowboy Cafe in Medora provide stiff competition.

NATURAL ESCAPES

INTERNATIONAL PEACE GARDEN Since 1932 this garden in Dunseith at the Canada border has paid tribute to the friendship between the US and Canada. The vast formal garden is a breathtakingly curated kaleidoscope of color with ponds, waterfalls and fountains. The International Peace Garden is in both the US and Canada, but there are no boundaries within the site in recognition of the countries' amicable relationship. While visiting, set aside time to pause at the Peace Tower and 9/11 Memorial. These striking structures stand in stark, powerful contrast to their lively floral surroundings.
www.peacegarden.com, 10939 Hwy 281

THEODORE ROOSEVELT NATIONAL PARK Campers, hikers and wildlife lovers alike will all find a treasure trove of pristine natural landscapes at this vast national park near Medora. View the badlands and an expansive canyon from the Painted Canyon Visitor Center. On the 36-mile Scenic Loop Drive, you'll see abundant wildlife as well as breathtaking views. Bizarre rock formations, streaked with a rainbow of red, yellow, brown, black and silver minerals, are framed by green prairie. Only the rush of rivers and the distant hoofbeats of animals interrupt the silence in this untouched terrain. While exploring the park, look out for prairie dog towns. *www.nps.gov/thro, off I-94*

ARTS, HISTORY & CULTURE

BONANZAVILLE Take a step back in time at this seasonal museum in West Fargo that celebrates antique Americana. Whether you're an automobile enthusiast, history buff or antique lover, you'll find something of interest here. Explore the seasonal pioneer village that includes a hotel, church, jail, barbershop, fire station, mansion, farmhouse, general store and much more. *www.bonanzaville.org*

ENCHANTED HIGHWAY Getting there really is at least half the fun when you're driving on the Enchanted Highway. Take exit 72 on I-94 near Gladstone to see a collection of the world's largest scrap-metal sculptures. The 32-mile outdoor art gallery showcases artist Gary Greff's massive, playful sculptures. *http://enchantedcastlend.com/enchanted-highway, 607 Main St, Regent*

★ ★ ★

ASK A LOCAL

'As a North Dakota native, I think Theodore Roosevelt National Park would be one of the top must-see destinations in the state. As someone who resides in Bismarck, I like to showcase Fort Abraham Lincoln State Park for the reason of its authentic history. General Custer's home, the earth lodges, and the scenery of the bluffs overlooking the Missouri River are legendary. North Dakota also has some fun cities with vibrant downtown opportunities. A few of my favorite stops would include the Red Pepper in Grand Forks and Drekker Brewing Company in Fargo. In Bismarck you'll want to stop at the Toasted Frog for the fried pickles, and if you're visiting Minot, 10 North Main is a popular stop, and be sure to order the pheasant!'
– *Fred Walker, North Dakota Department of Commerce*

Pictured left: Sunrise over the hills of Theodore Roosevelt National Park.

© Steven Liveoak / Shutterstock; Right: © Ace Diamond / Shutterstock

The state's major airports are in Fargo, Bismarck and Grand Forks. North Dakota does have some shuttles between towns and city bus service, but overall, the state is best explored by car to take in the sights. Once a day, Amtrak's Empire Builder service passes through the state.

FARGO AIR MUSEUM Aviation buffs flock to this Fargo museum with a collection of aircraft that spans decades of air history, including a replica of the Wright Brothers' flyer and one of the Midwest's largest aviation libraries. You might even see one of the exhibits in action, as many of the airplanes still take to the sky; 90% of the holdings remain in flying condition. *www.fargoairmuseum.org, 1609 19th Ave N*

FARGO THEATRE A beautiful art deco theater downtown is the center of the arts in Fargo. Listed on the National Register of Historic Places, it has screened films since 1926, and still presents indie flicks and documentaries. The theater also presents concerts and live events. *www.fargotheatre.org, 314 Broadway N*

LEWIS & CLARK ... & SACAGAWEA Learn about the Corps of Discovery Expedition and the Native Americans essential to the effort at Washburn's Lewis and Clark Interpretative Center. The same ticket gets you into Fort Mandan, a replica of the fort built by Lewis and Clark, 2.5 miles west of the center. The fort sits on a lonely stretch of the Missouri River marked by a monument to Seaman, the expedition's dog. To the west on ND-200 is the Knife River Indian Villages National Historic Site, where you can still see the mounds left by three earthen villages of the Hidatsas, resident here for more than 900 years. Stroll the park to see the village site where Lewis & Clark met Sacagawea. *www.fortmandan.com*

ON-A-SLANT VILLAGE Step back in time and experience the life of the Mandan tribe at Fort Abraham Lincoln State Park, site of this village that was home to the Mandans for over 200 years until a tragic smallpox epidemic. Here you'll find reconstructed earth lodges equipped

ITINERARY

Day 1
Start in the state's east in Fargo, best known for the eponymous Coen brothers film. You can take in movies at the Fargo Theatre in their honor.

Day 2
Start heading west with a stop at Jamestown, best known for being home to the World's Largest Buffalo and the National Buffalo Museum, and a night spent in state capital Bismarck, which has its own museums to boast of, downtown and in nearby Mandan.

Day 3
Your next destination is the beautiful Theodore Roosevelt National Park. Begin at the South Unit right off I-94, where you'll find a museum, park film, bookstore and Theodore Roosevelt's Maltese Cross Cabin. For unparalleled natural scenery, take the 36-mile scenic park drive through the badlands, admiring the bison herds.

Day 4
Find new views along the Enchanted Highway between Gladstone and Regent to see the world's largest scrap-metal sculpture.

From left: The historic Fargo Theatre in downtown Fargo; statue of Sacagawea on the North Dakota State Capitol grounds in Bismark.

with the housewares, tools and weapons that were part of the Mandans' daily life. *www.parkrec.nd.gov, 4480 Fort Lincoln Rd, Mandan*

FAMILY OUTINGS

FORT UNION TRADING POST
On the Montana–North Dakota border in Williston, the pearl-white Fort Union Trading Post is a reconstruction of the American Fur Company post built in 1828. It was the most important post along the upper Missouri River through the 1860s. A small museum discusses the fur trade, and there are interactive opportunities for kids. *www.nps.gov/fous, 15550 ND-1804*

JAMESTOWN This North Dakota city is perhaps best known for being home to the World's Largest Buffalo (a concrete, 60-ton piece of Americana) and the National Buffalo Museum. History buffs will enjoy a visit to the Fort Seward Military Post and the Stutsman County Memorial Museums, while outdoor enthusiasts can explore the nearby Jamestown Reservoir. *http://discoverjamestownnd.com*

NORTH DAKOTA HERITAGE CENTER & STATE MUSEUM Engaging and informative, this museum tells the state's rich history. If you're traveling with children, the museum hosts a plethora of interactive activities for kids. With everything from dinosaurs to Native American history, the museum is a worthwhile destination for all ages. *https://statemuseum.nd.gov, 612 E Boulevard Ave, Bismarck*

SCANDINAVIAN HERITAGE PARK The small Scandinavian Heritage Park in Minot is home to a Norwegian stave church and other structures. Stretch your legs and stroll the Scandinavian exhibits. *https:// scandinavianheritage.org, 1020 S Broadway*

© Posnov / Getty Images

OHIO

★ ★

POPULATION: 11.7 million | **SIZE:** 44,825 sq miles | **CAPITAL:** Columbus
WEBSITE: http://ohio.org

THE SEVENTH-LARGEST STATE BY POPULATION IS THE CORNERSTONE OF THE AMERICAN MIDWEST. Its three major cities stretch from Cleveland on Lake Erie to Cincinnati next to Kentucky, with Columbus holding down the state in the center. Myriad other cities boast their own charms. This is a 'swing state' through and through, where progressive artist enclaves and tech start-ups huddle in the shadow of the Rust Belt's former glory days while the nation's biggest Amish community holds to a traditional way of life just up the road. Top attractions like the Rock & Roll Hall of Fame lure steady streams of vacationers, but it is Ohio's wholesome patchwork of cities with a personality and culture all their own that will keep you coming back for more. Even its sole national park, Cuyahoga Valley, breaks the mold with a network of small rural towns inside its confines.

FOOD & DRINK

AMISH DAIRIES From slow-churned butter to specialized cheeses, Ohio's Amish use old techniques to create their dairy products. At Heini's Cheese Chalet, learn how Amish farmers hand-milk their cows and spring-cool (versus machine-refrigerate) their goods before delivering it each day. Grab abundant samples of the more than 50 cheeses they make and peruse the kitschy History of Cheesemaking mural. To see the curd-cutting in action through the big window, come before 11am (except on Wednesday and Saturday). *https://heinis.com, 6005 Hwy 77, Millersburg*

BUCKEYES The Buckeye State takes its moniker seriously, and every Christmas, bakers in the state create these chocolate-coated peanut butter fudge morsels that look exactly like buckeye tree nuts. OSU fans prepare them for game days in this football-mad state, and local sweet shops stock them as well.

CINCINNATI CHILI Spiced with chocolate and cinnamon and served 'five ways' – atop spaghetti and beans and garnished with cheese and onions – Cincinnati chili was developed by immigrant restaurateurs in the early 20th century, and is now known across the country. Get some at Skyline Chili, with locations all over the city.

ICE CREAM It must be all the local dairies, but buckeye residents sure do love their ice cream. Gourmet ice cream purveyor Jeni's has stores across the country now and wide distribution in grocery stores, but its origins are in Columbus' Short North district, where their scoop shop serves out flavors like brambleberry crisp. Rich and creamy, Jeni's sources its milk and ingredients directly from farmers. Graeter's also has locations throughout the state after an 1870 start in Cincinnati. Then there's Young's Jersey Dairy in Yellow Springs, whose famous ice cream shop, the Dairy Store, whips up what many say are Ohio's best milkshakes.

ITALIAN-AMERICAN CLASSICS Could America's best Italian restaurants be in Ohio? With a large Italian-American population, the feather-light, freshly made pasta in Cincinnati is a poignant reminder that the shells of dried macaroni in your pantry are better suited for arts and crafts. Cincy favorite Sotto bookends its primis with house-made charcuterie boards and puffy ricotta doughnuts in a cavernous wood-beamed space in the heart of downtown.

LAKE PERCH All along Lake Erie, lake perch feature as one of the most sought-after fish and a frequent fresh meal. The fish are caught daily and often swaddled in crunchy breading. The hole-in-the-wall spot New Sandusky Fish Co on the bay is terrific for lake perch and walleye sandwiches with a side of French fries.

LOCAL BREWS Cleveland brewery Platform Beer Co at Ohio City's southern edge has a tasting room overflowing with cheap pints of innovative saisons, pale ales and more. Meanwhile Cincinnati's German influence meant it was once a beer drinker's paradise. In the 1890s there were

★ ★ ★

FIRST IN FLIGHT

Forget North Carolina's license plate – it's Ohio that's the real home of aviation, as recognized by the US Congress. Brothers Wilbur and Orville Wright were from Dayton, Ohio, and while their plane took off from Kitty Hawk, North Carolina, historians believe they drafted and built the machine back in their home state. Furthermore, over 20 astronauts were born in Ohio, including Neil Armstrong and John Glenn; more than any other state.

From left: View of the Cincinnati skyline from the Over the Rhine District.

Photo credit along right edge: © Howard Grill /Getty Images; Left: © Luke.Travel / Shutterstock

★ ★ ★

GOETTA FEST

How many cities boast their own type of meat? Goetta (pronounced get-uh) is an herb-spiced, pork-and-oats breakfast sausage, and it's only found around Cincinnati. The city pays homage annually at Goetta Fest in August. Folks gather for goetta-eating contests and goetta ring toss games, and the world's lone Goetta Vending Machine provides one-of-a-kind souvenir meat rolls for a few bucks.

1800 saloons for 297,000 citizens, enabling them to guzzle two and a half times more beer than the rest of the country. Check out Rhinegeist Brewery, a hoppy clubhouse with beers on tap and a view of the bottling line. Ohio is reaching back into its past with moonshine distilleries as well; Hocking Hills Moonshine has a copper still that dates to the family's 1800s farm, and they still use the sweet spring water on their grounds.

NATURAL ESCAPES

CUYAHOGA VALLEY NATIONAL PARK

The Cuyahoga river wends through a forested valley here, earning its Native American name of 'crooked river'. The name is evocative, and hints at the mystical beauty of Ohio's only national park on a cool morning, when the mists thread the woods and all you hear is the honk of Canadian geese and the sound of a great blue heron flapping over its hunting grounds. Follow the park's Ohio & Erie Canal Towpath Trail to trace the historic route that linked Lake Erie to the Ohio River

in the 19th century. *www.nps.gov/cuva/ index.htm, 15610 Vaughn Rd, Brecksville*

HOCKING HILLS STATE PARK Hidden in Hocking County, Hocking Hills State Park is splendid to explore in any season (but especially lovely in autumn), with miles of trails for hiking and biking past waterfalls and gorges. It features several spectacular rock formations, whose gorges and recesses tempt explorers. Old Man's Cave is a scenic winner for hiking. *http://parks.ohiodnr.gov/hockinghills, 19852 Hwy 664, Logan*

JOHN GLENN ASTRONOMY PARK The Hocking Hills claim some of the country's darkest skies, and John Glenn Astronomy Park, named after the native son and astronaut, is an amazing opportunity for earthlings obsessed with the universe. A 28-inch permanent telescope, plus smaller movable telescopes, allow gazers to peer through a retractable roof at stars, planets, the moon, nebulae, galaxies and comets, with astronomers and other star experts

From left: Rhinegeist Brewery; Blue Hen Falls at Cuyahoga Valley National Park; the imposing Cleveland Museum of Art.

© Ian Dagnall / Alamy Stock Photo

nearby to interpret what you're seeing during the warmer seasons. *https://jgap.info, 20531 OH-664, Logan*

ARTS, HISTORY & CULTURE

400 WEST RICH More than 140 artists, designers and performers have studios in this cavernous, revamped industrial warehouse in Columbus. It's open to the public from 7pm to 10pm on the second Friday of each month, when it also hosts a cool craft market (part of a larger gallery hop in the surrounding artsy neighborhood of Franklinton). The collaborative venue also offers printmaking, painting and ukulele workshops; check the monthly calendar for the schedule of events. *https://400westrich.com, 400 W Rich St*

AKRON MUSIC SCENE The Black Keys, Devo and dozens of other acclaimed artists have roots in Akron, and the city has something to fit every taste in music, helped by a conservatory program at the university. Larger music venues, including

Akron Civic Theater, Lock 3, and EJ Thomas Performing Arts Hall, host the big names, but the best way to see emerging and well-known acts is to head to the more intimate establishments. In the Historic Arts District (home to the largest of the Akron Art Bomb Brigade murals) you'll find the award-winning BLU Jazz+, a cozy brick space reminiscent of a mid-century jazz club. The live music here pairs well with the Southern-inspired cuisine served up at the bar, and the club is putting Akron on the map as a preeminent destination for jazz enthusiasts.

CLEVELAND MUSEUM OF ART
Cleveland's whopping art museum houses an excellent collection of European paintings, as well as African, Asian and American art. Head to the 2nd floor for rock-star works from Impressionists and surrealists. Gallery One, near the entrance, holds a cool quick hit of museum highlights, though there's much more to unearth. Before or after your visit, be sure to stroll the Fine Arts Garden, set within

FUN FACT

Ohio's state flag is the only burgee-shaped one in the country (it's like a pennant with a triangle missing at the end).

★

© Lost Mountain Studio / Shutterstock: Left: © Ron Bouwhuis / Getty Images

Wade Park and designed by Frederick Law Olmsted. The Wade Park District where the museum is sited is listed on the National Register of Historic Places and houses several other cultural institutions, making for a rich day's sightseeing. *http://clevelandart.org, 11150 East Blvd*

HOPEWELL CULTURE NATIONAL HISTORICAL PARK

The area south of Columbus was a center for the ancient Hopewell people, who left behind huge geometric earthworks and burial mounds constructed from around 200 BC to AD 600. This national historical park tells their story. The visitors center provides intriguing background information, but the highlight is wandering about the variously shaped ceremonial mounds spread over 13-acre Mound City, a mysterious town of the dead. Don't miss the famous Serpent Mound 50 miles southwest of town. *www.nps.gov/hocu, 16062 Hwy 104, Chillicothe*

NATIONAL MUSEUM OF THE US AIR FORCE

Located at the Wright-Patterson Air Force Base near Dayton, this huge museum has everything from a Wright Brothers 1909 Flyer to a Sopwith Camel (WWI biplane) and the 'Little Boy' type atomic bomb (decommissioned and rendered safe for display) that was dropped on Hiroshima. The hangars hold miles of planes, rockets and aviation machines, and a spiffy new building adds spacecraft and presidential planes (including the first Air Force One). *www.nationalmuseum.af.mil, 1100 Spaatz St*

OVER THE RHINE NEIGHBORHOOD

Known as the most dangerous district in America only a decade ago, 'OTR' has become a resurgent neighborhood by prioritizing small businesses and sustainable growth. Today the Italianate row homes feature design boutiques and darling eateries. A street car service, narrated by Cincy native Nick Lachey,

---

★ ★ ★

GETTING THERE & AROUND

Cleveland has the state's busiest airport, followed by Columbus, Cincinnati (note its airport is technically in Kentucky) and Dayton. An Amtrak route links Cleveland, Cincinnati and Sandusky. To get around within and between cities, car is easiest.

filled to the brim with a private collection of commercial signs spanning the age of American consumerism. From mirrored glass and light bulbs to curlicues of pulsing neon, the ASM's highlights include ads for KFC and McDonald's, and retro road signs aplenty. *http://AmericanSignMuseum.org, Monmouth Ave, Cincinnati*

CEDAR POINT AMUSEMENT PARK

Cedar Point is one of the world's top amusement parks, known for its 18 adrenaline-pumping roller coasters set on a Lake Erie peninsula. Stomach-droppers include the Top Thrill Dragster, among the globe's tallest and fastest rides. It climbs 420ft into the air before plunging and whipping around at 120mph. The Valravn is the world's longest 'dive' coaster, dropping riders at a 90-degree angle for 214ft. *www.cedarpoint.com, 1 Cedar Point Dr, Sandusky*

OHIO AMISH COUNTRY Rural Wayne and Holmes Counties in central Ohio are home to the US's largest Amish community. Visiting here is like entering a pre-industrial time warp. Descendants of conservative Dutch-Swiss religious factions who migrated to the USA during the 18th century, the Amish continue to follow the *ordnung* (way of life), in varying degrees. Many adhere to rules prohibiting the use of electricity, telephones and motorized vehicles. *www.visitamishcountry.com*

ROCK & ROLL HALL OF FAME &
MUSEUM Cleveland's top attraction perches on Lake Erie like an overstuffed attic bursting with groovy finds: Jimi Hendrix's Stratocaster, Keith Moon's platform shoes, John Lennon's Sgt Pepper suit and a 1966 piece of hate mail to the Rolling Stones from a cursive-writing Fijian. It's more than memorabilia, though. Multimedia exhibits trace the history and social context of rock music and the performers who created it. *www.rockhall.com, 1100 Rock and Roll Blvd*

links stops throughout the neighborhood, including the Findlay Market, a boisterous conglomeration of artisanal vendors. *www.otrchamber.com*

THOMAS EDISON BIRTHPLACE MUSEUM

The tiny town of Milan, 15 miles southeast of Sandusky, is the birthplace of Thomas Edison. The small brick home where he was born in 1847 has been restored and is now a small museum demonstrating his inventions, such as the light bulb and phonograph. Guides take you through the rooms on a 25-minute tour, during which you'll also see plenty of Edison family photos and mementos. *http://tomedison.org, 9 N Edison Dr*

FAMILY OUTINGS

AMERICAN SIGN MUSEUM Like a monument to nostalgia more than a didactic museum space, this warehouse is

ITINERARY

Day 1
Start in Cincinnati, sipping beer from local breweries, strolling Fountain Square and checking out the arts and sports scenes. Don't forget to try Skyline Chili or goetta.

Day 2
Wander Cincy's Over the Rhine neighborhood, then visit the elaborate caves and gorges of beautiful Hocking Hills State Park.

Day 3
Enjoy Columbus' museums or visit the National Museum of the US Air Force in Dayton.

Day 4
Finish your north–south exploration of the state in Cleveland with a visit to the Rock & Roll Hall of Fame and Cleveland Museum of Art in this resurgent city.

Day 5
Venture to the Lake Erie coastline and ride the legendary roller coasters at Cedar Point in Sandusky, America's most overlooked, thrill-packed amusement park. Hikers can visit unique Cuyahoga Valley National Park instead.

From left: The Rock & Roll Hall of Fame in Cleveland; a display at the American Sign Museum in Cincinnati.

OKLAHOMA

★ ★

POPULATION: 3.9 million | **SIZE:** 69,960 sq miles | **STATE CAPITAL:** Oklahoma City
WEBSITE: www.travelok.com

OKLAHOMA GETS ITS NAME FROM THE CHOCTAW WORD MEANING 'RED PEOPLE.' ONE LOOK
at the state's vivid red earth and you'll wonder if the name is more of a literal than an ethnic comment,
but with 39 tribes located here, the state is a place with deep Native American culture and heritage.
Cowboys, the other side of the Old West coin, also figure prominently in the Sooner State. Although
pickups have replaced horses, there's still a great sense of the open range, interrupted only by Oklahoma
City and Tulsa. Oklahoma's share of Route 66 links some of the Mother Road's iconic highlights as it
visits myriad atmospheric old towns. With the third-largest Native American population in the country,
stunning natural beauty and effortless western charm, it's no wonder that this beautiful state's tourism
slogan is 'Oklahoma: Native America.'

© Richard G Smith / Shutterstock

FOOD & DRINK

CHICKEN-FRIED STEAK Steak is almost always on the menu in ranching-heavy Oklahoma. Battered, fried and served with a cream-based gravy, this popular dish is Oklahoma's official state food. Ann's Chicken Fry House on Route 66 serves an excellent version – be sure to order their black-eyed peas too. Kendall's Restaurant in Noble offers delicious fare and is three decades deep into the chicken-fried steak business, feeding generations of University of Oklahoma students along the way.

FRIED OKRA It's not just steak that gets fried in the Sooner State. Fried okra is another menu staple, though its vegetable base probably doesn't make it any better for you. This southern classic is an Oklahoma calling card for good reason.

OKLAHOMA WINE Oklahoma boasts a thriving wine industry with more than 52 wineries and vineyards. Enjoy sophisticated tasting rooms and warm Oklahoman hospitality at Woods & Waters Winery & Vineyard in Anadarko, with 11 varieties of Oklahoma grapes and over 600 acres of rolling hills and countryside.

THETA AND ONION BURGERS The Theta Burger gets its name from the University of Oklahoma's Theta sorority, whose members would order a burger topped with mayonnaise, pickles and hickory sauce so often that it spawned a new trend; the Theta is now served everywhere in Oklahoma. A popular location to try it is Johnnie's Charcoal Broiler in Oklahoma City. Not into mayo or pickles? Another local favorite is the fried onion burger, a thin patty of ground beef fried under a heavy pile of sliced onions, originally called a Depression burger.

NATURAL ESCAPES

BLACK MESA STATE PARK Named after the thick coating of black lava rock that covered the area 30 million years ago, this beautiful park in Kenton is ideal for camping, wildlife watching and hiking. Don't miss the Three Corners marker, where you can stand in Oklahoma, Colorado and New Mexico all at once. *www.travelok.com, County Rd 325*

TURNER FALLS PARK Located in the heart of the beautiful Arbuckle Mountains in Davis, this stunning state park is home to a 77ft waterfall, beaches, swimming holes, caves, hiking trails, campsites, cabin rentals and more. The streams are also packed with trout for fishing enthusiasts. This gorgeous natural oasis is a wonderful refuge. *www.turnerfallspark.com, US-77*

WICHITA MOUNTAINS WILDLIFE REFUGE The 59,020-acre refuge protects bison, elk, longhorn cattle and a super-active prairie dog town. Wildlife is abundant; observant drivers might even see a spindly, palm-sized tarantula tiptoeing across the road. At the visitors center, displays highlight the refuge's flora and fauna, and a massive glass window yields inspiring views of prairie grasslands. For a short but scenic hike, try the creek-hugging Kite Trail to the waterfalls and rocks at the Forty-Foot Hole. *www.fws.gov/refuge/wichita_mountains, Lawton*

★ ★ ★

The SOONER State

Oklahoma has been nicknamed the Sooner State since at least the 1920s. It comes from the 'sooner clause' established during the famous Land Run of 1889. The decisive clause stated that no person was allowed to enter the unclaimed lands of Oklahoma before a carefully designated date that the president was to declare that year. However, claimants often secretly camped on or near the unclaimed lands to illegally make a run for the land 'sooner' than the designated time. This gave them a head start over claimants who chose to follow the rules and enter from the border. 'Sooner' is now an unofficial name for all Oklahomans and serves as the name of the Norman-based state college football team, the University of Oklahoma Sooners. It's also their rallying cry: Boomer Sooner!

© Sean Pavone / Shutterstock; Left: © Walter Bibikow / Getty Images

ARTS, HISTORY & CULTURE

CHICKASAW CULTURAL CENTER

Visitors will experience Chickasaw history and culture at this expansive site in Sulphur, which traces Chickasaw history from involvement in the French and Indian War to the Trail of Tears and on to the present day. It's a unique opportunity to engage with Chickasaw traditions. *https://chickasawculturalcenter.com, 867 Cooper Memorial Dr*

FORT GIBSON

FORT GIBSON One of Oklahoma's most important historic sites, Fort Gibson was home to the removal commission in the 1830s and is where surviving Creek and Seminole Indians were brought after the forced march. From here they were dispatched around the Indian Territory. You can get a good sense of military life 180 years ago at the restored grounds and buildings. It was originally built as a frontier fort in 1824 and remains the oldest town in Oklahoma. *www.okhistory.org/sites/fortgibson, 907 N Garrison Ave*

GILCREASE MUSEUM

GILCREASE MUSEUM This world-class museum in Tulsa was founded by a Native American man named Thomas Gilcrease who discovered a vast oil reserve on his property. The museum holds one of the top collections of Native American art in the country and one of the largest collections of art from the American West in the world. *https://gilcrease.org, 1400 N Gilcrease Museum Rd*

JOHN HOPE FRANKLIN RECONCILIATION PARK

RECONCILIATION PARK On May 30, 1921 – Memorial Day – a white woman and an African American man were alone in an elevator in Tulsa when the woman screamed. This singular event incited three days of violent race riots in which scores were killed and Tulsa's main African American neighborhood was burned. One of the worst such instances in American history, this park serves as a memorial. *www.jhfcenter.org, 322 N Greenwood Ave*

OKLAHOMA CITY MUSEUM OF ART

Serving over 125,000 visitors annually

★ ★ ★

ASK A LOCAL

'Located on the 49th floor of Oklahoma City's Devon Tower, Vast restaurant serves upscale twists on local favorites, such as chicken-fried cauliflower. A highlight is the gorgeous city view offered by the restaurant's floor-to-ceiling windows. Take note that the attire is business casual, and settle in for a night on the town.'

© Marilyn Angel Wynn / Alamy Stock Photo

from over 30 countries and all 50 states, OKCMOA has a rotating cast of exhibits and the permanent collection includes one of the largest collections of Chihuly glass in the world. A full-service restaurant and roof terrace are on-site. *http://www.okcmoa. com, 415 Couch Dr*

OKLAHOMA CITY NATIONAL MEMORIAL MUSEUM
A poignant homage to the story of the 1995 Oklahoma City bombing, this somber memorial and museum tells the story of the country's largest incident of domestic terrorism. It avoids becoming mawkish and lets the horrible events speak for themselves. *https://oklahomacitynationalmemorial.org, 620 N Harvey Ave*

OKLAHOMA JAZZ HALL OF FAME
The best place to learn about jazz greats from Oklahoma and beyond, this Tulsa treasure is the perfect pit stop on your journey. With free Tuesday night jam sessions and weekly Sunday night concerts, this landmark both sustains and contains Oklahoma's rich jazz history. If you prefer folk to jazz, the nearby Woody Guthrie Center beckons. *www.okjazz.org, 111 E 1st St*

PRICE TOWER
Visit Bartlesville to tour the only Frank Lloyd Wright–designed skyscraper ever built, the 221ft Price Tower, completed in 1956. Inside and out it is like *Architectural Digest* meets *The Jetsons*. Wright shopped the design around for 30 years before he found clients willing to build it. All but abandoned in the 1990s, the building now houses a ground-floor art gallery and the Inn at Price Tower. *www.pricetower.org, 510 S Dewey Ave*

SPIRO MOUNDS
Set along the Arkansas River near Spiro, this 150-acre site with prehistoric mounds is one of the country's most important of its kind. Dating to the Mississippian period of AD 800 to 1540, it was a place of ceremonial significance that can still be visited today, though the museum could use a renovation. *www.okhistory.org/sites/spiromounds, 18154 First St*

FUN FACT

The official state poem is 'Howdy Folks,' an ode to Oklahoma cowboy Will Rogers by David Randolph Milsten.

★

From left: The Frank Lloyd Wright–designed Price Tower in Bartlesville; the Bricktown district of Oklahoma City; the Red Earth Powow.

© Christopher Winfield / Shutterstock; Right: © John Davis / Stocktrek Images

GETTING THERE & AROUND

Oklahoma City and Tulsa have the largest airports. Once here, the best way to maneuver across this broad state is to take a classic Route 66 road trip. If starting in Oklahoma City, the EMBARK system does provide public transport options via bus and ferry.

FAMILY OUTINGS

ADMIRAL TWIN DRIVE-IN A charming stop on the famous Route 66 (also known as the Will Rogers Highway after the Oklahoma native, or just the Mother Road), this old-fashioned drive-in movie theater is classic Americana at its finest. The theater is open from March through Halloween and has two screens playing the latest box-office hits. Plan an early arrival to ensure you get a spot. *http://admiraltwindrivein. com, 7355 E Easton St, Tulsa*

NATIONAL COWBOY & WESTERN HERITAGE MUSEUM Founded in 1955 this museum in Oklahoma City is the largest and most prominent collection of Western art and artifacts in the US. Focusing on the historical wonder that is the American West, its art collection is world-renowned. The museum also has a full-scale replica of a frontier village and an interactive children's space. *https://nationalcowboymuseum.org, 1700 NE 63rd St*

RED EARTH POWWOW Consistently ranked among the top public Native American powwows, the Red Earth Powwow in Oklahoma City is an event you will never forget. It is held in June of every year, hosting over 1200 Native American dancers and artists. More than 200 tribes are represented annually as they celebrate their traditions on a grand scale. *www.redearth.org, Cox Convention Center, 1 Myriad Gardens*

Day 1
Start in Tulsa, visiting the Gilcrease Museum or Oklahoma Jazz Hall of Fame. Entertainment for the evening awaits at the Admiral Twin Drive-In on Route 66.

Day 2
Move on to Oklahoma City via Route 66 and pay homage at the Oklahoma City National Memorial Museum to remember the lives lost during the Oklahoma City bombing. After lunch, tour the Stockyards City neighborhood to brush up against some real cowboys. For dinner, enjoy Oklahoma's official state dish, chicken-fried steak, at Ann's Chicken Fry House.

Day 3
South of Oklahoma City, stop at the Chickasaw Cultural Center and tour the state's many natural wonders at the Chickasaw National Recreation Area.

Day 4
If you have time, head further west on Route 66 to explore the famous road of yore en route to the glorious Wichita Mountains.

From left: Turner Falls; the Milky Way rises above the Wedding Party rock formation in the Black Mesa area.

OREGON

★ ★

POPULATION: 4.2 million | **SIZE:** 98,466 sq miles | **STATE CAPITAL:** Salem
LARGEST CITY: Portland | **WEBSITE:** www.traveloregon.com

OREGON HAS ENOUGH ECOSYSTEMS TO FILL A WHOLE CONTINENT, FROM THE IMMENSE SAND dunes of the Pacific coast to the fossil-covered high desert of the Columbia Plateau. In between lie vast tracts of temperate rainforest, rugged rivers, a verdant wine region and glacier-coated volcanoes topped by moodily magnificent Mt Hood. Outdoorsy Oregon offers the call of the open air: rafting on the Rogue River, hiking around Crater Lake and mountain biking on Mt Bachelor all beckon visitors. But Oregon is also offbeat and creative. Its biggest city, Portland, prides itself on being a bastion of budding microbusinesses, and nearby Beaverton is the nation's running capital and home of Nike. From frontier authenticity to hip urban vibes to magnificent natural vistas, the Beaver State offers plenty to chew on for visitors of all tastes and inclinations.

© Olena Yakobchuk / Shutterstock

FOOD & DRINK

CRAFT BEER With over 80 breweries within its city limits, Portland has earned its right to the sobriquet Beervana. This was one of the first places in the US to offer hop-heavy craft beer in the early 1980s, and while some of its leading brands have subsequently gone national, the city still guards a charismatic haul of local pubs and dives offering copious microbrewed IPAs, stouts and lagers on tap.

FOOD TRUCKS In a city where you can pay royally for gourmet food, give thanks for Portland's economical food trucks. Hundreds of these multiethnic kitchens on wheels cluster in busy pods around the city, plying a potpourri of quick-on-the-draw fusion food. Since many of the owners are recent immigrants, the carts act like an international potluck of mobile snack shacks stuffed with soul food from around the globe.

HAZELNUTS If you're traveling in Oregon, you may notice the hazelnuts. The state grows 99% of the nation's crop, most of it reaped from the orchards of the fertile Willamette Valley. Hazelnuts have crept onto the menus of progressive locavore restaurants like Paley's Place in Portland and Bistro Maison in McMinnville and also enlivened the beers of Newport's Rogue Ales.

PINOT NOIR Sharing a similar latitude and climate with Burgundy in France, Oregon's Willamette Valley is celebrated for its pinot noir, a light, fruity, medium-bodied red wine. Family-run wineries such as Eyrie

Vineyards helped kick-start Oregon's viticulture industry in the 1960s, and pinot noir has since gone on to become a wine-bar favorite, thanks in part to its starring role in the (Califonia-focused) film *Sideways*.

THIRD-WAVE COFFEE Long a proud purveyor of coffee purism, Portland has no shortage of third-wave coffee shops selling fair-trade beans. Locally founded Stumptown was one of the pioneers of lightly roasted, single-origin coffee in the 1990s, but it has since been joined by a generation of quality-obsessed coffee geeks on first-name terms with their farmers. Indeed, Oregonian coffee now has as many nuances as its wine.

NATURAL ESCAPES

BAGBY HOT SPRINGS Two hours' drive east of Salem, this old-fashioned Pacific Northwest 'spa' is bivouacked in the middle of the forest with rustic bathhouses capturing mineral-rich thermal water. You'll have to hike 1.5 miles along a wooded trail and pay a small entrance fee for the pleasure of soaking in one of its communal wooden tubs. *www.bagbyhotsprings.org*

CRATER LAKE NATIONAL PARK Oregon's only national park protects the country's deepest lake, a volcanic crater whose waters are sustained purely by snow and rain; it blazes a unique shade of blue on clear summer days. Whether you sail across it, coast along Rim Drive, or merely admire it from Crater Lake Lodge, the crater and its mirror-like lake is an unforgettable vista, scattered with some

★ ★ ★

THE OREGON TRAIL

The fabled Oregon Trail was a rough, unpaved wagon trail that ran from Missouri to present-day Oregon across the US, with an unofficial termination point in Oregon City, the first incorporated city west of the Rocky Mountains. The pioneering route was in use from around the time of the Lewis and Clark Expedition in the first decade of the 1800s to the birth of the transcontinental railroads in the 1860s. It is thought that around 300,000 fur traders, settlers, homesteaders, dreamers, missionaries and hopeful itinerants made the arduous journey across the landscapes of the Old West in search of better prospects. In the process they forged a new chapter of US history, and changed the lives of the local Native Americans forever.

Left: Cannon Beach.

© Bob Pool / Shutterstock; Left: © Zack Frank / Shutterstock

alluring hiking trails on the edges. www.nps.gov/crla

JOHN DAY FOSSIL BEDS NATIONAL MONUMENT
Oregon's geological diversity is never more vivid than in John Day, where a mini-rainbow of colored rocks, ranging from deep brown to golden yellow, are encrusted with fossilized animals and plants dating back 45 million years. Though spread out, the national monument in east–central Oregon is worth visiting for its paleontology center, historic pioneer ranch and short hikes through arid multicolored hills. www.nps.gov/joda

MT BACHELOR
Close to the high-energy outdoor activity capital of Bend, Mt Bachelor is a revered winter ski resort known for its piles of dry powder and abundant sunshine. The resort has long advocated cross-country skiing in tandem with downhill and it maintains 35 miles of groomed trails. In summer it transforms into a beacon for hikers and mountain bikers. www.mtbachelor.com

MT HOOD
Clearly visible from Portland, 11,249ft Mt Hood is an active stratovolcano that hosts a national forest, a 40-mile wilderness loop trail constructed by the Civilian Conservation Corps (CCC) in the 1930s, and America's only year-round lift-operated skiing area. Most excursions kick off from the Timberline Lodge, a National Historic Landmark that featured in the film *The Shining*. www.timberlinelodge.com

OREGON DUNES NATIONAL RECREATION AREA
It's often a case of two steps forward, one step back when hiking among these gigantic dunes rising to heights of 500ft on the Oregon coast just south of Florence. Comprising the largest expanse of oceanfront dunes in the US, the area is laced with trails and characterized by unusual ecosystems and diverse wildlife. www.fs.fed.us, 855 Hwy 101

SMITH ROCK STATE PARK
No discussion of American sport climbing omits mention of this glorious state park perched atop the rust-red high desert of central Oregon.

FUN FACT

Oregon is home to the world's largest living organism, a fungal colony in the state's Blue Mountains.

From left: John Day Fossil Beds National Monument; an orchard with Mt Hood in the distance; a van fully covered with artwork at the annual Hawthorne Street Fair in Portland.

© Dee Browning / Alamy Stock Photo

The region's walls, gullies, gorges and spires are renowned for advanced climbing opportunities; however, the 1800 marked routes include some easier ascents, and there are hiking trails for those who arrive without chalk and harnesses. *https:// smithrock.com, 9241 NE Crooked River Dr*

WILD ROGUE WILDERNESS One of the country's great wild rivers, the Rogue reaches its apex in the Wild Rogue Wilderness, a remote canyon where the turbulent waters throw up class IV rapids. Consistent water levels and an old riverside packhorse trail make the area ideal for rafting, hiking and fishing. Its star power is so strong that it even took central billing in the movie *The River Wild*, starring Meryl Streep and Kevin Bacon. *https://oregonwild.org/wilderness/wild-rogue-wilderness, Agness*

ARTS, HISTORY & CULTURE

DOUG FIR LOUNGE Since the demise of legendary punk-rock venue the Satyricon in 2010, the Doug Fir has taken up the mantle as Portland's go-to live music spot. Complementing the superb music facilities is an adjacent Northwest-flavored restaurant endowed with a log cabin aesthetic, where you can load up on deviled eggs while looking out for minor-league rock stars. *www.dougfirlounge.com, 830 E Burnside St*

KENNEDY SCHOOL It's hard to discuss Portland without mentioning McMenamins, the local craft brewer that has expanded into a multifarious chain with its finger in many different pies. Nowhere encapsulates the brand's distinct art nouveau-meets-psychedelic style as much as this erstwhile school that's been transformed into a hotel, bar, restaurant and arthouse movie theater. *www.mcmenamins.com/kennedy-school, 5736 NE 33rd St*

POWELL'S CITY OF BOOKS No surprise that erudite Portland exhibits the world's largest independent bookstore. Fuel up on caffeine from the in-store cafe and

★ ★ ★

KEEP PORTLAND WEIRD

Testament to Oregon's unashamed quirkiness is the unofficial slogan of its largest city, 'Keep Portland Weird.' Portlanders pride themselves on their quirkiness, self-expression and freedom to be pleasantly odd. The subtle signs are everywhere: bizarrely flavored doughnuts, a museum that pays homage to vacuum cleaners, an adult soap-box derby, and knitted sculptures posing as street art. Much of the singularity has been parodied in the TV comedy show *Portlandia*, while the slogan itself is displayed with a mixture of pride and irony on a downtown wall on the corner of Third Avenue and West Burnside Street.

© VW Pics / Getty Images: Right: © Greg Vaughn / Getty Images

Portland International is Oregon's main airport. The state has an extensive road network. Public transport, while plentiful along the I-5 corridor, is less comprehensive in the interior and on the coasts. Amtrak trains run between Portland, Eugene and Klamath Falls. Greyhound buses ply north–south along I-5 and head inland to Pendleton.

then lose yourself amid the never-ending shelves of cavernous Powell's while looking for that esoteric limited-edition copy of Allen Ginsberg's poems. *www.powells.com, 1005 W Burnside St*

FAMILY OUTINGS

CANNON BEACH It's hard to pick just one standout spot from Oregon's 362-mile-long coastline, but you can't go wrong starting in Cannon Beach close to the border with Washington and near Ecola State Park. The beach for which the artsy town is named is a stunner dominated by wave-lashed Haystack Rock, a 235ft-high sea stack that's part of Oregon Islands National Wildlife Refuge. *www.cannonbeach.org*

FOREST PARK The 'green lungs' of Portland might be better described as giant bellows. Stretching for 8 miles across the hillsides to the west of the city, this verdant space is one of the largest urban parks in the nation. Multiple walking trails are speckled with clusters of old-growth trees. *www.forestparkconservancy.org*

HIGH DESERT MUSEUM One of the country's great out-of-the-way museums, this hugely intriguing place 3 miles south of Bend combines artifacts left by 19th-century pioneers with illuminating geological displays and wildlife demonstrations. After soaking up Native American and Oregon Trail history, head outside for raptor shows and guided hikes. *www.highdesertmuseum.org, 59800 Hwy 97*

ITINERARY

Day 1
Kick off in the gateway city of Portland, a bastion of eccentricity known for its bold craft beer, micro-roasted coffee and delicious avant-garde food.

Day 2
Head east tracking the Columbia River, stopping off at the various attractions around Cascade Locks including the Bridge of the Gods crossing into Washington. Grab lunch in Hood River before circumnavigating the skirts of Mt Hood for a night in the fantastic Timberline Lodge.

Day 3
Plunge south to the outdoor adventure capital of Bend and Mt Bachelor, its nearby activity playground. Be sure to visit the excellent High Desert Museum while passing through.

Day 4
Descend on the mesmerizingly reflective blue waters of Crater Lake National Park.

Day 5
Finish off with a dose of Shakespearean culture or an outing on the Rogue River in pretty Ashland.

PENDLETON Site of the annual weeklong Pendleton Round-Up, a rodeo in the second week of September, Pendleton maintains its Old West ethos year-round. Stop into Pendleton Woolen Mills, manufacturing Western classics since 1863, tour the underground tunnels used by the Chinese population in the sundown era, and visit the Tamástslikt Cultural Institute, which details the impact of pioneers on Native American tribes in the region. Located on the Umatilla Indian Reservation outside Pendleton, its interactive exhibits educate visitors on Native history.
www.pendletonchamber.com

From left: Inside Pendleton Woolen Mills; lush oasis Forest Park in Portland.

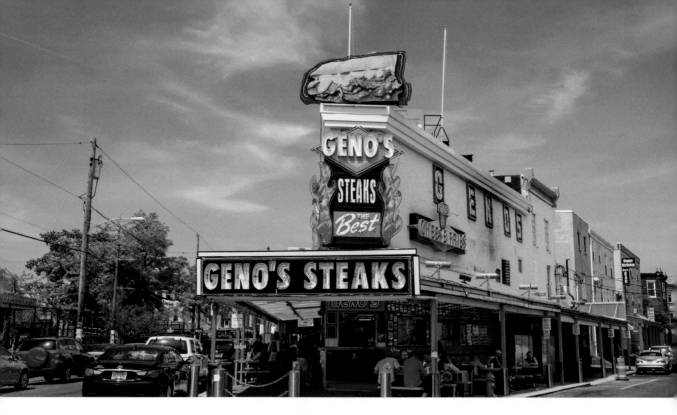

© f11photo / Shutterstock

PENNSYLVANIA

★ ★ ★ ★ ★ ★ ★ ★ ★ ★ ★ ★ ★ ★ ★ ★ ★ ★ ★ ★

POPULATION: 12.8 million | **SIZE:** 46,055 sq miles | **STATE CAPITAL:** Harrisburg
LARGEST CITY: Philadelphia | **WEBSITE:** https://visitpa.com

PENNSYLVANIA'S NICKNAME, THE KEYSTONE STATE, REFLECTS THE CENTRAL ROLE IT PLAYED in the nation's early years – both the Declaration of Independence and the Constitution were debated and adopted at Independence Hall in Philadelphia. Even beyond the Revolutionary period, many key events in US history played out in the state, from the Battle of Gettysburg to industrialization later in the 19th century. Don't assume, however, that a trip to Pennsylvania is all about visiting museums and historic sites. The varied neighborhoods of Philadelphia add up to an exciting, cosmopolitan city. Pittsburgh has emerged from its past as a steel town to become a dynamic tech hub. Natural beauty beckons in the Poconos, while cultural highlights include everything from Amish communities to one of modern architecture's most iconic buildings, Frank Lloyd Wright's Fallingwater.

FOOD & DRINK

APPLE DUMPLINGS It's easy to fall in love with this traditional Amish and Mennonite dish: whole apples are filled with brown sugar and cinnamon, then wrapped in pastry dough and baked. You'll find the dessert on many menus in Pennsylvania Dutch country, as well as in other parts of the state, though many places only serve it at the peak of apple season, in fall and early winter.

MICROBREWS Pennsylvania has a thriving microbrewery scene, with more than 200 craft breweries throughout the state. Some older ones found inspiration in the brewing traditions brought to America by German immigrants. While you could spend weeks tasting Pennsylvania's artisanal ales and lagers, Bullfrog Brewery is an established, award-winning favorite in Williamsport. The Brew Gentlemen brewery in the former steel town of Braddock is always coming up with new, flavorful innovations.

PHILLY CHEESESTEAKS Residents of Philadelphia have strong opinions about who makes the best cheesesteak, the city's signature dish: a roll filled with sautéed beef and onions, topped with melted cheese (or Cheez Whiz). We won't settle that debate but some popular favorites are no-frills Geno's Steaks on South 9th Street, Dalessandro's Steaks and Hoagies on Wendover Street, family-run Campo's on Market Street and Pat's King of Steaks on Passyunk Avenue, which has been serving the sandwiches since 1930.

PIEROGIES Pittsburgh's Polish community traces its roots back to the 18th century, and in the early 20th century, a third of the city's population was either first- or second-generation Polish. The community's culinary imports have been embraced by other Pittsburgh residents too. Pierogies Plus in McKees Rocks sells a variety of the Polish dumplings, while Cop Out Pierogies in the city is famous for its unusual fillings, like buffalo chicken or pumpkin spice, one of its dessert pierogies.

PRIMANTI'S SANDWICH Pittsburgh's counterpart to the cheesesteak is the Primanti's sandwich, created by the Primanti brothers, who opened their first restaurant in 1933. It soon became a popular favorite, serving sandwiches of grilled meat, melted cheese, coleslaw and french fries. There are now Primanti Bros locations throughout Pennsylvania, as well as in five other states, but a Primanti's sandwich should be on your agenda when you visit their hometown.

SCRAPPLE For some reason this Pennsylvania Dutch dish has never made significant inroads beyond the Mid-Atlantic. Perhaps it's because a description of it doesn't sound all that appetizing: pork scraps combined with spices and meal and formed into a loaf. The result is surprisingly delicious, however, and it's commonly served as a side or a sandwich, with condiments savory or sweet. Scrapple is a popular state fair favorite, though you can try it at any time of the year at Philadelphia's Reading Terminal Market.

SHOOFLY PIE The Pennsylvania Dutch (really the descendants of German immigrants) have a fondness for sweets,

★ ★ ★

PENNSYLVANIA READS

If you want to learn about Pennsylvania before your trip, here are a few books for your reading list.

An American Childhood by Annie Dillard is a touching memoir of the author's childhood in Pittsburgh.

Benjamin Franklin by Walter Isaacson is an engaging biography of perhaps the most appealing of the Founding Fathers, the Philadelphia-based inventor, entrepreneur, and statesman.

The Johnstown Flood by David McCullough recounts a tragic disaster, when a makeshift dam in Johnstown broke on May 31, 1889 and killed more than 2000 people. In the process he also creates a vivid portrait of Gilded Age America.

The Mysteries of Pittsburgh by Michael Chabon is the Pulitzer Prize–winning author's moving coming-of-age novel.

© George Sheldon / Shutterstock; Left: © Storms Media Group / Alamy Stock Photo

© George Sheldon / Shutterstock; Left: © Storms Media Group / Alamy Stock Photo

★ ★ ★

CROSSING THE DELAWARE

From Groundhog Day and the anticipation of whether or not Punxsutawney Phil will see his shadow to the Fourth of July festivities in Philadelphia, Pennsylvania has a calendar filled with unique events and celebrations. One of the more unusual ones is the annual reenactment of George Washington's crossing of the Delaware River on Christmas Day. On December 25, 1776, Washington led forces from the Continental Army across the river for a surprise attack on Hessian troops in Trenton, New Jersey, the following day. The reenactment takes place at 1pm, though there is also a dress rehearsal, usually two weeks in advance, if you have other plans on Christmas.

perhaps best illustrated by shoofly pie. Molasses, brown sugar, butter and spices are baked in a piecrust. It's worth making a detour to Ronks to try Dutch Haven's version, made using the bakery's original 1946 recipe. Beiler's Bakery, at Reading Terminal Market in Philadelphia, also sells this Pennsylvania favorite.

STROMBOLI A stromboli is, like a calzone, sort of a pizza-on-the-go, but while a calzone is folded, a stromboli is rolled. While many pizzerias in Pennsylvania serve the dish, Romano's in Essington (just south of Philadelphia) claims to have invented it. Dino's Pizza in Warminster may not have been the first to serve stromboli, but its version has been described by many as the state's best.

NATURAL ESCAPES

CHERRY SPRINGS STATE PARK If you think that you need to travel to the West to see the night sky in all its glory, you may be

surprised to learn that Pennsylvania has an International Dark Sky Park in the northern part of the state. At Cherry Springs, far from any urban centers, the stars shine brightly, to amateur astronomers' delight. *www.dcnr.pa.gov*

POCONOS The Pocono mountains – the fun-to-pronounce name comes from the Lenape for 'creek between two hills' – rise in rocky crusts and folds across the northeast corner of Pennsylvania, and contain some 2400 sq miles of mountains, streams, waterfalls, lakes and forests. The mountains are bordered on the east by the Delaware Water Gap, to the west by coal country, and to the south by the Lehigh Valley. *www.poconomountains.com*

ARTS, HISTORY & CULTURE

AMISH VILLAGE The story of the Amish is remarkable – a 17th-century religious sect that has maintained its traditions in contemporary America. With 30,000

From left: Reenacting crossing the Delaware; Amish country; the striking exterior of Fallingwater. Previous page: Geno's Steaks, Philly.

© Supercel7 / Getty Images

Amish residents, Lancaster County has one of the country's largest concentrations of this unique group. An unobtrusive way to learn about the Amish is by visiting the Amish Village in Ronks with its displays about their faith and way of life. *www. amishvillage.com, 199 Hartman Bridge Rd*

THE ANDY WARHOL MUSEUM The world's largest collection of works by Andy Warhol is in Pittsburgh, where he was born and raised. Many of the silk screens may be familiar given how many museums own at least a few Warhols. Still, seeing the entire span of his career in one building provides a new perspective on his life and work. *www.warhol.org, 117 Sandusky St*

BARNES FOUNDATION The Barnes Foundation, which opened at its current location on Philadelphia's Benjamin Franklin Parkway in 2012, has a remarkable collection of Impressionist and post-Impressionist works. The museum is also known for its unusual displays. African

masks and decorative items sit next to oil paintings, encouraging visitors to think in terms of shapes and colors, not styles and periods. *www.barnesfoundation.org, 2025 Benjamin Franklin Pkwy*

BRANDYWINE RIVER MUSEUM OF ART The illustrator and artist NC Wyeth settled in Chadds Ford in the Brandywine Valley and raised five children, three of whom also became artists – the most famous of them Andrew Wyeth. The museum's permanent collection includes many works by the Wyeths, including Jamie, Andrew's son, though it also hosts temporary exhibitions focused on other artists. *www.brandywine.org, 1 Hoffmans Mill Rd*

FALLINGWATER One of modern architecture's most famous buildings, Frank Lloyd Wright's Fallingwater is in Mill Run, roughly 90 minutes by car from Pittsburgh. The house was completed in 1939, and with its unique flow of indoor and outdoor spaces, it's one of Wright's

FUN FACT

Pennsylvania's small town of Indiana is known as the Christmas Tree Capital of the World, a testament to its status as one of the top suppliers of Christmas trees in the country.

ferrantraite / Getty Images; Left: © Delmas Lehman / Shutterstock

★ ★ ★

ASK A LOCAL

What is Philly's best sandwich?

'The Grilled Pork Bahn Mi #2 at Ba Le Bakery at 6th Street and Washington Avenue. The house-made baguettes are the greatest sandwich rolls ever made. They have a perfect level of crispy crunch on the outside, with a soft inside. The fresh veggies, jalapeño, sprigs of cilantro and grilled pork come together to make a sandwich I feel should overshadow all the other great sandwiches in Philly.'
– Joseph Frost, chef de cuisine at Terrain Cafe in Devon, PA

most important works. You can visit only on guided tours; reserve far in advance. *https://fallingwater.org, 1491 Mill Run Rd*

FONTHILL CASTLE AND MERCER MUSEUM At the peak of the Arts and Crafts movement, Henry Chapman Mercer accumulated a fortune producing his famous Moravian tiles. With his newfound wealth, he designed a distinctly American 'castle' folly near Doylestown, a mix of Gothic, Byzantine and other styles, and made of poured concrete. It stands today as a monument to an eccentric if largely forgotten visionary. The separate Mercer Museum showcases 40,000 objects from American life in the 18th and 19th centuries. *www.mercermuseum.org, 525 E Court St*

GETTYSBURG NATIONAL MILITARY PARK Even if you rarely visit battlefields, make an exception for Gettysburg. When General Robert E Lee marched Confederate troops into southern Pennsylvania in July

1863, their defeat by Union forces turned the tide against the Confederacy in the Civil War. The stories of 170,000 Americans, on both sides, who fought over three days are brought to life by the museum and battlefield walks and drives. Visit over July 5–7 to witness the annual reenactment. *www.nps.gov/gett, 1195 Baltimore Pike*

INDEPENDENCE HALL A stately brick building completed in 1732, Philadelphia's Independence Hall long housed Pennsylvania's Colonial government, but it is most famous as the setting of several key events in the country's early history. The Declaration of Independence and the Constitution were debated and adopted here, and Congress met in the nearby courthouse from 1790 to 1800. *www.nps.gov/inde, 520 Chestnut St*

LIBERTY BELL With its inscription 'Proclaim Liberty Throughout All the Land Unto All the Inhabitants thereof,' a line from Leviticus, this 2080lb bronze bell

From left: Gettysburg National Military Park; Philly's Museum of Art; colorful shopfronts in the Northern Liberties neighborhood.

© Darren LoPrinzi / Getty Images

cast in London in 1753 has been a powerful symbol of freedom for abolitionists, suffragists and others. The bell is a short walk from Independence Hall, so it's easy to visit both at once. *www.nps.gov/inde*

LONGWOOD GARDENS A modest farm in Kennett Square in the Brandywine Valley was transformed after its purchase by Pierre S du Pont in 1906 into a stunning botanical and display garden. Its 1000 acres include both a treasure trove of plant species and a series of beautiful formal gardens that are like a course on garden design over the last century. *https://longwoodgardens.org, 1001 Longwood Rd*

PHILADELPHIA MUSEUM OF ART You may recognize this museum even if you have never visited Philadelphia before, thanks to its appearance in *Rocky* (the cinematic scene is now commemorated with a statue of the boxer on the site). After climbing those famous steps, enter and explore an encyclopedic collection with everything from medieval armor and Old Master paintings to South Asian works, with a rotating schedule of blockbuster exhibitions. *www.philamuseum.org, 2600 Benjamin Franklin Pkwy*

VALLEY FORGE This little town in southeastern Pennsylvania was the site of the Continental Army's encampment from December 1777 to June 1778, making it the base of General George Washington's operations. Visitors today can see Washington's restored headquarters, reconstructions of the troops' log cabins, and a triumphal arch – somewhat out of place in its rural setting – completed in 1917. *www.nps.gov/vafo, 1400 N Outer Line Dr, King of Prussia*

FAMILY OUTINGS

CRAYOLA EXPERIENCE Crayola crayons are so ubiquitous, you may never have considered where they are made. The

★ ★ ★

A REBORN PENN MUSEUM

The Penn Museum in Philadelphia, part of the University of Pennsylvania, has long been known both for its excellent archaeology and anthropology collection, especially strong in Egyptian antiquities, and for the dated gallery spaces of its 19th-century building. There's a new reason to see the museum's ancient masterpieces, though: a recent renovation under the direction of New York architectural firm Gluckman Tang. Dark and narrow spaces are flooded with light from floor-to-ceiling windows, while the highlight is a new gallery that allows columns from the palace of Egyptian pharaoh Merenptah to be rebuilt at their full, imposing height.

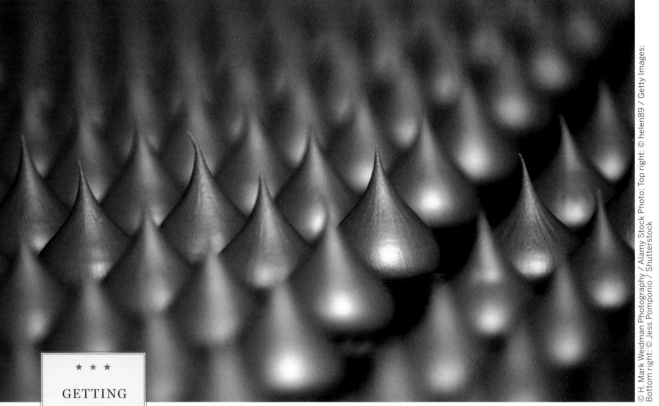

© H. Mark Weidman Photography / Alamy Stock Photo; Top right: © helen89 / Getty Images; Bottom right: © Jess Pomponio / Shutterstock

★ ★ ★

GETTING THERE & AROUND

The main air access points are the international airports of Philadelphia and Pittsburgh, and northeastern PA is near the giant hub of New Jersey's Newark Airport, with connections across the world. Trains serve many of its major cities, while buses service most towns. That said, with so many of this state's interesting sites lying off the beaten path, renting a car and driving around on your own is best.

company's headquarters is in eastern Pennsylvania. At nearby Easton the associated Crayola Experience gets kids excited about drawing with crayons – a challenge in this age of screens. There is, of course, a store on-site, and you should expect to leave with some new 64-packs. *www.crayolaexperience.com, 30 Centre Sq*

EASTERN STATE PENITENTIARY
This penitentiary in Philadelphia, which opened in 1829 and closed in 1971, was a model for other prisons with its groundbreaking radial design. A visit will intrigue kids, especially those fascinated by gangsters (Al Capone was incarcerated here) and ghost stories. But it's not recommended for children under seven. *www.easternstate.org, 2027 Fairmount Ave*

ECKLEY MINERS' VILLAGE MUSEUM
Many ghost towns were once mining settlements abandoned once the lode was exhausted, and such was the fate of Eckley, a village to the south of Wilkes-Barre. The town, founded in the 1850s, largely faded into obscurity in the 1920s after coal deposits were used up. Today the abandoned homes have been restored as a museum. *http://eckleyminersvillage.com*

HERSHEY
In 1905, candymaker Milton Hershey built the world's largest chocolate manufacturing plant and an eponymous company town to go along with it. Two years later, Hersheypark opened. It has grown over the decades into a wildly popular amusement park with 70 rides and other attractions, including roller coasters. Hershey Chocolate World, adjacent to Hersheypark and its adrenaline-pumping rides, attracts serious chocolate lovers with its chocolate-making tour. *www.hersheypa.com*

ITINERARY

Day 1
Start in the City of Brotherly Love, Philadelphia. Founded by William Penn, a Quaker merchant (and the source of the state's name), Pennsylvania's largest city is a mix of historic sites and lively neighborhoods. Walk in the footsteps of Benjamin Franklin and other Founding Fathers in the Old City and Society Hill, near Independence Hall. Rittenhouse Square is the city's most posh area, but others like Manayunk, with its repurposed factories and loft spaces, are worth a detour.

Day 2
Visit cultural highlights like the Philadelphia Museum of Art or the Barnes Foundation. For lunch there's Reading Terminal Market, where you can try a Philly cheesesteak or pastries made by Pennsylvania Dutch bakers. In the afternoon, explore Eastern Penitentiary, an eerie prison converted to a museum.

Day 3
Pennsylvania is too big to cover in one trip. One option is to drive west to the Brandywine Valley (home of Longwood Gardens and the Wyeth family of artists) and Lancaster County's rolling farmland, which houses one of the country's largest Amish communities. Or head north to Jim Thorpe, a historic town in the Poconos. If you choose the latter, stop in Bethlehem, a charming town with Moravian roots, or Easton, for a visit to the Crayola Experience.

Day 4
Drive across the state to its second-largest city, Pittsburgh. If you have chosen the southern route on day 3 (to the Brandywine Valley), then Gettysburg will be on your route.

Days 5 & 6
Pittsburgh has reinvented itself from a rough-around-the-edges industrial city into a tech center. New restaurants are opening and there's a positive energy that is palpable. The Andy Warhol Museum and the Carnegie Museum of Art are highlights. In this city of hard-core sports fans, cheer on the home team right downtown, with the Steelers at Heinz Field and the Pirates at PNC Park. And Fallingwater, Frank Lloyd Wright's masterpiece, is just over 90 minutes away by car, well worth a visit before leaving the region.

From left: Tempting Hershey Kisses; Crayola Experience in Easton; Eastern State Penitentiary.

RHODE ISLAND

★ ★

POPULATION: 1 million | **SIZE:** 1212 sq miles | **STATE CAPITAL:** Providence
WEBSITE: www.visitrhodeisland.com

RHODE ISLAND IS LIKE A LUMINOUS PIECE OF SEA GLASS, GLIMMERING ON THE EAST COAST. Its size (the smallest in the US) has long served to keep the state's natural beauty and myriad attractions a secret. Travelers often merely pass through Rhode Island to get to Boston or New York City. And the truth is, a lot of Rhode Islanders are happy that way. Tourists can come for the grandeur of Newport's mansions and then be on their way. Cities like Providence thrive just fine on local tastes for world-class cuisine and art. Block Island can remain a getaway for citizens of the state who are content to have the place to themselves. For better or worse, however, the part of the population who would have Rhode Island remain undiscovered is going to have to get used to sharing the state. The secret is out: Rhode Island is a destination all its own.

© diane39 / Getty Images

FOOD & DRINK

CLAMS APLENTY Fresh clams can be scooped straight from the shores of the Ocean State, so it's no surprise that the locals have learned all sorts of ways to make them delicious, starting with regional specialty clam cakes. Higher-end presentations include those at Al Forno, where the spaghettini with roasted clams is not to be missed. Seasonal clam shacks abound for quick bites in summer: Aunt Carrie's in Narragansett and Evelyn's Drive-In on the shore of Tiverton are two tasty options.

DEL'S LEMONADE It's not a trip to Rhode Island without sampling Del's at one of the many frozen lemonade stands throughout the state. While best enjoyed during the warmer months, this sweet and slushy drink is so popular that many of the iconic Del's Lemonade stands are open year-round. Del's green-and-yellow-striped cup is a Rhode Island icon.

DOUGHBOYS State fairs have their funnel cakes, New Orleans has beignets and Rhode Island has doughboys. Essentially fried dough as big as your head (though you can get them smaller), doughboys are available plain or with sugar if you really want to give your insulin-providing pancreas a run for its money. Try Iggy's in Narragansett for a world-class doughboy experience.

JOHNNYCAKE These treats (yes, the same as the cornmeal flatbread you read about in *The Cabin Faced West* and *Little House on the Prairie*) are a big draw in Rhode Island, and in many places can be ordered solo or in combination with breakfast sandwiches and omelets. Jigger's Diner in East Greenwich is a favorite for these culturally significant staples.

NATURAL ESCAPES

NEWPORT CLIFF WALK This 3.5-mile hike has stunning views of the rocky Atlantic shoreline on one side and Newport's mansions on the other. Most of the trail is paved and accessible from several points. Start at the north end (it's wheelchair- and stroller-friendly), and if you're wearing the right footwear and your party is feeling hearty, continue onto the more rugged parts. Dogs are allowed, but bicycles aren't. *http://cliffwalk.com*

SCHOONER *ADIRONDACK II* The state's 400 miles of coastline makes sailing a big deal in Rhode Island, and nothing beats a trip from Newport on the *Adirondack II* or her sister *Eleanor*. The captain tells stories and answers questions, but you can also tune out and just enjoy the voyage. There's no better way to appreciate the state's sailing culture than by taking part in it. *https://sail-newport.com, 30 Bowens Wharf*

ARTS, HISTORY & CULTURE

NEWPORT GILDED AGE MANSION TOURS Explore the historical vacation 'cottages' of America's richest. Interpretive resources range from audio to guided tours, with a children's option available at the Breakers. Don't miss: the Breakers (platinum walls, breathtaking ocean views); the Elms (considered modern for 1901);

★ ★ ★
FORT ADAMS FESTIVALS

Depending on your musical preferences, choose either the famous Newport Jazz Festival or the Newport Folk Festival. Both are Rhode Island summer events held at cool Fort Adams State Park, itself a worthy destination. Driving around Newport during festivals can be a hassle, so take the Newport Water Shuttle or do as the locals do: drop anchor and enjoy the music from a boat.

Left: The Block Island North Light.

© Travel Ink / Getty Images; Right: © Danita Delmont / Alamy Stock Photo

Marble House (giddily over the top; visit its teahouse but skip the food). Gift shops abound, but little differentiates them. *www.newportmansions.org/explore*

NEWPORT VINEYARDS Whether it's the beginning of your time in Newport or the end, Newport Vineyards in Middletown is a capstone experience. No reservations are needed for the tour, which takes you through every step of the wine-making process. Check the schedule for live music and events, and in nice weather, enjoy one of the reasonably priced bottles outside among the vines.
www.newportvineyards.com,
909 E Main Rd (Rte 138)

PROVIDENCE WALKING TOURS This super-strollable city has stories and charm for days, and self-guided walking tours are a great way to experience them. All routes (find them online) have their merits, but a favorite is the East Side including Benefit Street, with stops such as the Old Brick Schoolhouse, a monument to public education and progressive ideas, plus the Statehouse and the RISD Museum. *www.goprovidence.com*

RISD MUSEUM The Rhode Island School of Design (RISD) in Providence is one of the best schools for art and design in the world. Students aspire to have their work included in RISD's museum, and rightly so. RISD's art and design museum is as good as any of its peers, with an impressive collection of sculpture, paintings and antiquities, and really shines in the jewelry, furniture and textile departments. *https://risdmuseum. org, 20 N Main St*

FAMILY OUTINGS

BLOCK ISLAND Described lovingly by locals as 'like Martha's Vineyard, only

---

★ ★ ★

GETTING THERE & AROUND

Rhode Island is accessible by sea, air or land. Ferries serve several ports, TF Green Airport in Warwick serves the entire state, and roads are well-maintained and easy to navigate by car or bus. Amtrak stops in Providence and Kingston as well.

ITINERARY

Day 1
Roam the opulent
vacation homes of the
Gilded Age's richest 1%
in Newport, with a stop
in the scenic downtown
for lunch and a quick
spin on the Cliff Walk.
In summer, it's hard to
beat a sunset cruise to
end the day.

Days 2 & 3
Stop by Fort Adams
State Park if you enjoy
history (Del's Lemonade
can fuel your visit).
Then take the ferry to
Block Island to explore,
hike and relax along
the island's 17 miles of
shoreline.

Day 3
Head to state capital
Providence. Check
the schedule to see if
WaterFire is showing; if
not, you can still enjoy
a fascinating walking
tour of the city, check
out the Rhode Island
School of Design and
the neoclassical Rhode
Island State House.
Top it all off at one of
the best restaurants in
the state, Al Forno; the
Italian menu perfectly
complements a gondola
ride on Providence's
rivers (just pretend
they're canals).

tackier,' Block Island boasts 18 miles of beaches, hiking and biking trails, and two marinas. Kids will love the Glass Float Project and 1661 Farm and Gardens, while the supernaturally inclined can be on the lookout for the 'clock lady.' Experience stunning views – and a lot of steps! – at the must-see Mohegan Bluffs. Ferries are available daily from the mainland in Point Judith, Newport and Fall River. *www.blockislandinfo.com*

CRESCENT PARK CAROUSEL Recently put through a vigorous restoration, this grand carousel in Riverside has delighted visitors since it opened in 1895. Have a day out, 1900s-style, by taking a few turns on the carousel, snacking on some popcorn, enjoying a concert at the nearby park and having a bite at Blount Clam Shack across the road. It's open seasonally, as are many spots here. *www.crescentparkcarousel.org, 700 Bullocks Point Ave*

LA GONDOLA Kitschy? Maybe. Fun? Absolutely. Parties of up to six are regaled in this 'touch of Italy in Rhode Island' experience by singing gondoliers with plenty of personality. From spring through fall, tour the rivers of Providence and get a unique look at some of the city's famous landmarks while your tour guide spins yarns about their history and provenance. *www.gondolari.com, Gondola Landing, One Citizens Plaza*

WATERFIRE It's a sculpture and a show with music. Consisting of 100 wood fires artfully positioned on the rivers in Providence, WaterFire is awesome. Shows in the summer impress, but for a truly magical, almost primal, experience, bundle up a bit and visit in the fall. As an add-on, you can take the walking tour to get a behind-the-scenes look at the installation (plus priority viewing spots). *https://waterfire.org, Waterplace Park*

From left: The Breakers, in Newport, built by the Vanderbilts in 1901 and open to the public; the RISD Museum in Providence.

SOUTH CAROLINA

★ ★

POPULATION: 5 million | **SIZE:** 32,020 sq miles | **STATE CAPITAL:** Columbia
LARGEST CITY: Charleston | **WEBSITE:** https://discoversouthcarolina.com

CROSS THE BORDER FROM NORTH TO SOUTH CAROLINA AND YOU'RE OFFICIALLY IN THE DEEP South. The pace of life slows down here, and the accents thicken. Pockets of the state remain all about tradition, passed down through generations, and visitors will find history in every corner. Travel the sleepy byways from tiny fishing villages to antebellum cities to partake in the local culture and culinary delights. Most of South Carolina's better-known sights and activities are on the coast: the beaches of the Grand Strand, the Sea Islands where descendants of enslaved people still maintain their own food, culture and dialect, and the gardenia-scented cobblestones of Charleston, possibly the most charming city in America. But inland holds its own power. Explore tea-dark swamps, splendid old plantation houses with painful pasts, and marvelous upland hiking trails.

© Peter Unger / Getty Images

FOOD & DRINK

CHARLESTON CUISINE Charleston was always a foodie town, and Upper King St in particular has been named one of the top foodie neighborhoods in the country. One of the standouts is Husk, where everything on the daily-changing menu is grown or raised below the Mason–Dixon line, but chefs all over town are reinventing Southern food in dazzling ways.

FISH SHACKS Watch the sun set in pastel streaks over the water while tucking into a plate of seafood and a glass of wine. Fish-centric spots abound in the state from Edisto Island to St Helena Island to Charleston suburb Mt Pleasant, Shem Creek's popular dining district with a nostalgic mid-century vibe. Our favorite (though distinctly non-scenic) spot here is fried fish heaven The Wreck of the Richard & Charlene, in an old bait locker.

FROGMORE STEW More of a boil than a proper stew, the Frogmore stew is a regional delicacy of boiled shrimp, corn and other seafood, served dumped out on newspaper (no frogs included). Bowen's Island Restaurant in Folly Beach has been serving it since 1946.

LOWCOUNTRY CUISINE The coast of South Carolina is home to one of America's best regional cuisines: the seafood-rich, African-inflected Lowcountry fare. Classic Lowcountry dishes include creamy, sherry-spiked she-crab soup, okra-based gumbo, bacon- and tomato-flecked red rice, and shrimp and grits, a classic local fisherman's breakfast.

SOUTH CAROLINA BARBECUE TRAIL Most Southern states choose one barbecue sauce and stick with it. South Carolina keeps its options open, with four official sauces to top slow-smoked pulled pork: vinegary 'light tomato,' sweet 'heavy tomato,' tangy 'mustard' and spicy 'vinegar.' Choose your favorite (mustard is the most distinctively South Carolinian) on a road trip to the 220 finger-licking restaurants of the BBQ trail.
https://discoversouthcarolina.com/barbecue

TEA TIME South Carolina still has two working tea plantations, one outside Charleston and the other, Table Rock Tea, in the small town of Pickens. On sandy, subtropical Wadmalaw Island, Charleston Tea Plantation grows more than 300 varieties of black and green tea. Board a vintage red trolley to tour the fragrant tea fields, then learn about production at the factory before picking up boxes of Plantation Peach or Carolina Mint tea to take home. *www.charlestonteaplantation. com, 6617 Maybank Hwy*

NATURAL ESCAPES

ANGEL OAK Cross the Stono River and drive through the golden farm fields of Johns Island to reach this storied oak tree. Upwards of 500 years old and 28ft in circumference, its twisted, fern-covered branches reach all the way to the ground. Legend has it the spirits of former enslaved people visit this tree for solace.
3688 Angel Oak Rd, Johns Island

CONGAREE NATIONAL PARK South Carolina's only national park is the

★ ★ ★

Charleston's
HAUNTED STREETS

Ghost tours are a staple in Charleston, and the city thrives on rumors of spirits and hauntings such as the reputed ghost of Poogan's Porch restaurant. The city, founded in 1670, is one of the oldest in America. With its 18th- and 19th-century buildings, and silent gaslit streets, the city resembles Bath or Bristol, but palmetto trees and live oaks give it a distinct swampiness. The ancient cemeteries, with their wayward headstones and trees draped in Spanish moss, combine the settings for two different sorts of ghost story – the haunted English graveyards of MR James and Walter de la Mare, and African-inflected tales of voodoo. The combination reflects the region's heritage: colonized by the British, built and made rich by generations of African slaves. African beliefs persisted in another form: this is voodoo country, though the subject is veiled in secrecy.

© Dale Dudley / Shutterstock; Left: © The Washington Post / Getty Images

★ ★ ★

ASK A LOCAL

'In Charleston watch the sunrise at Waterfront Park. Stroll to City Lights Coffee, sit in the window and watch the world wake up. Walk to Fast and French for breakfast and local gossip at the communal table. Rent a bicycle and twist and turn through the narrow streets. Head out to Folly Beach to eat the most delicious tacos under an oak tree at the rustic beach shack, Chico Feo. Walk a block to the beach before heading to one of the oldest surf shops in the country, McKevlin's. For a true day adventure, take the 2-hour trip to Hemingway, SC for the best old-school BBQ at Scott's Bar-B-Que. On your way back, stop in historic Georgetown and walk the boardwalk.'
- *Artist Candace Patterson, owner of Dos Bandidos Art*

country's largest contiguous old-growth bottomland forest. Walk the elevated boardwalk beneath bald cypress trees dripping Spanish moss or kayak the waters of the Congaree River, keeping your eyes open for bobcats, otters and turtles, then camp beneath the canopy. Don't miss the world's tallest loblolly pine at 169ft tall. *www.nps.gov/cong, 100 National Park Rd, Hopkins*

FALLS PARK ON THE REEDY Make this your first stop in Greenville. Ridiculously picturesque Falls Park on the Reedy is a 32-acre park hugging the banks of the Reedy River as it splashes through downtown. In the 1800s its shores were a center of industry, lined with mills, textile factories and warehouses. Today inviting trails and manicured gardens are the draw, with shops and restaurants just a few steps away. The centerpiece of the park is 60ft Reedy Falls, best viewed from the graceful Liberty Bridge, a 355ft-long pedestrian suspension bridge just downstream. *http://fallspark.com*

FRANCIS MARION NATIONAL FOREST This 250,000-acre wilderness is named for Revolutionary War hero Francis Marion, aka the 'swamp fox,' famous for hiding in unsparing terrain. There are four different areas to the forest, including the delightfully named Hellhole Bay. You can camp, hike, or ride horses or bikes here, but the choice activity is canoeing the spooky blackwater swamps beneath ancient bald cypresses. *www.fs.usda.gov/scnfs, 2967 Steed Creek Rd, Huger*

HUNTING ISLAND STATE PARK Camp amidst the tangled maritime forest of this 5000-acre undeveloped barrier island. The beach is as pristine as they come, the waters blood-warm by midsummer. Paddle through the silent, humid marshes, bike the lagoonside trail, or climb the long-defunct 1875 lighthouse. So lush and dense is the foliage, the Vietnam War scenes from *Forrest Gump* were filmed here. No wonder it's the most visited state park in the state. *https://southcarolinaparks.com/hunting-island, 2555 Sea Island Pkwy*

From left: Scott's BBQ in Hemingway; the Angel Oak on Johns Island; Congaree National Park boardwalk. Previous page: Cobblestoned Chalmers Street in Charleston.

© Jason Yoder / Shutterstock

PALMETTO TRAIL Some 350 miles of this planned 500-mile cross-state hiking and biking trail are completed, running from the Lowcountry's Intracoastal Waterway through the upland mountains, passing through maritime forest, swamps and piney mountains, and along urban sidewalks and bike paths. It's divided into 26 sections ranging from 1.3 to 47 miles, so just bite off as much as you can chew. When finished, it will showcase each of South Carolina's distinctive ecosystems.
https://palmettoconservation.org/ palmetto-trail

TABLE ROCK STATE PARK Hoof it up Pinnacle Mountain, the aptly-named tallest peak in South Carolina, at this 3000-acre Blue Ridge park. Then fish for bass and bream in Lake Oolenoy, wade in icy Carrick Creek, or join monthly 'Music on the Mountain' bluegrass jam sessions at the Table Rock Lodge. For overnight stays, snag a rustic 1930s cabin.
https://southcarolinaparks.com/table-rock, 158 Ellison Lane, Pickens

ARTS, HISTORY & CULTURE

BEAUFORT Colonial Beaufort, all gracious antebellum homes shaded by magnolias and with a historic district frequently used as a set for Hollywood films, is one of South Carolina's most photogenic towns. Visit the John Mark Verdier House Museum, rifle through the downtown shops in this retreat on the Sea Islands, and then at low tide kayak out into the Beaufort River with a cooler of beer to drink with the locals on the famous sandbar. *www.beaufortsc.org, Port Royal Island*

BROOKGREEN GARDENS On a 9000-acre former rice plantation south of Myrtle Beach, these enchanting gardens explode with blue-purple hydrangea and plate-sized hibiscus, petal-pink azaleas and ruffled Confederate rose, firecracker-red quince and delicate apricot, all shaded by live oaks and magnolias and dotted with more than 2000 figurative sculptures by American artists. *www.brookgreen. org, 1931 Brookgreen Dr, Murrells Inlet*

FUN FACT

The official state dance is called the 'shag.' Quit your giggling, it's a form of the jitterbug.

© ovidiuhrubaru / Getty Images; Left: © James Kirkikis / Shutterstock

GULLAH CULTURE

The Gullah people are the descendants of Central and West African enslaved people who worked the rice and indigo plantations of the southeastern Sea Islands. Isolated from the outside, they developed their own Creole language, combining English with various African words and grammatical structures. Today many Gullah people still live on the land of their ancestors, maintaining their culture despite massive development of the Sea Islands. Travel the Gullah/Geechee (as the Gullah are known in Georgia) Corridor to learn about their crafts, art and food, such as sweetgrass basket weaving, quilting and rice-based dishes like okra soup or shrimp and red rice.

CHARLESTON HISTORIC DISTRICT

Stop first at Charleston's Rainbow Row, an irresistibly photogenic stretch of candy-painted rowhouses on lower E Bay St. Afterwards explore the enigmatic back alleys of this quarter, all wrought-iron gates and clouds of wisteria concealing the occasional tea house or antiquarian map shop. Finish at the harborside antebellum mansions of the Battery. *South of Beaufain and Hasell Sts*

FAT HAROLD'S BEACH CLUB
The culture of North Myrtle Beach still revolves around the shag, a jitterbug-like dance popular here since the 1940s. There's nowhere like this longtime club to see the dance in action, as couples of all ages take to the floor to swing to 'beach music,' a regional variety of R&B. There are lessons every Monday night at 7. *www.fatharolds.com, 212 Main St, N Myrtle Beach*

FORT SUMTER
Anyone remotely interested in US and Civil War history must visit this pentagon-shaped island in Charleston Harbor, from where the first shots of the conflict rang out in April 1861. The Union surrendered the fort after bombardment in the war's first skirmish, not recapturing it until near the war's end. Only 2.4 acres in size, the fort was built in response to perceived coastal vulnerabilities after the War of 1812. Though it's all ruins now – just a few antique arms and fortifications – the sense of historical importance remains. The only way to visit is by boat, itself a fun activity. *www.nps.gov/fosu*

GATEWAY WALK
See some of Charleston's most picturesque and historic churches in the aptly-nicknamed Holy City via a stroll down this hidden garden path. There's the white-columned St John's Lutheran with its handsome bell tower, the 17th--century St Philip's with its higgledy-piggledy graveyard, the towering Gothic Revival Unitarian and the round-turreted Romanesque Circular Congregational Church founded in 1681. *Between Archdale St and Philadelphia Alley*

From left: Sweetgrass baskets, a traditional Gullah craft; Fort Sumter outside Charleston; Folly Beach.

© Cvandyke / Shutterstock

MCLEOD PLANTATION Enslaved people from the Gullah culture worked the cotton fields of this James Island plantation from the 1850s, some staying on as tenants and servants to the McLeod family through the 1990s. Learn about their lives with a guided tour of the house and its gracious grounds, which focuses on the African American journey towards freedom. *https://ccprc. com/1447/McLeod-Plantation-Historic-Site, 325 Country Club Dr, Charleston*

MIDDLETON PLACE The most imposing of three plantations along Ashley River Rd outside Charleston, Middleton Place was built by 100 enslaved people in the mid-1700s. Visit the plantation house, then explore the enchanting if ghostly French gardens and rice paddies, by foot or by horse-drawn carriage. There's also an unexpected modernist hotel on-site, and a lauded Lowcountry restaurant. *www. middletonplace.org, 4300 Ashley River Rd*

OLD SLAVE MART MUSEUM Visiting South Carolina perforce means reckoning with its past. Formerly called Ryan's Mart, this building once housed an open-air market that auctioned African American men, women and children in the mid-1800s, the largest of 40 or so similar auction houses. This shameful past is unraveled in text-heavy exhibits illuminating the slave experience; the few artifacts, such as leg shackles, are especially chilling. *www.charleston-sc.gov, 6 Chalmers St, Charleston*

FAMILY OUTINGS

CHARLESTON CITY MARKET With more than 300 vendors hawking everything from sweetgrass baskets to piping-hot biscuits, this vibrant, open-air market is one of the nation's oldest, getting its start in 1804. Some travelers may feel it's a bit schlocky, but over its four blocks there are plenty of interesting finds and locally made products (all marked with a 'Certified Authentic Handmade in Charleston' seal). *www.thecharlestoncitymarket.com, 188 Meeting St*

★ ★ ★

SPOLETO FESTIVAL USA

All of Charleston gets decked out for this 17-day spring performing arts festival, when performers from around the globe come to put on plays, operas and musical performances of all stripes in venues across the city. Also expect poetry readings, film openings, kid's activities, gallery shows and streets full of artisans and food vendors.

© John Wollwerth / Shutterstock; Right: © Eric Murphy / Alamy Stock Photo

The state's three main gateways are Charleston International Airport, Greenville–Spartanburg International Airport and Myrtle Beach International Airport. Regional hubs include Columbia Metropolitan Airport and Savannah/Hilton Head International Airport, which is actually located in Georgia but is the major airport for the Hilton Head region. Amtrak and Greyhound serve a few of the major metropolitan areas.

FOLLY BEACH Popular with surfers and day-tripping Charlestonians, Folly Beach is blessed with warm white sand and mostly calm waters. Part of the island is a county park, with a pelican rookery tucked inside its precincts. Walk the 1000ft Folly Beach Pier to choose a fishing spot. You'll find the obligatory taffy and souvenir shops on Center St. *www.visitfolly.com*

HILTON HEAD ISLAND South Carolina's largest barrier island has come to be shorthand for a certain breed of upscale, polo-shirt-clad, golf-loving Southerner. Join them by renting a luxe vacation home on one of the island's 'plantations' (as its private neighborhoods are called in tone-deaf fashion), traveling by golf cart between the lovely white beaches. Save time for a daylong fishing charter. *www.hiltonheadisland.org*

MYRTLE BEACH To some, this sun-blasted welter of arcades, mini-golf courses, all-you-can-eat seafood buffets and daiquiri bars is hell on earth. To others, it's the classic American summer vacation. Decide which category you belong in with a trip to South Carolina's favorite beach town. At the very least you'll get in some primo outlet shopping and work on your tan. *www.visitmyrtlebeach.com*

SOUTH OF THE BORDER If you're headed down I-95 you'll see the billboards long before you arrive. They feature Pedro, a cartoon Mexican bandido, enticing you to stop at 'South of the Border.' What is this place? Conceived as a fireworks stand in 1950, it's now a sprawling roadside attraction featuring souvenir stalls, games, a sombrero-shaped restaurant and more. *www.thesouthoftheborder.com*

ITINERARY

Day 1

Start off in the 'Holy City' of Charleston, so-called for its wealth of stunning historic churches. Wander the gardenia-fragrant cobblestone streets of the Historic District, stopping to snap a selfie on Rainbow Row, and take a sunset walk on the peninsula's southern tip at the Battery.

Day 2

Take a morning boat out to the awe-inspiring ruins of Fort Sumter, where the Civil War started. In the afternoon, drive out to Ashley River to tour the grand home and gardens of Middleton Place plantation, and to learn about the dark history of the enslaved people who worked there.

Day 3

Head south toward agricultural Wadmalaw Island to take a trolley ride through the tea fields at the Charleston Tea Plantation and visit the heartbreakingly beautiful Angel Oak. Drive on to postcard-pretty Beaufort for dinner.

Day 4

Enjoy Hunting Island State Park's inviting cream-colored sand and explore its atmospheric marshes and lagoons.

From left: Hilton Head; Brookgreen Gardens.

SOUTH DAKOTA

★ ★

POPULATION: 869,666 | **SIZE:** 77,116 sq miles | **STATE CAPITAL:** Pierre
LARGEST CITY: Sioux Falls | **WEBSITE:** www.travelsouthdakota.com

FOR SOME PEOPLE THE SOUTH DAKOTA TERRITORY OFFERED THE PROMISE OF RICHES, AND for others it offered a new life. While South Dakota may now be best known for a mountain embellished with some famous carved portraits, there is so much more to see and do – although Mt Rushmore definitely deserves consideration on any travel itinerary. These days wagon-rutted roads have been replaced with interstates and paved highways, but the stories of those who traveled them still remain, including the region's Oglala Lakota Tribe. Gently rolling prairies through shallow, fertile valleys mark much of this endlessly appealing state. But head southwest and all hell breaks loose, in the best possible way. Badlands National Park is the geological equivalent of fireworks, while the Black Hills are like opera. South Dakota's landscapes are challenging, intriguing and majestic.

© Mark Read / Lonely Planet

FOOD & DRINK

CHISLIC Visitors are unlikely to leave the state without encountering its signature item: chislic, or as locals like to call it, mutton on a stick. With a name likely derived from Turkish shish kebab, these seasoned meat skewers are a favored menu item. Meridian Corner in Freeman is known to have an excellent version, but options aren't lacking to sample this South Dakota delicacy.

KOLACHES The dispute over who makes the best kolaches is legendary in South Dakota. Brought to the state by Czech immigrants in the 1800s, this round pastry (the name means 'wheel') made itself part of South Dakota tradition. While each family has its own recipe, you'll certainly find traditional-tasting kolaches at Tyndall Bakery in the town of Tyndall. After they get a sweet filling like apple, cherry or strawberry cream, these melt-in-your-mouth pastries are baked, glazed and sprinkled with streusel.

NATURAL ESCAPES

BADLANDS NATIONAL PARK Millions of years ago, a sea covered what is now South Dakota. The forces of erosion have stripped away the soft soil here in the state's southwest, leaving spires and sharp canyons of multicolored rock and dry, hard dirt. The Lakota people called the area *mako sica*, and the French traders who came through later named it *les mauvaises terres* – both translate, roughly, as 'bad lands.' If you love wildlife, be sure to include a stroll down Sage Creek Road during your visit to watch for buffalo and herds of bighorn sheep. The Badlands also include the Jewel Cave National Monument and Wind Cave National Park, with more than 335 miles of mapped passages between both caves. *www.nps.gov/badl*

CUSTER STATE PARK Custer State Park boasts some of the best American wildlife viewing outside of Yellowstone, as well as curvaceous mountain drives, serene lakeside retreats and plenty of open range. At the end of the 19th century, the number of buffalo in North America had plummeted to around 1000, and the species looked set for extinction. Today more than that live in the herd at Custer State Park alone, one of the largest free-roaming herds of American buffalo. This is due in part to President Theodore Roosevelt, who in 1905 started a campaign to save the remaining buffalo. After decades of habitat management and protection from poachers, conservationists now say the number of buffalo in North America has reached 500,000. *https://gfp.sd.gov/parks/detail/custer-state-park, 13329 US Highway 16A*

ROUGHLOCK FALLS STATE NATURE AREA Its rugged name belies the elegant beauty of this scenic park near Lead in the Black Hills, an evergreen island in a sea of high-prairie grassland. The region's name – the 'Black' comes from the dark ponderosa-pine-covered slopes – was conferred by the Lakota Sioux. Paved pathways and relatively nearby parking make for an accessible stroll past gorgeous woods (colorful in fall) and picturesque waterfalls. *www.blackhillsbadlands.com, Roughlock Falls Rd*

★ ★ ★

PINE RIDGE INDIAN RESERVATION

In the center of Pine Ridge Indian Reservation, a sign describes the events that took place here in 1890. Just a few years after Crazy Horse and the local tribes routed Lt General George Custer's battalion at Little Big Horn, the US 7th Cavalry Regiment entered Wounded Knee to disarm the Lakota tribe. When a deaf tribesman refused to give up his weapon, a shot rang out, and the 7th Cavalry opened fire from all sides. By the time the incident was over, at least 150 Lakota were dead (other reports put the number as high as 300 dead). Today a bare memorial marks the site, but exhibits elsewhere on the 3500-sq-mile Pine Ridge Indian Reservation better outline the massacre and the events of the larger Sioux Wars. The Historical Center at the Oglala Lakota College tells the history of the Oglala Lakota people, including what happened at Wounded Knee.

© robert cicchetti / Shutterstock; Left: © Alex Pix / Shutterstock

ARTS, HISTORY & CULTURE

CRAZY HORSE MEMORIAL The Crazy Horse Memorial has been under construction since 1948. Located in the Black Hills, it is the world's largest mountain carving. Visitors can learn about the culture and tradition of Native Americans at the museums of Crazy Horse Memorial. During warmer months the multimedia Legends in Light laser light show is presented nights after dark. *https://crazyhorsememorial.org, 12151 Ave of the Chiefs*

MINUTEMAN MISSILE NATIONAL HISTORIC SITE This first national park dedicated to the Cold War preserves one silo and its underground launch facility. In the 1960s and 1970s, a thousand Minuteman II intercontinental ballistic missiles, always at the ready in underground silos spread across the Great Plains, were just a 30 minute flight from their targets in the Soviet Union. The missiles have since been retired (though more modern ones still lurk underground across the northern Great Plains). An impressive visitors center has displays and films about the missiles and the Cold War, and there are tours of the nearby underground Launch Control Facility Delta-01, where two people stood ready around the clock to turn the launch keys. *www.nps.gov/mimi, I-90, exit 131*

MT RUSHMORE A trip to South Dakota feels incomplete without a stop at Mt Rushmore, near Keystone, though expectations are sometimes outsize. Conceived in 1927 as a way to draw tourists to the state, this national memorial continues to inspire wonder at just how lead sculptor Gutzon Borglum and his team of several hundred workers managed to carve the 60ft faces of Washington, Jefferson, Lincoln and Theodore Roosevelt from the

★ ★ ★

GETTING THERE & AROUND

South Dakota's two major airports are in Rapid City and Sioux Falls. Greyhound bus stations can be found throughout the state, but since South Dakota has 82,576 miles of roadway, much of which is scenic, you're likely better off driving your own car or renting so that you can explore at your own pace.

rock face. Hint: the majority of the work was done with dynamite. *www.nps.gov/moru, 13000 SD-244*

SANFORD LAB HOMESTAKE VISITOR CENTER

Gape at what open-pit mining can do to a mountain at the 1250ft deep Homestake Gold Mine in Lead. The mine's shafts plunge more than 1.5 miles below the surface and are now used for physics research. Homestake has been called the richest spot on earth; over 126 years, miners extracted more than 41 million ounces of gold and 9 million ounces of silver. *www. sanfordlabhomestake.com, 160 W Main St*

FAMILY OUTINGS

CORN PALACE The king of roadside attractions, the Corn Palace in Mitchell entices more than a half million people to pull off I-90 each year. Close to 300,000 ears of corn are used annually to create the building murals. Ponder the scenes and you may find a kernel of truth or just say, 'aw, shucks.' *https://cornpalace.com, 604 N Main St*

DEADWOOD So famous as a center of Wild West lawlessness that it spawned a tv show by the same name, Deadwood offers a number of museums and attractions that mine its history as the home of outlaw legends such as Wild Bill Hickok and Calamity Jane. Deadwood also has access to winter sports, good for when a reenactment of *The Trial of Jack McCall* (the play has been running in town since 1920) has lost its luster. Local Mt Moriah cemetery has bus tours to see the graves of the town's notable ne'er-do-wells. *www.deadwood.com*

INGALLS HOMESTEAD For fans of 'Half-pint' and her loving narration of prairie life, the Ingalls Homestead in De Smet will be a highlight of your South Dakota visit. Hands-on interactive activities help you experience life as it was for the Ingalls family. *www.ingallshomestead.com, 20812 Homestead Rd*

MAMMOTH SITE Budding paleontologists of all ages will enjoy the ongoing excavation site at Hot Springs. Hundreds of animals perished in a sinkhole here about 26,000 years ago, and you can walk around the active archaeological dig. The site is home to the world's largest mammoth research facility, and visitors have a hands-on adventure participating in indoor digs. *www.mammothsite.org, 1800 US-18 Bypass*

SIOUX FALLS The state's largest city lives up to its name at Falls Park, where the Big Sioux River plunges through a long series of rock faces. Stroll along the grass-lined paths to the city's namesake waterfall; just south lies a buzzing downtown district with a burgeoning foodie scene and some of the best eats in the region. *www.siouxfalls.org*

ITINERARY

Day 1
Begin with Mt Rushmore, then enjoy the scenic drive to the world's largest mountain carving at the Crazy Horse Memorial in the beautiful, pine-filled Black Hills.

Day 2
Spend the day at Custer State Park in the Black Hills. Take a safari 4WD ride and see herds of buffalo, deer, bighorn sheep and wild turkeys. Or take a guided horse-back ride on a trail.

Day 3
Spend the day absorbing vistas on your driving tour of Badlands National Park. Be sure to make frequent stops at the scenic overlooks for unforgettable views, and stop into the Historical Center on the Pine Ridge Indian Reservation, which features exhibits on Wounded Knee.

Day 4
Bring any science nerds in your group to the Mammoth Site for some live-action paleontology.

From left: Mt Rushmore at sunset; bison in the grasslands of Wind Cave National Park. Previous page: Rock formations at Badlands National Park.

TENNESSEE

★ ★

POPULATION: 6.7 million | **SIZE:** 42,143 sq miles | **STATE CAPITAL:** Nashville
WEBSITE: www.tnvacation.com

TENNESSEE MEANS MUSIC. MODERN COUNTRY WAS INVENTED HERE, AND NASHVILLE IS STILL the heart of the industry. Blues thrives in the humid towns of the west Tennessee Delta and on the streets of downtown Memphis, also a major fount of soul music. Folk songs ring out in the hollers of the Great Smokies, and gospel choruses praise the lord in churches across the state. You'll hear music in your ears long after you've left. The Volunteer State is geographically diverse, stretching from the muddy banks of the Mississippi through to the Cumberland Plateau and into the Appalachians. This means opportunities for nearly every kind of outdoor activity, from mountain hiking to grade A sandstone rock climbing to river rafting to laid-back fishing. And while Nashville and Memphis are big cities, most of the state is deeply rural. Road-trip through small towns with their own unique quirks and industries.

© Sean Pavone / Getty Images

FOOD & DRINK

HOT CHICKEN Spicy fried 'hot chicken' is a hyper-local mania in Nashville that's spread nationwide as of late. Go to the source – the unassuming North Nashville storefront known as Prince's – and order through the hole in the kitchen wall. Then wait 45 minutes for the chicken to be painstakingly panfried, before it's served up on white bread with pickles. It'll change your life, especially if you get the spiciest version. *www.princeshotchicken.com, 123 Ewing Dr*

RIBS In Memphis, 'barbecue' generally means ribs. Ribs can be 'dry,' with a rub of spices, or 'wet' with a sweet, tangy sauce. You could eat barbecue in Memphis for a week and never hit a bad joint. But for our money, the top long-standing spots include laid-back Cozy Corner BBQ for ribs and unique barbecued Cornish game hens, and the buzzy cellar dining room at Charlie Vergos' Rendezvous for dry-rubbed ribs perfected over seven decades.

TENNESSEE WHISKEY The 'Lincoln County Process' distinguishes Tennessee whiskey from bourbon; after distilling, the liquid is filtered through sugar-maple charcoal before aging. Tour a local distillery, or stop by the acknowledged giant. Jack Daniel's has been aging Tennessee whiskey in oak barrels around the Lynchburg hills since 1866. A quarter-million visitors pour through each year to tour the distillery and barrelhouse and sample the golden goods. Tour guides are full of salty stories. *www.jackdaniels.com, 133 Lynchburg Hwy, Lynchburg*

NATURAL ESCAPES

GREAT SMOKY MOUNTAINS NATIONAL PARK Days here are spent hiking past shimmering waterfalls and picnicking beside boulder-filled mountain streams, followed by evenings around the campfire as stars glimmer above the forest canopy. Book way, way ahead (like, a year) for the chance to spend a night atop Great Smoky Mountains National Park's Mt LeConte, in a rustic, electricity-free lodge that can only be reached by a quad-burning daylong hike. The lodge's supplies are packed in by llamas three times a week; catch them hoofing it up the Trillium Gap trail. *www.nps.gov/grsm*

NATCHEZ TRACE PARKWAY Pick up this glorious 444-mile scenic route just southwest of Nashville, driving beneath canopies of old-growth trees, stopping in shady hollows and at hidden springs. The former Native American footpath is also bikeable, and there are campsites along the way. But first fuel up with scratch-made biscuits and country ham at the famed Loveless Cafe, just at the northern entrance. *www.nps.gov/natr*

ARTS, HISTORY & CULTURE

BB KING'S BLUES CLUB There are a half-dozen BB King's clubs across the country, but this is the original, opened by the late blues legend in 1991. Amidst dozens of other venues on Memphis' storied blues row, it stands out for its quality house band, high-energy juke joint atmosphere and surprisingly decent food. *www.bbkings.com/memphis, 143 Beale St*

★ ★ ★

MUSIC FESTIVALS

CMA Music Fest Hundreds of the top names in country music and some quarter-million fans come to Nashville in June for this four-day festival, with concerts, autograph sessions and meet-n-greets all over town. It's a total scene, from the lively fan campgrounds to the packed arenas vibrating with screams.

Bonnaroo Well away from the lights of Nashville in an Eastern Tennessee field, the Bonnaroo music festival has a distinct whiff of patchouli. The four-day June event emphasizes jam band-y music (think Phish, Dave Matthews Band), though huge names from other genres play as well; past guests have included Kayne West, Arcade Fire and Bruce Spring-steen. Expect camping, vegan food trucks and macramé outfits.

Left: The Newfound Gap in the Great Smoky Mountains near Gatlinburg.

© pabradyphoto / Getty Images; Left: © ZUMA Press Inc / Alamy Stock Photo

★ ★ ★

PEABODY DUCKS

Daily at 11am sharp, five ducks waddle out of the lobby elevator of Memphis' storied Peabody Hotel and across the red carpet to the marble fountain, where they splash the day away. It's a tradition born from a 1930s hunting trip, no doubt involving whiskey. The ducks make the reverse trip at 5pm, to the delight of spectators. A former circus animal trainer served as The Peabody Duckmaster for fifty years, retiring in 1991. In their honor, the on-site restaurant doesn't serve any duck on its menu.

COUNTRY MUSIC HALL OF FAME
Hunkering over an entire city block of downtown Nashville, this is the kind of place where country fans could spend a week and even nonfans will wander happily for hours. Visitors are immersed in sound and history with listening booths, videos and touchscreens, as well as artifacts from Elvis' gold Cadillac to Johnny Cash's guitar. *https://countrymusichalloffame.org, 222 5th Ave S*

GRACELAND When in Memphis, visiting Elvis' white mansion is a nonnegotiable. By turns kitschy and sad, the audio tour takes you past the faux waterfall of the Jungle Room to the clubby yellow-and-black basement and out to the King's poolside grave. The upstairs toilet, where he actually died, is off-limits. Outbuildings house museum-like displays of history and memorabilia. *www.graceland.com, Elvis Presley Blvd*

GRAND OLE OPRY Everyone who's anyone in country, folk, bluegrass and gospel has played Nashville's Opry, a raucous, boot-stompin', laughter-filled live music stage show running for more than 90 years. Most shows are at the rather featureless Music City location, but it's way more fun to catch winter performances at downtown's iconic Ryman Auditorium. Both are open for tours too. *www.opry.com, 2804 Opryland Dr*

HATCH SHOW PRINT Half the bands in America have had concert posters made at this iconic letterpress shop, printing since 1879 and a mainstay of the country music industry. You'll recognize their bright graphic style when you see it. It's impossible to leave without a souvenir, whether a vintage playbill or a modern ad. Come too for regular letterpress workshops. *https://hatchshowprint.com, 224 5th Ave S, Nashville*

NATIONAL CIVIL RIGHTS MUSEUM
Inside the former Lorraine Motel, where Martin Luther King Jr was fatally shot in 1968, is this gut-wrenching museum

From left: Peabody Duckmaster Jason Sensat, and honorary duckmaster Paige Nowak, corral the hotel's ducks as they make their way to the hotel's lobby fountain; Robert's Western World sign on Broadway in Nashville; Elvis Presley's grave at Graceland.

© Rush Jagoe / Lonely Planet

detailing the ongoing struggle for African American equality in America. Exhibits are immersive – sit down at a segregated lunch counter or climb aboard a bus with Rosa Parks. It will leave you feeling reflective, but that's the point. *www.civilrightsmuseum. org, 450 Mulberry St, Memphis*

ROBERT'S WESTERN WORLD
Of all the honky-tonks lining Nashville's Lower Broadway, Robert's is our favorite. You can get a cheap beer, eat a fried bologna sandwich, buy a pair of quality cowboy boots and watch rousing country acts any day of the week. What more could you want? The weekend house band, Brazilbilly, is always a rockin' good time. *https://robertswesternworld.com, 416-B Broadway*

SHILOH NATIONAL MILITARY PARK
Some 23,000 soldiers died in this bloody 1862 battle, one of the most important of the Civil War. The Confederates eventually retreated, and the Union was able to advance deeper south. Tour the now-serene wooded battlefield by car, stopping at various monuments and the Cumberland River overlook where the Union reinforcements arrived by ship. *www.nps.gov/shil, 1055 Pittsburg Landing Rd, Shiloh*

STAX MUSEUM OF AMERICAN SOUL MUSIC
In 'Soulville USA,' the Memphis neighborhood that spawned way more than its fair share of soul stars, lies this funkadelic museum on the site of the former Stax Records recording studio. Check out Isaac Hayes' shag-carpeted 1972 Superfly Cadillac, walk through a recreated Delta church and hit the dance floor from the hit show *Soul Train*. *https://staxmuseum.com, 926 E McLemore Ave*

SUN STUDIO
This dusty storefront is ground zero for American rock 'n' roll music. Starting in the early 1950s, Sun's Sam Phillips recorded blues artists such as Howlin' Wolf, BB King and Ike Turner, followed by the rockabilly dynasty of Jerry

FUN FACT

Nashville's Grand Ole Opry hosts the longest continuously running live radio program in the world, broadcast every weekend since 1925.

Right: © IrinaK / Shutterstock; Right: © IrinaK / Shutterstock

Lee Lewis, Johnny Cash, Roy Orbison and, of course, the King himself (who started here in 1953). *www.sunstudio.com, 706 Union Ave, Memphis*

FAMILY OUTINGS

DOLLYWOOD East Tennessee patron saint Dolly Parton owns this wildly popular mountain livin'-themed amusement park in Pigeon Forge, all about the heart and soul of the Great Smokies (and great fun). Ride the Mystery Mine coaster, get historical with visits to a recreated one-room schoolhouse or Dolly's own Locust Ridge childhood cabin, or tour the bald eagle sanctuary. In summer add time for the Splash Country water park. *www. dollywood.com, 2700 Dollywood Parks Blvd*

GATLINBURG Love it or hate it, this East Tennessee town at the entrance to Great Smoky Mountains National Park is an Americana kitschfest like no other. We're inclined to adore the hillbilly-themed mini-golf courses, corn-dog-scented arcades, zip line rides and endless pancake houses. Riding the aerial tramway to Bavarian-themed Ober Gatlinburg ski area and amusement park is a must. *www.gatlinburg.com*

LOOKOUT MOUNTAIN An original American roadside attraction, Chattanooga's Lookout Mountain includes the 19th-century Incline Railway, which chugs to the top of the mountain, and Ruby Falls, the world's longest underground waterfall, complete with campy purple spotlights. You can allegedly see seven states from the Rock City summit, home to wholesome seasonal family activities like a corn maze and Christmas village. *www.lookoutmountain.com, 827 E Brow Rd*

★ ★ ★

GETTING THERE & AROUND

Both Nashville and Memphis have major airports with flights to many large and medium US cities and a handful of international ones. Amtrak only serves Memphis, via the City of New Orleans train from Chicago to New Orleans. Public transportation even in big cities is lacking, so you'll want a car.

Day 1
Start off in Great Smoky Mountains National Park. Spend the day hiking and stay at mountaintop LeConte Lodge or uber-kitschy Gatlinburg.

Day 2
On to Chattanooga for a day of sightseeing; the Tennessee Aquarium, riverfront strolls and Lookout Mountain.

Day 3
Drive to Nashville, with a detour to Lynchburg's Jack Daniel Distillery. Arrive in time to wander neon-spangled Lower Broadway, catching the latest and greatest at Robert's Western World or one of the other classic honky-tonks. Afterwards, Prince's Hot Chicken is open late for a spicy fried chicken fix.

Day 4
Hit the Country Music Hall of Fame and Hatch Show Print. If the Opry is on in the evening, swing by, y'all.

Days 5 & 6
In Memphis, enjoy two days of barbecue, Graceland, and visiting the National Civil Rights Museum. At night, it's Beale St blues clubs time.

From left: A wooden roller coaster at Dollywood; Ruby Falls, the US's longest underground waterfall.

LOST SEA Make like Indiana Jones with a boat ride across the eerie, jade-green water deep inside this enormous cavern. Covering four acres, it's America's largest underground lake. Look up to see delicate, needle-like formations known as 'cave flowers.' Outside, old-fashioned family activities like gem panning and glassblowing demos will keep the kids happy. *https://thelostsea.com, 140 Lost Sea Rd, Sweetwater*

TENNESSEE AQUARIUM Follow the journey of a raindrop from the Appalachians to the Gulf of Mexico in this massive riverside Chattanooga aquarium, one of the country's finest. Though specializing in the aquatic life of the American South, it's also got animals ranging from lemurs to penguins. Book ahead to join one of the educational cruises on the Tennessee River. *www.tnaqua.org, 1 Broad St*

TEXAS

★ ★

POPULATION: 28.7 million | **SIZE:** 268,581 sq miles | **STATE CAPITAL:** Austin
LARGEST CITY: Houston | **WEBSITE:** www.traveltexas.com

THINK BIG IN THE LONE STAR STATE. TEXAS WAS ITS OWN COUNTRY BETWEEN 1836 AND 1845, and still feels like one. It's not merely the mind-boggling size (larger than France and Switzerland combined), but that Houston, San Antonio and Dallas all rank among the US's ten most populous cities. The landscapes intensify the sensation: wind-blown plains, cactus-stippled desert, remote river-churned canyons and fields that span horizons. There is even a ranch here larger than the state of Rhode Island! Everywhere has a biggest on-the-planet boast, from Austin and its music scene (world live music capital, y'all) to Houston for its leading role in the aerospace industry (among the first words spoken from the moon were Texas-bound). Texan culture is bombastic, with legacies of cowboys, line dancing and barbecue to add pride. Add in economic prowess in oil and agriculture to give the state its distinct independent feel.

© Kris Davidson / Lonely Planet

FOOD & DRINK

AUSTIN FOOD TRUCKS Food trucks embody Austin's spirit, and the variety of cuisines served from them aptly reflect the city's cultural and culinary diversity. Most importantly, they serve affordable and tasty fare, which can be enjoyed in the Texas sunshine. The city's wacky and wonderful food truck culture is epitomized by the East Side King food trucks, which can be found in various locations around the city, but in general, if you see a crowd at a truck, it's worth checking out.

BRISKET Whether you pull into the first roadside spot you see or join the queue forming hours before opening at Austin's Franklin Barbecue (only open for lunch, from 11am until they run out of meat), the fatty brisket at the end is a fine prize. Lamberts, also in Austin, pushes boundaries with their inventively flavored sugar-and-coffee-rubbed brisket.

CRAFT BREWERIES Settle in for craft beers as epic as the state where they're brewed. Austin has beer nirvana Jester King Brewery, where what are generally considered the finest craft brews of the state get made. Some of the unique hoppy highlights here include their Terroir Project, fermented with Texas Syrah grapes, or their Snorkel, brewed with smoked sea salt and oyster mushrooms. Houston has Texas' oldest craft brewery, Saint Arnold Brewing Company, founded in the industry's nascent days of the mid-1990s, which has consistently produced great beers over the last quarter-century. It put Texas craft beer on the map, and brews like the Bishop's Barrel series, each beer aged in different barrels from bourbon to chardonnay, shows their inventiveness hasn't ceased. And that's just the top of the keg(s).

TACOS Texas doesn't share over 1200 miles of border with Mexico to no purpose. The state has some of the best tacos in the country, and you'll find fresh tortillas all over. Whether sampling the offerings in Laredo, San Antonio or Austin, two or three is a reasonable meal, but good luck tearing yourself away before consuming double that.

TEXAS BARBECUE Barbecue is synonymous with Texas dining. Every corner of Texas boasts its own distinct barbecue style. In East Texas, marinated beef brisket and pork is slow cooked until the meat falls off the bone. In Central Texas, brisket and ribs are spiced, seasoned and smoked over an oak- or pecan-wood fire. Thick molasses-like marinade is a trademark of South Texan barbecue, while over in West Texas, meat is smoked directly over a mesquite-wood fire. What unites Texas barbecue – and sets it apart from barbecue traditions elsewhere in the South – is that beef, not pork, is the main event, while homemade sausage is served as a side.

TEX-MEX Purists may scoff, but the joys of Tex-Mex (an entirely separate category from Mexican food) are legion. Joints like Houston's El Real Tex-Mex cafe announce themselves proudly and serve up sizzling fajitas, steaming enchiladas, sinful nachos and fluffy soft-shelled tacos among many standout choices. Typically cheese-smothered and rich, this

★ ★ ★

THE STATE FAIR OF TEXAS

Texas is certainly not short on agricultural events but the massive State Fair of Texas, where the best of the state's livestock are showcased, is a calendar highlight. Taking place in Dallas for almost a month from late September, this titanic celebration of farming has been running since 1886. Wear your cowboy hat and get high on one of the US's tallest Ferris wheels; corn dogs, supposedly invented here, are the must-try food.

Left: Two wranglers on horseback overlooking the Dixie Dude Ranch in Bandera.

© ShuPhotography / Shutterstock; Left: © stock_photo_world / Shutterstock

★ ★ ★

SXSW

Since South by Southwest (SXSW) kicked off in 1987, Austin has been transformed – both artistically and economically. Texas dance halls now sit in the shadows of high-rise apartment buildings; coffee comes with all variety of foams, syrups and flavors; and techies outnumber cowboys. Like it or loathe it, the massive craziness that descends upon Austin for 10 days during March has all the makings of an unforgettable time. The festival remains firmly at the center of Austin's best characteristics: a hub of creativity and art, a strong entrepreneurial spirit and that ongoing title of 'Live Music Capital of the World.' It's no secret that the festival has moved firmly into the mainstream, raising questions of how it is changing Austin as it grows. Capital One, Uber and Bud Light have been sponsors and Barack Obama has given the event's keynote.

unique merger of Mexican ingredients and American sensibilities may be a bit of a mutt, but it's 100% delicious (just don't tell your cardiologist). While Texas has foodie bonafides, and there's a bold new culinary concept by local James Beard–honored chefs for every 1980s Tex-Mex cafe holdout, there's still a place for the Tex-Mex classics.

TEXAS WINE TRAIL, HILL COUNTRY

In verdant, craggy Hill Country, stretching approximately from Austin to Fredericksburg and from New Braunfels up to Lampasas, lie some 53 wineries that have established Texas as one of the top five wine-producing states, both in size and in class. This wine trail takes you to each: a window not only into Texas winemaking, but into the beautiful bucolic landscapes and middle-of-nowhere towns en route. *www.texaswinetrail.com*

NATURAL ESCAPES

BIG BEND NATIONAL PARK The stunning 1250 sq miles of mountain, desert and

canyon here form a fittingly dramatic frontier between Texas and Mexico. Big Bend is extremely popular for its hiking, climbing and river-running opportunities (everyone knows that if you only visit one park out of the hundred-odd in the state, this should be it) but is huge enough to absorb them all. *www.nps.gov/bibe*

ENCHANTED ROCK STATE NATURAL AREA This pink granite mound swooping out of the Hill Country offers irrefutably dramatic views from its summit. But the 'enchanted' element stems from the Tonkawa people's belief that the crackling sound the rock makes, as it heats up during the day then cools off at night, were ghostly fires. *https://tpwd.texas.gov/state-parks/enchanted-rock*

GUADALUPE MOUNTAINS NATIONAL PARK This is one for real adventurers: sheltering the state's highest peak, Guadalupe Mountain (8751ft), this is a true wilderness area, with only basic campgrounds and unpaved tracks meaning

From left: Singer, songwriter, and rapper Anderson Paak performs at a concert during SXSW 2016; El Capitan of Guadalupe Mountains National Park; pecan pie is the official state dessert.

© Michael Grayson / Getty Images

hiking with gear is the only way to explore. The park's McKittrick Canyon is famous for its glorious fall foliage, with a popular 6.8-mile out-and-back trail, but there are 80+ miles of trails overall. *www.nps.gov/gumo*

PADRE ISLAND NATIONAL SEASHORE

The 60 southern miles of 'North' Padre Island that lie outside Corpus Christi city limits are all a protected part of the Padre Island National Seashore. Endangered Kemps ridley sea turtles nest in the park and are closely protected. If you're visiting in late summer, you might be able to take part in a turtle release. *www.nps.gov/pais/index.htm*

PALO DURO CANYON STATE PARK

Flanked by rock that glows a startling purple-red hue in the sharp sunlight, this is one of the Texas Panhandle's (and among the country's) natural highlights: the US's second-most extensive canyon, and a magnet for outdoor-lovers and artists alike. Named after the Spanish for 'hard wood' in reference to the groves of mesquite

hereabouts, it's a worthy detour south of where Route 66 passes through Amarillo. *https://tpwd.texas.gov/state-parks/palo-duro-canyon*

ARTS, HISTORY & CULTURE

THE ALAMO Nowhere induces a Texan's sense of pride like the Alamo, the poignant site where a few hundred Texan Revolutionaries battling for independence died defending the fort here in 1836 against thousands of Mexican troops. The revolutionaries' heroics – and Mexican General López de Santa Anna's cruelty – inspired Texans to victory at the subsequent Battle of San Jacinto. *www.thealamo.org, 300 Alamo Plaza, San Antonio*

AUSTIN MUSIC SCENE In the self-proclaimed world live music capital, is it Antone's nightclub that can lay claim to having contributed most to giving Austin the title? Since 1975 this venue has been a haven for live blues and R&B, and the

FUN FACT

The official state dessert is pecan pie, surely because the state is so rich in pecan trees (it's third in the nation for its pecan harvest). Ooey, gooey, and delicious, Lady Bird Johnson brought a recipe for this favorite Texas treat along to the White House when she became first lady.

© Kris Davidson / Lonely Planet; Left: © Juanmonino / Getty Images

★ ★ ★

RODEO FRENZY

The history of Texas and the rodeo harks back to at least the 16th century. Horses introduced by New Spain became commonplace here before they did elsewhere in the US, and Texas had more space for cattle farming than almost anywhere else in North America. Today there is a rodeo almost every week somewhere in the state, where competitors go head-to-head in such disciplines as calf roping, steed wrestling and barrel racing. Some of the biggest and best rodeos on the planet take place in Texas. Perhaps most famous is the Houston Livestock Show and Rodeo, which takes place for three weeks in late February and early March.

greats from BB King and Jimmy Reed have played here. Or is it the famed Continental Club, which considers itself granddaddy of the scene? In Austin, you can't pick musical favorites, though you can certainly try. Something of interest goes on in Austin nightly. *www.austintexas.org/music-scene*

BANDERA It's not always easy finding real, live cowboys in Texas, but the pickin's are easy in Bandera (pop. 857), which has branded itself the Cowboy Capital of Texas. There are certainly lots of dude ranches around, and rodeos and horseback riding are easy to come by. Another great reason to come to this vibrant spot in the Hill Country? Drinking beer and dancing in one of the many hole-in-the-wall cowboy bars and honky-tonk clubs, where you'll find friendly locals, good live music and a rich atmosphere. Giddy up! *www.banderacowboycapital.com*

BILLY BOB'S TEXAS Dubbing itself the world's largest honky-tonk (that's a country music venue), this Fort Worth

country music nightclub opened in 1981 and was soon attracting greats from Bob Hope to Johnny Cash and Willie Nelson. These days the colossal 100,000 sq ft of space makes room for live rock and blues besides country, alongside bull riding and a wall of fame with handprints of stars who have visited. *https://billybobstexas.com, 2520 Rodeo Plaza*

EL PASO MUSEUM OF ART Housed in a former Greyhound bus station, this is the only accredited art museum in a 250-mile radius, with a phenomenal collection of European 12th- to 18th-century paintings. Just as interesting is the contemporary southwestern US and northern Mexico art which, perched on such a controversial border as El Paso is, broaches many thought-provoking subjects, like migration. *https://epma.art, 1 Arts Festival Plaza*

GALVESTON HISTORIC DISTRICTS
Sitting on a barrier island near the northern end of a 600-mile-long Texas coastline, Galveston may not have the state's

From left: A young rodeo rider practices; Prada Marfa, a permanently installed sculpture by artists Elmgreen & Dragset, 26 miles northwest of the city of Marfa; entrance to Luckenbach Dance Hall.

© simon leigh / Alamy Stock Photo

favorite beaches, but there's nowhere else boasting such a beautiful combination of sun-drenched historic charms. Galveston Historic Downtown Cultural Art District boasts one of the country's few surviving turn-of-the-century theaters, The Grand 1894 Opera House, which has outlasted both the hurricanes that have battered the Gulf Coast and considerable periods of neglect and is now restored to its full glory. In the East End Historical District, Sacred Heart Church and the Victorian-style Bishop's Palace overflow with unique architectural flourishes. www.galvestonhistory.org

LUCKENBACH DANCE HALL Made famous by a Waylon Jennings song, and the spot to get the feel for a traditional Texas dance hall (though partisans of Gruene Hall near New Braunfels might disagree), this wood-built place has live music on almost nightly. The prettily preserved Luckenbach General Store, dating from 1849 and doubling as a saloon, completes the 19th-century feel across

the street. *www.luckenbachtexas.com, 412 Luckenbach Town Loop, Fredericksburg*

MARFA Founded in the 1880s, Marfa's two major cultural hallmarks date from the latter part of the 20th century. Its first taste of fame came when Rock Hudson, Elizabeth Taylor and James Dean arrived to film the 1956 film *Giant*; it's since served as a film location for *There Will Be Blood* and *No Country for Old Men*. Now Marfa is a pilgrimage destination for art-lovers, thanks to one of the world's largest installations of minimalist art at the Chinati Foundation Museum and the Judd Foundation. The museums have attracted galleries such as Ballroom Marfa, quirky lodging options and interesting restaurants. *www.visitmarfa.com*

MUSEUM OF FINE ARTS Houston stakes its claim for inclusion in any self-respecting list of US beacons of culture with this museum, boasting over 65,000 artworks. French impressionism and post-1945 American and European painting

★ ★ ★
EL PASO

El Paso is Texas' westernmost city, closer to four other state capitals than to Austin (Phoenix and Santa Fe in the US, Sonora and Chihuahua in Mexico). It's also known as Sun City, with over 300 days of desert sunshine a year. Yet more than anything else, it's a border town. Earlier part of Spanish- and Mexican-controlled New Mexico, El Paso wasn't US territory until post-1848. Texans, Mexicans, Tejanos, Indigenous Mexicans and Americans all called this place home.

© Nick Fox / Shutterstock; Left: © stock_photo_world / Shutterstock

★ ★ ★

TX IN TINSELTOWN

Paris, Texas by director Wim Wenders is a Texas road trip movie of an artsy sort.

I Love Dick, a tv miniseries, is a story about obsession and art in Marfa.

Boyhood by Richard Linklater is a boy's Texas coming-of-age story.

Friday Night Lights spotlights a small Texas town's football culture.

The Last Picture Show, the 1971 Best Picture winner about a West Texas town.

are especially impressive; Rembrandt and Picasso feature, and works by Rodin and Matisse are displayed in the nearby sculpture garden. Be sure to check out the MFAH's neighbors in the Museum District as well, particularly the Menil Collection and luminous Rothko Chapel. *www.mfah.org, 1001 Bissonnet St*

SIXTH FLOOR MUSEUM Site of the most notable assassination of all time, that of President John F Kennedy, this riveting museum has managed to remember and recreate the President's life, and the moments leading up to his death – all in the building from where the fatal shots were fired. Multimedia exhibits deal with official versions of events and conspiracy theories. *www.jfk.org, 411 Elm St, Dallas*

TEXAS STATE CAPITOL Of course, the Texas State Capitol would be the largest in the US, but this grand edifice, built in 1888 and finished in Renaissance revival–style red granite, strikes an impression in multiple ways. Gawk at the rotunda

beneath the dome; experience the whispering gallery created by the curved ceiling and peek at the government in action from the third-floor balcony. *https://tspb.texas.gov/prop/tc/tc/capitol. html, 112 E 11th St, Austin*

FAMILY OUTINGS

BARTON SPRINGS Hot? Not for long. Even when the temperature hits 100°F, you'll be shivering in a jiff after you jump into this chilly natural spring-fed pool set within Austin's Zilker Park. Draped with century-old pecan trees, the area around the pool has a lively social scene, and it gets packed on hot summer days. *https:// austintexas.gov/department/barton-springs-pool, 2201 Barton Springs Rd*

CADILLAC RANCH To millions of people whizzing across the Texas Panhandle each year, the Cadillac Ranch, also known as Amarillo's 'Bumper Crop,' is the ultimate symbol of the US love affair with wheels. A salute to Route 66 and the spirit of the

From left: Barton Springs in Austin's Zilker Park; the Cadillac Ranch; the Congress Avenue Bridge bat colony.

© Kushal Bose / Shutterstock

American road, it was created by burying, hood first, 10 west-facing Cadillacs in a wheat field outside town. *I-40, exits 60 & 62*

CONGRESS AVENUE BRIDGE BAT COLONY Every year up to 1.5 million Mexican free-tailed bats make their home upon a platform beneath the Congress Ave Bridge, forming the largest urban bat colony in North America. It's become an Austin tradition to sit on the grassy banks of Lady Bird Lake and watch the bats swarm out to feed on an estimated 10,000lb to 30,000lb (4536kg to 13,500kg) of insects per night. It looks a lot like a fast-moving, black, chittering river. Don't miss this nightly show; best viewing in August. *Congress Avenue Bridge, Austin*

KING RANCH Exploring a ranch as large as a US state (825,000-acre King Ranch is bigger than Rhode Island) is easier said than done, but well worth a go. The small section open to the public is a 10-mile driving tour: you can spy the breeds of cattle and horses the ranch is known for,

and see real-life *vaqueros* (cowboys), descendants of the workers that came here in the 1860s, in action. It's one of almost 250,000 farms and ranches in the state. *https://king-ranch.com; Hwy 141 W, Kingsville*

MCDONALD OBSERVATORY Free from the light pollution of big cities, the middle of west Texas has some of the clearest and darkest skies in North America, making it the perfect spot for an observatory. Some of the world's biggest telescopes are here, perched on the peak of Mt Locke (6791ft) and so enormous you can spot them from miles away. The popular star parties help you see the night sky in a whole new way. A day pass gets you a guided tour that includes close-up peeks at (but not through) the 8.91ft Harlan J Smith Telescope and the 36ft Hobby-Eberly Telescope, as well as a solar viewing, where you get to stare at the sun without scorching your eyeballs. *http://mcdonaldobservatory.org, 3640 Dark Sky Dr, outside Fort Davis*

★ ★ ★

Don't mess with
TEXAS

Texas is famed for its 'Don't Tread on Me' attitude, though the Gadsen flag famed for the phrase was never associated with Texas. But those 'Don't Mess With Texas' bumper stickers you see all over the state? The line was actually developed as part of an anti-litter campaign, even if it has become the state's unofficial motto. Be sure to admire the state's super-clean highways on any road trip.

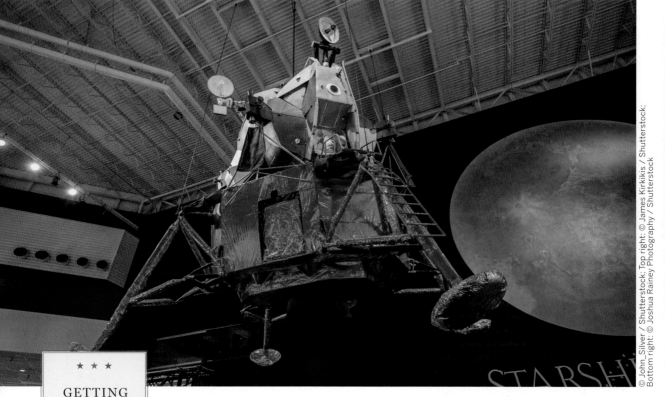

© John_Silver / Shutterstock; Top right: © James Kirkikis / Shutterstock; Bottom right: © Joshua Rainey Photography / Shutterstock

★ ★ ★

GETTING THERE & AROUND

The major international air hub is Dallas/Fort Worth International Airport, along with Houston's George Bush Intercontinental. Dallas-Fort Worth, Austin and Houston have local rail networks, but all connect only a limited number of destinations. Unsurprisingly for a state famed for gigantic, gas-guzzling pickup trucks, you will need your own wheels to get just about anywhere outside the main cities.

MISSION TEJAS STATE PARK El Camino Real, the royal road connecting missions between Mexico City and current-day Louisiana, ran right through Nacogdoches. At Mission Tejas State Park nearby, you can see a replica of the 17th-century Mission San Francisco de los Tejas, tour the 1820s Rice Family Log Home and hike in the footsteps of Davy Crockett on the Camino Real itself. *https://tpwd.texas.gov/state-parks, 105 Park Rd 44, Grapeland*

RIVER WALK San Antonio's charming River Walk has become an vital artery at the heart of city life, leading you 15 miles right through the center via most downtown attractions and riverfront cafes, over pretty stone footbridges and eventually out to connect with the city's historic missions (Mission San José is the most impressive of these). Explore it by hiking and by biking; it's the city's heart. *www.thesanantonioriverwalk.com*

SPACE CENTER HOUSTON Get as close to a moon landing as you will likely get: Space Center Houston sits alongside NASA's Johnson Space Center and tours include the old mission control (as in the Apollo 13 transmission, 'Houston, we have a problem') where planning for many space missions took place. Interactive exhibits include the chance to land a space shuttle. *http://spacecenter.org, 1601 NASA Pkwy*

STOCKYARDS There is no denying Fort Worth's real appeal: its fun Wild West–era Stockyards district, once home to one of the USA's largest livestock markets and today retaining the cowboy feel of yore. Big-hatted dudes saunter the streets, and there is a twice-daily cattle drive. Turn-of-the-century-style saloons and stores line the streets; dine at Cattlemen's Steak House, and see the hotel allegedly bearing the bullet holes from a Bonnie and Clyde shoot-out. *www.fortworthstockyards.org*

ITINERARY

Day 1

Fly into Dallas/Fort Worth Airport, where the metro area encompasses two of Texas' best attractions, Dallas' Sixth Floor Museum, site of JFK's assassination, and Fort Worth's trapped-in-time Wild West–style Stockyards district, where you can round off an evening at the globe's largest honky-tonk, Billy Bob's.

Day 2

Drive south through Hill Country toward Austin, perhaps following part of the Texas Wine Trail, through charming small towns like Fredericksburg and Luckenbach, with a picnic stop-off at Enchanted Rock State Natural Area. Consider overnighting out in the countryside hereabouts for a taste of rural Texas Hill Country life.

Day 3

Linger in state capital Austin, making the most of a downtown you can explore largely by foot. Don't miss the Texas State Capitol, the largest building of its kind in the US, and be sure to brave the queues for some of the planet's best barbecue at Franklin Barbecue. In Austin, one of the world's foremost cities for live music, choose from one of 500-odd gig venues for your evening entertainment.

Day 4

Head south to San Antonio to take a peek at the seventh-largest US city, brightened by the spectacular 15-mile River Walk. This passes by the state's most iconic attraction, the Alamo, where Texan revolutionaries died while defending a fort against a Mexican force that vastly outnumbered them. The River Walk leads you to several historic missions just outside the city.

Days 5 & 6

Journey out to Big Bend National Park, the state's most spectacular wilderness area. Stay overnight to truly savor this vast smorgasbord of mountains, deserts and canyons at a lodge like Chisos Mountains Lodge. Try a section of the 4.8-mile round-trip Lost Mine Trail for superb views. After, you'll need to start the 8.5-hour drive back to Dallas/Fort Worth Airport. But get one last meal of brisket to go.

From left: Lunar Module LTA-8 at Space Center Houston; the sign for Cattlemen's Steak House, a popular restaurant in the Fort Worth Stockyards; San Antonio's River Walk.

UTAH

★ ★

POPULATION: 3.1 million | **SIZE:** 84,899 sq miles | **STATE CAPITAL:** Salt Lake City
WEBSITE: www.visitutah.com

IS THIS AMERICA OR ANOTHER PLANET? FROM THE RIPPLED FORMS OF THE RED ROCK DESERT to the landlocked Great Salt Lake to the snowbound Rockies, Utah's landscapes defy belief. With world-class recreation (especially skiing), they also inspire play. Public lands blanket over 65% of the state, so the access is simply superb. Don't miss southern Utah, famous for the fantastic national parks known as the Mighty Five: Arches, Bryce Canyon, Canyonlands, Capitol Reef and Zion. Think brick-hued mesas, sorbet-colored spindles and seemingly endless sandstone desert interspersed with Mormon-influenced outposts. Explore the pioneer remnants, ancient rock art and dinosaur traces in wild, untamed country. The Wasatch Mountains, with pine forests and top-notch winter resorts, dominate northern Utah, where Salt Lake City and trendy Park City offer fine dining as well as vibrant urban culture without pretension.

© Chase Dekker Wild-Life Images / Getty Images

FOOD & DRINK

LIQUOR LAW LOOPHOLES Though not entirely dry, Utah comes pretty close. Anything over 4% alcohol by volume (ABV) is deemed liquor and can't be bought from a grocery or convenience store. You can be served in restaurants with the right license, however booze is prepared behind a 'Zion curtain' that obscures the action from view, and there's a limit of 1.5oz liquor in every mixed drink. It's a big improvement from the old 'members-only' bar limitations of years past. Salt Lake City even features its own Beer Bar, with 140 different beers on the menu.

PASTRAMI BURGER If Utahns love one thing more than a burger, it's a burger topped with pastrami. While it originated in California, the pastrami burger reigns supreme in Utah. Chain Crown Burger makes an excellent one, though the fight for the title is heated. Don't forget the fry sauce.

UTAH SCONES Not quite scones, not quite fry bread or sopapilla, this Utah treat gets fried and then topped with butter, honey or powdered sugar. It's not great for your arteries, but it's mighty tasty.

NATURAL ESCAPES

ARCHES NATIONAL PARK Though a dwarf alongside larger surrounding wilderness areas, Arches punches way above its weight. Wonder over the world's greatest concentration of sandstone arches, with huge sandstone ribbons framing the sky and trails scrambling over red rock. It's nothing short of magical. Arches is also highly accessible, with short hiking distances to incredible highlights. *www.nps.gov/arch, Moab*

BEARS EARS NATIONAL MONUMENT
Created in 2016, this national monument in southeastern Utah encompasses far more than the wooded mountaintop that bears its name. A stunning red rock wilderness holds ancient cliff dwellings, deep river canyons and countless rock carvings that will move you. Come explore: development has been minimal here, so route-finding is often part of the fun of an outing. The monument is jointly managed by the Bureau of Land Management, US Forest Service, and a coalition of five local Native American tribes. *www.fs.fed.us/visit/bears-ears-national-monument*

BRYCE CANYON NATIONAL PARK
Famous for its sunset-colored spires punctuated by tracts of evergreen forest, Bryce Canyon National Park is one of the planet's most exquisite geological wonders. Hike soft, winding trails beneath the sandcastle-like pinnacles known as hoodoos, through natural amphitheaters filled with thousands of what look like pastel daggers. You will feel like you've stepped into a fairy tale. *www.nps.gov/brca*

CANYONLANDS NATIONAL PARK
A crimson vision of ancient earth, this sprawling park has rugged, otherworldly terrain. Arches, needles, craters, mesas and petroglyphs are part of this immense playground covering over 500 sq miles. Accessed only by trail, Horseshoe Canyon shelters one of the most impressive

★ ★ ★

ASK A LOCAL

'Try to mountain bike the Wasatch Crest Trail in the fall when the colors peak. The views are sublime and the single track is a blast. It's one of those routes that satisfy the soul. You can pedal up Big Cottonwood Canyon from Salt Lake to the top of Guardsman Pass, get a shuttle to the top or come up from the Park City side. The trick is to pick an even-numbered calendar day to pedal all the way back down to the Salt Lake Valley. On odd-numbered days bikes aren't allowed on the upper Millcreek Canyon trails. Wait too late in the season and the snow flies, covering the upper miles. Bring a camera because you'll want to capture the 360-degree view.'
– *Francisco Kjolseth, professional photographer*

Left: Mesa Arch, Canyonlands National Park.

© Allison J. Hahn / Shutterstock; Left: © Tobin Akehurst / Getty Images

★ ★ ★

LOST IN THE DESERT

Everett Ruess, a young artist, explorer and vagabond, had incredible exploits in southern Utah and the Four Corners region in the early 1930s. He disappeared under mysterious circumstances outside Escalante in 1934, when he was 20, but his evocative letters bring to life a fascinating, somewhat forgotten Old West. Read them in the book *Everett Ruess: A Vagabond for Beauty*. Also based on real-life Utah adventures is the movie *127 Hours*, about the canyoneer Aron Ralston's accident and bloody escape.

collections of millennia-old rock art in the Southwest. The centerpiece is the Great Gallery, with pictographs dating back to 2000 BC. Elsewhere, hike slickrock trails, pedal the White Rim on fat tires or just float the snaking switchbacks of the calm Colorado River, taking it all in. *www.nps.gov/cany*

MOAB With the promise of a hot tub and pub grub after a dusty day on the trail, Moab is southern Utah's adventure base camp. This former uranium mining town has been reincarnated as the state's recreation capital, repurposing its vast network of back roads for unreal mountain biking, hiking access and 4WD adventures. Guided trips range from river running to canyoneering. *www.discovermoab.com*

SCENIC BYWAY 12 In a state of stunning drives, this might take the cake. Scenic Byway 12 runs from Capitol Reef to Bryce Canyon, traversing moonscapes of sculpted slickrock, crossing razor-thin ridges and climbing over an 11,000ft

mountain. Along the way it meets rural wagon trails and national parks and monuments, interspersed with farm-to-table dining and charming inns. *https://scenicbyway12.com*

ZION NATIONAL PARK Prepare for an overdose of awesome. Zion's soaring red-and-white cliffs are one of America's most majestic natural wonders. Wading the cool Virgin River under steep canyon walls on the Narrows or walking the dizzying, razor's-edge trail to Angels Landing is indeed amazing. There's also delicate beauty: 'weeping' rocks, tiny grottoes and meadows of mesa-top wildflowers. *www.nps.gov/zion*

ARTS, HISTORY & CULTURE

NATURAL HISTORY MUSEUM OF UTAH This SLC museum is a wonderful starting point for understanding Utah. Walk through a stunning architectural 'canyon' to explore cool exhibits on Indigenous cultures and natural history. Take in the full

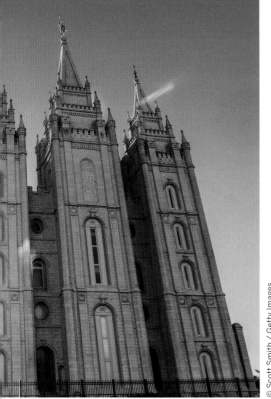

From left: Grand Staircase-Escalante; LDS temple in Salt Lake City's Temple Square; Pando quaking aspens in Fishlake National Forest.

© Scott Smith / Getty Images

breadth of prehistory with the Past Worlds paleontological displays, which contain a vast collection of dinosaur fossils. *https://nhmu.utah.edu, Rio Tinto Center, 301 Wakara Way*

SPIRAL JETTY Created by Robert Smithson in 1970, this beyond-cool art installation is a 1500ft coil of rock and earth spinning out from the northeastern shore of the Great Salt Lake. For years it was fully submerged. Since the early 2000s, drought has brought low water levels, making the work even more prominent and stirring. *www.spiraljetty.org, Golden Spike National Historic Site*

SUNDANCE RESORT Art and nature blend seamlessly at this magical resort-cum-artist-colony founded by actor Robert Redford. When it's not hosting the Sundance Film Festival, the resort is a prime spot to recharge your battery. You can immerse yourself in snow sports, horseback riding and fly-fishing. Spend the night in rustic luxury, hike Mt Timpanogos

and dine at the resort's excellent restaurants. The resort is in northern Utah, near Provo. *www.sundanceresort.com*.

THE TABERNACLE CHOIR Taking in the celestial sound of the world-renowned Tabernacle Choir is a heart-stirring experience and a must-do on any SLC bucket list. See the 360-person choir perform at the Tabernacle on Sunday, accompanied by the 11,000-pipe Tabernacle organ. Or drop in on Thursday evening public rehearsals for free (just check the website in advance). *www.thetabernaclechoir.org, Temple Square*

TEMPLE SQUARE Salt Lake City's most famous sight occupies a 10-acre block surrounded by 15ft-high walls. Latter-Day Saints (LDS) docents give free, 30-minute tours continually, leaving from the visitors centers at the two entrances on South and North Temple Streets. Sisters, brothers and elders are stationed every 20ft or so to answer questions. (Note that no one is

FUN FACT

Pando, a grove of quaking aspens in Utah's Fishlake National Forest, is one of the world's largest and oldest living organisms, linked through a shared root system.

© kyletperry / Getty Images; Right: © Per Breiehagen / Getty Images

going to try to convert you – unless you express interest.) *www.templesquare.com*

FAMILY OUTINGS

BEST FRIENDS ANIMAL SANCTUARY
Kanab's most famous attraction is 5.5 miles north of town. Surrounded by more than 33,000 mostly private acres of red rock desert, Best Friends is the largest no-kill animal rescue center in the country. It shows films and gives facility tours four times a day; call ahead for exact times and reservations. The 1½-hour tours let you meet some of the more than 1700 horses, pigs, dogs, cats, birds and other critters on-site. *https://bestfriends.org, 5001 Angel Canyon Rd*

CLEVELAND-LLOYD DINOSAUR
QUARRY Call it Utah's own Jurassic Park. This dinosaur dig site has yielded over 12,000 bones. A dozen species were buried here 150 million years ago, and the large concentration of meat-eating allosaurs has helped scientists worldwide draw new conclusions. Excavations are ongoing and there are hikes and excellent exhibits to check out. *www.blm.gov, off Hwy 10 near Price*

GOBLIN VALLEY STATE PARK
A Salvador Dalí–esque melted-rock fantasy, a valley of giant stone mushrooms, an alien landscape or the results of a cosmological acid trip? No matter what you think the stadium-like valley of stunted hoodoos resembles, one thing's for sure – the 3654-acre park is just plain fun. A few trails lead from the overlooks down to the valley floor. You can climb down, around and even over the evocative 'goblins' (2ft- to 20ft-tall formations). *https://stateparks.utah.gov, Hwy 24, Green River*

★ ★ ★

GETTING THERE & AROUND

Most flights land in Salt Lake City. Public transportation serves Salt Lake City and links to Park City and ski resorts. Despite some long-distance train and bus service, Utah's scenic byways and curvy back roads are best seen by car.

SNOWBIRD Taste the bluebird skies and champagne powder of Utah, and you will be effectively spoiled for life. With long, lazy groomers and vast acres of wide-open snow bowls, plus a wicked terrain park and steeps, Snowbird pleases all skiers. It has the longest season of Salt Lake City's resorts; lifts usually run from mid-November to mid-May. *www.snowbird.com, Little Cottonwood Canyon*

UTAH OLYMPIC PARK While it continues to host competitions, the site of the 2002 Olympic ski events in Park City offers an outsize dose of adrenaline to visitors too. In summer, zip lines and alpine slides offer thrilling rides, while the adults-only bobsled ride clocks 70mph on the course. In winter, you can even take bobsled, skeleton, free-jump and freestyle skate lessons. *www.utaholympiclegacy.com, 3419 Olympic Pkwy*

From left: Goblin Valley State Park; skiers at Snowbird.

ITINERARY

Day 1
In Salt Lake City, Mormon guides offer a glimpse of Utah's unique state history in Temple Square. Browse the booming downtown, check out shops and dine at one of many small, creative city restaurants. You could always add an extra day here to drive out to nearby Park City, charming even without the bustle of the annual Sundance Film Festival. This is your last chance to soak up urban vibes before heading out into Utah's amazing parks and wilderness areas. Or spend your second day exploring at Utah Olympic Park.

Day 2
Make the five-hour drive to Moab, your adventure hub for the next few days. Detour along the way to the info-packed Cleveland-Lloyd Dinosaur Quarry to see the Jurassic era come alive.

Day 3
In Moab, spend the cool morning hours on a mountain bike; the Slickrock Trail is considered a desert classic. After lunch, hit nearby Arches National Park, seeing formations along the 19-mile park road. Do make time for the 3-mile round-trip to Delicate Arch, the land-mark on Utah license plates.

Day 4
For a bird's-eye view of Canyonlands National Park, drive to the mesa top of Island in the Sky. Trails and panoramic views of the entire region abound, including the Colorado and Green Rivers, which can also be floated with a Moab outfitter. Pack a picnic lunch as there are no services in the park.

Day 5
With only half the volume of visitors received by other area parks, Canyonlands' Needles District takes you well off the beaten path. Take plenty of water to hike the wonderful Chesler Park–Joint Trail, an 11-mile loop that squeezes through a narrow slot canyon; sometimes you will have to step through sideways.

Day 6
On your way back to Salt Lake City from Moab, stop to view the amazing Spiral Jetty. The Great Salt Lake where this installation by Robert Smithson is based can be home to up to five million migrating shorebirds depending on the time of year, so bring your long lens if you love photography.

VERMONT

★ ★

POPULATION: 626,042 | **SIZE:** 9616 sq miles | **STATE CAPITAL:** Montpelier
LARGEST CITY: Burlington | **WEBSITE:** www.vermontvacation.com

VERMONT'S BLEND OF BUCOLIC FARMLAND, WOODED MOUNTAINS AND QUAINT VILLAGES
makes it an appealing refuge. Whether you visit for the brilliant fall foliage or its White Christmas
reputation as 'America's winter playground,' Vermont has you covered. It's an outdoor enthusiast's
paradise, from Green Mountain National Forest to Lake Champlain, yet indoor types find a lot to love
as well, thanks to cozy inns, excellent museums, and world-class historical sites. Go highbrow and buy a
case of champagne flutes from a world-renowned glass factory, or dive into delicious bites one ice-cream
scoop at a time. But most of all, what sets Vermont apart is its independent spirit: Vermont remains a
haven for quirky creativity, a champion of grassroots government and a bastion of 'small is beautiful'
thinking. Vermont is a solid old sugar maple that continues to thrive, surprise and dazzle.

© Sean Pavone / Shutterstock

FOOD & DRINK

BEN & JERRY'S Boasting as many feel-good vibes as the Vermont-born ice cream itself, Ben & Jerry's is a sure bet for all ages. Try to go for a cone at off-hours for the most rewarding experience – long wait times are far from groovy. A free scoop is included with the factory tour in Waterbury and can be enjoyed while perusing the cemetery of 'de-pinted' flavors.
www.benjerry.com,
1281 Waterbury-Stowe Rd (Rte 100)

CHEESE Vermont is famous for its cheddar, alpine and blue cheese varieties. Sample it straight from the source in one of Vermont's many dairies, buy a hunk at any general store or get a selection of cheeses after dinner. Try the cheese board in the tavern at the Dorset Inn in Dorset, Vermont's oldest continuously operated inn. If you take your cheese with more exclusivity, see what the chef at the Backroom, a reservations-recommended hot spot in Pittsfield, has in store.

HEN-OF-THE-WOODS MUSHROOMS Hen-of-the-woods mushrooms are employed to fine advantage in many of Vermont's farm-to-table restaurants. The best of these is, not surprisingly, Hen of the Wood, with locations in Waterbury and Burlington. Diners love specialties like hen-of-the-woods toast and duck breast.

KING ARTHUR FLOUR Serious bakers and lovers of serious baked goods flock to small Norwich, beautifully placed near the Connecticut River, to pay homage at the altar of flour. Founded in 1790 (the name dates to 1896), this employee-owned bakery supply company has expanded its reach from mere flour to lauded cookbooks and on-site baking classes. Everyone from beginners to professionals can hone their skills in the spacious instructional kitchens. A cafe and shop are on the premises for those wanting to sample the final product.
www.kingarthurflour.com, 135 US-5 S

MAPLE MAPLE EVERYWHERE No trip to Vermont is complete without a sampling of its maple syrup, the byproduct of deep forests of sugar maples. Enjoy it with pancakes or French toast, or in the form of candy, vegetable glazes or marinades. Offerings are everywhere, but a particularly memorable venue is Sugar & Spice in Mendon, where a delicious brunch is served in an authentic sugarhouse on a picturesque estate.

NATURAL ESCAPES

GREEN MOUNTAIN NATIONAL FOREST The largest contiguous public land area in the state hosts outdoorspeople of all abilities, with more than 400,000 acres of lakes, streams and hiking trails. Whatever you like to do outdoors – from hunting to horseback riding – Green Mountain National Forest delivers. Start at the Grout Pond Recreation Area in Stratton for a taste of everything the forest has to offer.
www.stateparks.com/green_mountain_ national_forest_in_vermont.html

LAKE CHAMPLAIN Comprising Vermont's northwestern border, Lake Champlain is one of the more stunning jewels in the state's crown. Enjoy serious fishing, relaxed

★ ★ ★

VERMONT MAPLE FESTIVAL

Maple syrup is celebrated everywhere and every day in Vermont, but no event celebrates the product like the Vermont Maple Festival in the small northern town of St Albans. Far from flashy (it's about as homespun as mittens knit by a relative), the three-day event has been held the last weekend in April since 1966. Tour sugarhouses and get free samples of maple products at every turn. Don't miss the festive face painting, parade, cooking contests, window displays and the crowning of the new king and queen Maple Ambassadors.

Left: Rural Vermont.

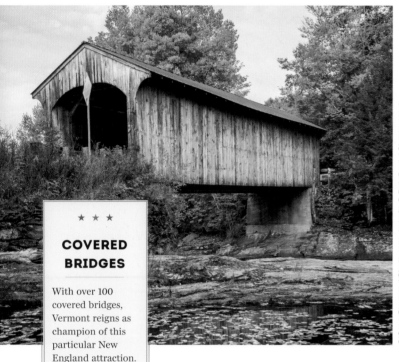

© Sean Pavone / Shutterstock; Left: © Bob Pool / Shutterstock

★ ★ ★
COVERED BRIDGES

With over 100 covered bridges, Vermont reigns as champion of this particular New England attraction. Some were reconstructed after fires and floods wrecked the originals, a hazard of wood bridges, but structures from the 19th century remain, many built by esteemed bridge builder Nichols (or Nicholas) Powers. Otter Creek's Hammond Covered Bridge was built in 1842; Arlington's Green Covered Bridge went up a decade later. The Brown Covered Bridge in Shrewsbury, dates to 1880 and retains its original lattice truss. Picking a favorite bridge is hard with the abundance of winning options dotting the state.

hiking, biking the lakeshore or simply watching sailboats go by. Paddleboarding and swimming in the crystal water are sure bets for summer, while kayaking or boating in the fall is ideal for viewing foliage. Burlington is a popular point of entry. www.lakechamplainregion.com

STOWE What better way to explore Vermont than from the top down? Stowe has long been a destination for downhill skiing, thanks to its proximity to Mt Mansfield, the state's highest point. Today the town has evolved and provides plenty to do year-round, including farmers markets, footraces, biking, and beer festivals. *Sound of Music* fans will enjoy a visit to the Trapp Family Lodge. www.gostowe.com

VINS NATURE CENTER AND QUECHEE GORGE Adjacent to striking, 164ft-deep Quechee Gorge with its dramatic vistas from Vermont's oldest surviving steel-arch bridge, this nature center in Quechee is a must for birders. See avian rehab in action,

with daily 'turtle time' and raptor feedings sure to fascinate even the young or uninitiated. Nearby picnic areas and hiking trails are part of the charm. https://vinsweb.org, 149 Natures Way

ARTS, HISTORY & CULTURE

CHURCH STREET MARKETPLACE Four blocks of downtown Burlington closed off to vehicles, the marketplace offers street entertainment, quirky dining and eclectic shops, with plenty of holdouts against the inevitable influx of global brands. Highlights include Lake Champlain Chocolates (eco-friendly, ethical and delicious: try the seasonal truffles) and cozy Crow Bookshop, known for helpful staff and resplendent with the smell of the printed word. www.churchstmarketplace.com

MORGAN HORSE FARM Open to visitors May through October, the Morgan Horse Farm in Weybridge is home to the world's oldest continuous Morgan horse breeding herd. Student tour guides share details of

From left: The Montgomery Covered Bridge, also known as the Lower Covered Bridge in Waterville; Church Street Marketplace in Burlington; Quechee Gorge.

© Robert Harding / Getty Images

bloodlines and pedigree as well as a history of the farm and its founder, Justin Morgan. Horses are even available for purchase; the gift shop offers easier-to-pack souvenirs. *www.uvm.edu, 74 Battell Dr*

PRESIDENT CALVIN COOLIDGE STATE HISTORIC SITE While most US presidents take their oaths of office in Washington, DC, Vermont's own Calvin Coolidge did so at his childhood home in Plymouth – by the light of a kerosene lamp. In addition to seeing the room where this happened, visitors can get a sense of the past with perfectly preserved buildings and even a working cheese factory. *https://historicsites.vermont.gov, 3780 Rte 100A*

ROBERT FROST STONE HOUSE MUSEUM Whose woods are these? They're Robert Frost's. This museum in Shaftsbury offers a glimpse into the domestic life of one of America's most influential poets, who lived in the stone house for nine years. Visitors can see the table where he penned his famous 'Stopping by Woods on a Snowy Evening' and remnants of the orchard Frost himself planted. *www.bennington.edu, 121 Historic Rte 7A*

SHELBURNE MUSEUM The word 'museum' doesn't adequately describe the 39 buildings and 100,000 items on display at this 45-acre site in Shelburne. Purists may balk at the hodgepodge collection, including a covered bridge, steamboat, and lighthouse imported from elsewhere in the Northeast, but there is unparalleled Americana here, including examples of folk and decorative arts. Museum founder Electra Havemeyer Webb found beauty in everyday American objects; visitors will find a kind of beauty in her collection. *https://shelburnemuseum.org, 6000 Shelburne Rd*

SIMON PEARCE In a state famous for its artisans, Simon Pearce is king. Visit the company's flagship store in Quechee, the Mill, to see thrilling glassblowing demonstrations, shop the collection of elegant glassware and even have a bite

FUN FACT

Vermont is the only state in the US to have its very own state flavor. That's right: it's maple.

© Danita Delimont / Alamy Stock Photo: Right: © Artazum / Shutterstock

Most destinations in Vermont are best reached by car, although the state is also well served by the Vermonter train, operated by Amtrak; the Ethan Allen Express serves Castleton and Rutland. The largest airport is Burlington International, supported by small regional airfields.

to eat. Dining here is recommended to experience the beautiful tableware and decor as well as the views of the Ottauquechee River waterfall and Taftsville Covered Bridge. *www.simonpearce.com, 1760 Quechee Main St*

FAMILY OUTINGS

ECHO, LEAHY CENTER FOR LAKE CHAMPLAIN
When one more covered bridge might be a bridge too many, ECHO is here for the entire family. This stunning aquarium and science center in Burlington has no shortage of hands-on experiences and activities. Visit sled dogs in the fall, encounter a real shipwreck and, in fine weather, dine on the patio with views of beautiful Lake Champlain. *www.echovermont.org, 1 College St*

HILDENE, THE LINCOLN FAMILY HOME
The reception here can be chilly, but the Manchester summer home of Abraham and Mary Todd Lincoln's son, Robert, is worth it. Visitors are welcome to roam the picturesque grounds, but finding an eager docent gets you a personal tour of the Georgian revival mansion, with fun facts about President Taft's sleeping habits, who was good friends with Robert. *https://hildene.org, 1005 Hildene Rd*

MONTSHIRE MUSEUM OF SCIENCE
This interactive science museum in Norwich has tons to do inside, but the real fun starts outside. During the summer, kids love the outdoor science park, teeming with water exhibits (bring swimsuits and towels), and aspiring astronomers get a sense of the enormity of the universe on the Planet

ITINERARY

Day 1
Start at beautiful
Hildene in Manchester,
home of Robert Lincoln,
followed by a visit to
the Green Mountain
National Forest. After a
hike, head to the Dorset
Inn for a bite to eat.

Day 2
Head east and north
to the Calvin Coolidge
State Historic Site in
Plymouth, then proceed
to Quechee Gorge to
view its steep sides and
cross the town's covered
bridge. If nature isn't
your thing, head to
Quechee proper for
shopping and the glass
at Simon Pearce.

Day 3
Take in the Montshire
Museum of Science
in Norwich and then
head to Ben & Jerry's in
Waterbury for a factory
tour. Have dinner in
Burlington and call it a
day. Vermont's largest
city would be tiny in
most other states, but
its relatively diminutive
size is one of Burling-
ton's charms.

Day 4
Enjoy Burlington's
Church Street Market-
place and explore Lake
Champlain, relishing in
its expansive waters.

Walk, a scale model of the solar system that starts with the sun and ends with Pluto. *www.montshire.org, 1 Montshire Rd*

PUTNEY GENERAL STORE A Vermont trip must include a visit to a general store. Putney boasts the state's oldest, operating since 1796. The store has Vermont cheese, maple syrup and souvenirs, plus sundry items necessary for locals: duct tape, paint thinner, you name it. The saying goes, 'If they don't have it, you don't need it.' *www.putneygeneralstore.com, 4 Kimball Hill Rd*

SHELBURNE FARMS LEARNING CENTER Respect and appreciation for the natural environment is at the heart of this kid-friendly learning center in Shelburne. The 1400-acre working farm has adopted the UN's Sustainable Development Goals, though young visitors will likely be more impressed by the happy-looking sheep, goats, pigs, rabbits and chickens that reside here than by the distinction. Stop by the Welcome Center and Farm Store to bring home cheddar, vegetables, eggs and maple syrup, all produced on the farm. *https://shelburnefarms.org, 1611 Harbor Rd*

From left: Glass-blowing at Simon Pearce; Hildene, the Lincoln family home.

VIRGINIA

★ ★ ★ ★ ★ ★ ★ ★ ★ ★ ★ ★ ★ ★ ★ ★ ★ ★ ★

POPULATION: 8.5 million | **SIZE:** 42,775 sq miles | **CAPITAL:** Richmond
LARGEST CITY: Virginia Beach | **WEBSITE:** www.virginia.org

LOOPING THROUGH THE OLD DOMINION STATE MEANS TAPPING INTO CULTURAL TOUCHPOINTS from every corner of the country compressed into one scenic and historic tract of land. Since English settlers established this as the first permanent British colony in the New World in 1607, the state has played a lead role in nearly every major American drama, from the Revolutionary and Civil Wars to the civil rights movement. Virginia's natural beauty is as diverse as its history and people. The wide sandy beaches of the Chesapeake Bay kiss the Atlantic Ocean, pine forests, marshes and rolling green hills form the soft curves of the central Piedmont region, and the rolling Blue Ridge Mountains and stunning Shenandoah Valley line its back. Visitors can enjoy Colonial Williamsburg, a foot-tapping mountain-music scene and an ever-growing network of wine, beer and spirit trails to follow.

© Zack Frank / Shutterstock

FOOD & DRINK

CHESAPEAKE OYSTERS If you're a fan of oysters, then make the pilgrimage out to coastal Virginia for oysters plucked straight from the source. The OG locale Rappahannock Oysters, right on the namesake Rappahannock River, brings bivalves to the table raw, or cooks them on an open grill.

COUNTRY HAM Slices of salty pinkish-brown cured country ham are a nonnegotiable part of a full Southern breakfast. Virginia is indisputably the country's leader in ham production, and Smithfield Hams are rightly famous. You can visit their Smithfield shop, or just order a side to start your day at any eatery in the state.

NATURAL ESCAPES

BELLE ISLE STATE PARK A small state park, Belle Isle boasts picnic areas, boat launches, hiking and biking trails and a host of other well-maintained amenities patrolled by soaring bald eagles. The eponymous on-site Georgian house, built in 1760, feels like a dictionary illustration pasted next to the word 'mansion.' Alas, it can only be admired from afar, as it's privately owned, but the other historic property in the park, the Bel Air House (no fresh princes, sadly), is available for overnight rentals. *www.dcr.virginia.gov, 1632 Belle Isle Rd, Lancaster*

CHINCOTEAGUE ISLAND Virginia shares claim to the Assateague Island National Seashore with neighboring Maryland. The bottom third of this wild pony habitat blends into Virginia's Chincoteague National Wildlife Refuge and Chincoteague Island, the main town for eating and lodging on the Eastern Shore in Virginia. It has become a bit hip in recent years, with a young and entrepreneurial slew of residents injecting energy into the community, but the main draw is still the access to the ponies. The wild ponies were made famous by the *Misty of Chincoteague* series of novels written by Marguerite Henry starting in 1947. *www.chincoteague.com*

SHENANDOAH NATIONAL PARK One of the most spectacular national parks in the country, Shenandoah is a showcase of natural color and beauty all year round: in spring and summer the wildflowers explode, in fall the leaves burn bright red and orange, and in winter a cold, starkly beautiful hibernation period sets in. Its singular ribbon of gray road, Skyline Drive, ambles through every green corner of the preserve as it follows the crest of the Blue Ridge Mountains. The 100-plus miles of track promise 69 lookout points over dozens of tree-filled valleys and cool lakes, each one worthy of a stop. *http://goshenandoah.com*

ARTS, HISTORY & CULTURE

ARLINGTON NATIONAL CEMETERY The 624-acre grounds at Arlington outside of DC contain the dead of every war the US has fought since the Civil War. Highlights include the Tomb of the Unknown Soldier, with its elaborate changing-of-the-guard ceremony; the grave of John F Kennedy

★ ★ ★

CIVIL WAR HISTORY

Virginia was a major locus in the Civil War. Manassas National Battlefield Park is now a green oasis, but on July 21, 1861, soldiers clashed here in the first major land battle of the war, watched by DC residents expecting a quick victory. The surprise Southern victory in the First Battle of Bull Run (known in the South as the First Battle of Manassas) erased any hopes of a quick end to the war. In the Second Battle of Manassas of August 1862, again the South won. More than 13,000 were killed in four battles fought in a 17-mile radius near Fredericksburg and Chancellorsville; visit the site where Stonewall Jackson was mortally wounded by friendly fire. At war's end, General Robert E Lee surrendered to General Ulysses S Grant in the town of Appomattox, now a National Historical Park comprised of over two dozen restored buildings.

Left: **Manassas National Battlefield Park.**

© brians101 / Getty Images; Left: © RosalreneBetancourt 14 / Alamy Stock Photo

★ ★ ★

THE
Crooked
ROAD

When Scots–Irish fiddle and reel joined with African American banjo and percussion, American mountain or 'old-time' music was born, later spawning such genres as country and bluegrass. The latter still dominates the Blue Ridge, and Virginia's Heritage Music Trail, the 330-mile-long Crooked Road, takes you through nine relevant sites, along with some Insta-worthy mountain scenery. Take a detour and join music-loving fans of all ages who kick up their heels (many arrive with tap shoes) at these festive jamborees. During a live show you'll witness expert elders connecting to deep cultural roots and a new generation of musicians keeping their heritage alive and evolving.

and his family, marked by an eternal flame; the Shuttle Challenger Memorial; and the Iwo Jima Memorial, displaying the famous raising of the flag over Mt Suribachi, is on the cemetery's northern fringes. *https://arlingtoncemetery.mil, Memorial Ave*

CARYTOWN While Richmond, the once-Confederate capital, may best be known for its Monument Avenue honoring Confederate figures, the Carytown district is firmly rooted in the present, awash in psychedelic colors covering its mismatched storefronts. Wander down the main commercial drag, Cary Street, to find curio shops, used bookstores, an old three-penny theater and a scatter of health-conscious eateries. *www.carytownrva.com, Cary St*

KING STREET The main artery in downtown Alexandria bears all the charm of a Nancy Meyers Christmas flick, and then some. Colonial brick and colored clapboard shutters adorn each facade – it

could take you almost an entire day to wander down the street, poking your head into each establishment to see what lurks within. Don't miss the Stabler-Leadbeater Apothecary Museum, a pharmacy preserved from the 1800s containing potions in dusky beakers and parchment prescriptions in towering wooden cabinets. *www.visitalexandriava.com/old-town-alexandria, King St*

MONTICELLO The house at Monticello is an architectural masterpiece designed and inhabited by Thomas Jefferson, founding father and third US president, who spent 40 years building his dream home. It was finally completed in 1809. The centerpiece of a plantation that once covered 5000 acres, today it is the only home in America designated a Unesco World Heritage Site. The 45-minute 'Slavery at Monticello' walking tour (included in ticket price) is the highlight of any trip. Guides don't gloss over the complicated past of the man who declared that 'all men are created equal' in the Declaration of Independence, while

From left: A performance at the Blue Ridge Music Center, one of the stops on the Heritage Music Trail; the changing of the guard at the Tomb of the Unknown Soldier, Arlington National Cemetery; King Street in Alexandria.

© Mark Summerfield / Alamy Stock Photo

owning slaves and fathering children with one of them, Sally Hemings. *https://home.monticello.org, 931 Thomas Jefferson Parkway*

MOUNT VERNON Mount Vernon was the beloved home of George and Martha Washington, who lived here from the time of their marriage in 1759 until George's death in 1799. Regular guided tours of the furnished main house give a fascinating insight into the Washingtons' daily life, and self-guided tours of the outbuildings and gardens offer plenty of opportunities to interact with actors offering first-person narratives of working and living on the 18th-century plantation. *www.mountvernon.org, 3200 Mount Vernon Memorial Hwy*

PENTAGON The Pentagon is the largest office building in the world and the headquarters of the US Department of Defense, the Army, the Navy and the Air Force. Outside the building is the Pentagon Memorial; 184 illuminated benches honor

each person killed in the September 11, 2001, terrorist attack on the Pentagon. To get inside the building, you'll have to book a free guided one-hour tour on the website and provide appropriate photo ID. *https://pentagontours.osd.mil/tours, Arlington*

TORPEDO FACTORY ART CENTER Once a munitions plant that stored sensitive government documents and dinosaur bones after WWII, the Torpedo Factory was purchased by the municipal government and transformed into artists' studios a decade later. Today, over 80 ateliers thrive in the airy, interactive space. Visit Lisa Schumaier, a native Alexandrian, who makes whimsical ceramic sculptures and relief paintings from unexpected items like used chewing gum. *http://torpedofactory.org, 105 N Union St, Alexandria*

UNIVERSITY OF VIRGINIA Founded by Thomas Jefferson, this 'Academical Village' is bustling with young college students. At the heart of this 'village' is the Lawn, a large gently sloping grassed field fringed

FUN FACT

Before colonists planted tobacco in Jamestown after a mulberry blight, silk was meant to be this colony's cash crop.

Virginia has regional airports in the four corners of the state, including Washington Dulles International Airport in the north, Richmond International Airport in the southeast, Norfolk International Airport in the east and Roanoke's regional airport in the southwest. Amtrak stops in Richmond, Fredericksburg, Charlottesville and Williamsburg among several other smaller stations.

by columned pavilions, student rooms, the Stanford White–designed Old Cabell Hall (1898) and Jefferson's famous Rotunda, modeled on Rome's Pantheon. *http://virginia.edu, Charlottesville*

VIRGINIA MUSEUM OF FINE ARTS

Richmond is a cultured city, and this splendid museum is the cornerstone of the local arts scene. Highlights include furniture and decorative arts by designers like Eileen Gray, Josef Hoffmann and Charles Rennie Mackintosh. Other galleries house one of the largest Fabergé egg collections and American works by O'Keeffe, Hopper, Whistler and Sargent. Be sure to walk around the 24ft-high *Chloe* sculpture. *www.vmfa.museum, 200 N Blvd*

FAMILY OUTINGS

COLONIAL WILLIAMSBURG The restored capital of England's largest colony in the New World isn't some phony, fenced-in theme park: Colonial Williamsburg is a living, breathing history museum with a painstakingly researched environment that evokes America in the 1700s. It contains 88 original 18th-century buildings and several hundred faithful reproductions, as well as an impressive museum complex. Townsfolk and 'interpreters' in period dress go about their colonial jobs, emulating daily life. *https://colonialwilliamsburg.org*

DINOSAUR KINGDOM II From artist and creative wunderkind Mark Cline, this

© Jouni Vikki / Getty Images

seasonal kitschy theme park transports visitors to an alternate reality: a forested kingdom where Union soldiers are attempting to use life-size dinosaurs as weapons of mass destruction against Confederate forces during the Civil War. The Styrofoam and fiberglass creations are lifelike enough to amaze younger kids, and the offbeat historic juxtapositions will entertain even the grouchiest of adults. *www.dinosaurkingdomii.com, 5781 S Lee Hwy, Natural Bridge*

HISTORIC JAMESTOWNE The original Jamestown site established in 1607 is the home of the first permanent English settlement in North America, though it quickly became the so-called 'lost colony,' whose disappearance remains a mystery. The ruins were rediscovered in 1994, and visitors can take a free guided tour of the excavations and 4000 artifacts. Note the plaque on John White's commemorative (but not complimentary) statue, calling him 'an arrogant and boastful man.' *https://historicjamestowne.org, 1368 Colonial Pkwy*

LURAY CAVERNS If you can only fit one cavern into your Shenandoah itinerary, head 25 miles south from Front Royal to the world-class Luray Caverns and hear the 'Great Stalacpipe Organ' – hyped as the largest musical instrument on earth. Tours can feel like a cattle call on busy weekends, but the stunning underground formations make up for all the elbow bumping. *https://luraycaverns.com, 101 Cave Hill Rd*

NAVAL STATION NORFOLK This is the world's largest navy base and one of the busiest airfields in the country. Hampton-based company Tidewater Touring works with the base to offer 45-minute bus tours conducted by naval personnel; tours must be booked in advance (hours vary). The Battleship *Wisconsin* is a highlight. *www.cnic.navy.mil/norfolksta, 9079 Hampton Blvd, Norfolk*

VIRGINIA BEACH With 35 miles of sandy beaches, a 3-mile concrete oceanfront boardwalk and nearby outdoor activities, it's no surprise that Virginia Beach is a prime tourist destination. The city has worked hard to shed its once-reputation as a rowdy 'Redneck Riviera,' and you'll find some lovely parks and nature sites beyond the crowded high-rises lining the shore. If you get tired of the crowds, head 30 miles south to the 112,000-acre wonderfully named Great Dismal Swamp National Wildlife Refuge, a marshy habitat that once covered more than one million acres of southeastern VA and northeastern NC. *www.visitvirginiabeach.com*

ITINERARY

Day 1
Start in historic Alexandria outside of Washington, DC, and spend the day wandering the cobbled colonial streets near the waterfront. You can take in Mount Vernon or Arlington National Cemetery before dining on King Street.

Day 2
Point your car to Luray Caverns and drive down the stunning turns of Shenandoah National Park's Skyline Drive.

Day 3
Head to Charlottesville, where colonial and college vibes intermix at the University of Virginia and the estate of Monticello beckons.

Day 4
Richmond is a southern city in transition with flecks of blue and red sprinkled around the city. Compare and contrast a stroll on Monument Avenue with one around Carytown.

Day 5
Hit the shoreline at Virginia Beach for fresher-than-fresh oysters and a distinctly mid-Atlantic beach vibe set near the world's most impressive naval base in Norfolk and the Great Dismal Swamp Wildlife Refuge.

Left: Historic Jamestowne's church.

W A S H I N G T O N

★ ★

POPULATION: 7.5 million | **SIZE:** 71,362 sq miles | **STATE CAPITAL:** Olympia
LARGEST CITY: Seattle | **WEBSITE:** www.experiencewa.com

FROM ITS ORIGINAL HEYDAY AS AN OUTPOST FOR PROSPECTORS HEADING TO THE KLONDIKE
Gold Rush, Washington has been populated with fiercely independent pioneers – ranchers and
homesteaders, business titans and tech innovators. When you're surrounded by alpine lakes, emerald
islands and snow-capped peaks, it's common sense to go to work in flannel shirts or hiking pants. Boeing
opened up shop in Seattle during WWI, and the state now hosts the likes of Microsoft, Amazon, and
Starbucks (and ongoing discussion about their impacts). Over 60% of the state's population lives in the
greater Seattle metro area, but it's the natural beauty that makes Washington stand out. The Olympic
Peninsula and the San Juan Islands duke it out for most perfectly lush, green Pacific Northwest scenery.
In the more sparsely populated plains of Eastern Washington over the Cascade Mountains, you may see
tumbleweeds blow past cattle ranches, Ice Age–carved scablands or lush apple orchards.

© KingWu / Getty Images

FOOD & DRINK

COFFEE AND MORE COFFEE Absolutely visit the original Starbucks at Pike Place Market (hint: it's not the true original). But, for the grand dame of the Starbucks-in-Seattle experience, head to the chain's paean to coffee on hustling, bustling Capitol Hill, or stop into one of the many excellent local cafes serving delicious lattes competing for your attention.

GEODUCK CLAMS As you sit alongside the dark and brooding Puget Sound in a tree-encircled bay eating freshly harvested geoducks (it's pronounced 'gooey-duck'), the Pacific Northwest will seep into your very bones. Or maybe that's just the rain. Founded in the 1890s, Taylor Shellfish Farms runs several oyster bars around the state that serve this Pacific Northwest native, the world's largest burrowing clam, which can reach a length of 3ft. *www.taylorshellfishfarms.com*

PIKE PLACE MARKET Fishmongers throw fish over ooh-ing and aah-ing tourists while locals maneuver past to pick up their goat milk, lacinato kale or stylish eyeglasses. To taste Washington's famous berries at this 1907 farmers market, try Ellenos marionberry Greek yogurt, chocolate-covered Chukar cherries, or in early summer, buy burstingly sweet Rainier cherries. *www.pikeplacemarket.org, 1st Ave and Pike St, Seattle*

SALMON The silvery rivers here teem with fat sockeye salmon, many of which find their way to local tables. It's classically grilled above cedar planks, a deliciously smoky preparation discovered by the Native Americans who first relished in the sea's bounty.

WALLA WALLA WINERIES The dark basalt soil that soaks up this southeastern region's sunshine is practically tailor-made to produce deeply flavorful wines that have poured this southeastern region on the oenological map lately. Add in a dose of Wild West history, farm-to-table restaurants, and winemakers like Charles Smith, and you've got yourself a microcosm of the best of Washington. *www.wallawalla.org/wineries*

NATURAL ESCAPES

DRY FALLS Cataclysmic Ice Age floods of 2000ft surges of ice rushing at 60mph cut near-instantaneous swathes through what are now dramatic scablands in Eastern Washington. Dry Falls once saw the equivalent of every river in the world's worth of water, but there's nary a drop of water in sight in this unexpectedly fascinating terrain. *http://parks.state.wa.us/251/Dry-Falls, 34875 Park Lake Rd NE, Coulee City*

MT RAINIER NATIONAL PARK In Seattle or Tacoma, 'The mountain is out today' is the equivalent of 'Nice day!' The impossibly grand, improbably snow-blanketed volcanic peak hosts bright swathes of midsummer wildflowers that share their land with dense packs of snow. *www.nps.gov/mora*

MT ST HELENS On May 18, 1980, Mt St Helens volcano erupted without

---

★ ★ ★

THREE HIKES *in the North Cascades*

Geology professor and climb leader Emma Agosta's favorite hikes are in Washington's North Cascades.

Heather-Maple Pass Loop This moderate 7-mile loop hike has 2000ft of elevation gain with nonstop mountain views, spectacular in the fall when the larches turn gold.

Hidden Lake Lookout An incredibly scenic 8-mile and 3300ft elevation gain hike that takes you above a secluded alpine lake and an old fire lookout with 360-degree views of the most scenic and iconic North Cascades.

Sahale Arm A very strenuous 12-mile trail takes you up over 4000ft to the base of the Sahale Glacier, with spectacular views of the glacier and rugged mountains. The high plateau on the trail's Cascade Pass is very *The Sound of Music*. Wildflowers in summer; fiery red foliage in fall.

© Sean Pavone / Shutterstock; Left: © Edmund Lowe Photography / Shutterstock

★ ★ ★

Local Voice:
THE PIG WAR

'Hike along the bays and prairie-covered ocean bluffs of American Camp at the San Juan Island National Historical Park. The site honors the Pig War, sparked by a British boar repeatedly plundering a Yank's potato patch, and a larger dispute about the border. Soon both countries mobilized their troops. The standoff lasted from 1859 to 1872, and bored soldiers started sharing picnics and horse races. Finally an arbitrator awarded the island to the US. The only casualty was the hog.'
– *Travel writer/ photographer Amanda Castleman*

warning, blowing off 14% of its height and killing 57 people. Now a national park, a permit is required for the summit, but the surrounding area provides plenty of scenery, hikes and elk viewing. *http://parks.state.wa.us/245/Mount-St-Helens, 3029 Spirit Lake Hwy, Castle Rock*

NORTH CASCADES NATIONAL PARK
Every color ever found in nature coalesce here: glacial blue alpine lakes in the winter, bursts of purple and yellow wildflowers in the spring, earthen reds and oranges in the fall, and so, so much green throughout the year. The road-trip highway of the gods (Highway 20) bisects the region, making visiting the rugged wilderness surprisingly easy. *www.nps.gov/noca*

OLYMPIC PENINSULA AND OLYMPIC NATIONAL PARK
Two-hundred-plus inches of rain a year on a mountainous peninsula in the already lushly forested Pacific Northwest adds up to some pretty spectacular scenery. Some favorites: the fairy tale–like setting of the Hoh Rainforest,

the 5-mile hike out to the Dungeness Spit lighthouse (stay a week as a lighthouse keeper!), or hiking blustery Hurricane Ridge. *www.olympicpeninsula.org*

SAN JUAN ISLANDS
In case of a zombie attack, the San Juans would be just about the safest spot. The ferry route maneuvers through hundreds of impossibly scenic islands and several territorial orca pods. Three main islands are filled with ecologically minded farms, and dozens of art galleries and farm-fresh restaurants would keep you well-fed and happy for years. *www.visitsanjuans.com*

SNOQUALMIE FALLS
You don't have to be a *Twin Peaks* fan to appreciate the rushing waterfall, but understanding the show is a start to understanding the culture of Western Washington. Stand on the viewing platform to get sprayed with the mist the Snoqualmie tribe recognized as sacred, or visit Salish Lodge & Spa next door (the 'Great Northern' from the iconic tv show). *www.snoqualmiefalls.com*

From left: Lime Kiln Lighthouse on the western side of San Juan Island; the Hall of Mosses Trail in Olympic National Park; the Museum of Glass in Tacoma. Previous page: Mt Shuksan in North Cascades National Park.

© Richard Cummins / Getty Images

ARTS, HISTORY & CULTURE

BURKE MUSEUM On the beautiful University of Washington campus, this natural history museum features exhibits on the landscape, paleontology and anthropology of the region. The highlight is Pacific Voices, a permanent exhibit about the many Native American tribes that have lived in the Pacific Northwest for thousands of years. *www.burkemuseum.org, 4300 15th Ave NE, Seattle*

CAPE DISAPPOINTMENT STATE PARK The Lewis and Clark Expedition reached its end in Washington State, finally arriving at Cape Disappointment as they became the first Americans to traverse the western half of the US from 1804 to 1806, with help from a 16-year-old Shoshone woman named Sacagawea. The Lewis & Clark Interpretive Center in the park brings to life their groundbreaking perilous journey at the spot where it ended. *http://parks.state. wa.us/187/cape-disappointment, 244 Robert Gray Dr, Ilwaco*

GATES FOUNDATION DISCOVERY CENTER Seattleites' rain-chilled hearts can't help but warm with pride when visiting the Bill & Melinda Gates Foundation's public showcase. The very best of American innovation, ingenuity and charity are on display in exhibits about the foundation's work around the world. *www.discovergates.org, 440 5th Ave N*

MOHAI Seattle and Washington's history are both inextricably tied to its industry. At the Museum of History and Industry on Seattle's Lake Union, there are exhibits on everything from the founding of Seattle and the Seattle Fire of 1889 to the history of Seattle hip-hop and the innovative goings-on today at Microsoft, Boeing or Amazon. *www.mohai.org, 860 Terry Ave N*

MUSEUM OF GLASS The Museum of Glass, with its slanted tower called the Hot Shop Amphitheater, is Tacoma's tribute to native son Dale Chihuly. It holds art exhibits and glassblowing demonstrations. Chihuly's characteristically elaborate and

FUN FACT

Pub trivia in Seattle might host a picture round of salmon; Washingtonians are expected to know their spawning chinook from non-spawning coho.

© artran / Getty Images; Left: © Stephen Saks / Getty Images

★ ★ ★

SPOKANE

Washington's second-biggest population center (edging out Tacoma by about 7000 people) is a welcome break after the treeless monotony of the eastern Scablands. Situated at the nexus of the Pacific Northwest's 'Inland Empire,' this understated yet confident city sits clustered on the banks of the Spokane River. Though rarely touted in national tourist blurbs, Spokane hosts the world's largest mass-participation running event (May's annual Bloomsday Run), a stunning gilded-age hotel in the Davenport, and a spectacular waterfall throwing up angry white spray right downtown.

colorful Bridge of Glass walkway connects the museum with the enormous copper-domed neobaroque 1911 Union Station. *www.museumofglass.org, 1801 Dock St*

PIONEER SQUARE The Klondike Gold Rush toward Alaska and Canada in the late 1890s resulted in boom times in Seattle, and are commemorated in the Klondike Gold Rush Historical Park, housed in the refurbished former Cadillac Hotel. While few prospectors eked out a living up north, hundreds of Washingtonians became wildly rich outfitting them. Pioneer Square is still a bustling neighborhood filled with the redbrick architectural delights built after the 1889 Great Fire, and a totem pole with one heck of a story as the centerpiece. *www.nps.gov/klse, Yesler Way, Seattle*

SEATTLE CENTER Built in 1962 for Seattle's Space Age World's Fair, the Space Needle is the most distinctive landmark of the city. The Seattle Center offers much more than just the Space Needle, though. The complex under this instantly

recognizable icon features the Chihuly Garden and Glass museum, the MoPOP pop culture museum and a mesmerizing giant musical water fountain. *www.seattlecenter.com, 305 Harrison St*

VANCOUVER NATIONAL HISTORIC RESERVE Situated within easy walking distance of Vancouver's city center (that's not Vancouver, Canada, by the way) is its most important historical monument, itself one of the most important statewide. Comprising an archaeological site, the region's first military post, a waterfront trail on the Columbia River and one of the nation's oldest operating airfields, the complex's highlight is the reconstructed Fort Vancouver National Historic Site, a 19th-century fur-trading post. It's a worthy detour from nearby Portland for history buffs. *www.clark.wa.gov, 750 Anderson St*

WING LUKE MUSEUM OF THE ASIAN PACIFIC AMERICAN EXPERIENCE Since the late 1800s, Asian pioneers

From left: Riverfront Spokane; the Museum of Pop Culture, located under the Space Needle in Seattle; small town Leavenworth in winter.

© Checubus / Shutterstock

have helped build and shape Seattle and its culture. The Wing Luke is a living part of Seattle's International District neighborhood, and offers walking tours of the neighborhood's sites, foods, and most famous resident: movie star and martial arts master, Bruce Lee. *www.wingluke.org, 719 S King St*

FAMILY OUTINGS

BALLARD LOCKS Here at the Hiram M Chittenden Locks in Ballard, the fresh waters of Lake Washington and Lake Union drop as much as 26ft into saltwater Puget Sound. You can stand inches away and watch the boats rise or sink (depending on direction). Construction of the canal and locks began in 1911; today 100,000 boats pass through them annually. Located on the southern side of the locks, the fish ladder was built in 1976 to allow salmon to fight their way to spawning grounds in the Cascade headwaters of the Sammamish River, which feeds Lake Washington. Keep an eye out for the migrating salmon during spawning season (mid-June to October). *www.ballardlocks.org*

GAS WORKS PARK Seattle isn't just surrounded by nature – it also contains endless parks, from old-growth forest at Seward Park to this quirky gem on the banks of Lake Union. Once the Seattle Gas Light Company, the ruins and rehabilitated industrial buildings are now part of a public space for exploration and relaxation. Lake Union is accessible for exploring by kayak as well. *www.seattle.gov/parks/find/parks/ gas-works-park, 2101 N Northlake Way*

LEAVENWORTH In the 1960s, town leaders in this down-and-out logging town chose a tourism makeover by becoming a Bavarian village to fit the alpine scenery of the Cascades. Even the hospital is Bavarian-themed now. Schnitzel and sausage restaurants rub elbows with wine tasting rooms and carriage rides, flanked by world-class skiing and snowshoeing. Leavenworth is at its best from Oktoberfest through Christmas. *www.leavenworth.org*

★ ★ ★

THE SPACE NEEDLE

In 2018 the Space Needle got a $100 million facelift. Built on an 18-month timetable for the World's Fair, it was completed mere days before the fair opened. Per one of the original structural engineers, Gary Noble Curtis, '55 years ago, when we built it, it felt real modern. But it was really getting tired'. The result? A fully rotational viewing platform with panoramic views and exposed gear mechanism.

© Richard Cummins / Getty Images; Right: © Mint Images / Getty Images

★ ★ ★

GETTING THERE & AROUND

Washington's major international airport is SeaTac (SEA), although there is a small international airport in Spokane. The outlandishly scenic Amtrak Cascades service runs from Eugene, Oregon through Tacoma and Seattle to Vancouver, Canada. The ferry system is comprehensive, but few excursions can beat riding a seaplane to the San Juan Islands.

MUSEUM OF FLIGHT Seattle's second gold rush was the aerospace and aviation industry, so it's no surprise it has one of the best museums around dedicated to the history of air and space flight. Exhibits detail 100 years of flight, from the Wright Brothers to lunar modules, with plenty of hands-on activities and special events. *www.museumofflight.org, 9404 E Marginal Way*

WILD BEACHES Though their cold waters and grey skies aren't the most inviting for swimmers, Washington's beaches on the Pacific and Olympic coasts have a wild beauty. At Olympic National Park's Ruby Beach, a short path leads down to a large expanse of windswept shore embellished by polished black stones and strewn tree trunks. Known for its more raw, untamed beaches, La Push's Rialto Beach and First Beach are popular with surfers and sea kayakers, as well as fans of the *Twilight* franchise. On the Pacific coast, 28-mile Long Beach lives up to its name.

ITINERARY

Days 1 & 2
Tour Seattle's Pike Place
Market, and check out
its fishmongers, pro-
duce stalls and artists.
At the Seattle Center,
check out the Chihuly
Museum or let kids run
off steam at the musical
fountain while waiting
for your Space Needle
visit (timed preferably
just before sunset).
See Seattle from Lake
Union: rent kayaks or a
wooden boat to explore
on your own. Warm
up in the lakefront
MOHAI for exhibits on
Seattle's history and
industry roots. Head up
to Scandinavian Ballard
for the Nordic Museum
and a seafood dinner
before getting drinks in
hopping Capitol Hill.

Days 3 & 4
Take to the waters,
either on a seaplane
or a ferry. Head to the
Olympic Peninsula
for a windswept hike,
San Juan Islands for
orca spotting, or take
a quick ferry to nearby
Bainbridge or Whidbey
Islands.

Days 5 & 6
Throw on some hiking
shoes and go into the
wild. Hike the alpine
lakes in the North
Cascades (stopping by
Taylor's Shellfish Farms
on the way) and camp
on mighty Mt Rainier.

**From left: Museum of
Flight; Ruby Beach.**

WEST VIRGINIA

★ ★ ★ ★ ★ ★ ★ ★ ★ ★ ★ ★ ★ ★ ★ ★ ★ ★ ★ ★

POPULATION: 1.8 million | **SIZE:** 24,038 sq miles | **STATE CAPITAL:** Charleston
WEBSITE: www.wvtourism.com

NEARLY 75% OF THE MOUNTAIN STATE IS COVERED BY FORESTS, AND AS YOUR CAR SWOOPS INTO the wooded mountains, most likely on a two-lane road, the truth of West Virginia's official hashtag – #AlmostHeaven – is confirmed. The Appalachian Mountains ripple across the horizon, the New and Cheat Rivers smash through leafy gorges, and Seneca Rocks reaches toward the sky, blessings from a temperamental Mother Nature. Yes, you'll probably lose cell service at least once on your drive, but several outdoor adventures in the state rank among the best in the country, from rafting the Gauley River during the fall dam release to hiking the tundra-like plains of Dolly Sods. Homegrown is the catchword at farm-to-table restaurants and indie shops from Morgantown to Charleston to Lewisburg. Gorgeous scenery and wild and wonderful adventures keep the state's Appalachian pride strong.

© ESB Professional / Shutterstock

FOOD & DRINK

APPLES Some of America's crispest, juiciest apples come from the golden mountains of West Virginia, where the lush, cool climate provides ideal growing conditions and has even produced popular varietals. The Golden Delicious is native to the state, and at family-run Orr's Farm in Martinsburg, you can pick your own bushel, then nibble an apple cider doughnut and sip hot apple cider.

JQ DICKINSON SALT-WORKS An ancient sea sleeps below the Appalachian Mountains on the outskirts of Charleston, and the region has a long history of mining salt from its briny waters. Brother-and-sister team Lewis Payne and Nancy Bruns, who are seventh-generation salt producers, mine and sell small-batch salt in Malden – it's a favorite of gourmet chefs nationwide. We bet you'll buy a jar after the tour. *www.jqdsalt.com, 4797 Midland Dr*

PEPPERONI ROLLS They say an Italian immigrant – Giuseppe 'Joseph' Argiro – invented West Virginia's favorite hearty snack: the now-ubiquitous pepperoni roll, found on convenience store counters across the state. Argiro, a coal miner turned bakery owner, was looking for an easy-to-hold meal for miners. After some experimentation he found that a soft bread roll loaded with pepperoni – a cured meat – did the trick. It could be eaten with one hand and stayed edible all day. For a sample, head to Fairmont, the birthplace of the treat, where you can dig in at Country Club Bakery. Another good option is Chico Bakery in Morgantown.

NATURAL ESCAPES

COOPERS ROCK STATE FOREST The overlook at Coopers Rock near Morgantown is one of the most photogenic spots in West Virginia. Here a stone-and-log fence clings to a sandstone cliff top soaring high above the Cheat River Gorge. The leafy drive to the viewpoint is ablaze with color in fall. The Rock City Trail (0.7 mile one-way) barrels through a wonderland of boulders. *www.wvstateparks.com, 61 County Line Drive, Bruceton Mills*

DOLLY SODS WILDERNESS Red spruce trees, windswept boulders, valley views and boggy forests set a striking scene in the northern reaches of this remote but popular wilderness perched atop the Allegheny Plateau. The alpine landscape in Monongahela National Forest near Davis is dotted with pine and offers breathtaking views. With 47 miles of trails crisscrossing its 17,371 acres, Dolly Sods is ready for adventure. *www.fs.usda.gov/mnf, Fire Rd 19*

NEW & GAULEY RIVERS White-water rapids hurl paddlers downstream on the New and Gauley Rivers near Fayetteville, a national hot spot for wet-and-wild excursions. Trips on the New River are appropriate for families as well as thrill seekers, while the fall dam release on the Gauley is one of the most exciting white-water adventures in the US. Your essential photo? The New River Gorge Bridge. *www.nps.gov/neri*

SENECA ROCKS A striking rock formation rising 900ft above a fork of the Potomac River, Seneca Rocks in Monongahela

★ ★ ★

BRIDGE DAY FESTIVAL

On the third Saturday in October, hundreds of BASE jumpers parachute from the 876ft-high New River Gorge Bridge, which is closed to vehicles for the event. Pedestrians can stroll the bridge, watch the action and shop at the many vendors. Set in the Appalachian Mountains, this dizzyingly tall bridge was the longest single-span arch steel bridge in the world for years (it now ranks fourth). The festivities include live music in Fayetteville over the same weekend.

Left: New River Gorge Bridge.

© MarkVanDykePhotography / Getty Images: Right: © ablokhin / Getty Images

West Virginia's Eastern Panhandle begins 60 miles northwest of Washington, DC; Morgantown is 75 miles south of Pittsburgh, Pennsylvania. Amtrak stops in Charleston and Harpers Ferry, and Charleston has a small airport. You will need a car to explore the state and will likely be accessing most mountain towns and parks on two-lane roads.

National Forest is one of the most recognizable natural features in the state. Rock climbers have scaled its sandstone walls since the mid-1930s. Today there are more than 370 mapped climbing routes. A 1.5-mile hiking trail leads to an observation platform near the top of the formation. *www.fs.usda.gov/mnf, Hwy 28/55*

ARTS, HISTORY & CULTURE

GREENBRIER BUNKER TOUR
In the 1950s a top-secret relocation center was built into the mountain below the posh Greenbrier resort in White Sulphur Springs for Congress to use in the event of a nuclear war. Kept secret for 30 years, the Cold War bunker is now open to the public. Tours of this nuclear age relic last 90 minutes and reservations are required. *www.greenbrier.com, 300 W. Main St*

HARPERS FERRY
History lives on in this cobblestoned town, framed by the Shenandoah Mountains and the confluence of the Potomac and Shenandoah Rivers. The lower town is an open-air museum managed by the National Park Service, with many exhibits spotlighting abolitionist John Brown's attempt to spark a slave uprising here in 1859. The Appalachian Trail and the C&O Canal bike path unfurl nearby. *www.nps.gov/hafe*

PURPLE FIDDLE
Bluegrass culture and hipster day-trippers from the urban South and Northeast mash up at this rustic mountain store in the hamlet of Thomas for a stomping good time. There's live music every night; consider purchasing tickets for weekend shows in advance. The artsy Fiddle is an unexpected but fun surprise. *http://purplefiddle.com, 96 East Ave*

TRANS-ALLEGHENY LUNATIC ASYLUM
For maximum chills, join the evening paranormal tour at this former hospital for the mentally ill in Weston, 60 miles south of Morgantown. The Gothic-style

★

ITINERARY

Day 1
Start at Coopers Rock State Forest. From here, join the West Virginia University students in downtown Morgantown for lunch. Afterward, stroll the Monongahela River, then take a tour of the goosebumps-inducing Trans-Allegheny Lunatic Asylum.

Day 2
Start a walking tour of downtown Charleston by the state capitol's gold dome. After lunch, take scenic Route 60 east to JQ Dickinson Salt-Works, the Mystery Hole and Hawks Nest State Park.

Day 3
It's all about outdoor adventure in the New River Gorge National River and Fayetteville: white-water rafting, hiking, mountain biking or rock climbing. Or hold tight on a tour of the catwalk under lofty New River Gorge Bridge.

Day 4
Route 60 continues east to Lewisburg, where the historic downtown is packed tight with indie shops and innovative restaurants. A bunker tour at the Greenbrier fallout shelter in White Sulphur Springs reveals Cold War secrets.

From left: Harpers Ferry; Green Bank Observatory.

19th-century building, which closed in 1994, stretches nearly a quarter of a mile. Despite the insensitive name of the place (it was later renamed Weston State Hospital), the daytime history tours thoughtfully discuss the inhumane medical practices that regularly occurred in the asylums of yesterday. *http://trans-alleghenylunaticasylum.com, 71 Asylum Dr*

FAMILY OUTINGS

BECKLEY EXHIBITION COAL MINE
This small museum in Beckley spotlights the region's coal heritage, which while dwindling, is still part of its identity; the state supplies 15% of the country's coal. Visitors can ride a train 1500ft into a former mine, peruse exhibits about mining life and explore the coal town village. Don't like enclosed places? You can see everything but the mine for a lower admission. If you do go in the mine, bring a jacket; it's cold underground! *https://beckley.org, 513 Ewart Ave*

GREEN BANK OBSERVATORY The observatory in Green Bank is a radio telescope, so you won't be looking at the stars through any lenses here. But you can learn about radio astronomy and get a closer look at the powerful telescope, which catches radio waves. The dish's surface could hold two football fields. Because the dish is finely attuned to catch radio waves, the surrounding 13,000-sq-mile region has been designated a National Radio Quiet Zone to minimize interference. *https://greenbankobservatory.org, 155 Observatory Rd*

MYSTERY HOLE Stopping at the Mystery Hole, where gravity and the known limits of tackiness are gloriously defied, is a must (though it's closed seasonally). In fact this kitschy place is one of the great attractions of roadside America. Everything inside this madhouse tilts at an angle! It's open May through October in Ansted, 10 miles north of Fayetteville. *http://mysteryhole.com, 16724 Midland Trail*

WISCONSIN

★ ★

POPULATION: 5.8 million | **SIZE:** 65,498 sq miles | **STATE CAPITAL:** Madison
LARGEST CITY: Milwaukee | **WEBSITE:** www.travelwisconsin.com

VISITORS TO WISCONSIN WILL DISCOVER MANY WONDERS, WHETHER THEY'RE EXPLORING the craggy cliffs and lighthouses of Door County, kayaking through sea caves at Apostle Islands National Lakeshore, soaking up the urban delights of Milwaukee and Madison, or throwing cow chips at the annual festival in Prairie du Sac. Sure, there's bowling, beer and brats, but Wisconsin also has a world-class university system, a thriving arts scene and more than 15,000 lakes, prime for winter ice-fishing. Sports are the lifeblood of this state, but the warm people here won't hesitate to pull over for a stranded car on the highway, even if it's got Bears or Vikings plates. Wisconsin is your party-loving big brother with a heart of gold and a lake house, offering you indulgence and clarity all in the same weekend. And don't forget the cheese.

© Matt Anderson Photography / Getty Images

FOOD & DRINK

BEER It's not for nothing that Milwaukee's baseball team was christened the Brewers: beer is central to this heavily Germanic state. Founded in 1855, the historic Miller facility preserves Milwaukee's beer legacy. Though the mass-produced beer may not be your favorite, the factory impresses on popular free tours with its sheer scale: you'll visit the packaging plant where 2000 cans are filled each minute, and the warehouse where a half-million cases await shipment. Beer connoisseurs have plenty of more high-brow options, from Lakefront Brewery in Milwaukee to Potosi Brewing Company in Potosi, which began brewing beer in 1852.

BUTTER BURGERS The Wisconsin town of Seymour claims the invention of the hamburger, but other contenders beg to differ. All's not lost in bragging rights, though: the state came together to perfect the burger in the form of the butter burger. Thin patties are served on a toasted bun with a pat of butter in the center (because it's Wisconsin). There's no better place for a butter burger than Kroll's in Green Bay. Enjoy with a cup of booyah (think chicken stew), and cheese curds (get the white ones).

CHEESE CURDS Wisconsin is synonymous with cheese, and though labels such as Pleasant Ridge and Evalon win international awards, nothing wins hearts quite like cheese curds. These golden nuggets of cheese can be found at any self-respecting gift shop or tavern. The locals will tell you that fresh ones 'squeak' as you eat them, and everyone has a favorite place for the fried variety. Kohler's Horse & Plow has great ones, as do the Wisconsin State Fair and the Milwaukee Brat House. If all else fails and you can't make it to the cheese emporium at Kenosha's Mars Cheese Castle, the fast-food variety at Culver's and A&W are pretty good too.

DANE COUNTY FARMERS MARKET On Saturdays a food bazaar takes over Capitol Square in Madison. It's one of the nation's most expansive markets, famed for its artisanal cheeses and breads set out in front of the State Capitol from April through November. Craft vendors and street musicians add to the festivities. In winter the market moves indoors to varying locations. *https://dcfm.org*

DOOR COUNTY CHERRIES Door County is rightfully famous for its delicious cherries. You can get cherry pancakes, cherry jams, cherry salsas, cherry wine and more at just about any restaurant or gift shop. Wood Orchard Market in Egg Harbor has every possible configuration you could possibly purchase, or if you're not looking to take home a bushel of cherry products, have the cherry-stuffed French toast at the White Gull Inn in Fish Creek.

NATURAL ESCAPES

APOSTLE ISLANDS NATIONAL LAKESHORE It's hard to argue that Lake Superior is anything but the greatest of the Great Lakes, and the Apostle Islands near Bayfield showcase it brilliantly. There are caves (ice caves in winter!), trails and

★ ★ ★

ASK A LOCAL

'I always look forward to my visits to Big Bay State Park on Madeline Island, where I've hiked, biked, kayaked and taken many a photograph. Even among the most spectacular natural landscapes in America, the Apostle Islands are a unique treasure. The 21 islands and 12 miles of mainland coast allow visitors to explore the majesty of Lake Superior across all seasons, from walking along windswept beaches in summer to hiking through old-growth forests in fall to observing sea caves of frozen waterfalls under a chandelier of icicles in winter. As one of only four national lakeshores operated by the National Park Service in the entire country, the Apostle Islands hold a singular place in the conservation of the American landscape, providing a window to the largest freshwater lake in the world.'
— *US Senator Tammy Baldwin*

© Ali Majdfar / Getty Images; Left: © RWI FINE ART PHOTOGRAPHY / Alamy Stock Photo

★ ★ ★

FISH BOIL

Tradition has it that the spectacle of a fish boil began with Scandinavian fisherfolk coming off Lakes Michigan and Superior with their daily haul. Today the fish is usually just as fresh; it's cut into pieces and thrown into a huge cauldron with boiling water, potatoes and onions. Spectators thrill as the story-teller/fire-tender throws kerosene on the fire, causing flames to shoot 30ft into the air and the cauldron to boil over. The result is flaky and delicious whitefish, usually accompanied by coleslaw and a piece of Door County cherry pie.

lighthouses to explore, and while the lake is not warm enough for swimmers, exploring is invigorating via kayak or boat. Bring what you can; convenience store prices are very high. *www.nps.gov/apis*

CAVE POINT COUNTY PARK This park in Sturgeon Bay doesn't change by the season but by the days. Some days you can wade 50ft into the calm waters of Lake Michigan; others, you can't go near it due to the force of the crashing waves. Don't miss this wild and beautiful place and the thimbleberries that grow here. *www.doorcounty.com/experience/cave-point-county-park, 5360 Schauer Rd*

NATURAL BRIDGE STATE PARK Balance the tourist-induced mayhem of the Wisconsin Dells with the tranquility of nearby Natural Bridge State Park in North Freedom. The 'bridge' is made of sandstone and is a remnant of the last Ice Age. Nearby there's a rock shelter used by Native people over 10,000 years ago, making it the oldest documented site of human

occupation in the Upper Midwest. It's an inspiring place for a day out. *https://dnr.wi.gov, E7992, County Hwy C*

NUGGET LAKE There's gold in that there lake, and gemstones too! The lake is at the site of a long-ago meteor collision, and the gold and gemstones are the result of the meteor's impact. Near Plum City, it is considerably more secluded than better-known destinations, so it's a perfect choice for camping, hiking, cross-country skiing and kayaking. Kids love the thrill of prospecting for gold as well as the modern playgrounds nearby. *www.co.pierce.wi.us, N4351, County Rd HH*

WASHINGTON ISLAND A 45-minute ferry ride from Northport on the mainland across the strait of Death's Door (named for its many shipwrecks) takes you to this delightful refuge, the largest of Door County's islands and the only one with a year-round resident population. Take the Cherry Train Tour or go solo and rent a moped. Schoolhouse Beach is beautiful but

From left: Traditional Scandinavian fish boil on Washington Island in Door County; Cave Point County Park; Green Bay Packers fans tailgate outside Lambeau Field.

© Jeff Bukowski / Shutterstock

rough (no sand, just rocks); it's adjacent to some of the world's most beautiful lavender fields, celebrated in the numerous lavender-themed gift shops. Lighthouses, hiking trails and galleries round out the experience. *https://washingtonisland.com*

ARTS, HISTORY & CULTURE

DR EVERMOR'S SCULPTURE PARK

The doc welds old pipes, carburetors and other salvaged metal into a hallucinatory world of futuristic birds, dragons and other bizarre structures. The crowning glory is the giant, egg-domed Forevertron, once cited by Guinness World Records as the globe's largest scrap-metal sculpture. The doc is in poor health now and isn't around much, but his wife, Lady Eleanor, usually is. The park is about 8 miles south of Baraboo, in Sumpter; finding the entrance is tricky. It is behind Delaney's Surplus; look for a small road just south of Delaney's leading in. Hours can be erratic, so call to confirm that it's open. *www.worldofdrevermor.com, S7703, US Hwy 12*

LAMBEAU FIELD Is a football stadium really a cultural attraction? In Green Bay it is. You don't need to care about football to be fascinated and touched by the history here. Take the stadium tour (almost always led by an older gentleman who was there for the Ice Bowl in 1967), peruse the Hall of Fame, have poutine at 1919 Kitchen & Tap, and visit the Pro Shop, a monument to branding. *www.packers.com/lambeau-field, 1265 Lombardi Ave*

MILWAUKEE ART MUSEUM You have to see this lakeside institution, which features a stunning wing-like addition (actually a sunscreen) by Santiago Calatrava. It soars open and closed every day at 10am, noon and 5pm (8pm on Thursday), which is wild to watch; head to the suspension bridge outside for the best view. There are fabulous folk and outsider art galleries, plus a sizable collection of paintings by Georgia O'Keeffe. A 2015 renovation added photography and new media galleries to the trove of art in the holdings. *https://mam.org, 700 N Art Museum Dr*

FUN FACT

The Green Bay Packers are owned by the people of Green Bay (pop. just over 100,000). The football team is a nonprofit whose fans support it, and the team supports them with a bolstered economy, plenty of charitable giving and even a Lombardi Trophy from time to time.

Milwaukee has the biggest airport, with Madison following, but you might score cheaper airfare if you look to the smaller airports, like Appleton and Green Bay. Public transport is not the state's strong suit. Buses and trains are not an easy option for visitors with limited time, so hop in a car and see the state, one family farm at a time!

TALIESIN Believe it or not, the same state that's home to the Mars Cheese Castle was also home to famed architect Frank Lloyd Wright, who lived in Spring Green. Tour the entire estate (including houses, a school, barn, restaurant and Romeo and Juliet windmill) or just get the highlights with Taliesin (Wright's home) itself. Come prepared for serious walking around the grounds. *www.taliesinpreservation.org, 5481 County Rd C*

VILLAGE OF KOHLER What began as a hub for immigrants seeking employment with the Kohler company (toilets, sinks and more) has evolved into a five-star destination, with the company having veto power over village improvements. Visitors can tour the design showroom to plan their perfect bathroom, eat at the Immigrant (jacket required) and stay at the gorgeous Kohler-owned American Club. World-class golf and a spa are available too. At its prettiest in winter, Kohler is certainly the most elegant place in Wisconsin. It takes Wisconsin's collectivist impulses to an impressive extreme. *www.us.kohler.com*

FAMILY OUTINGS

BAY BEACH At this amusement park in Green Bay, treat the entire family to a fun day out for less than $20. With kids' rides costing a mere quarter and the roller coaster topping out at $1, Bay Beach is a great way to spend an active day outdoors.

© Dennis K. Johnson / Getty Images

Michigan, packing in the fetching towns of Jacksonport, Baileys Harbor, Egg Harbor, Fish Creek, Ephraim and Sister Bay to welcome travelers. Summer is prime time: only about half the businesses stay open through winter. *www.doorcounty.com*

MARIEKE GOUDA Cute cows and a clean facility give you a good feeling about the dairy industry in Wisconsin at this Thorp-based farm. Gouda is its specialty, but samples of all kinds of cheese are on offer here. The baby calves are a bonus. See how cheese gets made, come away with a greater appreciation for the whole process and meet the farm's mouse mascot, Wheyd. *www.mariekegouda.com, 200 W Liberty Dr*

STATE STREET No trip to Madison would be complete without a stroll on State Street, a seven-block pedestrian mall that runs between the state's majestic Capitol and the University of Wisconsin–Madison campus. Unique local shops, bars and restaurants line the streets, and an ever-present blend of students, families, professionals and free spirits create a vibrant atmosphere. Stop at the Madison Museum of Contemporary Art, which is free and fabulous. *www.visitdowntownmadison.com/shop, State St*

TITLETOWN ENTERTAINMENT DISTRICT If you go to only one place in Green Bay, choose the newly developed Titletown, an entertainment complex near Lambeau Field in Green Bay. Stay at Lodge Kohler or at least have a bite to eat on the balcony with views of the stadium. In winter you can go ice-skating and tubing; it feels like you're in a swank ski resort town. In summer outdoor entertainment abounds. Titletown exemplifies the economic development model of the Green Bay Packers. *www.titletown.com, 1065 Lombardi Ave*

Located right on the bay, the park helps locals escape the summer heat and provides cheap food, picnic spots and a playground. Your budget will love it. *https://greenbaywi.gov, 1313 Bay Beach Rd*

DOOR COUNTY This is Wisconsin's answer to Cape Cod, and some will argue it's all-around better. Rocky coastlines, picturesque lighthouses, cherry orchards and small 19th-century villages make Door County pretty dang lovely. Honeymooners, families and outdoorsy types all flock here to take advantage of the parkland that blankets the area and to explore hamlets packed with winsome cafes, galleries and inns. The county spreads across a narrow peninsula jutting 75 miles into Lake

ITINERARY

Day 1
Tour the State Capitol in beautiful Madison and enjoy time on Monona Terrace. Head over to nearby Spring Green afterward to visit Frank Lloyd Wright's Taliesin.

Day 2
Enjoy your time in lakeside Milwaukee at the stunning Milwaukee Art Museum, designed by Santiago Calatrava, and take in the brewing culture at one of the local beer halls.

Day 3
Tour the Village of Kohler on your way up to Green Bay. Once in Titletown, enjoy the food and culture and let your enthusiasm for football (or not) inform your points of interest. Fans will want to beeline for Lambeau Field, home of the Packers.

Day 4
Head north to scenic Door County and spend the day shopping, eating and visiting stunning Cave Point.

Day 5
Take the ferry from Northport to Washington Island in Door County, passing through once-perilous Death's Door, taking in its food, cultural attractions and beautiful stone beaches.

Left: Taliesin, home of Frank Lloyd Wright.

W Y O M I N G

★ ★ ★ ★ ★ ★ ★ ★ ★ ★ ★ ★ ★ ★ ★ ★ ★ ★ ★ ★

POPULATION: 586,107 | **SIZE:** 97,914 sq miles | **STATE CAPITAL:** Cheyenne
WEBSITE: www.travelwyoming.com

WIND WHISTLES ACROSS THE SAGE FLATS AND CLOUDS GALLOP THE BLUE HEAVENS OF THIS BIG western state dotted with ranches, wilderness, winter resorts and old mining towns. Wyoming is the distillation of America's rural West. Its dinosaurs left only tracks, but cowboy culture is alive and kicking. Swing open the saloon doors of Cody and Cheyenne to a world of rodeos and powwows. Outdoor playgrounds Jackson Hole and Lander embrace a world of fat-tire bikes, espresso drinks and microbrews. Nature takes center stage everywhere: foremost is the mind-blowing beauty of Yellowstone National Park, with its rainbow pools, spurting geysers and herds of bison and wolves. The foreboding, jagged summits of Grand Teton National Park form the backdrop for stunning hikes and paddles. Don't forget the wild charm of the Wind River and Medicine Bow ranges, deep in the blessed heart of nowhere.

© Kris Wiktor / Shutterstock

FOOD & DRINK

BUFFALO JERKY Yellowstone National Park is home to one of America's largest buffalo herds, and the giant ruminants are a state icon. Wyoming Buffalo Company in downtown Cody sells the kind of savory buffalo jerky cowboys might have chewed on 150 years ago.

JACKSON HOLE FINE DINING Home to magnates and celebrities, and a destination for upper-crust vacationers from all over, Jackson Hole has an après-ski scene like few others. The local cuisine caters to a discerning palate (and heavy wallet). You'll find a lively urban buzz and a refreshing variety of foods. Glorietta in Jackson serves high-class Italian, while those wanting a more casual night out may travel to nearby Wilson for the Stagecoach Bar, open since 1942.

NATURAL ESCAPES

DEVILS TOWER NATIONAL MONUMENT Rising a dramatic 1267ft above the Belle Fourche River, the nearly vertical monolith of Devils Tower is an awesome site. Known as Bears Lodge by some of the 20-plus Native American tribes who consider it sacred, it's a must-see if you are traveling between the Black Hills (on the Wyoming–South Dakota border) and the Tetons or Yellowstone. *www.nps.gov/deto*

GRAND TETON NATIONAL PARK Almost intimidating in their grandeur, the imposing glacier-carved summits of the Tetons have captivated human imagination throughout the ages. The toothy Grand Teton (13,775ft)

is a prize for climbers; just south of Yellowstone, the park is also a prime destination for hiking, with wildflower meadows and gemstone alpine lakes. For something different, try dogsledding over nearby Togwotee Pass. *www.nps.gov/grte*

MEDICINE BOW-ROUTT NATIONAL FOREST Covering nearly 2.9 million acres from northern Colorado to central and northeastern Wyoming, this national forest encompasses the lovely Snowy Range nd the Medicine Bow Mountains, including Medicine Bow Peak at 12,013 ft. At this elevation, year-round snowfields glisten even in summer. It's the perfect place to escape the crowds of the national parks. Camp within its bounds, or stay in nearby Laramie. *www.fs.usda.gov/mbr*

NATIONAL ELK REFUGE This national wildlife refuge protects Jackson's herd of several thousand elk by providing a winter habitat and forage. On a winter day, visitors can take horse-drawn sleigh rides through the snow-covered meadows for close-up views of the herd. Layer up for warmth! The refuge is located on the edge of Jackson. *www.fws.gov, 675 E Broadway Ave*

WILD MUSTANGS What could be more Wild West than the thunder of hooves on the plains? By the southeast gateway to Yellowstone, the Wind River Wild Horse Sanctuary is a Bureau of Land Management eco-sanctuary on the Wind River Indian Reservation. Cody Wyoming Adventures also has wild mustang tours to the badlands refuge of the McCullough Peaks Wild Horse Range. *www.blm.gov*

★ ★ ★

ASK A LOCAL

'If you want to see old Wyoming, head to the Buckhorn Bar in Laramie. Grab a seat at the bar to check out the bullet-riddled mirror. And yeah, you can still get dollar drafts on Tuesdays. Tell me, what on earth can you get for a dollar anymore?'
– *Brett Baker, Wyoming native*

Left: Elk in Grand Teton National Park.

© GJ-NYC/Shutterstock; Right: © littlenySTOCK / Shutterstock

The major airport in Wyoming is Jackson Hole. There's little in the way of public transportation, so renting a vehicle is necessary to see the sights. Major interstate highways through Wyoming avoid the most interesting northwestern area entirely, but state roads are generally in good shape and fast-moving.

YELLOWSTONE NATIONAL PARK

America's iconic first national park wows over 4 million visitors each year. It's home to over 60% of the world's geysers, which erupt in towering explosions of boiling water and steam, set alongside Technicolor hot springs and bubbling mud pots. The surrounding wilderness, teeming with elk, bison, grizzly bears and wolves, is no less impressive. Partly in Idaho and Montana as well, the bulk of the park is in Wyoming. *www.nps.gov/yell*

ARTS, HISTORY & CULTURE

BUFFALO BILL CENTER OF THE WEST

This sprawling complex of five museums in Cody showcases everything western, from the spectacle of Wild West shows and galleries of frontier artwork to the visually absorbing Plains Indian Museum. The Draper Museum of Natural History explores the Yellowstone region's ecosystem. Inside, look for Teddy Roosevelt's saddle and one of the world's last buffalo tepees. *www.centerofthewest. org, 720 Sheridan Ave*

CENTER FOR THE ARTS

Well-heeled Jackson is the de facto cultural hub of Wyoming, drawing artists of international renown. The best spot to take in cultural and creative activity in Jackson Hole is the Center for the Arts. This state-of-the-art performance center in downtown Jackson hosts everything from singer-songwriters to classical performances to gospel soul. *https://jhcenterforthearts.org, 240 S. Glenwood St*

NATIONAL MUSEUM OF WILDLIFE ART

Major works by Bierstadt, Rungius, Remington and Russell breathe life into their subjects in impressive and inspiring ways at this Jackson museum – almost better than seeing the animals in the

ITINERARY

Day 1
Home to both ski bums
and celebrities, Jackson
is a different side of
Wyoming, as seen by its
petite downtown with
galleries. In nearby Wil-
son, the Stagecoach Bar
has fun theme nights.

Day 2
From Jackson, head out
to Grand Teton National
Park. Hike along Jenny
Lake to Inspiration
Point for a taste of
grandeur.

Day 3
Continue exploring
the Tetons today. In
Moose, rent a canoe or
stand-up paddleboard
to explore String Lake.
Spend sunset at Willow
Flats to spot wildlife.

Day 4
Drive into Yellowstone
National Park via the
southern entrance, pass-
ing the Continental Di-
vide into geyser country
for the day. Old Faithful,
Grand Prismatic Spring
and Mammoth are the
major highlights.

Day 5
Head out early to the
east end of Yellowstone
for wildlife watching.
Start in Lamar Valley
before Hayden Valley
and its herds of bison.
Stay at the Lake Yellow-
stone Hotel.

**From left: Mammoth
Hot Springs in
Yellowstone; The
Wrangler in Cheyenne.**

wild. Almost. The outdoor sculptures and building itself (inspired, oddly, by a ruined Scottish castle) are worth stopping by to see even if the museum is closed. *www.wildlifeart.org, 2820 Rungius Rd*

WYOMING TERRITORIAL PRISON In Laramie, explore the only prison ever to hold Butch Cassidy, who served time here for grand larceny from 1894 to 1896 before becoming one of history's greatest robbers. His story is told in thrilling detail in a back room, while the faces of other 'malicious and desperate outlaws' haunt visitors as they explore the main cellblocks. *http://wyoparks.state.wy.us/index.php/ places-to-go/wyoming-territorial-prison, 975 Snowy Range Rd*

FAMILY OUTINGS

CHEYENNE FRONTIER DAYS During the last full week in July, the world's largest outdoor rodeo and celebration of all things Wyoming features 10 days of roping and riding. All generations participate. There's also singing and dancing between air shows, parades, melodramas, carnivals and chili cook-offs. Check out the lively Frontier Town, Indian Village and free morning 'slack' rodeos too. If you need an outfit, stop by The Wrangler in Cheyenne's historic downtown to pick up the requisite cowboy boots and hat. It's the most hopping week of the year. *www.cfdrodeo.com, 4610 Carey Ave*

JACKSON HOLE MOUNTAIN RESORT
Jackson Hole is larger than life. With over 4000ft of vertical rise and some of the world's most infamous slopes, its 2500 acres and average 400in of snow sit at the top of every serious shredder's bucket list. In summer it becomes a major mountain-biking destination, with tram connections to fine Teton hiking. *www.jacksonhole.com*

INDEX

ABOUT THE AUTHORS

Amy C. Balfour (West Virginia) has hiked, paddled and skied her way across West Virginia. She has written or co-written more than 50 Lonely Planet guidebooks.

Alison Bing (Arizona and California) specializes in travel predicaments – including accepting dinner invitations from cults and trusting the camel to know the way. She's survived to write 52 Lonely Planet guidebooks.

Harmony Difo (Nebraska and Oklahoma) is a moveable feast, a writer, reviewer, journalist and slow traveler experienced in short and longform travel content for all formats and on all continents.

Jay Gentile (Illinois, Indiana, Iowa and Michigan) is an award-winning freelance journalist, travel writer and frequent Lonely Planet contributor specializing in US-based travel.

Holly Hurst (South Dakota and North Dakota) is a freelance writer who seeks out the best in food, wine, and live music across the country.

Adam Karlin (Alabama, Florida, Hawaii, Louisiana, Maine, Maryland and Mississippi) was born in Maryland, lives in New Orleans, and has covered the USA from Maine to Hawaii for Lonely Planet.

Lauren Keith (Kansas) is a writer, editor and Kansas native who wishes that getting home was as easy as clicking your ruby slippers.

Barbara Noe Kennedy (Georgia) is a travel journalist based in Arlington, Virginia.

Alex Leviton (North Carolina and Washington) has spent many years in Durham, North Carolina and hiking the trails around the Pacific Northwest.

Emily Matchar (Kentucky, Massachusetts, New Mexico, South Carolina, and Tennessee) is a writer based in Hong Kong and Chapel Hill, North Carolina. Her work has appeared in the *New York Times*, the *Atlantic*, the *New Republic*, the *Washington Post* and other publications.

Carolyn McCarthy (Colorado, Utah and Wyoming) has contributed to over 50 titles for Lonely Planet, including Colorado and the Southwest. Her website is *www.carolynmccarthy.org*.

John Newton (Connecticut, Delaware, Montana, New Hampshire, New Jersey and Pennsylvania) has written travel stories for *AFAR, Condé Nast Traveler, GQ, New York Post, Men's Journal, Travel+Leisure* and others.

Elizabeth Paulson (Rhode Island, Vermont and Wisconsin) has been to all 50 states and a dozen countries. She's never met a volunteer museum interpreter she hasn't liked.

Brandon Presser (Minnesota, New York, Ohio, Virginia and Washington, DC) has spent time in over 120 countries, and has written over 50 books about travel. He contributes to publications including *Bloomberg, Departures,* and *The Daily Beast*, and was a host on Bravo's television series, *Tour Group*.

Brendan Sainsbury (Alaska and Oregon) has been researching the Pacific Northwest region for Lonely Planet for 15 years. He has a special affection for Alaska.

Zuzanna Sitek (Arkansas) is Poland-born and New Jersey-raised, but has never felt more at home than she does in Northwest Arkansas.

Kaidi Stroud (Idaho) is an educator and freelance writer in Idaho. Travel these days includes spouse, kids, and pooch – preferably out of cell range.

Kerry Walker (Missouri and Nevada) is an award-winning British travel writer, author, photographer and translator, and a lover of mountains, cold places and true wilderness.

Luke Waterson (Texas) is a novelist and travel writer based in Wales who writes for travel publishers Lonely Planet as well as the *Telegraph*, the *Independent*, BBC Travel, Adventure.com and others. Find out more about his writing at *https://lukeandhiswords.com*.

The Westport Library
Westport, Connecticut
203-291-4800

The Unique States of America
September 2019
Published by Lonely Planet Global Limited
CRN 554153
www.lonelyplanet.com
10 9 8 7 6 5 4 3 2 1

Printed in Singapore
ISBN 978 17886 8641 9
© Lonely Planet 2019
© photographers as indicated 2019

Managing Director, Publishing Piers Pickard
Associate Publisher Robin Barton
Art Director Daniel Di Paolo
Designer Kristina Juodenas
Editor Nora Rawn
Print Production Nigel Longuet

Although the authors and Lonely Planet have taken all reasonable care in preparing this book, we make no warranty about the accuracy or completeness of its content and, to the maximum extent permitted, disclaim all liability from its use.

All rights reserved. No part of this publication may be reproduced, stored in a retrieval system or transmitted in any form by any means, electronic, mechanical, photocopying, recording or otherwise except brief extracts for the purpose of review, without the written permission of the publisher. Lonely Planet and the Lonely Planet logo are trademarks of Lonely Planet and are registered in the US patent and Trademark Office and in other countries.

Lonely Planet Offices

Australia
The Malt Store, Level 3,
551 Swanston St, Carlton, Victoria 3053
T: 03 8379 8000

USA
124 Linden St, Oakland,
CA 94607
T: 510 250 6400

Ireland
Digital Depot, Roe Lane (Off Thomas Street)
The Digital Hub,
Dublin 8, D08 TCV4

Europe
240 Blackfriars Rd,
London SE1 8NW
T: 020 3771 5100

STAY IN TOUCH lonelyplanet.com/contact

Front cover photo: © fotoVoyager / Getty Images. Back cover photo: © Justin Foulkes / Lonely Planet.
Front cover thumbnails from left: © Matt Munro / Lonely Planet; Kris Davidson / Lonely Planet; Kris Davidson / Lonely Planet; Sivan Askayo / Lonely Planet; Matt Munro / Lonely Planet; Gary Latham / Lonely Planet. Back cover thumbnails from left: © Matt Munro / Lonely Planet; Matt Munro / Lonely Planet; Sivan Askayo / Lonely Planet; Justin Foulkes / Lonely Planet; Lottie Davies / Lonely Planet; Kris Davison, Lonely Planet.

Paper in this book is certified against the Forest Stewardship Council™ standards. FSC™ promotes environmentally responsible, socially beneficial and economically viable management of the world's forests.

THE WESTPORT PUBLIC LIBRARY
34015072493974

DATE DUE

MAR 4 — 2020

MAR 0 4 2022

PRINTED IN U.S.A.

DAT